Praise for *Be Gay, Do Crime*

"The history of queer people is marked by resistance and resilience against significant hostility and harassment from those in power. *Be Gay, Do Crime* explores the strategic use of arrests and police violence as tools to suppress individuals who bravely refused to go back into the closet. This almanac highlights incredible acts of defiance in the face of power and shows us all on whose shoulders we stand."
—Erin Reed, transgender activist and journalist

"Day by day, the collective vigilance of queer people in the US and around the world has led us on paths toward liberation. This book of days names the names—some renowned and many forgotten—and celebrates quotidian victories, one day at a time. This daybook is a keeper!"
—Rahne Alexander, intermedia artist and writer from Baltimore

"Without an understanding of trans/queer insurgent history, it's hard to imagine beyond the cage of gay pragmatism. As necessary remedy, this collection invites us all to know collective revolt's past so that we might also make its future."
—Eric A. Stanley, author of *Atmospheres of Violence: Structuring Antagonism and the Trans/Queer Ungovernable*

"It takes a multiplicity of tactics and histories to make liberation, and we can only win by struggling persistently together, day by day. *Be Gay, Do Crime* offers insight to forge queer and trans revolt and inspires new futures by naming our collective past. Use this book!"
—Emily K. Hobson, author of *Lavender and Red: Liberation and Solidarity in the Gay and Lesbian Left*

"*Be Gay, Do Crime* is a beautiful collection of daily bite-sized lessons in queer history. It serves as an excellent reminder of those who have come before us and what they have endured. As LGBTQ+ people continue to face challenges today, we must return to our roots and Be Gay, Do Crime."
—Allison Chapman, LGBT+ activist and legislative researcher

"The short queer histories throughout this book culminate into a larger picture of the dire importance of queer history and activism. *Be Gay, Do Crime* is illuminating, eye-opening, and a much-needed text to understand our past and present. Reading it should reignite anyone's commitment to social justice."
—Beck Banks, transgender media studies scholar and activist

"*Be Gay, Do Crime* is a provocation. What if learning about queer and trans histories was an everyday practice? What if we marked time by honoring the lives of queer and trans activists past and present, instead of the birthdays of saints or presidents? What if queer and trans people had an accessible way to place themselves in the larger story of liberation? Organized like a daily calendar rather than a history textbook, this unique and useful book brings together stories that are usually separated by centuries: the birth of Emma Goldman in Lithuania on June 27, 1869, for example, appears alongside the launch of the first Trans Pride March in Toronto on June 27, 2009. By disrupting our commonplace ideas about chronology and progress, *Be Gay, Do Crime* offers a way to think about history differently: not as a straight line leading to a single inevitable present, but as a queer tangle, spawning multiple possible futures. Help get queer and trans history out of the ivory tower and into the chaotic share houses where it belongs: Buy this book for everyone on the Signal chat, have arguments about it, and let it inspire your next wave of mischief."
—Cassius Adair, assistant professor of media studies, The New School

"*Be Gay, Do Crime* is an encyclopedia I could get into! This clever book shifts the way many understand what kind of queer history deserves to be recorded, and it is an important reminder (for those who need reminding) that state violence has always been central to queer experience. I learned so much from reading, and I can't wait to share it with others."
—Karma R. Chávez, member of Against Equality and author of *Queer Migration Politics: Activist Rhetoric and Coalitional Possibilities*

"This book brought me to tears. The historical repression of the gay community runs so deep, and the resistance to that repression rises so high. This book reminded me of many things I had forgotten, and taught me many things I had never had the privilege to learn. I am emboldened by the historical and continued refusal to quietly go into the closet or shadows, to love and exist openly and freely. It is an honor to read this history and stand with the gay community as the struggle against bigotry continues to this day. Reading this book is essential to understand how far we've come and how much danger still exists. Up the Queers!"
—Eric King, author of *A Clean Hell: Anarchy and Abolition in America's Most Notorious Dungeon* and coeditor of *Rattling the Cages: Oral Histories of North American Political Prisoners*

"Packed full of radical queer history for each day of the year, *Be Gay, Do Crime* is the book you've been waiting for. The love, compassion, empathy, and rage of the queer community in the face of white supremacist violence and ignorance shows us the way forward. Learning and sharing this history of radical resistance is as urgent now as it has ever been. Do yourself a favor—steal this book and learn our history, which has been hidden for far too long."
—Josh Davidson, coeditor of *Rattling the Cages: Oral Histories of North American Political Prisoners* and Certain Days calendar collective member

"When conventional gender and sex behaviors become enshrined in law, queers must become lawbreakers. This book reminds us that we are bound across time and space with others who challenged and continue to challenge the criminalization of difference. Ours is a collective struggle over what is possible. Let's be gay, let's do crime, and let's build queer worlds—together."
—Craig Jennex, coauthor of *Out North: An Archive of Queer Activism and Kinship in Canada*

BE GAY, DO CRIME

EVERYDAY ACTS OF QUEER RESISTANCE AND REBELLION

Edited by Zane McNeill, Riley Clare Valentine, and Blu Buchanan

Foreword by Cindy Barukh Milstein

Introduction by Working Class History

WCH

PM

Be Gay, Do Crime: Everyday Acts of Queer Resistance and Rebellion
© 2025 Zane McNeill, Riley Clare Valentine, and Blu Buchanan
This edition © 2025 PM Press

Entries attributed to Working Class History in the endnotes originally appeared on the Working Class History website and have been edited and reprinted here with permission. The entries for January 27, 2025 and February 13, 2025, written by Zane McNeill, were originally published by *Truthout* and are reprinted in modified form here under Creative Commons (CC BY-NC-ND 4.0).

ISBN: 979–8–88744–130–6 (paperback)
ISBN: 979–8–88744–143–6 (hardcover)
ISBN: 979–8–88744–131–3 (ebook)

Library of Congress Control Number: 2025931260

Cover by John Yates / stealworks.com
Interior design by briandesign

10 9 8 7 6 5 4 3 2 1

PM Press
PO Box 23912
Oakland, CA 94623
www.pmpress.org

Printed in the USA.

Contents

Using This Book

We live in a time when something new is emerging. Amid the joy of new connections, mutual aid, and deepening relationships—of ways to love and care for one another—we also find ourselves facing foes old and new. Forces of domination like capitalism, white supremacy, and fascism seem to be entrenching themselves against the gains and organizing of liberatory movements around the globe. Genocides are happening regularly all around us, and we see people shutting down business as usual for peace and justice. This book is a bit of historical sustenance, to be shared among friends, lovers, and family of all kinds. We hope it helps to transform despair into action, into a recommitment to live in caring and just ways in the face of unjust and uncaring systems.

With that in mind, this book should not be read alone. Like all kinds of sustenance, we imagine this shared around the table, in the many spaces we turn into our homes. In a time when queer people, particularly queer people of color, are being written out of history and our public spaces, we hope that this book situates readers within a larger pattern of struggle—not a struggle for rights and inclusion but a deeper struggle against systemic violence and dehumanization. These systems of violence starve us of connection—to one another, but also to our own histories. This book endeavors to feed those connections and to rejuvenate us with the realization that we have never been in this alone, that all systems are products of their time, and thus that they can be dismantled and new systems put in their place.

This book records not only moments of triumph in our collective struggle but also the moments when queer politics were tested, and often galvanized, under the pressure of vigilante or state violence. While queer people are not defined by the violence they experience, we hope that recording and sharing these experiences develops a communal historical memory to draw on in times of crisis. Few of us are born into a family knowledgeable about queer history, and for queer people this often leads to enormous gaps in what we know about our struggle and its intersection with other organizing efforts. Those gaps help to pit LGBT+ folks against other movements, because austerity narrows our viewpoint—suggesting that the only way for us to succeed is on the backs of others. Rather than fighting for scraps tossed from the opulent table of domination, this book aims to show how important we are to getting one another cared for and fed.

The process of crafting this book has itself been a practice in transparency, care, and patience. It has been a much more circuitous process than expected; we've added and removed contributors, scoured libraries and the internet for sources, and stretched our own knowledge of radical queer history. Finding entries for every day is hard! It turns out that June is chock-full of events, but March is a slow month for those of us organizing for liberation. Sometimes this has meant adding fewer radical entries, which are not themselves radical events but are part of the broader context in which radical queers have done their work. However, the "Be Gay, Do Crime" slogan is our provocative and playful way to invite readers to join our elders in resisting compulsory heterosexuality and the systemic oppression of the queer community. These moments of resistance have looked different throughout time—sometimes visible protests, "die-ins," marches, and riots and sometimes finding community under the threat of criminalization, such as gay societies, balls, cruising, and bars. Additionally, our tactics and goals have shifted. For some queer organizers, liberation looked like the end of capitalism and the military-industrial complex, while for others the repeal of antigay laws, such as anti-obscenity and antisodomy laws, were their goals. While we are sometimes personally critical of so-called assimilatory tactics, we have included these moments in this collection as well to show what resistance has looked like to a variety of activists in multiple countries across hundreds of years.

We also recognize that these limitations emerge from the extent of our own editorial knowledge. Some of these limitations are based on our positionality; for example, we are much more immersed in the history of radical queer resistance in the United States, because of our own roots. Some are based on the historical archives themselves, because not every struggle is written about, saved, and preserved for future folks. We have tried to address these limitations as best as possible by stretching our source knowledge across international boundaries and the projects of race, gender, and class. It is our hope that this book serves as a starting point rather than a definitive encyclopedia—it is a survey, one we hope inspires you to engage in the practice of collective memory in your own homes and communities. Our small offering is the joy of connecting to others in the struggle, our movement's past and future ancestors.

An Amulet, a Rose, and a Dagger

Cindy Barukh Milstein

These days, one often sees the slogan "Protect Trans Kids" emblazoned on T-shirts, painted across banners, or chanted on the streets during a demonstration. Radicals have added a twist, interspersing illustrations of a rose and a dagger between those three simple words, giving them a more edgy feel. Yet a fifteen-year-old queer anarchist friend of mine recently shared their critique of this popular phrase, adamantly declaring, "We can defend ourselves!"

Their assertion points to the superpowers of many young folks today, as least as witnessed from my vantage point as an older queer anarchist on Turtle Island. They already know, at an early age, that they don't fit into heteronormative boxes. They already seem openly comfortable in who they are, in so many fabulous gender-nonconforming and even gender-abolition ways. And as teenagers and even preteens, they are already both bashing back and striving to create their own queer utopias.

Yet these youths are frequently unaware that their fighting spirit isn't so different from that of their ancestors, nor is their dedication to community self-defense. Take just one quote from this wide-ranging sampler of everyday acts of queer resistance and rebellion, proclaimed by gay anti-fascist Willem Arondeus as he faced execution for militant direct actions against Nazism (Netherlands, July 1, 1943): "Homosexuals are not cowards."

In fact, many of us adults don't know our own histories-from-below either. History, as the truism goes, is written by those in power, intentionally scheming to solidify their coercive and violent hold by erasing all that doesn't conform to their narrative. The victorious hegemons—whether colonialism and capitalism; states, police, and prisons; or homophobes, transphobes, and fascists—in essence put our grassroots histories into a closet and lock the door.

Or so they think.

Be Gay, Do Crime, with its abundance of calendrical offerings, acts like a bolt cutter. Each entry snaps open another padlock, allowing us to steal back what is ours. To reappropriate the many scraps of our bottom-up legacies of good troublemaking that otherwise would be "lost" to top-down histories, and use those glorious remnants, those fag ends, to figuratively craft our own amulets of mutualistic protection. And to share those talismans of remembrance freely with accomplices, coconspirators, and other visionary heretics as the material that sustains our unsanctioned, unabashedly magical world-building.

Thanks to its editors Zane McNeill, Riley Clare Valentine, and Blu Buchanan, this book is indeed a form of communal protection—a theme that threads its way throughout these pages. It's the kind of protection that comes from learning about radical history and revolutionary predecessors, thereby drawing strength from knowing that we've done this before, and not just one or two times. For centuries, we've resisted and rioted, made strides, grieved beloveds, experimented and sometimes failed, carved out autonomous spaces, graffitied walls and blockaded buildings, chosen our own kinship, lent our hearts and solidarity, lived dangerously and danced illegally, acted up and come out, fought back, defied borders and smashed binaries, remained illegibly subversive, and so much more.

As piece after piece reminds us, when push comes to shove, we defend each other, and wisdom doesn't disappear, even if the powers that be connive to bury our stories. "We're here, we're queer, we won't disappear" (Norway, June 25, 2022). And whether we're young, old, or anywhere in between, as this book underscores, we persist in everyday acts of reciprocity that reduce harm and alleviate suffering, within and outside our circles.

Or as poet Federico García Lorca put it (Spain, August 18, 1936), "I will always be on the side of those who have nothing and who are not even allowed to enjoy the nothing they have in peace."

But *Be Gay, Do Crime* is far more than a mere protective charm, much as you'll yearn to gather around a bonfire with friends under a glittery sky and read aloud various entries as if incantations to shield ourselves from the many brutalities of this world. This book is a flower and a weapon too.

Each "on this day in history" piece is a rose, and the more you read, the bigger the bouquet you'll be gifted by this collection. The editors have taken evident care in showering us with a myriad of colorful, beautiful, healing varieties of tales, not limited by time or place.

For instance, they take us on dates that stretch backward to the year 1365 and forward to 2025. They also extravagantly drag us across geographies, ranging from the United States, Canada, and Mexico to Ireland, Catalonia, and Greece, to Egypt, Kenya, and South Africa, to India, Hong Kong, and Australia, to Ecuador, Uruguay, and Chile. And they tenderly create an arrangement abloom with differentiated "inside" and "outside" political strategies, marked by expansive notions of sex, sexuality, and gender, while not forgetting to add sprigs of all the interrelated isms that we have battled together.

By being able to so fully "smell the roses" through the breadth of queered resistance touched on here, we—as readers and hopefully social actors—can more clearly pick our own place in what it means to self-organize toward liberation, beyond this book's pages. For there is so much sweetness to be experienced in *Be Gay, Do Crime*—joy and delight, desire and deliciousness, mischief and sensuous playfulness—all the inspiration that we ourselves directly engender and embody through our everyday practices of dreamy disobedience.

In turn, that refusal to acquiesce or assimilate to a deadening social order—depicted so compellingly in this book—is a weapon. It is wielded fiercely in so many of the historical moments herein, through a diversity of badass tactics, in order to smash fascism, dismantle empires, and cancel cops. Yet it is done so with pride, the kind that can neither be commodified nor contained. Because the aim—so loudly articulated by the examples within this book—isn't to add to the pain and misery of this world. It isn't to use our weapon of ungovernability to bring more chaos and violence into people's lives. It is to continually take stabs at what dreamy time-spaces of freedom would and should look like for everyone.

History becomes a weapon here because, as queer rebels declared during an occupation of New York University (September 25, 1970), "if you're ready to tell people that you want to be free, then your [sic] ready to fight."

But more than fight. *Be Gay, Do Crime* shows, repeatedly and lovingly, that queer, trans, and gender-nonconforming people have weaponized themselves and others in service of life—lives worth living, whole and sacred ones, not lives cut short. "The fire will not consume us. We take it and make it our own" (New York City, October 31, 1992).

August 31, 2024
Montreal, Quebec

Introduction

Working Class History

Despite the COVID-19 pandemic, 2020 was a year of mass protest and upheaval, particularly in the United States in the wake of police and vigilante murders of unarmed Black people, including George Floyd, Breonna Taylor, and Ahmaud Arbery. The Black Lives Matter movement reemerged and swept the country, and in just two months over 4,700 protests had taken place in 2,500 towns and cities, with between seven and twenty-six million participants.[1]

That same year, we released our first book, *Working Class History: Everyday Acts of Queer Resistance and Rebellion*, containing a curated selection of stories from our archive of "on this day in history" events that we had been gathering since our founding in 2014.

The book seemed to strike a chord with thousands of people, who were wanting to learn from the past to gain inspiration and tactics for the struggles going on in the present.

As we acknowledge in that book's introduction, the book did not pretend to be a comprehensive account of our collective history of struggle, and it was biased both by our geographical location, the availability of sources, and the languages we are able to speak.

In the book, we did try to highlight the intersections between class and other types of oppression, exploitation, and discrimination, including issues like race, sexuality, gender and gender identity, disability, and immigration status, among others. However, we were unable to do justice to any of these huge topics in a single book.

Given this, and the success of the book, we started to think about other ways we could help uncover and popularize lesser-known and more hidden parts of our history. And it turned out that our copublishers, PM Press, had been thinking the same thing. Together, we came up with the concept of a series of books, each highlighting everyday acts of resistance and rebellion of different groups.

PM connected us with Zane, Riley, and Blu, and together they compiled *Be Gay, Do Crime: Everyday Acts of Queer Resistance and Rebellion.* They have done a fantastic job, putting together a huge range of different types of stories, mostly from the US and Europe, but with a broad selection around the world as well. We are delighted to be releasing this work as the first additional title in this *Everyday Acts* series.

Since the Stonewall Rebellion of 1969 and the birth of the modern gay liberation movement, LGBT+ people around the world have been organizing, fighting, and winning many improvements to our rights and conditions.[2] But in recent years, in many countries, queer and trans people are under a new onslaught of attacks,[3] from both the far right and, in places like the UK, even the left of the political spectrum.[4]

In particular, in addition to everyday violence and discrimination at work, trans people are being subjected to a wave of hatred and fear-mongering, of the type that was previously directed at gay, lesbian, and bisexual people in the 1960s and '70s.[5] Couched in the language of "protecting" children and cis women,[6] right-wing capitalist interests, with the collaboration of much of the media, governments, the world's richest man, and transphobic left-wingers and self-declared "feminists," are demonizing trans people, taking away their health care, and attempting to legislate them out of existence.[7]

In the US in 2023, at least 510 anti-LGBT+ bills were introduced by state legislatures around the country—up from 180 the previous year,[8] and in the 2024 election, Republicans spent $215 million in advertising attacking trans and nonbinary people.[9] Again in power, the administration of Donald Trump has unleashed a slew of executive orders and other directives targeting transgender, intersex, and other people with differences in sex development.[10] In the name of fighting what it calls "gender ideology," the government now only recognizes two binary sexes, which it declares are unchangeable.[11] It is also attempting to erase the history of marginalized peoples, including Native Americans, Black people, women, and LGBT+ people, deleting tens of thousands of pages from government websites.[12] Mentions of trans people were deleted from the website of the Stonewall National Monument, and the acronym "LGBTQ+" was changed to "LGB."[13] Even mention of the Enola Gay aircraft that dropped the atomic bomb on Hiroshima was removed from Defense Department writings.

In the UK, the Conservative government temporarily banned health care for trans children, and when Labour was elected, Health Secretary Wes Streeting made the ban permanent.[14] The Supreme Court later overturned over two decades of legal precedents on transgender rights and unanimously ruled that transgender women with gender recognition certificates were not legally women as defined by the Equality Act 2010.[15] LGBT+ rights are also being rolled back in countries like Hungary, Russia, Italy, Uganda, and Indonesia.[16]

Civil rights activist and socialist Dr. Martin Luther King Jr. commented that "the arc of the moral universe is long, but it bends towards justice."[17] This may generally be true, but the arc does not bend by itself. It can only be bent by the concerted and deliberate action of millions of us, ordinary people. And we cannot be complacent. Any gains won by one generation can easily be taken away by governments of the next if people are not prepared to fight to protect them.

We hope that this book serves as a reminder of all those people in the past who have fought, organized, struggled, and sacrificed for what we have today. And we hope that we can both be inspired by their examples and learn from their successes, as well as their failures, in our organizing today.

JANUARY

1 **January 1, 1962** As part of an overall reform to its criminal code, the Illinois legislature repealed its "crime against nature" statute. The American Law Institute suggested the removal of this statute in its 1955 recommendations, and its repeal was the first of its kind in the US.[1]

January 1, 1965 The Council on Religion and the Homosexual, a group formed "to facilitate a conversation between clergy and homosexuals in San Francisco," sponsored a New Year's Eve ball. Although the group filed permits and met with the San Francisco Police Department, over twenty officers showed up to harass ball attendees, including photographing them and blocking off the intersection outside the event. While this type of police harassment was common for the time, this raid played an important role in demonstrating the role of police in anti-queer violence.[2]

January 1, 1967 Patrons of Los Angeles's Black Cat Tavern, a well-known queer watering hole in the neighborhood of Silver Lake, dared ring in the new year with a kiss. What followed was a police raid ending in the arrest of fourteen people and the charging of six with lewd conduct. Community organizers followed up on February 11 with a protest outside the Black Cat, part of a larger group of actions happening that day against police violence and harassment in Los Angeles.[3]

2 **January 2, 1971** "These racist attitudes oppress all gays," read a Gay Liberation Front flier. The GLF held a rally outside the Red Room, a local Houston gay bar, protesting its policy, imposed by the owner, of refusing service to Black people. The full text of the flier is as follows:

> BOYCOTT THE RED ROOM—The Gay Liberation Front of Houston regrets that the gay brothers and sisters of Houston are not together. The management of the local Gay Bar, the Red Room unfortunately refuses service to blacks. The discriminatory actions of the Red Room management are clearly racist moves that are a continuation of the repressive and racist attitudes of white Houstonians. These racist attitudes oppress all gays as long as the Red Room and others discriminate against blacks. Disposal of oppressive attitudes is a necessity and a demand. We are all prisoners of the Amerikan death culture.

The Red Room's management called the Houston Police Department, complaining of protesters outside the establishment. This was especially odd considering police regularly raided establishments catering to homo-sexuals. Management seemed to flip from being at odds with police to colluding with them when they thought their clientele were getting out of line.[4]

3 **January 3, 1990** Halfway through New York Governor Mario Cuomo's State of the State address, members of the AIDS Coalition to Unleash Power (ACT UP) had every eye turned on them. G'dali Braverman interrupted Cuomo's speech with the cry, "Mario, you missed the point, there's not been enough action!" While Cuomo ceded time to allow Braverman to speak, the state police still arrested eleven members of ACT UP that day, including Braverman. The other ten members were outside the assembly chamber blocking access with a rousing sit-in. All pleaded guilty to disorderly conduct and "related offenses."[5]

4 **January 4, 1982** In July 1981, American newspapers were reporting the rise of a "gay cancer" spreading in the community. By January, approximately eighty gay men came together to found New York City's Gay Men's Health Crisis organization (GMHC). Including Nathan Fain, Larry Kramer, Lawrence Mass, Paul Popham, Paul Rapaport, and Edmund White, these men worked together to coordinate the all-volunteer organ-ization focused on providing community care and support for those who found themselves sick. Rodger McFarlane, former director of the center, said, "We were forced to take care of ourselves because we learned that if you have certain diseases, certain lifestyles, you can't expect the same services as other parts of society." The organization has continued its work for over forty years, expanding its services to include intravenous drug users, children, and heterosexual men and women.[6]

5 **January 5, 1974** A turning point in radicalizing Canadian gay and lesbian organizing, the arrest of the Brunswick Four—Adrienne Potts, Pat Murphy, Sue Wells, and Heather (Beyer) Elizabeth—was one of the first moments in which violence against queer people was discussed on the national Canadian stage. The group was named after Toronto's Brunswick House tavern, where another patron approached the four and became belligerent when his advances were turned down. After the man poured beer on Adrienne Potts's head, it was the women who were removed from the tavern when they began singing their own, homemade lyrics to the Broadway classic "I Enjoy Being a Girl." Apparently, their new rendition, "I Enjoy Being a Dyke," was enough to get them thrown into police custody, harassed, and denied the right to a lawyer.

After a brutal stint under police watch, the women were released. Following this, they attempted to get justice through the courts but were stymied by the thin blue line practices of the Toronto police. Still, this event consolidated and radicalized Canadian gay and lesbian politics, focusing attention on resisting discrimination and ending police harassment.[7]

6 **January 6, 1863** Emma Johanna Elisabeth Trosse was born. She was a German educator and school leader, initially trained as a teacher and later qualified as a principal after passing an examination. Trosse started her career both in public schools and as a private tutor.

In 1895, she authored one of the earliest scientific treatises on homosexuality, advocating for legal safeguards for folks in the LGBT+ community, and also became the first woman known to scientifically examine lesbianism. Additionally, she published works delving into ancient medical practices among medieval Europeans, Greeks, and Egyptians.

Emerging from a distinguished lineage of scientific authors advocating for queer identities, she cemented her legacy with the term *Sinnlichkeit*, the precursor to the modern term *asexual*. Not only did she acknowledge the presence of people whom today's community identifies as asexual or demisexual, she also included herself among them.[8]

January 6, 1967 Both the US Civil Service Commission and the FBI worked to actively exclude gay and lesbian people from government employment during the Cold War. This was part of the "Lavender Scare," a period in which homosexuality was deemed dangerous to the American state and the "efficiency" of its operations. The Mattachine Society of New York lobbied to change this employment policy at the local level, and their efforts paid off when New York City's Civil Service Commission changed its policy in 1966 to protect the hiring of gay and lesbian workers. On this day in 1967, it officially made that policy change public. The US Civil Service Commission wouldn't change its policy until 1975.[9]

7 **January 7, 1949** "University of Missouri secret haven for homosexuals!" That could have been the university's slogan at the end of the 1940s. However, despite the perception of friendliness on campus, Missouri's state government classified homosexuality as a crime against nature. This led the university to engage in a concerted crackdown on homosexuality. Among those caught up in this suppression were four men: Warren W. Heathman, Harry J. Sohn Jr., Willie D. Coots, and Joe Byers. On this day in 1949, all four were convicted of "homosexual offenses" and put on probation for four years. Importantly, these four were only part of a larger campaign to suppress and surveil homosexuality by the state. While universities are often talked about as sites of "free speech," it is also important to grasp how they have served as agents of state violence.[10]

8 **January 8, 1962** In North Carolina, two men were arrested for participating in an "abominable act and detestable crime against nature." The two men, Max Perkins and Robert McCorkle, were tried. While McCorkle pleaded guilty and got the minimum sentence at the time—five to seven years—Perkins refused to plead guilty. In retaliation, the court found him guilty and sentenced him to twenty to thirty years in prison. He appealed this decision and was eventually found not guilty, on the grounds that the law specifically outlawed "buggary" and not fellatio.[11]

9 **January 9, 1946** Black American poet, novelist, children's writer, and playwright Countee Cullen, particularly well known during the Harlem Renaissance, died.

Cullen maintained a high level of secrecy about his personal life. Many of his friends, such as Alain Locke, Harold Jackman, Carl Van Vechten, and Leland Pettit, were openly gay. Later, his first wife revealed that their divorce stemmed from Cullen's attraction to men. Today, Cullen's poetry is frequently examined within the framework of queer culture.[12]

January 9, 1978 After multiple attempts to be elected, Harvey Milk was finally inaugurated as a San Francisco city supervisor. Milk's election was groundbreaking in a number of ways, as he was the first openly gay man to be elected to political office in California and one of the most publicly outspoken sources of opposition against a rising tide of antigay political and legal organizing from the newly formed "Moral Majority."

It is not only his election that marks a milestone in radical queer history, but also the major public organizing that consolidated under his political efforts. As figures like Anita Bryant (see June 14, 1977) and others were campaigning for the criminalization of homosexuality in the public sphere—arguing that simply being publicly homosexual was "grooming" children into "deviant lifestyles"—Milk and his fellow organizers were pushing back to include gay and lesbian people within public life.[13]

10 **January 10, 1982** Raymond Broshears, founder of the Lavender Panthers, passed away. Broshears, a minister and community organizer in San Francisco, formed the Lavender Panthers in July 1973 following an Independence Day attack that left him unconscious outside Helping Hands, his community center.

The Lavender Panthers were "an armed group who would patrol Polk Street and South of Market, with the intention of defending members of the gay community against attack." While Broshears did not advocate seeking out violent confrontation, he and the Lavender Panthers argued that it was necessary to safely navigate the streets during a period of frequent gay bashing. He is an example of that oft-quoted phrase, "We keep us safe."[14]

11 **January 11, 2007** The state of Coahuila in northern Mexico passed a law recognizing same-sex relationships. The law, called the *pacto civil de solidaridad* (PCS), provided expanded protections to couples. Congresswoman Julieta López Fuentes said, "The PCS represented a sensible response to the existence of citizens who traditionally have been victims of discrimination, humiliation, and abuse. This does not have to do with morality. It has to do with legality. As human beings, we have to protect them as they are. It has to do with civil liberty."

While this was a major breakthrough for those experiencing state-sanctioned violence, the bill had mixed results—even as it allowed couples inheritance rights and property rights, it simultaneously barred them from adopting children.[15]

12 **January 12, 1977** *The Advocate* published a stunning expose in which it was revealed that the Central Intelligence Agency had been tracking and storing information on approximately three hundred thousand people in the US who had been arrested for engaging in same-sex sexual activity. The inquiry uncovered an unsettling history of institutional monitoring of queer people, many of whom had been criminalized under discriminatory and outdated laws. The discovery surprised civil rights groups, LGBT+ activists, and privacy activists alike, demonstrating just how pervasively the institutionalization of homophobia had infected federal intelligence operations.[16]

13 **January 13, 1958** The case of *ONE, Inc. v. Oleson* was finally decided by the US Supreme Court. The Los Angeles postmaster had imposed a moratorium on using the postal service to send "obscene materials." This decision put all materials related to homosexuality under the umbrella of obscenity and made it impossible for groups like ONE, Inc. to reach their constituencies. The Supreme Court ruled in favor of ONE, Inc. and their LGBT+ magazine *ONE: The Homosexual Viewpoint*, the first gay publication in the United States. The court decided that the magazine and its contents fell under First Amendment rights to freedom of speech.[17]

January 13, 2014 Black trans organizer and prison abolitionist CeCe McDonald (see May 26, 1989) was released following her incarceration for defending herself against racist and transphobic violence. CeCe was jailed for nineteen months in a men's prison in Minnesota.

Although her supporters celebrated her release from incarceration, they note that "we question the system that put her there." CeCe has contributed to major works like *Captive Genders: Trans Embodiment and the Prison Industrial Complex*. Her work around prison abolition has highlighted how the prison-industrial complex comes together to erase and dehumanize those it entraps. It has also helped to shed light on how the struggle for trans liberation is intimately bound up with other struggles to uproot the prison-industrial complex.[18]

14 **January 14, 1975** The Civil Rights Amendments bill of 1975 was introduced by Representative Bella Abzug of New York and cosponsored by four other representatives. It was the first proposed US federal bill to protect people based on sexual orientation. Its scope was broad, and it intended to use the Civil Rights Act to create additional protections against discrimination. In general, it "prohibits discrimination based upon such affectional or sexual preference in the following areas: (1) public accommodations; (2) public education; (3) equal employment opportunities; (4) the sale, rental and financing of housing; and (5) education programs which receive Federal financial assistance."

While the bill was referred to the House Judiciary Committee, where it was killed, it was the first attempt to codify protections based on sexual orientation at the national level. It represented an increasing pressure from below by organizers to address the problems of discrimination and second-class treatment by both society and the state.[19]

15 **January 15, 1909** *Akademos*, likely the first Francophone queer magazine, debuted. While its run only comprised twelve monthly issues, its brief existence brought together a network of queer intellectuals from across France and Europe.[20]

16 **January 16, 1956** Carlos T. Mock was born in San Juan, Puerto Rico. Mock began his organizing work within the field of medicine, as he saw the discrimination that LGBT+ doctors faced within their profession during his time at the Glen Ellyn Clinic. The experiences of these other doctors, as well as his own personal experiences, pushed him to join the board of Equality Illinois and work tirelessly to help pass the Human Rights Act of Illinois. This bill, passed in 2005, prohibited discrimination based on sexual orientation and gender identity.[21]

17 **January 17, 1969** D'Arcy Drollinger, entertainer and artist, was born in San Francisco. Drollinger is a powerhouse: a founding member of post-punk group Enrique, owner of the Oasis nightclub, and creator of the body- and sex-positive dance fitness brand Sexitude. Combining historical performances of high-camp drag and vaudeville theatrics, Drollinger has been a major influence on the queer scene of San Francisco and beyond (see May 18, 2023).[22]

18 **January 18, 1928** Betty Berzon was born in St. Louis. She was among the first psychotherapists to assist gay clients, a service she provided after she came out as a lesbian in 1968. She took this visibility even further, coming out as the first public lesbian psychotherapist in 1971 at the UCLA conference "The Homosexual in America." Alongside her work organizing gay and lesbian professionals within the American Psychiatric Association, she also helped to found the Los Angeles Gay and Lesbian Community Services Center.[23]

January 18, 2023 Tortuguita, a queer, nonbinary, and Indigenous Venezuelan and much-beloved environmentalist and organizer, was killed trying to stop the installation of what would come to be known as "Cop City," a development intended to fuel the militarization of domestic police by providing them with the tools to train alongside international military experts. It was these same police, specifically Atlanta police during a SWAT operation, who shot and killed the twenty-six-year-old.[24]

19 **January 19–20, 2017** DisruptJ20 protesters and militant queers interrupted the inauguration of Donald Trump as US president. More than two hundred were arrested on the streets of Washington, DC.[25]

20 **January 20, 1857** Charlotte Frances Payne-Townshend was born. Payne-Townshend was an Irish political activist, feminist, and member of the Fabian Society, a British organization historically tied to left-wing radical politics. In 1898, she married the playwright George Bernard Shaw. Their marriage was a highly celibate one, leading to speculation that Shaw was aromantic and asexual and that Charlotte was asexual.[26]

January 20, 1944 Pat Parker, a Black lesbian poet and organizer, was born. Involved in the Black Panther Party as well as the Black Women's Revolutionary Council, she worked diligently to combat homophobia, end domestic violence, and fight against white supremacy.

She gave her first public poetry reading in 1963 in Oakland, California. Her work emerged as an essential part of American Black poetry, and her work is often cited as a critical source for lesbian poetry. Her poem "Don't Let the Fascist Speak" has continued relevance today. It's been reproduced, in part, below:

> every citizen
> is entitled to
> freedom of speech
> my mind remembers
> & my innards churn
> conjure images
> of jews in camps—
> of homosexuals in camps—
> of socialists in camps—
> "Let the Nazis speak."
> "Let the Nazis speak."
>   faces in a college
>   classroom
> "You're being fascist too."
> "We want to hear what
>   they have to say."[27]

21 **January 21, 1966** Police in Forest Town, Johannesburg, raided a private home where over three hundred gay and gender-nonconforming white men (and almost certainly some trans women) were having a party. Nine people described as men were arrested for "masquerading as women."

Conservatives in South Africa were outraged by the January 21 arrests and called for tighter laws to criminalize white, male, and predominantly Afrikaner sexuality.

The incident triggered a national debate, and many gay and gender-nonconforming people began to speak out and argue, albeit anonymously, in favor of LGBT+ rights. While some stricter laws were passed, in some respects the new laws could be interpreted to decriminalize sexual acts between consenting adult men in private, although prosecutions for homosexuality did continue through the 1970s. Same-sex relationships in the Black working class, which were widespread especially in places like mining communities, were largely ignored by the apartheid authorities, who were more concerned with "corrupting" influences on white masculinity.[28]

22 **January 22, 1898** Sergei Mikhailovich Eisenstein, a Russian film director, screenwriter, film editor, and film theorist, was born. Almost all his contemporaries believed that Eisenstein was gay, but Eisenstein confessed that he was asexual to his close friend, Marie Seton: "Those who say that I am homosexual are wrong. I have never noticed and do not notice this. If I was homosexual I would say so, directly. But the whole point is that I have never experienced a homosexual attraction, even towards Grisha, despite the fact I have some bisexual tendency like, for example, Balzac or Zola, in the intellectual field."[29]

January 22, 1953 For neither the first nor the last time, Bayard Rustin (see March 17, 1912) would be targeted and arrested by local police. On this day in 1953, he was arrested in Pasadena, California, for "lewd vagrancy" and sentenced to sixty days in jail. This sentencing had a major impact on his relationship to movement-building work—his connection with the Christian pacifist organization Fellowship of Reconciliation (FOR) was severed following his conviction. The FOR said, "To our great sorrow, Bayard Rustin was convicted on a 'morals charge' (homosexual) and sentenced to 60 days in the Los Angeles County Jail on January 23, 1953.

As of that date, and at his own suggestion, his service as an FOR staff member terminated."

They framed this as a moral failing on the part of Rustin, a "problem" that he was struggling with and that through "rigorous discipline" and "growth" he could control while aiding the nonviolence movement. Historian John D'Emilio says, "The FOR distributed the statement widely among pacifists. In doing so, it ensured that a story buried deep within the local southern California press became common knowledge among the circles of people who mattered most to Rustin. Thus ended his dozen years of service to a Christian organization dedicated to peace and social justice."[30]

January 22–23, 1991 There just isn't money for AIDS programs! ACT UP protested US President George H.W. Bush, who had argued there was no money for AIDS programs while initiating a "billion-dollar-a-day" war in the Persian Gulf. As ACT UP was known for, organizers disrupted the *CBS Evening News* live broadcast on the night of January 22, shouting, "Fight AIDS, not Arabs!" Building on this energy, there were actions the next night all across New York City, coalescing in an action at Grand Central Station.[31]

23 **January 23, 1882** Who invented the term *homosexuality*? On this day in 1882, Károly Mária Kertbeny was born in Vienna as Karl Maria Benkert. It was he who coined the word, first using it in a Berlin pamphlet arguing against the antisodomy laws enforced by the state at the time. A man inclined to wander, Kertbeny spent significant time traveling across Europe, from Italy to France to Brussels, as well as across Germany, spending time in Dusseldorf, Munich, and Cologne before ending up in Berlin. He was part of a broader movement to decriminalize what was termed "sodomy" at the time, although Kertbeny did not intend for his new term, *homosexualität*, to identify any innate or biological group. Rather, sociologist Judit Takács argues that he coined the term to extend privacy protections that existed around sexual activity to include those engaged in same-sex activities.[32]

24 **January 24, 1915** Josef Kohout, also known as Heinz Heger, was born in Vienna. Kohout's story was the first published account of a gay survivor of the Nazi camps, a story that can be found in the book

The Men with the Pink Triangle. His story, alongside those of many gay men who were interned by the Nazis, shaped narratives of queer resistance to fascism for generations and continues to be a call to resist inclusion within projects of state violence. It is also the source of the reclaimed pink triangle used in ACT UP imagery—usually with the phrase SILENCE = DEATH.[33]

25 **January 25, 1962** In the United States, prom is a big deal. No matter how it might be remembered, the celebration has been established as a major rite of passage for high schoolers. Like all rites of passage, it is also a site for regulation, violence, and power. On this day in 1962, Aaron Fricke was born. Growing up in Pawtucket, Rhode Island, Fricke was the first American to challenge prom's heteronormative policies in court. He not only won the right to attend prom with his same-sex partner, but the court also ordered that the school had to provide an environment that would be safe for them to attend. While anti-LGBT+ policies would continue to persist around prom, this legal battle set the groundwork for the legal right of students to bring partners of any gender with them to the occasion.[34]

26 **January 26, 2011** David Kato, founder of Sexual Minorities Uganda, was killed. Kato was a teacher and LGBT+ rights organizer who organized in South Africa against apartheid and antisodomy legislation and then brought it back home to his community in Uganda. He said, "In South Africa I fought for their liberation in Johannesburg, so when I came home—that was in 1998—I had the same momentum. I tried to liberate my own community." He had just won a legal decision against Uganda's *Rolling Stone* newspaper, which had been printing the names and photographs of those it accused of being gay, including Kato, alongside a headline that read "Hang Them." Kato's win meant the paper was forced to stop targeting people for their perceived sexual orientation. Although he passed away far too early at forty-two, his legacy continues to resound in Uganda's queer circles and beyond.[35]

27 **January 27, 2025** A transgender woman in federal prison sued US President Donald Trump over an executive order he issued on his first day back in office seeking to define "sex" in a way the lawsuit said is "intentionally designed to discriminate against transgender people" and "deny them equal treatment."

The complaint, filed under the pseudonym Maria Moe, claims that Executive Order 14166 has caused Moe "significant distress" and "raises serious concerns for her safety and well-being going forward." The lawsuit sought an injunction to block the enforcement of Trump's executive order and require the Trump administration to restore Moe's previous housing and medical care as it was before January 20.

On January 21, the day after Trump signed the order, prison officials removed Moe from the general population at the low-security federal women's prison where she was housed, according to the suit. They placed her in solitary confinement and informed her she would soon be transferred to a men's facility. Being transferred to a men's facility would place her "at an extremely high risk of harassment, abuse, violence and sexual assault," the lawsuit said.[36]

28 **January 28, 1961** Have you ever agreed to the "terms and conditions" without reading everything over carefully? It turns out, something similar is how Illinois became the first state to rescind its antisodomy law. In 1961, Illinois passed a new criminal code, the product of "an eighteen-member joint committee of the Chicago and Illinois Bar Associations comb[ing] through the 148 chapters and 832 sections of the old statute books, using the American Law Institute's 1956 Model Penal Code as a guide." This model penal code did not criminalize sexual behavior between consenting adults, and this difference between present-at-the-time Illinois law and the model seems to have gotten lost in the shuffle. So when the new criminal code was passed into law on January 1, 1962, the state became the first to eliminate antisodomy laws from its criminal code. Oops![37]

January 28, 2024 Two gay leather bars in Seattle's Capitol Hill neighborhood were raided by authorities and issued "lewd conduct" violations that owners say were based on patrons' clothing choices, which included being shirtless as well as wearing a jockstrap.[38]

29 **January 29, 2017** One hundred forty-four crosses were erected on Copacabana Beach in Rio de Janeiro for those killed in anti-trans violence across Brazil in 2016. Rede Trans Brazil, an NGO focused on supporting trans people, gathered statistics that suggest Brazil is one of the top countries for anti-trans violence. Trans advocates there have worked to combat what they term a "culture of violence," seeking to abolish the conditions under which non-cis people experience discrimination, exclusion, and physical violence.[39]

30 **January 30, 1997** Nonbinary organizer and poet Leah Juliett was born. A survivor of abuse, they founded the March Against Revenge Porn, which raises awareness about sexual abuse facilitated by the internet and other technology. This organizing isn't just about raising awareness in a civil, polite way—Juliett led a march across the Brooklyn Bridge in 2017 to draw attention to the issue by disrupting the everyday life of New York City. In addition to their work addressing sexual abuse and revenge porn, Juliett has also signed an open letter to Congress calling for members to address the rampant issue of gun violence in the US.[40]

31 **January 31, 1989** Stop AIDS Now or Else! Both a group name and call to action, Stop AIDS Now or Else took over San Francisco's Golden Gate Bridge. About eighty members of the group shut down the bridge for thirty minutes, drawing a banner across both directions of traffic. The action was disrupted by police, who arrested between twenty and thirty organizers, but the message had been delivered to the state and the San Francisco community: Stop AIDS Now or Else![41]

FEBRUARY

1 **February 1, 1901** Poet, social activist, novelist, playwright, and columnist James Mercer Langston Hughes was born in Joplin, Missouri. Langston Hughes is best known as a leader of the Harlem Renaissance.

Scholars debate Hughes's sexuality, with some interpreting homosexual undertones in his works and others discovering unpublished poems referencing a supposed relationship with a Black male lover, suggesting he may have been homosexual. However, his primary biographer, Arnold Rampersad, writes that while Hughes displayed a preference for Black men in both his literary and personal life, he likely identified as asexual.[1]

February 1, 1950 Ted Brown was born on Long Island in New York. His mother, Dorothy Walker, a Jamaican woman, was deported from the US along with Ted and his sister because the FBI had declared her a "troublemaker" and because of her participation in "disturbances instigated by the NAACP." Brown says that it was from her that he learned the spirit of revolutionary love and rejection of bigotry. She would go on to move them first to Canada and then to the UK, when Ted was nine years old.

In November 1970, after watching *The Boys in the Band*, he got an invitation to attend a Gay Liberation Front (GLF) meeting. This meeting, the third ever for the newly formed group, set him on the path to organizing in the community—through GLF, the Black section of Galop (the Gay London Police Monitoring Group), and his work founding Black Lesbians and Gays Against Media Homophobia. He remarks that for him the "nascent gay liberation movement was intrinsically intertwined with the civil rights movement for racial justice."

That original impulse to understand the intersections of oppression didn't mean Brown only found solidarity within LGBT+ organizing spaces. "There was a considerable amount of patronising, rather than hate-filled racism. Some people considered black people as novelties. Most white LGBT people shared the same ignorant ideas as the general population," he explains. "[But] there were a few people of colour like me involved at the start, who were determined to have a black presence in the campaigns, tackling homophobia and racism together."

And tackle he does; Brown continues to organize alongside Black and Brown queer folks across London.[2]

2 **February 2, 1988** Four lesbians rappelled from the balcony into the UK House of Lords in protest at an ongoing debate about introducing the homophobic Section 28 law that would come into effect that May.

Section 28 of the Local Government Act 1988 prohibited local authorities, including schools, from teaching "the acceptability of homosexuality as a pretended family relationship."

Those who took part in the action were Olivia Butler, Rachel Cox, Angela Nunn, and Sally Frances. In 2017, four other lesbians climbed onto the Houses of Parliament in order to put up a blue plaque commemorating the 1988 action.[3]

3 **February 3, 1975** The first five of the Lexington Six, four lesbians and one gay man, were subpoenaed to appear in front of a grand jury in Kentucky on this day in 1975. After a month of waiting in jail, all six of the group would refuse to answer the questions of the grand jury, be held in contempt of court, and end up being jailed. As historian Josephine Donovan describes, each of them were "handcuffed, put in chains, and sent off in pairs to Kentucky county jails scattered across the state."

So, what sparked this instance of state repression? Five years before, antiwar activists robbed a bank in Brighton, Massachusetts; two of them were young, white, college-educated women who would become lovers and fugitives as they tried to escape the clutches of the FBI. These two women found a home in a feminist community in Lexington, Kentucky, and grew roots within the queer community there. After they both left, the FBI instituted a dragnet of the lesbian and gay community in the area, starting first with questions about the specific individuals and their whereabouts, but, as Donovan notes, "The questions broadened to include questions about the lesbian community in general—who was in it, who was involved with whom, who were friends with whom, the tenor of their political beliefs, and the nature of their lifestyles and 'sexual preferences.'"

After finding the conditions of the Madison County Jail "intolerable," two of the Lexington Six capitulated and agreed to cooperate with the grand jury. Three more spent two months in jail, until they were pressured to comply with the grand jury questions. But one woman held out the entire twelve-month convening of the grand jury and was eventually freed on May 3, 1976. All six acted to protect their community from state violence and surveillance, and their work inspired others—primarily women—to resist harassment by the FBI and federal and state organizations.[4]

4 **February 4, 2004** The Massachusetts Supreme Judicial Court argued that only full, equal marriage rights for gay couples would be constitutional: "Because the proposed law by its express terms forbids same-sex couples entry into civil marriage, it continues to relegate same-sex couples to a different status.... The history of our nation has demonstrated that separate is seldom, if ever, equal."

While some states across the United States had extended "civil union" status to same-sex couples, Massachusetts's highest court argued that this constituted a separate but equal system. This decision came amid a significant federal and national push to delegitimize gay relationships, with things like the so-called Defense of Marriage Act being passed in 1996 and President George W. Bush continuing to state that decisions like the court's were "deeply troubling" and calling for constituents to undermine the ruling. While this decision entrenched the idea that only marriage should provide legal protections, it also served as an important harm reduction decision that made things like medical care easier to get for some queer people.[5]

5 **February 5, 1981** Four Toronto bathhouses—the Barracks, the Club, Richmond Street Health Emporium, and Roman II Health and Recreation Spa—were raided late on this day in 1981. Targeted by police using the moniker "Operation Soap," the raids on the four bathhouses involved approximately two hundred police officers. Police claimed they were attempting to end sex work and "indecent" acts in each establishment, but what emerged was a targeted attack on patrons for their sexuality. Two hundred eighty-six men were charged for being found in a "common bawdy house" (a brothel), and twenty others were charged with operating a bawdy house. Historians have argued that this raid, one of the largest of its kind in Canadian history, was a turning point in activating the gay community to resist police oppression and harassment.[6]

6 **February 6, 1936** Angela Bowen was born. Bowen was an American dance teacher, English professor, writer, and activist for lesbian rights. She emerged as a prominent advocate for gay rights in the 1980s and '90s, assuming a position on the board of the National Coalition of Black Lesbians and Gays. Her commitment to the cause propelled her to eventually ascend to the role of cochair within the organization. Additionally, Bowen took on the responsibility of editing the group's magazine, *Black/ Out*, further solidifying her dedication to advancing LGBT+ rights.[7]

7 **February 7, 1970** "F*g*ts Stay Out." This sign, prominently displayed behind the bar of Barney's Beanery in West Hollywood, California, prompted a gay liberation march on this day in 1970. Morris Kight and Troy Perry, two key figures of gay organizing well known within the organizing circles of Los Angeles, worked together to coordinate the action, calling the sign a violation of civil rights. The sign represented the views of the Beanery's ownership, as the owner's daughter notes the sign had been up since 1959 and her father was recorded stating that he thought homosexuals should be shot. Organizers took to the streets to confront the homophobia in their community—and built that community through their coordinated actions together.[8]

8 **February 8, 1917** Civil rights leader and pacifist Igal Roodenko was born. Roodenko, a gay Jewish activist, was an early member of the Committee for Nonviolent Revolution and was involved with the pacifist organization the War Resisters League.

In April 1947, a group of eight Black and eight white men embarked on a two-week interstate bus journey from Washington, DC, into the upper South, known as the "Journey of Reconciliation," sponsored by the FOR (Fellowship of Reconciliation) and CORE (Congress of Racial Equality). Seating themselves side by side regardless of race, they aimed to challenge segregation in areas where local laws still enforced it, testing the newly established Supreme Court ruling of *Morgan v. State of Virginia*, which declared laws requiring segregation on interstate travel unconstitutional.

During their stop in Chapel Hill, North Carolina, four riders—Bayard Rustin, Igal Roodenko, Joe Felmet, and Andrew Johnson—were arrested for violating state law. Rustin and Roodenko were both found guilty at their trial. Rustin received a thirty-day sentence on a North Carolina chain gang. Addressing Roodenko, the judge remarked, "Now, Mr. Rodenky [*sic*], I presume you're Jewish." "Yes, I am," replied Roodenko. "Well," said the judge, "it's about time you Jews from New York learned that you can't come down bringing your n*gr*s with you to upset the customs of the South." And to teach him "a lesson," the judge sentenced him to ninety days on a chain gang—three times the length of Rustin's sentence.[9]

9 **February 9, 1874** Amy Lawrence Lowell was born. Lowell was an American poet, editor, and translator associated with the imagist movement, advocating for a revival of classical ideals in poetry. While historically contentious, many argue that Lowell was a lesbian poet. Her posthumous recognition came in 1926 when she was awarded the Pulitzer Prize for Poetry.[10]

10 **February 10, 1990** Director Bill Sherwood, best known for his sole feature film, the critically acclaimed *Parting Glances* (1986), passed away from AIDS-related complications at the age of thirty-seven. *Parting Glances* is recognized as one of the first American films to address the AIDS crisis with frankness and realism, offering a detailed portrayal of gay life in 1980s Manhattan. One of the earliest American films to depict gay life with emotional nuance and without moralizing overtones, the film offered a rare and intimate look at the lives of gay men in New York City at the height of the AIDS crisis.[11]

11 **February 11, 1916** Emma Goldman, feminist, anarchist, and organizer (see June 27, 1869), was arrested for giving a talk about family planning. The police targeted Goldman using the Comstock Law, accusing Goldman of participating in the transportation of "obscene, lewd and/or lascivious" materials. This included anything discussing contraception. Goldman had this to say following her incarceration: "When a law has outgrown time and necessity, it must go, and the only way to get rid of the law is to awaken the public to the fact that it has outlived its purpose. And that is precisely what I have been doing and mean to do in the future." Her journey did not end there. Her work continued to demonstrate the unnecessary nature of the state and the patriarchy, as well as the violence of social stratification.

She was a strong early advocate for LGBT+ rights—especially notable in an era when even many progressive movements ignored or actively marginalized queer individuals. She publicly defended homosexual love as natural and valid, criticized the criminalization of same-sex relationships, and supported the work of early gay rights activists like Magnus Hirschfeld.

In terms of her own sexuality, Goldman had intense and often unconventional relationships with both men and women, though historical records focus mostly on her relationships with men. Some scholars speculate about the possibility of queer desire or affinity in her life, but there's no definitive evidence to claim she was queer by modern definitions. Still, her politics were deeply aligned with queer liberation, and many in queer and anarchist communities today claim her as an ancestor because of that.[12]

February 11, 1954 A concentration camp was opened in Tefía, Canary Islands, which was soon used to intern LGBT+ people imprisoned when Spain banned homosexuality later that year. It was established as an agricultural labor camp in an inhospitable, desert environment. One of the first gay men to be imprisoned there was Octavio García. He later testified that guards constantly humiliated, insulted, and viciously beat prisoners, while they were given inadequate portions of rotting food.[13]

February 11, 1967 A protest against police repression was held outside the Black Cat Tavern in Los Angeles. It was part of a series of demonstrations against police raids and harassment of countercultural young people held that night around the city. The Black Cat was chosen as the location of one of the protests due to it being the site of a violent police raid on January 1, when police attacked customers, arresting fourteen people for same-sex kissing. The protest was endorsed by gay rights group PRIDE (Personal Rights in Defense and Education), which was formed the previous year, marking what may be the first use of the term "pride" in the LGBT+ rights movement.[14]

12 **February 12, 1928** "Daddy" Alan Selby, future founder of Mr. S Leather in the SoMa district of San Francisco, who would earn the nickname "the Mayor of Folsom Street," was born in London. While there have been debates about kink in queer spaces, Selby demonstrated how these two have always played an important role in explicitly linking desire and physicality to the struggle for collective liberation.[15]

13 **February 13, 2025** The National Park Service erased references to queer and transgender people from the Stonewall National Monument website, sparking outrage among transgender activists.

The monument commemorates the historic New York City gay bar where LGBT+ activists—including transgender trailblazers Marsha P. Johnson and Sylvia Rivera—waged an uprising that was a turning point for the modern LGBT+ rights movement (see June 28, 1969).

The New York Times reported that the Park Service's public affairs department said the website changes were made to comply with Donald Trump's anti-trans executive order, aimed at "restoring biological truth to the federal government." The department also referenced a second order issued in January by the acting secretary of the interior.

"The Stonewall Inn and The Stonewall Inn Gives Back Initiative are outraged and appalled by the recent removal of the word 'transgender' from the Stonewall National Monument page on the National Park Service website," the Stonewall Inn said in a statement. "This blatant act of erasure not only distorts the truth of our history, but it also dishonors the immense contributions of transgender individuals—especially trans-gender women of color—who were at the forefront of the Stonewall Riots and the broader fight for LGBTQ+ rights."[16]

14 **February 14, 1991** Valentine's Day can be a hard time, especially for queer people. On this day in 1991, Queer Nation, a radical queer organization often engaged in direct action, had "kiss-in" demonstrations across the US. One particular action in Seattle featured Jonathan Darci and about a dozen other men and women drawing attention to the lack of inclusion in the holiday, and more specifically in the traditions and American education system writ large. Darci said, "If you're not sure what your feelings mean or you're hiding your sexuality and pretending to be straight, as most gay and lesbian youth do, you feel even more isolated than other days. It's like icing on the cake of your oppression."[17]

15 **February 15, 1820** Susan B. Anthony, a prominent American social reformer and advocate for women's rights, was born. Historian Lillian Faderman found Anthony had relationships with women through-out her life, often documented through touching and intimate letters. Raised in a Quaker household dedicated to social justice, she began her activism by gathering antislavery petitions at just seventeen years old. By 1856, Anthony had assumed the role of New York state agent for the American Anti-Slavery Society.[18]

16 **February 16, 2020** America has a booming prison-industrial complex, a carceral system that targets marginalized populations for erasure and exploitation. On this day in 2020, Black and Pink, an organization focused on providing support for incarcerated queer and trans people, opened Lydon House in Omaha, Nebraska. The house is meant to serve formerly incarcerated folks, as well as those living with HIV and AIDS. Dominique Morgan, executive director of Black and Pink, said, "We now know how to how to create loving spaces for the people that we really want to be a part of our community."[19]

17 **February 17, 1977** The Canadian Broadcasting Corporation of Nova Scotia refused to advertise a public announcement about the Gay Alliance Toward Equality's "GayLine" resource. This prompted the local LGBT+ community to protest outside the organization's headquarters. Around twenty people marched together in the first recorded public protest of its kind in Nova Scotia. Although the CBC ended up doubling down on their position, this was a major moment of organizing for the local community and brought national attention to the censoring of LGBT+ organizations.[20]

February 17, 1994 Well into the 1990s, queer Canadian spaces were still being targeted by local police. On this day in 1994, the KOX/Katakombes bar in Montreal was raided by police, who arrested everyone in the bar for being in a "bawdy house," a Canadian legal term for a brothel. This was yet another clear instance in which public queerness was associated with indecency—an association we still see today.[21]

18 **February 18, 1934** Audre Lorde, American writer and daughter of Caribbean immigrants, was born. Lorde described herself as a "Black, lesbian, mother, warrior, poet." She was also a factory worker, social worker, X-ray technician, artisan, writer, civil rights activist, communist, and much more.

In the 1960s, she graduated from Columbia University and began to participate in the feminist, LGBT+, and civil rights movement of the time, where she contested the class discrimination and racism existing in the feminist movement, which was generally focused on the experiences of white women.

Lorde identified the wide and varied experiences of women in matters of class, race, age, sex, and even health, which is often referred to today as "intersectionality," noting that "there is no thing as a single-issue struggle because we do not live single-issue lives."

In 1980, together with Cherríe Moraga and Barbara Smith, she founded Kitchen Table: Women of Color Press, the first publisher for women of color in the US. Later, she developed *Farbe Bekennen* (Showing Our Colors), an important work of revolutionary activism in the Afro-German movement, when she taught at the Free University of Berlin.

She passed away in 1992 after a long struggle with breast and liver cancer.[22]

February 18, 1966 While the Mattachine Society is one of the earliest examples of gay organizing in the US, it operated using a cell-like structure, building local connections and lacking a significant national organization. On this day in 1966, we saw the first meeting of a group who would take gay and lesbian organizing onto the national stage.

This first meeting, in Kansas City, Missouri, would bring together a coalition of gay rights groups who were looking to coordinate their local efforts into a national organization. This would evolve into the North American Conference of Homophile Organizations (NACHO). While NACHO would eventually dissolve by the early 1970s under pressure from groups who were more intersectional and better organized, it served as an important step toward a coordinated articulation of queer liberation.[23]

19 **February 19, 2002** Sylvia Rivera, a prominent American activist for gay liberation and transgender rights, died. Renowned as a dedicated community worker in New York, Rivera initially identified as a drag queen for much of her life before later embracing her identity as a transgender person. She actively participated in demonstrations alongside the Gay Liberation Front. In collaboration with her close friend Marsha P. Johnson, Rivera cofounded the Street Transvestite Action Revolutionaries (STAR), an organization committed to supporting homeless young drag queens, gay youth, and transgender women.[24]

20 **February 20, 1988** Twenty thousand people in Manchester marched against Margaret Thatcher's homophobic Section 28 law, which made it illegal for public bodies to "promote" homosexuality, which included banning schools teaching the "acceptability of homosexuality as a pretended family relationship." The law was abolished in 2003, although later Conservative Prime Minister David Cameron voted against the complete scrapping of the ban. Another later Conservative prime minister, Boris Johnson, voted in favor of repealing Section 28, although he had previously compared gay marriage to bestiality in a book he published and had referred to gay men as "tank-topped bumboys" while working as a journalist.[25]

February 20, 2023 The National LGBTQ Task Force hosts a conference every year, bringing together government leaders, activists, and organizers. The conference, called "Creating Change," is a key networking event—but more importantly it is meant to embody the kind of organizing it aims to see enacted elsewhere. But during this event in 2023, trans, gendernonconforming, and intersex workers, volunteers, and attendees found that it was not a safe place to organize or labor.

These attendees came together as the "Trans Action Collective" and, alongside trans activist Angelica Ross, protested in order to get their nine grievances addressed. The demands included taking accountability for harassment and discrimination by hotel staff, compensation for volunteers, accessibility for the neurodivergent and disabled communities, and creating new awards categories to fully recognize the work of members of all communities.

"I heard that, you know, we needed a demonstration and a protest because some shit wasn't going down the way that it was supposed to go down," Ross told the audience. "When my brothers and sisters were telling me what was going on, I was like, 'You got to be kidding me. This is still going on?' So, we're not asking. These are demands."[26]

21 **February 21, 1903** Undercover New York police officers raided the Ariston Hotel Baths, the first raid of a gay bathhouse in US history. More than seventy men were inside at the time. Twenty-six were arrested, twelve were charged, and seven were convicted of sodomy. The men who were convicted faced prison sentences ranging from four to twenty years.[27]

February 21, 1933 Nina Simone was born. Simone was an American singer, songwriter, pianist, composer, arranger, and civil rights activist. Her music spanned styles including classical, folk, gospel, blues, jazz, and rhythm and blues.

Simone's consciousness on racial and social discourse was prompted by her friendship with the playwright Lorraine Hansberry. Simone, who was likely bisexual, stated that during her conversations with Hansberry, "We never talked about men or clothes. It was always Marx, Lenin and revolution—real girls' talk." The influence of Hansberry planted the seed for the provocative social commentary that became an expectation in Simone's repertoire. One of Nina's more hopeful activism anthems, "To Be Young, Gifted and Black," was written with collaborator Weldon Irvine in the years following the playwright's passing, acquiring the title of one of Hansberry's unpublished plays.

Simone's social circles included notable Black activists such as James Baldwin, Stokely Carmichael, and Langston Hughes; the lyrics of her song "Backlash Blues" were written by Hughes.[28]

22 **February 22, 1943** Hans Scholl, his sister Sophie Scholl, and their friend Christoph Probst were executed by guillotine for their role in organizing nonviolent resistance against Adolf Hitler and the Nazi Party. As university students in Munich, the Scholls and Probst formed the core of the White Rose, a clandestine group of young people who authored and distributed anonymous leaflets denouncing the regime's atrocities and calling on Germans to rise up against fascism. Their words ring powerfully true, even—perhaps especially—now:

> But the present "state" is the dictatorship of evil. "Oh, we've known that for a long time," I hear you object, "and it isn't necessary to bring that to our attention again." But, as I ask you, if you know that, why do you not rouse yourselves, why do you allow these men in power to rob you step by step, both openly and in secret, of one of your rights after another, until one day nothing, nothing at all will be left but a mechanized state system presided over by criminals and drunkards? Is your spirit already so crushed by abuse that you forget it is your right—or rather, your moral duty—to eradicate this system?

In 1937, Hans Scholl was implicated in a same-sex relationship after a former acquaintance reported him to authorities. He was subsequently arrested and held in solitary confinement, where he acknowledged the truth of the accusations. The following year, he stood trial under Paragraph 175, the Nazi law criminalizing homosexuality. Despite the serious nature of the charges, Hans was unexpectedly acquitted. Though he avoided formal punishment, the experience left a profound mark on Hans. The betrayal, isolation, and criminalization of his sexuality only sharpened his growing skepticism of the Nazi regime.[29]

23 **February 23, 1943** Carl Wittman was born in New Jersey. Wittman was a pivotal organizer, working first as a part of the national governing body of Students for a Democratic Society (SDS). During his time in in SDS during the early 1960s he worked on the issue of civil rights in the South, and he cowrote "An Interracial Movement of the Poor" in 1963. Although he was passionate in his work with SDS, he left the organization because of homophobia and went on to work in LGBT+ activism, writing *Refugees from Amerika: A Gay Manifesto* in 1970.[30]

24 **February 24, 2025** A State Department directive instructed US consular staff across the globe to refuse entry to transgender athletes applying for visas to participate in sports events. The guidance also called for permanent bans on applicants whose stated gender is judged to conflict with the sex assigned to them at birth.[31]

25 **February 25, 1982** Wisconsin Governor Lee Dreyfus signed Assembly Bill 70 into law, the first American law to make it illegal for private businesses to discriminate against people based on sexual orientation. The bill was a major win for queer folks in the state, as organizers had been attempting to pass legislation like it since 1967. Building grassroots support through religious leaders and local community made it possible, and another state wouldn't institute similar legislation for another nine years.[32]

26 **February 26, 1960** In what would later be dubbed the "gayola" scandal, San Francisco Police Sergeant Waldo Reesink was arrested on charges of extorting the owner of a gay bar, the Handlebar, for illicit payoffs to avoid raids. Despite the technical legality of gay bars, activities such as hand-holding or dancing together could still prompt closures.

After Reesink's arrest, owners of other gay bars came forward to reveal widespread corruption, and by the end of May, eight police officers in total had been charged with taking bribes. Reesink was sentenced to a year in jail.[33]

February 26, 2024 At least forty students from Owasso High School in Owasso, Oklahoma, staged a walkout to protest a widespread culture of bullying with minimal accountability at their school. The protest came after Nex Benedict, a sixteen-year-old transgender student, died on February 8 following a bathroom fight. In body camera footage from a police officer's interview with Nex, he recounted how three students jumped him after he splashed water on them in response to their bullying of him and his friend over their attire.[34]

27 **February 27, 2004** In New Paltz, New York, Mayor Jason West performed same-sex marriages for about a dozen couples, the first in the state. In June, the Ulster County Supreme Court issued a permanent injunction that stopped him from officiating these marriages. West's actions demonstrate that it's community recognition, not state sanctioning, that plays a role in recognizing important queer relationships.[35]

28 **February 28, 1994** The Clinton administration officially began enforcing the "Don't Ask, Don't Tell" policy, which was enacted by a significant majority in Congress. This legislation required openly lesbian, gay, and bisexual military service members to conceal their sexual orientation while serving. While this policy was critiqued by mainstream LGBT+

organizations for discriminating against lesbian, gay, and bisexual members, queer organizers attested that the military-industrial complex itself should be dismantled.[36]

29 **February 29, 1940** Black actor Hattie McDaniel was not allowed to sit with her white costars during the twelfth Academy Awards ceremony.

McDaniel, who, according to Mikelle Street in *Out* magazine, "most historians agree … lived her private life as a bisexual woman," won Best Supporting Actress for her performance in the film *Gone with the Wind*. In doing so, she became the first African American to receive an Academy Award. However, while her white costars sat at a table near the main stage, she was only allowed to sit at the back of the room.

The venue hosting the ceremony, the Cocoanut Grove nightclub at the Ambassador Hotel, had a strict policy of refusing admission to Black people. McDaniel was only granted entry after the producer, David Selznick, called in a special favor with hotel management.

McDaniel, who was born to two parents who had been enslaved, stated in her acceptance speech: "I shall always hold it as a beacon for anything I may be able to do in the future. I sincerely hope that I shall always be a credit to my race and the motion picture industry."

Over her career, McDaniel appeared in hundreds of films, mostly uncredited. Of her ninety-four credited roles on the Internet Movie Database, seventy-four of them were playing domestic workers, often as a stereotypical "Mammy" character.

Before she died, aged just fifty-seven, her final wish was to be buried in the Hollywood Cemetery, but this was not permitted, due to it not admitting Black people.[37]

MARCH

1 **March 1, 1990** In the beginning of 1990, ACT UP organized three protests in the state capital of Albany, New York, including one on this date, under the banner of "NY Disaster Zone." These demonstrations involved entering the capitol building and covering various objects with red tape, symbolizing the inefficiency and delays associated with bureaucracy.[1]

March 1, 2023 Over forty-seven Iowa schools saw students walk out in protest of proposed anti-LGBT+ legislation. The legislation reflected a copy-pasted attempt to pass bills that would "out trans students to their parents, prohibit teachers from discussing gender identity and sexual orientation in classrooms through eighth grade, and amend the state constitution to effectively ban same-sex marriage."

Students responded by organizing a "We Say Gay" walkout, demanding that legislators listen to what the youth of Iowa want. One organizer said that the walkout emerged because governmental officials had heard expert testimony about the harmfulness of these bills and did not seem to care or be swayed by the detrimental effects of the proposed laws.[2]

2 **March 2, 1982** Wisconsin became the first state to prohibit discrimination based on sexual orientation. Considering the impact that sexual orientation discrimination continues to have today, this was an important harm reduction step for queer people in the state.[3]

3 **March 3, 1973** Castro Camera, the photography shop established by Harvey Milk and Scott Smith, commenced operations at 575 Castro Street. The establishment of Castro Camera was more than just a neighborhood camera store opening—it was the heartbeat of a nascent queer liberation movement. The store started out as a simple storefront but transformed into an unofficial community center for San Francisco's LGBT+ community, particularly at a time when visibility, solidarity, and access to public space were limited and revolutionary for queer people.

Castro Camera was where Harvey Milk initially sowed the seeds of his political life. The store not only kept him afloat economically but also acted as a gathering place where neighbors could meet, plan, and envision a different future. Activists, artists, drag queens, working-class queers, and curious locals walked through the shop's doors. It was in this setting that Milk became known as "the Mayor of Castro Street," building the connections and believability that would later launch him into elected politics as one of the first openly gay elected officials in the United States.[4]

March 3, 1970 Jearld Moldenhauer, an organizer for the University of Toronto Homophile Association, was fired from his lab tech position on this day because of his LGBT+ activism. Moldenhauer played a foundational role in shaping Canada's gay liberation movement. In 1968, while studying in the US, he helped establish one of the first gay rights organizations on a university campus. After moving to Canada, he was instrumental in launching the country's first gay activist group following the Stonewall Uprising, as well as the first queer organization at a Canadian university. Moldenhauer went on to found Glad Day Bookshop, now recognized as the world's oldest LGBT+ bookstore (see April 21, 1982), and contributed significantly to landmark initiatives such as *The Body Politic* newspaper, Toronto Gay Action, and the Gay Alliance Toward Equality. He also helped preserve the movement's legacy through his involvement in what is now known as the ArQuives: Canada's LGBTQ2+ Archives. In 1972, he made history as the first openly gay activist to speak at a national political party convention in Canada. Alongside his activism, Moldenhauer used photography to chronicle the early years of queer resistance and community-building across the country.[5]

4 **March 4, 1948** Jean O'Leary, founder of Lesbian Feminist Liberation, codirector of the National Gay and Lesbian Task Force, and cofounder of National Coming Out Day, was born in Kingston, New York. While O'Leary has a checkered past, including significant moments of trans antagonism, she eventually realized that her original position was wrong. O'Leary's position suffered from the same issues as the second-wave feminism in which she was immersed: reinforcing notions of biological essentialism through the language of liberation. Still, her legacy as a community organizer remains an important one.[6]

March 4, 2023 Following the death of queer organizer Tortuguita (see January 18, 2023), forest defenders in Atlanta coordinated a week of action starting on this day. The first of the series of actions was a music festival event with approximately five hundred attendees. Alongside the event, a group of people took over a security outpost used to surveil the forest and burned a police vehicle.

This first day of action not only demonstrated how organizers have acted in strategic, militant ways to disrupt the installation of a police-military apparatus but also highlighted the way joyful celebration can be incorporated into actions of resistance.[7]

5 **March 5, 1971** A group of militant lesbians and supportive men inter-rupted an anti-abortion meeting held by an association called Laissez-les-vivre (Let Them Live) at a conference center in Paris's fifth arrondissement, showing that working together is the foundation for building a shared vision of a liberatory future. The group would formalize later that month (see March 10, 1971) as Le Front homosexuel d'action révo-lutionnaire (FHAR, or "Homosexual Revolutionary Action Front").[8]

6 **March 6, 1987** Melvin Boozer died at the age of forty-one, leaving an imposing legacy as an activist, scholar, and trailblazer. A college professor and zealous advocate of racial justice, LGBT+ activism, and AIDS awareness, Boozer brought the model of an intersectional lens to activism in an era in which this type of work was the exception and was often marginalized.

As an openly gay Black male during an era of rampant discrimination, Boozer used his voice and visibility to challenge systems of oppression on multiple fronts. He emerged as a national name in 1980 when he was nominated for vice president by the Socialist Party USA. That year, he was also invited to serve as an openly gay speaker for the Democratic National Convention, and he gave a historic address urging the party to treat LGBT+ rights with gravitas.

Boozer was also a vigorous participant in early AIDS activism, helping to fight the struggle against stigma and calling for government action during the early days of the epidemic. He served as president of the Gay Activists Alliance of Washington, DC, and set the local and national agenda regarding public health, equity, and the dignity of individuals living with HIV/AIDS.[9]

March 6, 2023 Four University of South Florida students were arrested while protesting Florida Governor Ron DeSantis's positions on racial justice and diversity programs in education as well as the treatment of LGBT+ subjects and people in public schools. The protest specifically focused on Florida's HB-999, legislation that intended to eliminate majors and minors in academic disciplines related to race and gender, institute new general education requirements, expand university board powers, and end tenure.

A public statement posted to social media alleged that the police "slammed protestors against the ground and on walls, sat on them, pulled their hair, pulled, shoved and scratched students, and placed protestors in choke holds." Police claimed they were attacked first with "objects" and an "unidentified liquid." However, video footage from protesters shows the police using unprovoked force to detain and arrest students. The four students arrested were charged with felonies and misdemeanors, including trespassing, battery of law enforcement, resisting an officer, and disrupting a school campus or function.[10]

7 **March 7, 2023** Mauree Turner, a Black Muslim and nonbinary lawmaker, was censured by the Oklahoma House of Representatives. The reason given by their fellow representatives was that they had "impeded a law enforcement investigation into an alleged assault on another House member and on an Oklahoma Highway Patrol trooper." The local news reported that someone protesting a ban on gender-affirming care was arrested after throwing water at a state representative and a state trooper. Turner offered the protester's spouse their office to process what had happened—something that would get them accused of "harboring a fugitive and repeatedly lying to officers."

Turner refused to apologize, saying, "I think an apology for loving the people of Oklahoma is something that I cannot do."[11]

8 **March 8, 1970** Diego Viñales was injured on this day. The former Argentinian student was swept up in an early-hours police raid on the Snake Pit gay bar in New York's Greenwich Village. The raid at the Stonewall Inn that had sparked rioting and gay activism had occurred the previous summer, but such raids were still common. After being taken to the police station, Viñales, who was on an expired student visa and fearful of deportation, tried to escape by jumping out of a second-floor window. He landed on the spikes of an iron fence. Viñales suffered grave injuries, but he survived and was arrested. Protest marches in response to the day's events were led by gay activist groups formed in the wake of Stonewall and helped spark greater community awareness and interest in the upcoming Christopher Street Liberation Day events scheduled for June 28 to commemorate the first anniversary of the Stonewall Rebellion.

Marty Robinson, a member of the Gay Activists Alliance (GAA), was credited with originating the "zap" protest tactic—using loud, theatrical, and impossible-to-ignore direct actions—after five hundred protesters marched on an NYPD station house at around 9:00 p.m. on the same day as the Snake Pit raid. The GAA had distributed a flyer earlier in the day with these words, written by Robinson: "Any way you look at it—that boy was PUSHED. We are ALL being pushed."[12]

9 **March 9, 1969** For years, the Dover Hotel, often simply referred to as "the Dover," served as a popular overnight haven for Los Angeles's burgeoning LGBT+ community. Operated and maintained by members of the United States Mission, a gay religious organization based in LA, it provided an affordable and accessible option for lodging, socializing with fellow members of the gay community, and engaging in sexual encounters. Operating akin to a gay bathhouse, the Dover regularly attracted police attention, leading to frequent raids.

Tragedy struck during one such police raid on this day in 1969, when nurse Howard Efland, according to witnesses, was fatally beaten outside the hotel. Officers claimed Efland had groped them, leading to him being dragged downstairs naked before the assault. The officers said that Efland was being transported to a police station when he kicked the door of the vehicle open and was subsequently thrown onto the Hollywood Freeway, resulting in his death. The Los Angeles County Coroner ruled the death an "excusable homicide."[13]

10 **March 10, 1867** Lillian D. Wald was born. Trained in nursing, Wald directed her efforts toward providing top-notch medical care to residents of New York City's Lower East Side. She founded the Henry Street Settlement, which accomplished this through its team of "visiting nurses," who resided in the settlement and attended to residents in their homes. By her retirement in 1933, Wald had overseen the employment of over 260 nurses and the treatment of more than a hundred thousand patients.

Within the communal living quarters of the settlement, Wald fostered a familial atmosphere with her fellow female residents and colleagues. As a pioneer of the "New Women" movement at the turn of the century, Wald eschewed traditional gender norms, shaping a unique paradigm for domestic and familial life. Though Wald never openly identified as lesbian, she cultivated profound platonic and romantic bonds with several women at Henry Street. Moreover, she maintained social connections with prominent LGBT+ figures in the reform movement, many of whom frequented the settlement to discuss social reform. They included Jane Addams and her partner, Mary Rozet Smith; M. Carey Thomas, president of Bryn Mawr College; and Wellesley College professors Vida Scudder and Florence Converse.

In addition to quietly fostering a supportive environment for LGBT+ women and advocating for impoverished immigrants, Wald championed various social causes. She was a staunch supporter of women's rights and played a role in the women's suffrage movement while advocating for access to birth control. Wald also ardently supported labor protections, especially for children. In 1909, alongside colleagues W.E.B. Du Bois and Jane Addams, she was a founding member of the National Association for the Advancement of Colored People (NAACP), extending her activism to New York City's burgeoning Black communities.[14]

March 10, 1971 A group of protesters attracted public attention by disrupting and stopping a public Radio Luxembourg broadcast hosted by Ménie Grégoire on the topic of homosexuality. Thirty people stormed the podium, shouting, "Liberty! Liberty!" and "Fight! Fight!" into the microphones. Later that evening, the group would formalize under the name Le Front homosexuel d'action révolutionnaire (FHAR, or "Homosexual Revolutionary Action Front").[15]

11 **March 11, 2004** The California Supreme Court unanimously mandated that San Francisco cease conducting same-sex marriages, a practice the city had started on February 12. In August, the court would rule that by issuing the licenses, the mayor had overstepped his authority, and would then void the four thousand same-sex marriages the city had sanctioned.[16]

12 **March 12, 2020** After being jailed for refusing to testify to a grand jury investigating the whistleblower media organization WikiLeaks, transgender woman and data analyst Chelsea Manning was released. Despite being released, she was still told to pay over a quarter of a million dollars in fines because of her resistance efforts. Her attempts to stand up to state repression and surveillance made her a key figure among those trying to bring attention to US governmental overreach and surveillance.[17]

13 **March 13, 1990** *Paris Is Burning* premiered in New York City. The film was hailed by critics as an invaluable documentary capturing the conclusion of the "Golden Age" of New York City drag balls, while also providing a profound examination of race, class, gender, and sexuality in America. In 2016, the Library of Congress selected the film for preservation in the National Film Registry, recognizing its cultural, historical, and aesthetic significance.[18]

14 **March 14, 1868** Magnus Hirschfeld was born in Kolberg, Germany. Hirschfeld, a German Jewish doctor, was one of the leading forces behind attempts to decriminalize homosexuality. His work made Germany one of the foremost sites of scientific research into sexuality and gender, with an Institute for Sexual Science (see July 6, 1919), significant medical research into queer and trans people's lived experience, and a number of organizing groups attempting to overturn Paragraph 175, which was the country's antisodomy statute.

It was because of both Hirschfeld's work and his Jewish identity that he was targeted by the Nazis. These attacks were not limited to newspaper smear campaigns: Hirschfeld was badly beaten in 1921. The Holocaust Encyclopedia says, "A newspaper article celebrated the assault and warned that 'the next time his skull might be crushed.'" The threat facing Hirschfeld and his work continued to increase, until in 1930 he went on a worldwide tour to the US, Japan, China, the Philippines, Indonesia, India, Egypt, and Palestine. His ideas about sexology are not above critique by the left either; Laurie Marhoefer argues in *Racism and the Making of Gay Rights: A Sexologist, His Student, and the Empire of Queer Love* that Hirschfeld drew from a number of racist, imperialistic, and eugenic ideas—the bread and butter of European (and American) thought during this period.

After Hitler came to power, Hirschfeld fled the country, never to return. He died in 1935 in Nice.[19]

March 14, 1971 Bringing together groups from around New York state, people took to the streets of Albany to demand the repeal or reform of laws against sodomy. Approximately two and a half to three thousand participants from across the political spectrum participated—from the more conservative Mattachine Society to the revolutionary Street Transvestite Action Revolutionaries (STAR). The action had a list of demands, as follows:

1. Scrapping the sodomy law, which defined homosexual sex as a sex crime.
2. Repeal of the solicitation law, which criminalized expressions of sexual interest between people of the same sex.
3. An end to the statutes against cross-dressing and impersonation.
4. Fair employment equal opportunity legislation for gays.
5. Legislation outlawing discrimination against gays in housing and public accommodations.
6. Repeal of the loitering laws used to entrap gay men who were seen as "cruising for sex."

Many of these demands would not be met until decades later, and some remain demands for the current generation of queer and trans organizers.[20]

March 14, 2024 Joan Gibbs, a multifaceted American activist, died. She had worked as an attorney, writer, and speaker and had played a crucial role in advancing social and economic justice in the US since the late 1960s. Gibbs was deeply involved in various movements, advocating against racism, fighting for women's rights, and supporting LGBT+ rights.

As a cofounder of Dykes Against Racism Everywhere and a former staff attorney at the Center for Constitutional Rights, Gibbs dedicated her legal career to championing constitutional and civil rights. Her clients ranged from organizations to individuals, including notable figures such as ACT UP; People United for Children; the late Sarah E. Wright, author of *This Child's Gonna Live*; and the late Herman Ferguson, a Black political prisoner, among others.[21]

15 **March 15, 1942** The US Army codified and expanded its psychiatric screening procedures by officially including individuals described as having "sexual perversion," a term then used to encompass homosexuality, within the scope of its exclusionary criteria. This step codified and intensified efforts to screen out gay men and others perceived to be sexually nonconforming from military service. The new rules amounted to the deliberate institutionalization of anti-LGBT+ discrimination, following broader wartime policy in consolidating narrow constructions of masculinity, national service, and moral value.[22]

16 **March 16, 1987** Mark Cagaanan Aguhar was born on this day. An activist, writer, and artist based in Houston, Texas, Aguhar used a multimedia practice to create powerful, critical art that exposed systems of power and violence. As a trans femme Filipina, she explored themes of intimacy and domination—not only as opposing forces, but as deeply entangled with each other:

> My work is about visibility. My work is about the fact that I'm a genderqueer person of color fat femme fag feminist and I don't really know what to do with that identity in this world. It's that thing where you grew up learning to hate every aspect of yourself and unlearning all that misery is really hard to do. It's that thing where you kind of regret everything you've ever done because it's so complicit with white hegemony. It's that thing where you realize that your own attempts at passive aggressive manipulation and power don't stand a chance against the structural forms of domination against your body. It's that thing where the only way to cope with the reality of your situation is to pretend it doesn't exist; because flippancy is a privilege you don't own but you're going to pretend you do anyway.

While she passed away by suicide in 2012, her work continues to inspire and ignite queer artists of color. We can see her lasting impact in the work of writer Roy Perez, who writes about Aguhar's influence and message in their publication "Proximity: On the Work of Mark Aguhar."[23]

17 **March 17, 1912** Bayard Rustin was born in West Chester, Pennsylvania. Rustin, a Black gay community organizer, would go on to organize the 1963 March on Washington alongside A. Philip Randolph. He worked closely with other civil rights leaders to promote Black civil and labor rights, also helping to coordinate the Southern Christian Leadership Conference as well as the Freedom Rides of 1961.

Although Rustin was enormously influential through his civil rights work, that influence was curbed by the threat of outing, with his 1946 arrest in Manhattan's Morningside Park for "solicitation to commit a lewd act" and his 1953 arrest in Pasadena, California, for "sexual perversion."

While Rustin did not organize along the lines of gay rights, his efforts for racial and labor justice set the stage for later organizing for sexual liberation.[24]

18 **March 18, 1967** When exactly did the iconic Stonewall Inn become a watering hole for queer and trans people? It was first opened on this day in 1967 as a "private" gay club by Mafia member Fat Tony Lauria.

Before this, it had served as a stable, a bakery, a speakeasy, and a restaurant. The Stonewall operated as a "private" club in order to avoid New York State Liquor Authority regulations and was one of the few places where queer and trans people could dance publicly.[25]

19 **March 19, 1983** Members of the Dublin Gay Collective held a protest march to remember the death of Declan Flynn. Flynn was beaten to death in Dublin's Fairview Park in 1982, and his killers were given suspended sentences in March 1983. Joni Crone of Liberation for Irish Lesbians recounts how Flynn's murder affected the local community: "[It] sent shock waves through the community and also strengthened the bonds that exist between activists campaigning for gay rights, women's rights and worker's rights." The Fairview march was a major turning point in organizing, shifting the number of participants around the issue from fewer than one hundred to approximately four to five hundred people.[26]

20 **March 20, 1990** Incensed by the rising instances of antigay and anti-lesbian violence in public spaces, as well as discrimination in the arts and media, sixty people from the LGBT+ community assembled at the Gay and Lesbian Community Services Center (now known as the Lesbian, Gay, Bisexual & Transgender Community Center) in the Greenwich Village neighborhood of New York City. Their objective was to establish a direct-action organization to address these issues head-on. The organization they formed would eventually be named Queer Nation.[27]

21 **March 21, 2025** The University of Maine System, covering seven state universities, was deemed compliant with US President Donald Trump's anti-trans executive order excluding transgender girls and women from participating in sports aligning with their gender. By codifying a definition of sex that would exclude transgender women from legal status in sports, the order was a drastic rollback of trans-inclusive policies and was seen as part of a broader effort by the Trump administration to rescind the rights of LGBT+ communities, namely trans youth and students.[28]

22 **March 22, 1972** The Equal Rights Amendment, which prohibits discrimination based on sex, was passed by the US Senate. That it has never been adopted and made part of the US Constitution is an indictment of the state system, which continues to expose queer people to various forms of discrimination.[29]

23 **March 23, 2011** Actress Elizabeth Taylor, who had become a powerful advocate for people with AIDS, passed away at the age of seventy-nine. Taylor stood out as a remarkable exception to celebrities who shied away from the disease in the 1980s. She served as host of the first celebrity AIDS benefit, in 1985; she helped establish the American Foundation for AIDS Research (now known as amfAR); she took her advocacy to the Senate in 1986, calling for increased funding for AIDS research; and she made heartfelt visits to AIDS wards and hospices in Los Angeles and San Francisco.[30]

24 **March 24, 1987** Two hundred fifty members of new AIDS rights direct-action group ACT UP demonstrated on Wall Street in New York City, demanding greater access to treatments and for national action to fight the disease. Seventeen participants were arrested.[31]

March 24, 2018 Gays Against Guns (GAG), a national queer-directed coalition focused on "nonviolently breaking the gun industry's chain of death," participated in the March for Our Lives event on this day in 2018. One of its cofounders, John Grauwiler, spoke to why this issue is essential to queer liberation: "Historically, queer people have challenged the status quo, and we have led the way because we recognize our outsiderness, and we take that and turn it to action."

Another GAG organizer, Cathy Marino-Thomas, said, "We as grown-ups let these kids down. We ought to be ashamed of ourselves, because [the kids] are organized, they got us off our butts, and they are doing it. I want to be there to support them."[32]

25 **March 25, 1998** The Trevor Project was founded to provide suicide prevention and crisis resources to young people—especially LGBT+ youth. Drawn from the work of Celeste Lecesne, Trevor was a character that featured in the one-person show *Word of Mouth*. Peggy Rajski and Randy Stone adapted Trevor into a short film that launched a national movement. Out of the attention this garnered, the founders developed enough funding to start the first national crisis intervention and suicide prevention hotline. This hotline, called the Trevor Lifeline, has helped hundreds of thousands of youths in crisis get connected to lifesaving resources.[33]

26 **March 26, 1977** A delegation of fourteen LGBT+ activists, among them George Raya from San Francisco, convened with President

Jimmy Carter's staff to address LGBT+ concerns. This was the first meeting with LGBT+ representatives ever held at the White House. During this period, Raya also wrote a paper on the health issues caused by hepatitis in the gay community, which helped secure federal funding for a hepatitis research project in San Francisco and laid important groundwork for AIDS researchers in the years to come.[34]

27 **March 27, 1943** Gay antifascist resistance fighter Willem Arondeus led a group in bombing the Amsterdam Public Records Office, which the Nazis had used to identify Jewish people and verify documents.

At 10:15 p.m., the group of around ten people, all wearing police uniforms, overpowered guards, sedated them, and dragged them to the garden. Five explosions were then heard, and the building was set ablaze. Firefighters then deliberately waited a long time before attempting to put out the fire, and when doing so they used large amounts of water, presumably in order to damage more papers. The attack destroyed thousands of files that could be used to check if documents forged by the resistance were genuine or not.[35]

March 27, 2023 In the face of increasing anti-trans and anti-queer legislation sweeping both the nation and Texas in particular, organizers rallied in front of the Texas Senate building to protest Senate Bill 12. *Truthout* shares that SB 12 "would criminalize performances by people exhibiting as the opposite sex assigned at birth in front of a minor or in a public space if it 'appeals to the prurient interest in sex.' Violators would face a Class A misdemeanor carrying a penalty of up to a year in jail, a $4,000 fine or both. The bill would also let the state fine businesses $10,000 if they allow minors to attend so-called prurient drag performances." A number of other bills attempting to criminalize queer and trans people were also being heard by the Texas legislature that day—a deluge of legislative organizing that queer and trans people were fighting because of its consequences on trans youth, bodily autonomy, and the public criminalization of gender nonconformity. Protesters filled three levels of the rotunda next to the hearing room.[36]

28 **March 28, 1969** Leo Laurence, president of the Society for Individual Rights, and his lover were featured in the *Berkeley Barb*, a weekly alternative newspaper. The Society for Individual Rights was a homophile group focused on community events and coordination in San Francisco and had deep ties to Bay Area politics. Laurence called on gay and lesbian community members to "come out" and participate in the many left-wing movements in the community—from the Black Panthers to other leftist organizations.[37]

29 **March 29, 1932** The New York Women's House of Detention was established in Greenwich Village. During the twentieth century in New York City, tens of thousands of women and transmasculine people found themselves incarcerated at the notoriously harsh women's prison, known as "the House of D." Author Hugh Ryan explains that many of these inmates were arrested for offenses related to their gender-nonconforming behavior: "Drunkenness, waywardism, disobedience to their parents, being out at night by themselves, wearing pants, accepting a date from a man, accepting a ride from a man ... all of these things could have gotten you arrested if you were perceived as the 'wrong kind of woman.'"[38]

March 29, 1973 Jill Johnston's collection of essays, *Lesbian Nation*, was published. The book advocated for the formation of a distinct lesbian movement independent from the broader gay rights movement, as well as from the straight feminist movement, which occasionally displayed prejudice against lesbians.[39]

30 **March 30, 1964** GAY, Canada's first gay periodical, published its first issue. This Toronto tabloid featured letters to the editor, gossip columns, fiction and poetry, clip art and photography, and articles discussing serious issues.[40]

31 **March 31, 2022** Trans women in Islamabad, Pakistan, organized a rally and vigil in response to widespread discrimination and violence. The community, called the *khawaja sira*, organized the event and have worked together to assist one another.

The rally and vigil followed the public death of at least five members of the community. Although Pakistan has recognized the community as a third gender category in Pakistan since 2012, the violence, harassment, and discrimination facing this community remain rampant. One attendee, Gudiya, said, "The community is excluded from education and therefore has few options for work other than begging, dancing and sex work.... If we had opportunities and alternatives we would not have opted [for] these options, and the irony is that these very reasons are then used to humiliate and murder us."

In the face of this violence, the khawaja sira aim to bring public attention to what's happening and, more than that, build resources and support for the community.[41]

March 31, 2023 Although a court ruling in February had allowed trans people in Hong Kong to change their gender documents, the government dragged its feet implementing the ruling. On this day in 2023, trans protesters gathered outside the administrative building. One, Henry Tse, the founder of the group Transgender Equality Hong Kong, said, "The government is using administrative tactics to deliberately delay the whole process." The immigration department responded to the organized protest, stating that it was reviewing the law and would complete a policy review "in a reasonable time."[42]

March 31, 2024 Queers Undermining Israeli Terrorism! (QUIT!) held a march in solidarity against the Israeli genocide in Gaza. The group demanded that Israel end its bombardment of Gaza, withdraw all military forces, and end the occupation of Palestine.[43]

APRIL

April 1977 The Combahee River Collective was a Black feminist lesbian socialist organization active in Boston from 1974 to 1980. The collective stated that the white feminist movement and the civil rights movement did not address their needs as Black women and as Black lesbians: the mainstream white feminist movement was racist, and the mainstream civil rights movement was not inclusive of feminist or gay liberation.

The collective emerged from the National Black Feminist Organization (NBFO). The NBFO was formed by Black feminists Florynce Kennedy and Margaret Sloan-Hunter among others and responded to the failures of mainstream white feminist groups to deal with the racism that Black women experienced in the US. The NBFO sought to focus on and address Black women's voices, perspectives, and issues. Members of the group who felt the need for a more radical vision informed by socialism, feminism, and gay liberation created the Combahee River Collective.

Early on, members met weekly in Cambridge, Massachusetts. Later, the collective held retreats throughout the northeast US at which members wrote articles developing a political framework specific to the intersections of their identities as Black women, feminists, socialists, and lesbians. The final statement of the collective's politics, dated April 1977, was drafted by Barbara Smith, Demita Frazier, and Beverly Smith. In the process of drafting this statement, the collective developed the theory of intersectionality, in which social and political identities impact the ways in which one is perceived, treated, and understood in the world. It was the first group to formally recognize and state that interlocking systems of oppression reinforce one another. "The Combahee River Collective Statement" is considered a definitive statement on identity politics, and the collective's articulation of intersectionality developed a framework for building coalitions that are antiracist and anticapitalist in nature.[1]

April 1, 1969 Homosexuals Intransigent! (HI!) was established, predating the Stonewall riots by almost three months and preceding the emergence of the gay liberation movement. It originated as a student organization at the City College of the City University of New York. L. Craig Schoonmaker, the founder of HI!, is often credited with coining the term "gay pride" for events commemorating Stonewall, including the inaugural march in New York City in June 1970. HI! produced several editions of a mimeographed newsletter, hosted dances on campus, and wielded considerable influence over the trajectory of the gay movement.[2]

April 1, 1998 Coretta Scott King was an organizer in her own right. Even after the assassination of her husband, Dr. Martin Luther King Jr., she continued to work for civil rights in the US, including the rights of gay and lesbian people. On this day in 1998, she addressed attendees of a Lambda Legal Defense and Education Fund event, saying, "Homophobia is like racism and anti-Semitism and other forms of bigotry in that it seeks to dehumanize a large group of people, to deny their humanity, their dignity and personhood."

Her longstanding commitment to bringing together issues of racial, gender, and sexual justice made her a powerful voice in a political field that often pitted marginalized people against one another. At a 2002 event, she went on to say, "We need more funding for diversity education so young people are inoculated against the toxic viruses of racism, sexism, and homophobia before they enter the work force."[3]

2 **April 2, 1974** Kathy Kozachenko became the first openly LGBT+ person to be elected to public office in the US, winning a seat on the Ann Arbor City Council in Michigan. Even with this early representation, the state system tokenizes queer representation in electoral politics and remained intractable to significant changes in law for decades following Kozachenko's election.[4]

3 **April 3, 1942** Tony DeBlase, also known as Fledermaus, a writer in the leather and S&M subcultures and creator of the leather pride flag, was born in Portland, Oregon. He was also the founder and publisher of *DungeonMaster* magazine.[5]

4 **April 4, 1928** Maya Angelou, a renowned American writer, poet, and civil rights leader, used her life and work to illuminate the realities of racism, resilience, and identity. Her groundbreaking memoir *I Know Why the Caged Bird Sings* marked a turning point in American literature, as she candidly recounted her experiences growing up Black in the segregated South. Through her powerful storytelling, Angelou became widely recognized as a champion of Black life and culture.

Over the course of her career, she authored seven memoirs, multiple collections of poetry, and several volumes of essays. Beyond her literary achievements, Angelou was deeply involved in the civil rights movement, lending her voice and efforts to the work of both Dr. Martin Luther King Jr. and Malcolm X.

Angelou's support for LGBT+ rights was bold and deeply intersec-tional. During a 1996 appearance before an LGBT+ audience in Florida, she declared, "I am gay. I am lesbian. I am Black. I am white. I am Native American. I am Christian. I am Jew. I am Muslim," expressing solidarity across identities. Later, in 2009, at the age of eighty-one, she personally contacted several New York state senators to encourage their support for marriage equality, which would be passed two years later.[6]

April 4, 1981 Paris's first Pride parade took place. The march was led by CUARH (Comité d'urgence anti-répression homosexuelle), an organization that fought against the repression of homosexuals.[7]

5 **April 5, 1997** Pioneering gay Jewish Beat generation poet Allen Ginsberg died at age seventy in New York City. In his personal life, Ginsberg took part in various protest movements in the 1960s and '70s, for example against the Vietnam War and against the US propping up the dictatorship of the Shah of Iran. In 1969, he visited the Stonewall Inn on the third night of the LGBT+ rebellion there against police harassment and told a reporter, "We're one of the largest minorities in the country, it's about time we did something to assert ourselves." He also observed of the community, "They've lost that wounded look." He was once expelled from Cuba after describing Che Guevara as "cute."

His poetry spoke of the underground counterculture and movements of the 1950s, '60s, and '70s, including the gay rights and later gay liberation movement. His publishers were prosecuted for obscenity for publishing his poem "Howl," which glorified anal sex, declaring, "The asshole is holy!" They were later exonerated.[8]

6 **April 6** This is International Asexuality Day (IAD). IAD is a campaign with four themes: advocacy, celebration, education, and solidarity. The campaign promotes the ace umbrella, including but not precluding demisexual, gray-asexual, and other ace identities.[9]

April 6, 2001 Robert Sloan Basker died. Basker was born September 30, 1918, in the East Harlem neighborhood of New York City. He joined the US Army after the attack on Pearl Harbor in December 1941. After his tour, he became an active participant in the civil rights and anti–Vietnam War movements.

In 1961, Basker assisted in securing a home for the first Black family in the all-white suburb of Skokie, Illinois. He was instrumental in the fight for integrated housing. In 1965, Basker cofounded Mattachine Midwest, and he served as its first president under the assumed name Bob Sloane. He also established the Mattachine Midwest telephone hotline for various social services for the LGBT+ community. He also worked with numerous LGBT+ organizations across the US, including participating in the 1965 conference of the East Coast Homophile Organizations (ECHO).

After Basker left Chicago and moved to Miami, Florida, he helped organize that city's first Metropolitan Community Church, the Miami Gay Activist Alliance, and Gay Community Seniors of South Florida. In 1976, he worked with eleven LGBT+ groups to create the Dade County Coalition for the Humanistic Rights of Gays, and collectively they lobbied and passed an antidiscrimination ordinance. Before his death, Basker lived in San Francisco and continued his work in gay rights, peace, civil liberties, women's rights, and antiracist organizing.[10]

7 **April 7, 1872** Marie Equi was born in New Bedford, Massachusetts. She grew up in a working-class immigrant family. She received a medical degree in 1903. Equi moved to Portland, Oregon, and built a successful practice that provided birth control and abortions. She was an out lesbian.

Equi participated in strikes for women workers' rights and frequently spoke at local town halls advocating for militant direct action. In 1916, she traveled to Seattle to provide medical care to wounded union members who had been attacked during a lumber strike, also known as the Everett Massacre.

As World War I drew close, Equi vociferously decried the war, ultimately leading to her arrest and conviction for sedition in 1918. Equi served nearly a year in San Quentin State Prison before returning to Portland in 1921, where she remained committed to labor rights, women's rights, and social justice.[11]

April 7, 1891 Martha May Eliot was born in Boston. Eliot was a leading pediatrician and public health specialist, served as an assistant director for the World Health Organization, and played a pivotal role in designing New Deal and postwar initiatives for maternal and child health.

Eliot shared her personal life in a deep and enduring domestic partnership with Ethel Collins Dunham, another pioneering female pediatrician. Dunham made history as the first female member of the American Pediatric Society and was honored with its highest award, the Howland Medal, in 1957.[12]

April 7, 1912 Harry Hay, a gay rights activist, communist, and labor rights activist, was born. He was raised in Chile and California, attended Stanford University, pursued acting, and subsequently joined the Communist Party USA.

Hay married Anita Platky, a Marxist activist, in 1938, and they adopted two daughters together. However, Hay pursued relationships with men outside of his marriage, which ended in divorce in 1951. Hay formed the Mattachine Society during his time in Los Angeles. At the time, it was illegal in California for homosexuals to gather in public. The American Psychiatric Association defined homosexuality as a mental illness. Hay wrote a manifesto, "The Call," and in it he was the first to take the position that homosexuals were an "oppressed minority."

Hay and other members of the Mattachine Society fought a case of police entrapment and were acquitted, which contributed to the spread of the organization across the US. It also led to Hay's expulsion from the Communist Party due to his sexuality. Hay maintained a vocal anti-assimilationist stance when it came to LGBT+ rights and cofounded the Los Angeles chapter of the Gay Liberation Front.

After his expulsion from the Communist Party, Hay joined various West Coast progressive political movements, such as the antiwar, anti-draft, and Indigenous rights movements. He would go on to found the Radical Faeries (see August 31, 1979) with Don Kilhefner and Mitchell L. Walker.[13]

April 7, 2018 Russian police detained as many as thirty gay rights activists, who had gathered in Palace Square in St. Petersburg in defiance of a ban on LGBT+ gatherings. The activists had requested to hold a parade and were denied. Each participant protested alone to prevent the protest from being called a gathering.

Police detained protesters who held rainbow flags or signs. In 2013, Russian authorities had passed a law banning gay "propaganda," leading to the criminalization of LGBT+ events.[14]

April 7, 2023 University of Florida students organized an "inject-in" to protest legislation by Florida Governor Ron DeSantis's administration, such as House Bill 1421 and Senate Bill 254, which would ban gender-affirming care for minors. *The Alligator*, an independent Florida newspaper, broke down the content of the bills:

> HB 1421 seeks to ban gender-affirming care for minors, prohibit the use of private insurance coverage for the treatment and bar a person's biological sex from being changed on their birth certificate.
>
> SB 254 would criminalize parents and doctors who provide minors with gender-affirming care and grant the state the ability to claim jurisdiction over children who have parents that allow them to receive gender-affirming care treatment. The bill would also ban the use of public funds to subsidize gender-affirming care through state-funded entities.

The protest was organized by the student group UF Queer Liberation Front and had speakers from University of Florida alumni, Gators for Gender-Affirming Care, and Gainesville's National Women's Liberation chapter. Students injected HRT, inspired by transgender activist Lindsey Spero, who injected testosterone in front of the Florida Boards of Medicine and Osteopathic Medicine on February 10, 2023. DeSantis's administration had conducted an audit on January 18 mandating that Florida public universities report the number of patients receiving gender-affirming care. According to *The Alligator*, "The audit reported a steady increase of gender-affirming care patients through UF Health."[15]

8 **April 8, 1974** The American Psychiatric Association removed the classification of homosexuality as a mental disorder, adopting the following resolution:

> Homosexuality per se implies no impairment in judgment, stability, reliability, or general social and vocational capabilities; Further, the American Psychological Association urges all mental health professionals to take the lead in removing the stigma of mental illness that has long been associated with homosexual orientations.

The organization then went on to publicly decry discrimination against homosexuals and supported civil rights legislation. Unfortunately, just as it was decriminalizing homosexuality, it crafted gender identity disorder to shift stigma from homosexuality to trans people.[16]

9 **April 9, 1936** Drew Shafer, an American gay activist from Kansas City, Missouri, was born. Shafer's openness about his sexuality, particularly notable for the time and place, marked him as a vocal advocate. In the mid-1960s, he delivered speeches on gay rights at various college campuses and spearheaded the establishment of a local chapter of ONE, Inc.

In February 1966, Shafer addressed the National Planning Conference of Homophile Organizations in downtown Kansas City, emphasizing the significance of communication and unity. His advocacy extended to a local radio show, which nearly cost him his clerical job at a Caterpillar Tractor Company plant. Thankfully, the intervention of the United Auto Workers union safeguarded his employment, highlighting that Shafer's activities outside business hours were not grounds for dismissal.

In March 1966, Shafer disbanded his ONE, Inc. chapter and founded the Phoenix Society for Individual Freedom, boasting approximately twenty founding members, with Shafer serving as president until 1968. Simultaneously, he launched *The Phoenix: Midwest Homophile Voice*, marking the inception of the Midwest's first LGBT+ magazine. The publication's reach gradually extended to states like Iowa and Nebraska. Additionally, in August 1966, Shafer commenced printing and distributing for another organization, the North American Conference of Homophile Organizations (NACHO), running the publishing clearinghouse out of his basement.[17]

April 9, 2020 Phyllis Lyon, the pioneering activist who cofounded the first lesbian rights organization in the US, passed away in San Francisco at the age of ninety-five. Lyon and her partner, Del Martin, established the Daughters of Bilitis from their home in 1955. In 1956, they founded *The Ladder*, the first nationally distributed lesbian publication.

In the 1960s, they fought to decriminalize homosexuality, forming the Council on Religion and the Homosexual. They went on to join the National Organization for Women (NOW) and advocated for lesbian recognition within the group. They participated in the campaign that led the American Psychiatric Association to redact homosexuality as a mental illness. Lyon assisted in defeating the 1978 Briggs Initiative in California, officially known as Proposition 6, a ballot proposition that would have banned gay and lesbian teachers from California schools. Lyon and Martin would later work with Old Lesbians Organizing for Change and act as delegates to the White House Conference on Aging.[18]

10 **April 10, 1880** Frances Perkins was born. Perkins was an ardent advocate for workers' rights and held the position of the fourth US secretary of labor, from 1933 to 1945. A member of the Democratic Party, Perkins made history as the first woman to serve in a presidential cabinet.

Perkins pursued studies in economics at the Wharton School of the University of Pennsylvania and later obtained a master's degree from Columbia University. Her dedication to reforming labor laws was ignited by her firsthand witnessing of the tragic Triangle Shirtwaist Factory fire in New York City, one of the deadliest industrial disasters in American history.

Her steadfast support of President Franklin D. Roosevelt solidified labor issues as a cornerstone of the emerging New Deal coalition. Remarkably, she was one of only two cabinet members to serve throughout Roosevelt's entire presidency.

Instrumental in shaping FDR's New Deal, Perkins played a pivotal role in crafting and advocating for legislation aimed at alleviating the effects of the Great Depression. Her remarkable achievements include the establishment of pensions, unemployment and workers' compensation programs, the introduction of a minimum wage and overtime regulations, the standardization of the forty-hour workweek, enactment of child labor laws, creation of new job opportunities through public works initiatives, and the formulation of the blueprint for the Social Security Act—a monumental achievement in her career.

Amid Hitler's ascent to power, Perkins also facilitated the entry of tens of thousands of immigrants to the US, with a significant portion being European Jews fleeing persecution by the Nazis.

In her personal life, Perkins shared a profound and enduring romantic relationship with Mary Harriman Rumsey, the founder of the Junior League. The two, close friends of Eleanor Roosevelt, resided together in Washington, DC, until Rumsey's passing.[19]

11 **April 11, 1964** The Association for Social Knowledge (ASK), the first homophile organization in Canada, released its first newsletter today.[20]

April 11, 1978 San Francisco Mayor George Moscone signed the most sweeping gay rights law in the US at the time, banning discrimination based on sexual orientation in employment, housing, and public accommodations in the private sector. The ordinance introduced by the publicly out gay City Supervisor Harvey Milk passed by a ten-to-one vote, with only Dan White, who would murder both Milk and Moscone on November 27, voting against it.[21]

12 **April 12, 1888** William Dorsey Swann battled arrest for "female impersonation" at his thirtieth birthday ball, half a mile from the White House in Washington, DC. Born into slavery in Maryland, Swann became the first American on record to take legal and political action to defend the rights of LGBT+ people to assemble and express themselves. He organized a succession of secret drag balls in the 1880s and 1890s for formerly enslaved Black men, often in defiance of police raids and public scrutiny. Calling himself the "queen of drag," Swann's defiant expression of queerness, Blackness, and joy in the middle of the nation's capital positions him as a progenitor of both queer liberation and Black freedom movements. After he was arrested in 1896, he requested a presidential pardon—the first documented legal attempt to defend the right to queer assembly in the United States.[22]

13 **April 13, 1970** The first public "zap" by the Gay Activists Alliance (GAA) occurred in front of the Metropolitan Museum of Art during its one-hundredth-anniversary celebration. New York Mayor John V. Lindsay was invited to participate in a morning ceremony on the museum's front steps. The zap took the form of repeated interruptions of Lindsay's speech, in which activists such as Marty Robinson, Jim Owles, Arthur Bell, Arthur Evans, and Morty Manford confronted the mayor on his lack of public support for gay rights. The GAA had been trying to engage with Lindsay over police harassment and employment discrimination against the LGBT+ community. Before the event, on March 8, the police had raided the Snake Pit, a gay bar, and the mayor had refused to engage with the GAA (see March 8, 1970).[23]

April 13, 1990 Queer Nation held its first "Nights Out" action, at Flutie's Bar in South Street Seaport, New York City, to demonstrate that LGBT+ people will not be limited to gay bars as spaces for socializing and for public displays of affection.[24]

14 **April 14, 1954** Following a 1954 case involving the sexual assault and murder of a young boy, a wave of moral panic swept through Iowa. In response, the state passed a "sexual psychopath" law permitting the involuntary commitment of individuals charged with public offenses if they were believed to exhibit tendencies toward committing sex crimes. In 1955, twenty gay men from the Sioux City area were institutionalized under this law, despite having no ties to the original incident.[25]

April 14, 1964 Environmental activist Rachel Carson, known for writing *Silent Spring*, died. Carson led a complex life, as reflected in her connection with Dorothy Freeman. The pair wrote over nine hundred letters to each other. In one correspondence, Freeman expressed, "I love you beyond expression.... My love is boundless as the Sea." Carson reciprocated in another letter, stating, "Reality can so easily fall short of hopes and expectations, especially where they have been high. My dear one, there is not a single thing about you that I would change if I could!" Many of their letters were destroyed by Carson and Freeman shortly before Carson's passing in 1964.[26]

15 **April 15–16, 2000** ACT UP and Health GAP held a demonstration in Washington, DC, along with the global justice movement. The groups participated in direct actions, which led to mass arrests, against the IMF and World Bank. ACT UP, Health GAP, and other organizations pushed for debt reduction, so that countries could use funds instead to fight AIDS and pay health workers.[27]

April 15, 2014 *Against Equality: Queer Revolution Not Mere Inclusion*, edited by Ryan Conrad and published by AK Press, was released. The book challenges mainstream gay rights struggles for inclusion into mainstream society. For example, it questions whether queer people's inclusion into the US military truly helps LGBT+ people, or whether that inclusion furthers imperialism and harms LGBT+ people around the world.[28]

16 **April 16, 1882** Rose Schneiderman, the first woman elected to a national office in an American labor union, was born in Poland. Starting work at the age of thirteen after her family emigrated to New York City's Lower East Side and her father died, she began her journey in union organizing at twenty-one. By 1906, Schneiderman had risen to the position of vice president of the New York Women's Trade Union League (WTUL), and she played a pivotal role in organizing the Uprising of the 20,000 for the International Ladies' Garment Workers' Union in 1909. Progressing further, she assumed the presidency of the New York WTUL in 1917 and later became president of the national WTUL in 1926.

Established in 1903, the WTUL emerged as a nationwide entity, aiming to forge a coalition between working-class women and their wealthier supporters, united in their efforts to enhance labor conditions for women. Within the WTUL, a homosocial environment was fostered, providing a platform for activist women to champion the cause of social justice. Schneiderman collaborated with several other prominent activists within the WTUL, including Mary Dreier, Helen Marot, Frieda Miller, Pauline Newman, and Maud O'Farrell Swartz. Schneiderman's long-term partnership with Swartz, with whom she shared a home for many years, has been recognized by LGBT+ historians as part of her legacy. Their relationship, though often understated in historical records, offers important insight into the queer dimensions of early twentieth-century labor feminism.

Schneiderman's close bond with Eleanor Roosevelt and their discussions on labor matters led President Franklin D. Roosevelt to appoint Schneiderman to the National Labor Advisory Board in 1933. In this role, Schneiderman advocated fiercely for the inclusion of domestic workers in Social Security and campaigned for wage parity among women workers.

"The woman worker needs bread, but she needs roses too," Rose Schneiderman said in 1911. For nearly fifty years, Schneiderman dedicated herself tirelessly to enhancing wages, working hours, and safety measures for women in the American workforce. She viewed these essentials as the "bread," fundamental human rights that every working woman deserved. However, she also strived for the provision of "roses," such as educational institutions, recreational amenities, and professional networks for women in trade unions, firmly believing that working women deserved far more than mere subsistence.[29]

April 16, 1892 Dora Rudolfine Richter, a transgender woman, was born in Germany. Richter was the first known person to undergo full male-to-female gender-affirming surgery, predating Lili Elbe, widely known as one of the procedure's first recipients, and was part of a cohort of transgender individuals under the guidance of Magnus Hirschfeld at Berlin's Institute for Sexual Science during the 1920s and early 1930s.[30]

April 16, 1967 Essex Hemphill was born in Chicago. A prominent American poet and activist who openly identified as gay, Hemphill was renowned for his influential presence in the Washington, DC, art scene during the 1980s. His work boldly confronted the intersecting realities of racial and sexual marginalization, centering the experiences of the Black gay community.[31]

April 16, 1977 A New York judge ruled that transgender tennis player Renée Richards was eligible to play in the women's division of the United

States Open tennis championships without undergoing a chromosome test. According to *The New York Times*, New York State Supreme Court Justice Alfred M. Ascione found the test to be "grossly unfair, discriminatory and inequitable, and violative of her rights under the Human Rights Law of this state.... It seems clear that defendants knowingly instituted this test for the sole purpose of preventing plaintiff from participating in the tournament."[32]

17 **April 17, 1943** Black students from Howard University staged a sit-in at the Little Palace Cafeteria, a segregated restaurant in Washington, DC. One of the organizers of this and other sit-ins in the city at the time was Pauli Murray, a young Black activist and feminist who identified as part female and part male and whose only significant romantic relationships were with women (see November 20, 1910). Murray helped organize another sit-in the following year at a Thompson's cafeteria, but after that the university ordered its students to desist. Washington, DC, eventually banned segregation in restaurants in 1953.[33]

April 17, 1965 During what is believed to be the first demonstration for gay rights, a group of ten people picketed the White House to protest the US government's discriminatory treatment of gays and lesbians. Primarily, the group advocated for the rights of gays and lesbians to maintain their employment within the government.[34]

18 **April 18, 1970** In the spring of 1970, a group known as Chicago Gay Liberation organized a series of dances on the University of Chicago campus in which same-sex couples could freely dance together. On this day, the group held a public dance at an arena off campus, and two thousand people attended.

The subsequent weekend, activists inspired by the success of the dance protested at the Normandy Inn, a popular gay bar. They demanded that same-sex couples be permitted to dance together and advocated for the relaxation of dress codes, which discouraged wearing attire associated with the opposite gender due to potential police intervention. In response to the pressure, the bar owners acquiesced, which prompted similar policy changes at other establishments.[35]

April 18, 2010 African activists crafted the African LGBTI Manifesto/ Declaration at a roundtable discussion in Nairobi, Kenya. Drafted at a time when homosexuality remained criminalized in over thirty African nations and stringent antigay legislation had been enacted in countries like Uganda and Nigeria, the manifesto boldly confronted conservative notions regarding African identity, disputing the idea that LGBTI identity was inherently "un-African" or merely a byproduct of European influence or colonial legacy. The manifesto also reshaped prevailing narratives surrounding African liberation and asserted that the LGBTI struggle was an integral and pressing component of Pan-Africanism's history and the ongoing movements for Black empowerment and sovereignty.[36]

19 **April 19, 1978** On the steps of the state capitol in St. Paul, Minnesota, fifteen hundred people rallied to oppose the proposed repeal of a gay rights provision within the city's human rights ordinance. Voters would go on to repeal the provision by a two-to-one margin.[37]

20 **April 20, 1990** Queer Nation staged a presence at Macy's Herald Square department store in Manhattan during Olympic gold medalist Greg Louganis's promotion of a new swimsuit line. Members of the queer community arrived with Wheaties cereal boxes featuring the swimmer's image affixed to the front, in remembrance of the occasion when the cereal company declined Louganis as a spokesperson, purportedly due to his sexual orientation.[38]

21 **April 21, 1966** Members of the Mattachine Society orchestrated a "sip-in" at the New York City bar Julius' to challenge the State Liquor Authority's discriminatory policy of revoking licenses from bars serving known or suspected gay men and lesbians.

This widely publicized event, during which patrons were denied service after disclosing their sexual orientation, marked one of the earliest public actions for LGBT+ rights preceding the Stonewall riots. It also played a significant role in advancing the establishment of legitimate LGBT+ bars in New York City.[39]

April 21, 1982 Glad Day Bookshop, the oldest surviving LGBT+ bookstore in Canada, was the subject of a series of raids conducted by the Toronto Police Services. Kevin Orr, a young employee, faced charges for "possession of obscene material for purposes of resale." On March 4, 1983, he was convicted and received a conditional discharge along with two years of probation.

John Scythes and Thomas Frank Ivison, owner and manager of Glad Day, respectively, were subsequently convicted in the 1990s for the distribution of *Bad Attitude*, a lesbian erotic magazine featuring BDSM themes.[40]

22 **April 22, 1944** Two hundred young Black people, mostly students at Howard University, held a sit-in demonstration at Thompson's, a segregated restaurant in Washington, DC—where Jim Crow laws were not in effect but segregation by custom existed. After effectively slashing the number of paying customers, the restaurant was ordered by its headquarters to begin serving Black patrons. The university, in fear of losing federal grants, subsequently directed its students to cease direct action, and Thompson's promptly restored segregation. One of the key organizers of the action was Pauli Murray, a young student and activist who identified as part male and part female and whose romantic relationships were with women (see November 20, 1910).[41]

April 22, 1973 The first LGBT+ rights protest in Chile took place when forty young people wearing striped sweaters demonstrated in the Plaza de Armas in the capital, Santiago, demanding an end to police harassment.

The organizer of the protest was a twenty-six-year-old sex worker and fortune teller known as La Gitana, who was described by the press as a "transvestite" but used female pronouns and was likely a trans woman. Another participant, Luis Troncoso Lobos, who self-identified as a transvestite known as La Raquel, described police treatment of gay and gender-nonconforming sex workers in a 2011 interview with *The Clinic*, a weekly newspaper: "The police were chasing us a lot. They saw us and took us to Altiro, detained for offenses to morals and good customs. The First Police Station in Santo Domingo was like a hotel for us. There they beat us and shaved us to zero. And that was what hurt the most. Later, one was embarrassed to look in the mirror and the clients did not even give you the time."

Women bystanders to the protest covered the eyes of their children, while men hurled homophobic abuse, calling the demonstrators "disgusting sodomites." The media described the participants as "deviants" and "weirdos" and falsely claimed that the protesters were demanding the right to have same-sex marriage.

In the wake of the protest, La Gitana began to experience increased police repression and harassment, until eventually one day she disappeared and was never seen again. Media attacks on gay, gender-nonconforming, and transgender people escalated, and later that year the right-wing coup of General Augusto Pinochet occurred. The LGBT+ rights movement was driven back underground, to reemerge in 1984 with the foundation of the lesbian and feminist Ayuquelén Collective.[42]

23 **April 23, 1946** LGBT+ activist Arthur Gursch was born. As a member of the Chicago Gay Liberation Front (GLF), he crossed paths with his future partner, Ortez Alderson, in 1970. With the dissolution of the local GLF group in 1971, Art transitioned to the Gay Activists Alliance, and he later joined the Socialist Workers Party (SWP). Despite his efforts to promote the party's involvement in the growing gay and lesbian liberation movement, he ultimately parted ways with the SWP due to its reluctance to fully engage in this cause.

Gursch was involved in significant events such as the 1979 March on Washington for Lesbian and Gay Rights, contributed to organizations like Black and White Men Together in New York, and demonstrated his commitment to the fight against AIDS through his involvement with ACT UP.

Gursch was also involved with the Gay Liberation Network from its inception, actively participating in planning meetings and events advocating for LGBT+ rights. Consistent with his lifelong commitment to solidarity, he ardently championed various causes including women's rights, workers' rights, immigrant rights, Palestinian rights, and the antiwar movement, both within the LGBT+ community and beyond.[43]

April 23, 1967 The Student Homophile League of Columbia University, the first officially recognized gay student organization in the United States, having received its charter only four days earlier, picketed and disrupted a panel of psychiatrists discussing homosexuality. In pushing against the psychiatric establishment's pathologizing of homosexuality, the protest was a moment of critical early campus-based LGBT+ activism. The action challenged not only institutional homophobia on the campuses of medicine and academia but also asserted queer students' very presence and agency on campus—demanding to be seen and respected and have a right to define their own identity.[44]

24 **April 24, 1941** Ernestine Eckstein, a prominent leader in the New York chapter of the Daughters of Bilitis, was born. Drawing from her involvement in the civil rights movement, she advocated for the Daughters of Bilitis to shift to organizing public demonstrations.

Eckstein worked alongside activists such as Phyllis Lyon, Del Martin, Barbara Gittings, Franklin Kameny, and Randy Wicker and became involved in the organization Black Women Organized for Action in the 1970s.[45]

April 24, 1993 The inaugural Dyke March took place in Washington, DC, coinciding with the March on Washington for Lesbian, Gay, and Bi Equal Rights and Liberation. Led by the Lesbian Avengers, this historic event saw the participation of over twenty thousand women.

Inspired by its success, the New York Lesbian Avengers took the initiative to organize their own march in June 1993. In addition to parading through the city, the Avengers distributed a manifesto and crafted a unique "float": a bed mounted on wheels, occupied by kissing dykes. A makeshift banner, now a fixture at the forefront of the march each year, was hastily created at Bryant Park using markers and tagboard. That same month, Atlanta and San Francisco also hosted their inaugural Dyke Marches.[46]

25 **April 25, 1965** Protesters orchestrated a sit-in at a Dewey's restaurant in Center City, the downtown business district of Philadelphia, advocating for equal access to public accommodations for lesbian, gay, bisexual, and transgender individuals. After three teenage protesters were arrested, the Janus Society, a group dedicated to promoting gay and lesbian rights, distributed around 1,500 leaflets over five days before organizing a second sit-in on May 2.[47]

April 25, 1993 A huge protest took place in Washington, DC, as an estimated one million people marched for LGBT+ rights. The protest began at 4:00 p.m., with demonstrators calling for an end to discrimination against LGBT+ people, particularly in the military, and for increased funding to fight against the AIDS epidemic.[48]

April 25, 2016 At least fifty-four protesters were arrested at the North Carolina statehouse in Raleigh for protesting House Bill 2. This law implemented a statewide policy prohibiting individuals from using public bathrooms that did not align with their biological sex. Additionally, it prevented cities from enacting antidiscrimination ordinances aimed at protecting gay and transgender people.[49]

April 25, 2023 Hundreds of drag performers and their supporters gathered in Tallahassee, Florida, to protest the passage of a bill by the

Republican-led state legislature prohibiting children from attending "adult live performances." LGBT+ advocates asserted that this legislation specifically targeted drag shows.[50]

26 **April 26, 1968** During his time as an architecture student at the University of Pennsylvania, civil rights, antiwar, gay liberation, and HIV/AIDS activist Kiyoshi Kuromiya (see May 9, 1943) and a group of friends held a demonstration against the use of napalm in Vietnam. They announced plans to burn a dog alive with napalm in front of the university library, which prompted thousands to gather in protest. However, instead of witnessing such a gruesome act, people in the crowd were handed a leaflet that read: "Congratulations on your anti-napalm protest. You saved the life of a dog. Now, how about saving the lives of tens of thousands of people in Vietnam."[51]

27 **April 27, 1953** Starting in the late 1940s, the US federal government embarked on a deliberate campaign to remove homosexuals from the civil service, famously known as the "Lavender Scare," which peaked with the issuance of Executive Order 10450 on this day in 1953 by President Dwight D. Eisenhower. The ramifications of this executive order persisted well into the 1970s. It wasn't until 1975 that the US Civil Service Commission lifted the ban on homosexuals in federal civil service. Subsequently, in 1977, the Department of State also abolished its ban within the Foreign Service. Finally, in 2017, President Barack Obama officially repealed Executive Order 10450 with Executive Order 13764.[52]

28 **April 28, 1990** Following a pipe bomb explosion at Uncle Charlie's, a gay bar in New York City's Greenwich Village, three people were injured. In response, Queer Nation swiftly rallied a thousand members of the queer community, who gathered within hours. Enraged marchers flooded the streets, brandishing a banner bearing the message "Dykes and Fags Bash Back."[53]

29 **April 29, 1945** US forces liberated the Dachau concentration camp in Germany. However, when the Allies took control of the concentration camps, some of those interned for homosexuality were not freed but rather were required to serve out the full term of the sentences they had received under the homophobic Nazi penal code. Thousands of LGBT+ people were interned in concentration camps, most made to wear a pink triangle. Many of them were subjected to medical experiments, castrated, or murdered.

After "liberation," the US Army handbook for the occupation of Germany established that, while most Holocaust survivors should be released from concentration camps, "criminals with a prison sentence still to serve will be transferred to civil prisons." Gay and bisexual men and trans women had been convicted under Paragraph 175 of the criminal code, which had been strengthened by the Nazis, and were therefore considered common criminals. Homosexuality was also against the law at that time in Allied countries, including the US, the UK, and the USSR.

One prisoner, Hermann R., who was detained at Landsberg Fortress, southwest of Dachau, joined liberation celebrations. But two weeks later, a US military commissioner told him, "Homosexual—that's a crime. You're staying here!"

US occupation authorities kept the Nazi version of Paragraph 175 on the books, and in the first four years after the end of the war, around 1,500 men per year were arrested under it. Later, West Germany kept it as well and convicted over fifty thousand men before it was finally revoked in 1969. East Germany, on the other hand, reverted to the pre-Nazi Paragraph 175 and convicted some four thousand men before revoking it in 1968.

LGBT+ people were not recognized as victims of the Holocaust and had their pension entitlements as victims of fascism reduced for the time they spent interned in concentration camps, with most never receiving any compensation.[54]

30 **April 30, 1989** Nearly thirty thousand demonstrators took to the streets of Austin, Texas, demanding the repeal of the state's sodomy laws and calling for enhanced funding for AIDS programs. The following day, members of ACT UP encased the state capitol in red tape as a symbol of their discontent with the state's bureaucratic processes, which, as one activist pointed out, "is often harder on people with AIDS than the disease itself."[55]

1 **May 1, 1996** Urvashi Vaid published *Virtual Equality*. Vaid was an LGBT+ rights activist, lawyer, writer, and consultant. She argues in *Virtual Equality* that lesbian, gay, bisexual, and transgender equality will occur only when the larger institutions of society and the family are transformed. *Virtual Equality* was published in the midst of the rise of gay conservatives, the end of the ban on gays in the military, also known as "Don't Ask Don't Tell," and a rise in antigay legal initiatives across the US. Vaid wrote that the gay rights movement needed to reconsider its tactics and shift from advocacy of civil equality to social change. The gay rights movement had focused on the limited goal of tolerance, and Vaid challenged activists to return to the pursuit of fundamentally changing the sociopolitical landscape. *Virtual Equality* won a Stonewall Book Award in 1996.[1]

May 1, 1997 Cathy Cohen published "Punks, Bulldaggers, and Welfare Queens: The Radical Potential of Queer Politics" in *GLQ: A Journal of Lesbian & Gay Studies*. Cohen argues that queer politics should shift from focusing on the dichotomy between queer/heterosexual and move toward coalition building beyond the basis of sexual orientation. Cohen notes that the sexual behavior of nonnormative cisgender heterosexual people has also been policed, such as women with children who utilize government assistance, or "welfare queens," as US President Ronald Reagan termed such women, and individuals who participate in BDSM, among others. Such cisgender heterosexuals are seen as sexually deviant and face discrimination. Cohen's piece links the discrimination and struggle of queer people to that of other marginalized peoples.[2]

May 1, 2016 "The African Trans Feminist Charter" was published in *Transgender Studies Quarterly*, the preeminent trans studies journal. L. Leigh Ann van der Merwe, a trans woman born in rural South Africa, wrote the introduction to the text and described the purpose of the charter as "an act of resistance and resilience, and mostly to position African trans women within feminist discourse on the continent and globally."

The text states that its framework is built on the values of embracing diversity, cooperation, transparency, inclusivity, respect, dignity, openness, support, integrity, commitment, creativity, loyalty, acceptance, excellence, empathy, and professionalism.

The charter aimed to develop an analysis of African culture and the ways in which it manifests in African trans women's lives. It was also intended to be a living document to be reviewed and amended as needed to serve trans women's contextual needs. The charter was adopted at a meeting in Johannesburg by trans women from Namibia, Botswana, Zimbabwe, Zambia, Lesotho, Uganda, Kenya, Tanzania, and South Africa to "plan and envision a movement driven by ourselves to articulate our politics and obtain conceptual clarity on working with feminist ideas."[3]

2 **May 2, 2023** The Texas Freedom Network (TFN) and All In for Equality Coalition led a protest in the Texas capitol building in Austin in response to Senate Bill 14, a piece of legislation that would prohibit minors in Texas from receiving new gender-affirming medical treatment and eventually bar doctors from providing gender-affirming medical treatment to minors altogether. Protesters held a "sing-in" during the debate over SB 14.

Republican House Speaker Dade Phelan promptly ordered state police to clear the gallery, writing on Twitter, "Rules matter in the TX House. Today's outbursts in the gallery were a breach of decorum & continued after I warned that such behaviors would not be tolerated. There will always be differing perspectives, but in our chamber, we will debate those differences w/ respect."

Police physically restrained Adri Pérez, the nonbinary organizer of TFN. First police grabbed them from behind and proceeded to drag them to the ground. In footage of the arrest, three officers appear to kneel on Pérez's back and legs, pinning them to the floor. Pérez was charged with assaulting a peace officer, a second-degree felony, and misdemeanor charges of disrupting a meeting and resisting arrest. TFN reported the charges were later dropped.

Sofia Sepulveda, the community engagement and advocacy manager of Equality Texas, was also forcibly removed and banned from the capitol for a year after a banner drop inside the capitol's rotunda reading "Let Trans Kids Grow Up." Protester Evan Wienck was charged with "assault by contact" and released at the scene.[4]

3 **May 3, 1879** Maud O'Farrell Swartz, an Irish American labor organizer, was born in Ireland. She moved to the US at the age of twenty-two. In 1905, she married the printer Lee Swartz. However, the union proved fleeting and discontented, leading to separation, though divorce was declined due to religious convictions. In 1912, she forged a deep bond with Rose Schneiderman, which endured until her passing.

She assumed the presidency of the Women's Trade Union League from 1922 to 1926, and in 1931 she made history by becoming the first woman and trade unionist to be appointed as secretary of the New York State Department of Labor, under Industrial Commissioner Frances Perkins.[5]

May 3, 2023 Fourteen protesters were arrested after occupying Florida Governor Ron DeSantis's offices for nearly seven hours in response to a series of anti-LGBT+ legislation from GOP lawmakers, including restrictions on transgender health care and the discussion of gender identity in public schools.[6]

4 **May 4, 1958** Keith Haring, an American pop artist, was born. Haring first received public attention for his graffiti in subways, though his work was also featured in over one hundred solo and group exhibitions throughout his career. Haring was diagnosed with AIDS in 1988. A year later, he founded the Keith Haring Foundation to fund AIDS organizations. He died on February 16, 1990, of AIDS-related complications.[7]

5 **May 5, 1725** Dutch sailor Leendert Hasenbosch was marooned on the uninhabited Ascension Island as punishment for sodomy, of which he was convicted the previous month. To survive, he drank the blood of turtles and seabirds, as well as his own urine, and kept a diary of his time. In January 1726, British sailors arrived on the island and found his diary and camp. But it appeared that Hasenbosch had died after around six months. His remains were never found, but his diary was translated into English that year and published under the title *Sodomy Punish'd*.[8]

6 **May 6, 1933** The Institute for Sexual Science (see July 6, 1919), an academic foundation in Berlin dedicated to sexological research and the advocacy of gay and transgender rights, was broken into and occupied by the German Student Union, a collective of Nazi-supporting youth.[9]

7 **May 7, 1365** Giovanni di Giovanni was tortured to death as one of the youngest victims of the campaign against homosexuality in fourteenth-century Florence, Italy. The campaign against homosexuality occurred shortly after the Black Death, the breakout of bubonic plague that had ravaged the city two years earlier. Bernardino of Siena, a significant priest and confessor, blamed "sodomites" for bringing the wrath of God upon the people of Florence. The remedy was to purify the city through fire, leading to burnings at the stake and other punishments.

Di Giovanni was called "a public and notorious passive sodomite" and was convicted by the Podestà court of being the partner of numerous men. His punishment was to be paraded around town on the back of an donkey, then publicly castrated. Finally, he was to have a red-hot iron inserted into his anus. Di Giovanni did not survive the punishment.[10]

8 **May 8, 1920** Touko Valio Laaksonen, known by the pseudonym Tom of Finland, was born. He was a Finnish artist known for his highly masculinized homoerotic art. He worked in advertising, becoming a member of the Helsinki bohemian set. However, he avoided the Helsinki gay subculture at the time.

In 1965, Laaksonen submitted his drawings to the American body-building magazine *Physique Pictorial*. The editor accepted the work and featured Laaksonen's drawing of a lumberjack on the cover of the magazine's Spring 1957 issue. The openness and visibility of Laaksonen's drawings were striking in a time when the US heavily criminalized homosexuality.

His work was set in parks, forests, locker rooms, bars, and prison cells. As noted on Back2Stonewall, "Tom's men seem to wander an array of secluded public spaces but usually not far from small groups of interested onlookers. Their denim bound erections, bursting buttons, and turned up short-sleeves can barely conceal the irrepressible optimism of a gay liberation that was yet to come."

Laaksonen's work became increasingly sexual over time, paralleling the gay liberation movement and the subsequent relaxation of censorship of queer media. Eventually, his art depicted full nudity, S&M scenes, and leather accoutrements. Laaksonen died in 1991.[11]

9 **May 9, 1943** Kiyoshi Kuromiya, a Japanese American author and activist in the civil rights, antiwar, gay liberation, and HIV/AIDS movement, was born in the Heart Mountain internment camp in Wyoming.

Kuromiya came out on July 4, 1965, at the first Annual Reminder protest, one of the first protests on record for gay rights in the US. In 1969, he cofounded the Gay Liberation Front (GLF) with Basil O'Brien. The GLF organized with the Black Panther Party and the Young Lords to advocate for gay rights. In 1970, Kuromiya represented the GLF as a gay delegate to the Black Panther Party's Revolutionary People's Constitutional Convention at Temple University in Philadelphia, where he received significant support and solidarity.

Once the AIDS epidemic began in the US in the early 1980s, Kuromiya founded the Philadelphia chapter of ACT UP. He was invited to participate in National Institute of Health alternative therapy panels due to his knowledge of HIV and AIDS. He developed ACT UP's *HIV Adult Standard of Care*, a guide that provided education for health care professionals on how to best help HIV-positive patients.

Kuromiya continued his advocacy and work in the HIV/AIDS movement when he contributed to the *Reno v. ACLU* Supreme Court case. The case challenged the indecency provisions of the Communications Decency Act, which had made it a criminal offense to provide sexually explicit information on HIV/AIDS through the internet. The case was ultimately successful and protected people's freedom of speech online.[12]

May 9, 1968 Bucks County Community College (BCCC) in Newtown, Pennsylvania, was the site of one of the earliest protests for LGBT+ rights before Stonewall. Approximately two hundred students gathered in a campus courtyard to protest the college president's cancellation of a lecture by gay movement leader Dick Leitsch, the president of the Mattachine Society of New York.

Ralph Sassi Jr., president of the student government, approved a request from the cultural affairs committee to bring Leitsch to campus. Leitsch had earlier challenged New York City's ban on serving LGBT+ people in bars. Students advocated for the event; however, the college began to experience pushback from faculty who considered homosexuality to be "perversion," as well as local clergy.

Charles E. Rollins, BCCC's president, canceled Leitsch's speaking engagement three hours before it was supposed to occur. Two hours after the announcements, students began to rally together. Reports are mixed as to precisely how it was carried out, but all agree that students walked out of classes after hearing a call that Leitsch's talk was canceled. Roughly a sixth of the student body met in the courtyard.

The student attendees were a mixture of LGBT+ people and heterosexuals. The demonstration is hailed as an example of changing perceptions of the gay community among young, college-aged students. BCCC now recognizes and praises the students as a part of the college's history.[13]

10 **May 10, 1904** Dutch cellist, conductor, lesbian, and anti-Nazi resistance member Frieda Belinfante was born in Amsterdam. Belinfante excelled in her field as a cellist and was the first woman in Europe to be artistic director and conductor of an ongoing professional orchestral ensemble. She also made weekly appearances as a guest conductor on Dutch National Radio and acted as a guest conductor of orchestras in the Netherlands and northern Europe.

However, the rise and spread of the Nazis across Europe caused Belinfante to pause her professional pursuits as a musician and orchestra conductor. As the Nazis limited what Dutch artists could do, she began to find allies she could work with politically. Eventually she was asked to represent musicians in a gay resistance group called CKC.

Belinfante forged documents, specifically focusing on false ID cards for those who needed them. One of the most successful missions of the CKC was to destroy the population register in Amsterdam's city hall. The German Nazi occupation began to retaliate and arrested members of the group. After a raid on her home, Belinfante created an ID card under the name of "Hans." She deepened her voice, borrowed a suit, visited a barber, and lived for three months as a man. She traveled around the Netherlands, living with allies and friends, while continuing to distribute false papers.

In December 1943, Belinfante escaped to Switzerland before emigrating to the US.[14]

May 10, 1933 German Nazis held their first book-burning celebration in Bebelplatz, a public square in Berlin. Nazis burned the library of the Institute for Sexual Science (see July 6, 1919) founded by Jewish physician Magnus Hirschfeld, which advocated for gay and transgender rights. The library had been seized, and the institute destroyed, on May 6.

In Bebelplatz, forty thousand people assembled to hear Joseph Goebbels deliver a speech declaring, "No to decadence and moral corruption!" Book burnings were also held in thirty-four university towns around Germany.

In addition to the institute's library, thousands of other books around the country were burned, including many works by Jewish authors, such as Albert Einstein, Karl Marx, and Sigmund Freud. Also burned were many works by socialists, such as Jack London, Ernest Hemingway, and Helen Keller.[15]

May 10, 2000 Gay rights activists in Glasgow climbed on top of a Stagecoach bus and covered it with pink paint until the police arrived. The bus was owned by Brian Souter, the chairman of Stagecoach bus and train services. Souter had given more than £500,000 to a campaign against lifting Section

28, which was a series of laws across Britain that prohibited the "promotion of homosexuality." It was passed by Margaret Thatcher's government and was in effect in Scotland from 1988 to 2000.

Souter's donation was in response to the Scottish communities minister, Wendy Alexander, pledging to repeal the law that prevented schools and educators from discussing homosexuality in a positive or neutral light. Souter funded a TV and newspaper advertising campaign and was condemned by political parties and activist groups.

OutRage!, a gay rights lobby group, was one of those to condemn Souter and call for a boycott of Stagecoach.[16]

11 **May 11, 1935** Richard Joseph Leitsch, also known as Richard Valentine Leitsch or Dick Leitsch, was born in Louisville, Kentucky. After moving to New York City in 1959, Leitsch met Craig Rodwell while cruising on Greenwich Avenue. Rodwell, who would go on to become his partner, introduced Leitsch to the Mattachine Society. Leitsch advocated for the gay rights movement to be inspired by and model themselves after the civil rights movement and started "sip-ins." He and others would go to bars that excluded gay people, particularly gay men, and order drinks.

During the Stonewall Rebellion, Leitsch was the first gay journalist to cover the riot. He wrote in *The Advocate* in September 1969:

> Momentarily, 50 or more homosexuals who would have been described as "nelly" rushed the cops and took the boy back into the crowd. They then formed a solid front and refused to let the cops into the crowd to regain their prisoner, letting the cops hit them with their sticks, rather than let them through. It was an interesting side-light on the demonstrations that those usually put down as "sissies" or "swishes" showed the most courage and sense during the action. Their bravery and daring saved many people from being hurt, and their sense of humor and "camp" helped keep the crowds from getting too nasty or too violent.[17]

12 **May 12, 1990** Queer Nation created the first "Queer Shopping Network." The group traveled to the Newport Mall in Jersey City, New Jersey, with leaflets offering information on LGBT+ people, safe sex tips, and a list of famous queer people throughout history. The leaflets were titled "We're here, we're queer, and we'd like to say hello!"[18]

13 **May 13–14, 1976** Between the late hour of May 13 into the early morning of May 14, Montreal police launched a synchronized and mass raid on queer nightlife venues, similar to the earlier "Operation Soap" raids in Toronto. These raids, as part of a larger campaign of state-sanctioned harassment, targeted various gay and lesbian clubs throughout the city, including the Taureau d'Or, Studio One, the Stork Club, the Crystal Baths, and Jilly's, a well-known lesbian bar. Among the most significant of these was the 1:00 a.m. raid on the Neptune Sauna—one of Montreal's best-known gay bathhouses, located downtown. At the Neptune, eighty-nine men were apprehended by the police, and many were humiliated. It was reported that officers came in with cameras and used forceful tactics, following patterns at earlier raids meant not just to police sexuality but also to shame and frighten queer communities for all to witness.[19]

14 **May 14, 1974** Bella Abzug and Edward Koch introduced the Equality Act to Congress. Although the bill did not pass, it aimed to ban discrimination against lesbians, gay men, unmarried people, and women in employment, housing, education, financial services, and public accommodations and facilities.

In a move that foreshadowed current hate crime laws, the act established penalties for those who deliberately caused harm to, threatened, or obstructed individuals because of their sex, marital status, or sexual orientation. It also authorized the US attorney general to pursue civil remedies in response to such discriminatory actions.[20]

15 **May 15, 1897** Dr. Magnus Hirschfeld founded the Scientific-Humanitarian Committee (S-HC) in Berlin. During its height, it held five hundred members and twenty-five chapters across Europe. It advocated against Germany's homophobic laws, such as Paragraph 175, which criminalized sexual acts between men. Signatories to S-HC's petition included Albert Einstein and Leo Tolstoy.

Hirschfeld advocated for a theory of biological determinism to explain sexuality; this work advanced awareness and scholarship on LGBT+ people. It further led to the crafting of policies and data to advocate for LGBT+ people.

As the Nazis came into power, Hirschfeld's work was targeted for elimination. It was destroyed in 1933, during the infamous book-burning rally in Bebelplatz (see May 10, 1933). Roughly twenty thousand books and journals as well as five thousand images were destroyed. Hirschfeld's work came to an abrupt end, and the elimination of this resource damaged emerging work on sexuality and gender identity. The Gestapo arrested more than 8,500 gay men, possibly using information from Hirschfeld's work.[21]

16 **May 16, 1981** Police in Helsinki arrested and charged over twenty people participating in the Vapautuspäivät (Liberation Days) gay rights march for allegedly "encouraging lewd behavior."[22]

17 **May 17, 2004** On this day, Tanya McCloskey and Marcia Kadish were the first same-sex couple to be legally married in the US. McCloskey's endometrial cancer came out of remission shortly after their marriage. Due to the new marriage laws, Kadish was able to spend time with her wife in the hospital. Kadish stated in an interview with NPR, "I was very grateful.... There was never a time that I couldn't see her in the hospital. I pretty much didn't leave her side for almost a year. And we were respected. It was a beautiful thing, the support. It was an awful, ugly thing, the sickness."[23]

18 **May 18, 2023** D'Arcy Drollinger, a well-known drag artist and night-club owner (see January 17, 1969), was established as San Francisco's drag laureate, the nation's first. Drollinger's role is to promote and uplift drag and LGBT+ culture. Her duties include producing and participating in drag events, serving as a spokesperson for San Francisco's LGBT+ community, and helping officials ensure the city's drag history is preserved and recognized.

Drollinger owns the Oasis nightclub, which hosted "Meals on Heels" during the COVID-19 pandemic shutdown, wherein drag performers brought food, cocktails, and socially distant lip-synching performances to homebound people.[24]

19 **May 19, 1904** Daniel Guérin was born in Paris. He is well known for his book *Fascism and Big Business*, which examines the connections between Nazis, fascists, and corporations. Guérin was an out bisexual and a leading figure in the French left from the 1930s until his death in 1988.

He was consistently focused on practical efforts to further leftist goals. Once Franco triumphed in the Spanish Civil War, Guérin worked with other organizers to rescue members of the Workers' Party of Marxist Unification from possible internment. Later, as World War II broke out, he worked with German Jewish exiles in France to develop a German paper, *Arbeiter und Soldat*, to attempt to organize resistance activity among soldiers occupying France. Guérin continued his work by writing and campaigning in support of victims of French colonialism, even having dinner with Ho Chi Minh during Minh's visit to Paris to negotiate the future of Indochina. His support for countries that had been colonized by France extended to Algeria, which he enthusiastically supported. Nonetheless, he was consistently critical of regimes that appeared to be repressive, including Stalinist and Trotskyist nations.

Once Guérin took a public stance as a bisexual man in support of gay rights, he began to experience significant backlash from the French left.

In 1965, Guérin wrote an article about the Kinsey Reports in support of Alfred Kinsey's research. His article was published in the journal *France-Observateur* alongside letters in which gay people were described as "perverts." Leftist journals frequently refused to publish his work on sexuality or censored his articles.

Guérin's work on sexuality consistently focused on intersectionality and the importance of solidarity for collective liberation.[25]

May 19, 1930 Lorraine Hansberry was born in Chicago. Hansberry wrote *A Raisin in the Sun*, which was the first play on Broadway to have been written by a Black woman. The play was influenced by her family's fight against segregation in the US Supreme Court case *Hansberry v. Lee*, which overturned segregation based on restrictive covenant laws.

Hansberry moved to New York City in 1950, first living in Greenwich Village, then in Harlem. While living in Harlem, she became a journalist at Paul Robeson's newspaper, *Freedom*, where she worked alongside W.E.B. Du Bois. Hansberry joined the Communist Party USA and faced retaliation by the FBI. They took her passport and surveilled her heavily, starting in 1952.

At the same time, she met Bobby Nemiroff at a protest, and they later married in 1953. During this period, Hansberry began to work on *A Raisin in the Sun* and also began to write queer stories such as the unpublished play *Flowers for the General*, in which a college student falls in love with her classmate and then attempts suicide due to being outed.

Hansberry and Nemiroff separated and divorced in 1964. Hansberry joined the lesbian organization Daughters of Bilitis and hosted group founders Del Martin and Phyllis Lyon at her home. Records of Hansberry's diaries show her listing "my homosexuality" as something she loved and hated about herself during her late twenties. She became increasingly a part of New York City lesbian life.

Hansberry regularly contributed to *The Ladder*, a magazine run by the Daughters of Bilitis. She began to write of the "homosexual viewpoint" for the magazine *ONE* as well, and all the while *A Raisin in the Sun* became increasingly popular. She had relationships with numerous women in New York City and was in love with Dorothy Secules, a resident of a building Hansberry bought with money she earned from *Raisin*, until Hansberry died in 1965.[26]

20 **May 20, 1885** Karl M. Baer was born in Germany. Baer was a Jewish author, social worker, reformer, and suffragist. Baer was intersex and, though assigned female at birth, came out as a transgender man in 1904 at the age of twenty-one. In December 1906, he made history as the first transgender person to undergo sex reassignment surgery, followed by obtaining full legal recognition of his gender identity with the issuance of a male birth certificate in January 1907.

Baer collaborated with sexologist Magnus Hirschfeld, providing insights into his experience of growing up female while identifying as male. Their collaboration resulted in the semifictional, semiautobiographical *Memoirs of a Man's Maiden Years*, published under the pseudonym N.O. Body, which achieved widespread popularity and was adapted into films in 1912 and 1919.[27]

May 20, 1936 The first issue of *Mujeres Libres* (Free women), a Spanish anarchist feminist magazine by the group of the same name aimed at ending the "triple enslavement of women to ignorance, to capital and to men," was published.

One of its cofounders, Lucía Sánchez Saornil, a writer, poet, and lesbian who was active in the anarcho-syndicalist CNT union, described the majority of her male comrades as follows: "Even as they rail against property, they are rabidly proprietorial. Even as they rant against slavery, they are the cruellest of 'masters.' . . . The lowliest slave, once he steps across his threshold, becomes lord and master. His merest whim becomes a binding order for the women in his household. He who, just ten minutes earlier, had to swallow the bitter pill of bourgeois humiliation, looms like a tyrant and makes these unhappy creatures swallow the bitter pill of their supposed inferiority."

The group went on to play an important role in the Spanish Revolution, which broke out later that year. In particular, they initiated a huge education campaign to address high illiteracy rates among women and girls, established collective childcare in factories and communities, worked with the CNT to train women for roles in the salaried workforce, and fought for equal pay. A number of members of Mujeres Libres were also among the women who volunteered to fight at the front against nationalist forces in the Spanish Civil War.[28]

21 **May 21, 1925** Franklin Edward Kameny was born in New York City. He was hired in July 1957 by the US Army Map Service as an astronomer, and once they learned of his San Francisco arrest for engaging in a sexual encounter with another man, he was questioned by his superiors. He refused to provide information about his sexuality and was promptly fired. In January 1958, he was barred from future federal employment. While he challenged his firing in court, the US Supreme Court declined to consider the case. Kameny then dedicated himself to gay rights activism.

In 1961, he cofounded the DC branch of the Mattachine Society with Jack Nichols. They launched protests at the White House in 1965 and worked with the Daughters of Bilitis and the New York chapter of the Mattachine Society to expand their protests to the Pentagon, Civil Service Commission, United Nations, and Philadelphia's Independence Hall. Kameny wrote to President John F. Kennedy, asking the president to reconsider the purging of LGBT+ persons from federal employment:

> The homosexuals in this country are increasingly less willing to tolerate the abuse, repression, and discrimination directed at them, both officially and unofficially, and they are beginning to stand up for their rights and freedoms as citizens no less deserving than other citizens of those rights and freedoms. They are no longer willing to accept their present status as second-class citizens and as second-class human beings.... I take the stand that not only is homosexuality, whether by inclination or overt act, not immoral, but that homosexual acts engaged in by consenting adults are moral, in a positive and real sense, and are right, good and desirable, both for the individual participants and for the society in which they live.

In 1971, Kameny became the first openly gay candidate for Congress. He was defeated by Democrat Walter E. Fauntroy. Kameny then created the Gay and Lesbian Alliance of Washington, DC, which continues to advocate for equal rights.[29]

May 21, 1990 ACT UP New York organized a national action to "Storm the NIH" (National Institutes of Health) in Maryland. The protest was the culmination of months of ACT UP formally requesting Anthony Fauci, then the chief of the National Institute of Allergy and Infectious Diseases, to be a part of the government's development process for AIDS drugs.

Over a thousand protesters arrived. Chants included "NIH, you can't hide, we charge you genocide." Other groups carried mock coffins to represent the mounting death toll of AIDS. Protesters held signs reading "Red Tape Kills Us" and "NIH—Negligence, Incompetence, and Horror." The protesters marched toward a row of police and held torches with rainbow-colored smoke. Members of ACT UP refused to leave until Fauci responded to their demands.

The official demands included testing all potential treatments immediately, devoting more research to opportunistic infections, an end to the underrepresentation of women and people of color in clinical trials, and a price reduction of AZT, the only AIDS-fighting drug approved by the FDA at the time.

A secondary goal of ACT UP's Treatment and Data Committee was to become incorporated into government committees, where it would have more power for long-term change. The men who led the Storm the NIH action were successful in their goal to join government committees, and they developed new practices for AIDS research that continue to be used.[30]

22 **May 22, 1930** Harvey Milk was born. Milk enlisted in the US Navy but resigned in 1955 after being questioned about his sexual orientation. Following his resignation, he served as a public school teacher on Long Island, a stock analyst in New York City, and a production associate for Broadway musicals. During the 1960s and '70s, Milk became involved in politics and advocacy through demonstrations against the Vietnam War.

In 1972, Milk moved to San Francisco, where he opened a camera store on Castro Street, the site of the city's growing gay community. Milk quickly became a neighborhood figure and ran for the San Francisco Board of Supervisors but lost. However, the race ushered him into local politics. In 1977, in his third bid, he easily won the election for supervisor. Milk's policies were supported by a broad constituency. He advocated not only for antidiscrimination laws for LGBT+ people, but also for day care centers for working mothers and increased library services, among other neighborhood issues. Milk and his supporters overturned a California ballot initiative, Proposition 6, also known as the Briggs Initiative, that would have mandated the firing of gay teachers in the state's public schools.

On November 27, 1978, Dan White, a former city supervisor, assassinated Milk. Milk had recorded several versions of his will in case he was murdered. According to the Milk Foundation, one such version included him saying, "If a bullet should enter my brain, let that bullet destroy every closet door." White was acquitted of murder charges and given the sentence of manslaughter, which led to the White Night riots in May 1979.[31]

23 **May 23, 1908** Annemarie Schwarzenbach, a bisexual Swiss German photographer, writer, antifascist, and androgynous style icon, was born. A prominent character in the prewar Bohemian Berlin, during the rise of fascism Schwarzenbach rejected her pro-Nazi family, began financing the antifascist literary review *Die Sammlung*, and photographed the rise of fascism in Europe.[32]

24 **May 24, 2008** Firestorm Cooperative opened its doors in downtown Asheville, North Carolina. The space organized explicitly as a queer and trans project, focusing on creating a space for grassroots community building and organizing. The collective later restructured its work and from 2018 to 2019 organized around fighting gentrification in West Asheville. It partnered with the Steady Collective to assist community members and provide free meals. Firestorm then came under scrutiny, and the city's zoning administration accused the cooperative of operating as a homeless shelter in violation of zoning code. With the support of national and local actors, the collective was able to combat the claims and continues to exist as a thriving community space.[33]

May 24, 2023 Members of the transgender and *travesti* communities in Argentina marched in Buenos Aires, demanding financial compensation for people who were tortured, raped, and killed during the military dictatorship between 1976 and 1983. During this era, potentially four hundred LGBT+ people were abducted, imprisoned, or killed in the infamous "Dirty War" and have yet to be acknowledged.

Argentina became a pioneering country in terms of queer rights in the early 2010s. In 2010, it was the tenth country to legalize same-sex marriage. In 2012, Argentina passed a gender identity law, allowing for people to change their legal gender identities without medical diagnoses, gender-affirming surgeries, or a judge's opinion. Since the implementation of the law, there have been increased efforts for legal representation of nonbinary gender identities such as travesti.

Argentina expanded trans rights in 2021 when the nation passed a law ensuring 1 percent of public sector jobs are held by trans people. Notably the law is titled the Cupo Laboral Travesti-Trans law, thereby including the travesti gender identity.[34]

25 **May 25, 1895** Socialist author Oscar Wilde (see October 16, 1854) was imprisoned for two years' hard labor for "indecency" for having sex with men. Though many potential witnesses refused to testify against him, he was convicted, and upon sentencing the judge stated, "It is the worst case I have ever tried. I shall pass the severest sentence that the law allows. In my judgment it is totally inadequate for such a case as this. The sentence of the Court is that you be imprisoned and kept to hard labour for two years." Wilde's detention would cause him serious health problems that eventually contributed to his untimely death.

In his essay "The Soul of Man Under Socialism," he declares, "Disobedience, in the eyes of any one who has read history, is man's original virtue. It is through disobedience that progress has been made, through disobedience and through rebellion."[35]

26 **May 26, 1989** CeCe McDonald, a Black trans woman and LGBT+ activist, was born in Chicago.

On June 5, 2011, twenty-three-year-old McDonald and four friends were walking past Schooner Tavern in Minneapolis. A group of at least four inebriated white people outside the bar began harassing McDonald and her friends. The drunken group called her friends—all of whom were Black—racial, homophobic, and transphobic slurs. The two groups began to fight, and McDonald was slashed in the cheek with broken glass. One of the assailants followed her as she tried to leave. McDonald took a pair of scissors out of her purse and stabbed the assailant in the chest in self-defense. He later died from the wound.

McDonald was arrested and only received care for her wounds after two months in prison. She was initially charged with first-degree manslaughter and refused to plead guilty. Then she was charged with second-degree intentional murder, which carries a potential forty-year sentence. But before her trial started, the prosecution offered to reduce the charge to second-degree manslaughter. McDonald pleaded guilty and was sentenced to forty-one months. She was housed in two men's prisons and faced immense structural transphobia while incarcerated. During her time in prison, a petition prompted "the state department of corrections to give her the full regimen of hormones she needed."

McDonald was released from prison in January 2014 after serving nineteen months. She now advocates for criminal justice reform.[36]

May 26, 2019 The University of Winnipeg hosted the Two-Spirit Archives, a collection of historical items highlighting Indigenous gender diversity in North America. The collection includes photographs, videotapes, journals, newspaper clippings, textiles, correspondence, and art, among other artifacts.

Albert McLeod, a codirector of Two Spirited People of Manitoba Inc. and member of the archive's advisory council, accumulated the original material beginning in 2011. In an interview, McLeod stated, "There was an intention to erase any history of Indigenous people in Canada through colonization, the residential school era, and I think queer Indigenous people were definitely not seen as something that the colonial state wanted." McLeon described the Two-Spirit identity as "aboriginal people who assume cross- or multiple-gender roles, attributes, dress and attitudes for personal, spiritual, cultural, ceremonial or social reasons," which predates colonization.

The mission of the Two-Spirit Archives is to develop an internationally renowned center for research that supports the Two-Spirit community. It seeks to document the Two-Spirit movement in Manitoba and throughout North America.[37]

27 **May 27, 1960** The Daughters of Bilitis held its first convention in San Francisco from May 27 to 30. Two hundred women attended the conference, along with San Francisco police officers, who arrived to check whether members were wearing men's clothing.[38]

28 **May 28, 2004** *That's Revolting! Queer Strategies for Resisting Assimilation* was published by Soft Skull Press. The anthology challenges whether gay mainstream movements are advocating for genuine progress or simply the attainment of straight privilege, and thereby cultural assimilation. This collection looks explicitly at methods to highlight queer resistance. Authors address such normative ideas as the naturalization of queerness taking away from the subversive quality of queerness. They raise questions about whether it matters if someone chooses to be gay or trans over being straight and cisgender. The anthology purposefully intends to overwhelm and disrupt its readership. Editor Mattilda Bernstein Sycamore describes it as "a queer intervention in the culture wars." Inspiring and unabashedly irreverent, it stands as an essential piece of queer thought.[39]

29 **May 29, 1979** Los Angeles passed ordinances prohibiting discrimination against homosexuals in private sector employment and in patronization of business establishments in the city. The bills were signed by Mayor Thomas Bradley and would be implemented on July 2, 1979.[40]

30 **May 30, 1926** Christine Jorgensen was born in the Bronx, New York. Jorgensen was one of the first American transgender women to achieve fame due to her transition. She tried to enlist in the US Army during World War II but was denied due to her size and weight. Drafted just months later, she hid her attraction to men during her time in the military and served as a clerical worker. After the war, she went to photography school in New Haven, Connecticut, and later to dental assistant school in New York City.

Jorgensen began to look to books to understand her identity, and when reading *The Male Hormone*, she began to take estrogen. She then consulted with doctors in Europe about gender-affirming surgeries. She traveled to Denmark and met endocrinologist Dr. Christian Hamburger, who agreed to perform the surgical procedure for free. He was the first person to diagnose her as transsexual rather than homosexual.

Jorgenson underwent hormone treatment, psychiatric evaluations, and finally genital surgery. Once she returned to the US, she was on the front page of the December 1, 1952, edition of the *New York Daily News* under the headline "Ex-GI Becomes Blonde Beauty: Operations Transform Bronx Youth."

Jorgenson continued to be interviewed, and headlines emphasized her GI background as well as her "long legs, blonde hair, and high fashion clothes." She went on to become an entertainer and performer at various nightclubs.[41]

31 **May 31, 1975** The George Jackson Brigade was founded. This group was based in Seattle, Washington, and named after George Jackson, a Black Panther member who was shot and killed during an alleged escape attempt at San Quentin State Prison. The majority of the group members were queer. Half of the organization were women, and half of the women were lesbians.

The majority of leftist groups, particularly guerrilla groups, in the 1960s and '70s were unwelcoming to queer people. Many organizations would not work with queer people at all. Brigade member Rita Brown stated the Seattle Liberation Coalition, an umbrella group of leftist organizations, was not allowed to use the word *lesbian* in any material.

The George Jackson Brigade conducted numerous actions, from armed bank robberies and attacks against prisons and jails to placing a pipe bomb in a Safeway grocery store in Seattle, among other bombings. The group released detailed communiqués after each action. During their operations, they tried to avoid harming civilians. During the Safeway grocery operation, Ed Mead, a prominent member, called the Safeway store to report the bomb. However, the store believed it was a prank. The explosion injured civilians and the group faced criticism for the action.

By 1978, most of the members had been arrested, charged, or imprisoned.[42]

JUNE

1 **June 1, 1987** Three hundred fifty people gathered in Lafayette Park in Washington, DC, to protest a lack of funding for AIDS research and the slow pace of federal education programs. Sixty-four of them were arrested, many of whom had AIDS, after blocking traffic on Pennsylvania Avenue in front of the White House.

The protesters scaled a concrete barricade in front of the White House. They sat in the middle of Pennsylvania Avenue chanting, "Testing is not a cure for AIDS" and "Reagan, Reagan, too little, too late." The demonstrators were charged with disorderly conduct and released after paying a fifty-dollar fine.

The protest was sponsored by ACT UP, who had members attending the Third International Conference on AIDS at the same time.

After the first protest, there was a secondary protest at the site of the conference, the Washington Hilton hotel, which was hosting six thousand researchers and attendees. The protest specifically pinpointed President Ronald Reagan's plan to expand routine AIDS testing for prisoners, marriage license applicants, immigrants, and people seeking treatment for addiction and sexually transmitted illnesses.[1]

June 1, 1999 Blockorama, the first Black queer space in Toronto Pride, began in a parking lot across from the Wellesley subway station. It has expanded into an all-day dance party and stage to celebrate Black queer history, creativity, and activism.

Jamea Suberi, a Trinidadian lesbian, feminist, educator, and activist, first thought of Blockorama in 1998. Suberi felt that Pride was similar to Trinidadian Carnival with its colors and costumes but lacked the presence of people of color. She reached out to friends Angela Roberston, Camille Orridge, Junior Harrison, and Douglas Stewart with the idea of developing a Carnival section in Toronto's Pride parade called *pelau*, made up primarily of queer people of color. The idea did not come to fruition, but it did evolve into Blockorama—an all-day party with drag, steelpan, drummers, dancers, and DJs.

In 1999, the group formed a coordinating committee called Blackness Yes! Nik Red, a long-term presence at Blockorama, describes the unfair treatment experienced by the organizers and the progress since:

> The founding members of Blackness Yes! had to work really hard to convince Pride Toronto to let them have a space for Blocko, a third of the Wellesley Parking Lot. After 20 years, people at Pride

Toronto actually know we exist now.... Blackness Yes! broke down a lot of barriers at Pride and began sowing the seeds for other community-led initiatives like the Trans March and Yes, Yes, Y'all to be part of Pride. Blockorama was and continues to be living, breathing proof that we need community-led spaces to express and celebrate the diversity of the LGBTQ communities in Toronto.

Blockorama remains a significant space at Toronto Pride and has continued to "reinsert Black diasporic queerness."[2]

2 **June 2, 1990** Queer Nation protested at New York City's White Horse Tavern after the establishment's management refused to come to the aid of a queer person being assaulted outside of the bar.[3]

3 **June 3, 1906** Josephine Baker was born in St. Louis, Missouri. As a child, Baker experienced the East St. Louis massacre, in which white Americans murdered between 39 and 150 Black people in late May and early July 1917 in response to a claim that a white man had been murdered by a Black man. As a teen, she experienced violence at the hands of the white families she worked for, as well as homelessness. Baker struggled to gain a permanent role in traveling Black performance troupes in the US due to racist hiring practices, so she decided to move to Paris.

At Théâtre des Champs-Élysées, Baker performed in *La Revue Nègre*, a show of all-Black artists. She became famous for her "Danse Sauvage," in which she would perform wearing a skirt made of a string of artificial bananas. Baker became a French citizen in 1937 when she married Jean Lion, though throughout her life she was rumored to have affairs with women, including Frida Kahlo. There is significant speculation as to her relationships with women; however, being out as queer would have been damaging to her career and safety.

Once World War II reached France, Baker became a spy for the French Resistance. She carried messages written in invisible ink on her sheet music and hid pictures of German military buildings in her underwear. She also hid weapons and Jewish refugees in her château. Baker was honored with the Croix de Guerre, a French medal recognizing bravery, and the Legion of Honor, given to those demonstrating a dedication to equality and liberty, with a Resistance rosette.

Josephine Baker refused to perform in the US at any place where Black people could not attend. She was not able to perform in St. Louis until February 1952, when the Kiel Auditorium finally allowed desegregated audiences to see her. During her performance, she spoke to the audience, saying, "People are dying so that you will be able to live in peace. Try to understand and love each other before it is too late."

In the 1950s, Josephine Baker raised funds for France's International League Against Racism and Anti-Semitism. She was the only woman to speak at the 1963 March on Washington. She continued to work off and on from 1959 to 1975, when she passed away. Roughly twenty thousand mourned her death in the streets of Paris.[4]

June 3, 1926 Allen Ginsberg, considered to be one of the twentieth century's foremost American poets, was born. He was a founding figure in the Beat Generation, a literary movement that challenged and explored US politics and society after World War II.

In 1953, Ginsberg moved to San Francisco, where he met Peter Orlovsky, his lifelong partner. While living in San Francisco, Ginsberg was approached by Wall Hedrick, a painter and cofounder of the Six Gallery, to arrange a poetry reading. Although he initially refused, Ginsberg later relented and read a rough draft of "Howl," which was considered obscene due to its discussion of casual sex and homosexuality. The poem and the publisher would later be the subject of a trial around obscenity and freedom of expression.[5]

4 **June 4, 2016** The Namibian city of Swakopmund held its first LGBT+ Pride parade. It was attended by around 150 people, who paraded down the city's main road waving rainbow flags. They then gathered for speeches in an amphitheater and held an afterparty. One activist, Florence Khaxas, told MambaOnline that the organizers hoped to open "a political and social space for the LGBT community in Namibia and to start a conversation as to the ways we organize ourselves." A law banning homosexuality, implemented by British colonial authorities, is still on the books in Namibia, although it is not believed to have been utilized since Namibia achieved independence in 1990.

Several Pride protests in Namibia are referred to by various sources as the first to occur in the country's history, but many of these are inaccurate. Some sources incorrectly describe the 2017 march in Windhoek as the first, while others claim the first occurred in 2013. (Working Class History found a planned Pride march in Keetmanshoop in 2009 but was unable to verify if it in fact occurred.)[6]

5 **June 5, 1994** Homocore Chicago was a group of queer punks who throughout the 1990s brought together the queer community once or twice a month. They organized their events as the AIDS epidemic increasingly impacted the queer community and at a time when the majority of US states still had laws against sodomy. The mainstream movement advocated for assimilation. Homocore rejected mainstream gay culture and instead advocated for an anticapitalist and anti-assimilationist message.

During Chicago's 1994 Pride parade, held on this day, the group protested the event. Banners read "Stonewall was a riot, not a brand name."[7]

6 **June 6, 1976** While leaving the Stonewall Tavern in Tucson, Arizona, Richard Heakin was stopped by thirteen teenagers, who began taunting him. Four of the boys then beat him, and a blow to his neck sent him to the hospital, where he died. The four attackers were sentenced to probation. The local outrage led to Tucson becoming one of the first cities in the US to add sexual discrimination to its antidiscrimination laws the following year.[8]

June 6, 1990 Queer Nation called for a "Youth Visibility Day" at Martin Luther King High School and La Guardia High School in Manhattan. Queer Nation member Henry Diaz, a seventeen-year-old La Guardia student, wrote a pamphlet on gay youth that would later inspire several students to come out.[9]

June 6, 1991 Sònia Rescalvo Zafra, a Spanish trans woman, was murdered in a brutal beating by a group of neo-Nazis in the Parque de la Ciudadela in Barcelona. Her murder acquired great relevance for being "the first crime of a transsexual by the mere fact of being one of which there is information and evidence in Spain."

On the night of her brutal murder, six skinheads of extreme right-wing ideology sneaked into the Parque de la Ciudadela in Barcelona through a hole in the gate, heading to the "musician's gazebo," a regular meeting place of LGBT+ people. There they found Sònia and a fellow trans woman, Dori Romero, both asleep. The skinheads took turns kicking the women with steel-toe boots. Dori survived the assault, but Sònia was killed by the multiple kicks to her head and a blow to the chest with a broomstick. The investigation served as a turning point for the treatment of hate crimes and discrimination in Barcelona, which eventually led to the creation of a specialized prosecutor's office.

In 1993, a commemorative plaque was placed on the bandstand that presides over the gazebo where Sònia was murdered. In 2013, the gazebo was renamed "Glorieta de la Transsexual Sònia" and acquired a new, more visible sign that reads: "To Sònia Rescalvo Zafra, who was brutally murdered on October 6, 1991, in this gazebo by a group of neo-Nazis because of her gender identity. The city of Barcelona condemns this crime and rejects any attitude or action that violates the rights contained in the Universal Declaration of Human Rights." It wasn't until 1995 that the people who attacked and murdered Sònia were sentenced to 310 years in prison; however, a year later the Supreme Court halved the sentence they were given. All six of the culprits have since been released from jail.[10]

7 **June 7, 1954** British mathematician Alan Turing, who helped the Allies win World War II by decoding encrypted Nazi communications, died of cyanide poisoning at the age of forty-one.

In 1952, he was convicted of "gross indecency" for homosexuality and sentenced to chemical castration by the state as punishment. Years of campaigning against the legacy of British state homophobia eventually resulted in Turing receiving a posthumous pardon in 2013, as well as the passing of the so-called Turing's Law, which granted posthumous pardons to nearly fifty thousand other men convicted of gross indecency for same-sex relations.[11]

June 7, 1990 Little Sister's Book & Art Emporium is a queer bookstore in Vancouver. It was established in 1983. A few years after opening, owners Jim Deva and Bruce Smythe began to notice irregularities with shipments that primarily came from the US. Many books never made it to the store, some books that made it through customs had pages ripped out, and some shipments were held indefinitely at the border (see December 8, 1986).

Meanwhile, other bookstores with heterosexual erotic literature had their shipments come through promptly and undamaged.

Eventually, Deva and Smythe sued the Canada Border Services Agency, arguing it was violating the store's freedom of expression rights.

Once at the Supreme Court of British Columbia, the judge ruled that the CBSA did wrongly destroy the store's material. Nonetheless, the judge stated it was justified under Section 1 of the Canadian Charter of Rights and Freedoms, which guarantees rights and freedoms within "reasonable limits prescribed by law."

In 2000, the case went to the Supreme Court of Canada, where it was ruled the CBSA had unjustifiably discriminated against Little Sister's solely based on it being a gay and lesbian bookstore. The ruling additionally stated that customs can screen and censor media at the border, provided it screens all content equally and without regard to sexual orientation. Customs now must prove confiscated materials are obscene, whereas previously the importer needed to prove otherwise.[12]

8 **June 8, 1974** Lambda Rising bookstore opened in Washington, DC. The bookstore was founded by Deacon Maccubbin in 1974 with 250 titles. It was well known for its expansive collection of LGBT+ theory and erotica, as well as movies, music, and gifts. Lambda Rising created the *Lambda Book Report* in 1987 and the annual Lambda Literary Awards, known as the "Lammys," in 1989. In 1996, Lambda Rising turned those projects over to the new nonprofit Lambda Literary Foundation.

In December 2009, Maccubbin announced the closure of the DC store and a second location in Delaware. He stated that the goal for the bookstore had been accomplished:

> When we set out to establish Lambda Rising in 1974, it was intended as a demonstration of the demand for gay and lesbian literature. We thought … we could encourage the writing and publishing of LGBT books, and sooner or later other bookstores would put those books on their shelves and there would be less need for a specifically gay and lesbian bookstore. Today, thirty-five years later, nearly every general bookstore carries LGBT books. We said when we opened it: Our goal is to show there's a market for LGBT literature, to show authors they should be writing this literature, to show publishers they should be publishing it, and bookstores they should be carrying it. And if we're successful, there will no longer be a need for a specialty gay and lesbian bookstore because every bookstore will be carrying them. And thirty-five years later, that's what happened. We call that mission accomplished.[13]

9 **June 9, 2019** Protesters at Sacramento Pride gathered in response to police being allowed to march in uniform during the event. The protest followed a series of decisions by the LGBT Community Center about police marching, particularly in uniform, at Pride. At first, uniformed police were banned from the event; however, the decision was reversed shortly before the parade. The center stated it had reached an agreement with the Sacramento Police Department, but more than a dozen staff members objected and demanded the board president's resignation.

Performers and participants stated they would no longer participate. Ebony Ava Harper, a transgender rights activist and one of the grand marshals for Sacramento Pride, stepped down from the position due to the acceptance of police.

Protesters argued the last-minute change to include police officers did not recognize the trauma some members of the queer community have experienced from interactions with police.

Additionally, protesters pointed out that Pride commemorates the Stonewall riots, which are known for people fighting back against police who attempted to raid the gay bar. Organizers said Pride is not about mainstream gay acceptance: It was and always has been a protest.

Protesters were able to successfully block multiple entrances to the parade and drew national attention to the conflict.[14]

10 **June 10, 2017** No Justice, No Pride blocked Washington, DC's 2017 Capital Pride Parade on three separate occasions. The protesters delayed the parade and forced participants to use alternative routes. The protest was in response to the inclusion of police officers and corporations in Pride.

No Justice, No Pride held its own march down the initially planned route with signs reading "Rainbows Don't Cover Death Merchants" and "No Pride in Police Violence."

Jen Deerinwater, a participant and Two-Spirit member of the Cherokee Nation, stated to journalists that Capital Pride's sponsors included organizations that contributed to the genocide of Indigenous peoples: the FBI, the NSA, the CIA, Wells Fargo, Lockheed Martin, Northrop Grumman, and the Federal Bureau of Prisons. The protesters were able to disrupt the Lockheed Martin and Wells Fargo floats.

No Justice, No Pride sponsored its own series of events as alternatives to Capital Pride. Before the protest, it had unsuccessfully lobbied organizers to reject sponsorships from corporate groups and ban police officers from marching in uniform. The group also uncovered an article from Capital Pride's president in which he wrote that transgender bathroom laws are unnecessary because "truly trans" people would pass undetected. The president resigned after these statements were made public.

Throughout the protest and Capital Pride, members of each group argued with one another. Capital Pride participants believed No Justice, No Pride was disrupting their celebration, whereas No Justice, No Pride pointed out that Stonewall was a riot against police violence toward the queer community, and the inclusion of police officers as well as specific corporate and governmental organizations contradicted the origins of Pride.[15]

11 **June 11, 1943** Karl Gorath, a twenty-year-old gay German nurse, was deported to the Auschwitz concentration camp. He was first arrested for homosexuality after being denounced by a jealous lover in 1939 and was given a prison sentence. After his release, he was sent to the Neuengamme concentration camp, where he was made to wear a pink triangle denoting LGBT+ prisoners. While working in the camp's health department, with some comrades he attempted to smuggle food to Russian prisoners, who were being starved to death. Their plan was discovered by the Nazis, who then sentenced Gorath to transportation to Auschwitz as a criminal and political prisoner, to be denoted with a red triangle.

Despite contracting dysentery, Gorath managed to survive the war and was released in 1945. But within a few months, he was arrested again by West German authorities, who had kept the homophobic Nazi laws intact. His case was overseen by the same judge, who greeted him with the words, "You are already here again!" and gave him the maximum sentence of five years. His lawyer requested that Gorath's time served in the concentration camps be counted as part of this, but his request was denied. After his release, because of his convictions he was unable to get a job for a decade. And when the time came to draw his pension, his years interned in concentration camps were deducted from his allowance, as were his unemployment payments.[16]

June 11, 2013 Russian police in Moscow detained over twenty gay rights activists involved in a "kissing protest" outside the parliament building, where legislators were preparing to pass a bill banning homosexual "propaganda."

The protesters were outnumbered by around two hundred antigay activists who surrounded them. The antigay protesters threw rotten eggs at the gay protesters, kicked them as they fell to the ground, chanted "Russia is not Sodom," and sang Orthodox Christian prayers while crossing themselves.[17]

12 **June 12, 2018** Two years after the mass shooting at the Pulse in Orlando, Florida, a popular LGBT+ nightclub, activists held a "die-in" on the Capitol lawn in Washington, DC. They laid roses on the lawn overlooking the Washington Monument. Following that, they dropped to the ground for twelve minutes, to symbolize one second for every mass shooting that had occurred up to that moment.

Amanda Fugleberg, a lifelong Orlando resident and protest organizer, recounted the trauma of the Pulse attack, which occurred fifteen minutes from her home: "It was the first news I saw when I woke up that day and I remember the death toll just rising.... It brought me to tears to know something like that happened so close." The organizers of the event were largely student activists who advocated for the day to be a national die-in action to draw attention to gun violence.[18]

13 **June 13, 2022** Jennicet Eva Gutiérrez publicly turned down a presidential invitation to the White House Pride celebration. Gutiérrez is a community organizer at Familia: Trans Queer Liberation Movement, a grassroots group based in Los Angeles.

In a letter, she described her reasoning for rejecting President Joe Biden's offer: "At the start of your administration you pledged to protect LGBTQ+ people worldwide, but it's a commitment that you have failed to uphold at home." The Biden administration failed to assist transgender migrants. She noted that Biden could easily use his executive powers to help transgender people in Immigration and Customs Enforcement (ICE) custody, saying, "The reality is that as this celebration is taking place, trans people currently in ICE custody will be in unsafe conditions."

During interviews, Gutiérrez stated that "having access to the White House" was not a priority as LGBT+ asylum seekers were being deported, transgender people were under attack and being criminalized across the US, and transgender immigrants were facing ongoing detainment in detention centers with inhumane conditions. At the US-Mexico border, trans people in detention centers were reportedly being misgendered, denied health care, or blocked from entering the country. Gutiérrez argued that Biden's executive orders that established some protections against anti-LGBT+ discrimination were not enough.[19]

14 **June 14, 1974** FannyAnn Viola Eddy, a prominent LGBT+ activist from Sierra Leone who established the Sierra Leone Lesbian and Gay Association, was born. In April 2004, she delivered a speech at the

United Nations in Geneva, urging support for the Brazilian Resolution, which sought to recognize the human rights of LGBT+ people. Eddy was brutally murdered in her office in Freetown in September 2004, and to this day the crime remains unsolved.[20]

June 14, 1977 Miss America Anita Bryant arrived in Chicago for a concert. The concert had been booked months earlier, before Bryant became a national anti-LGBT+ figure. Bryant was a leader for an anti-LGBT+ initiative in Dade County, Florida, where citizens voted to repeal an anti-discrimination ordinance, passed by the county commission earlier that year, that prohibited discrimination on the basis of sexual orientation in employment, public service, and accommodations.

The vote occurred on June 7, 1977. Bryant planned to visit Chicago only seven days later, and a group of Chicago LGBT+ activists decided to organize a picket. According to Albert Williams, one of the organizers, they were "warned by gay establishment leaders that it would be an embarrassing failure. Back then, it seemed, the only time LGBTQ people turned out en masse was for the Pride Parade."

However, over three thousand people showed up for the impromptu picket. The protest drew out people across different communities, from political activists to people who frequented bars to people who lived in the suburbs.

Protesters chanted, "Pray for Anita" and sang "The Battle Hymn of the Republic." According to historian John D'Emilio, demonstrators held signs reading "God Drinks Wine, Not Orange Juice" and "Anita Is McCarthy in Drag." A police spokesman noted, "The gays were noisy but peaceful."

The protest lasted for three hours, and eight demonstrators were arrested. Some of the protesters marched to the Tribune Tower, home of the *Chicago Tribune*, to protest a series of articles written by reporter Michael Sneed, who falsely linked a child pornography ring to the Chicago gay community.

Coverage of the protest made the front page of the *Tribune*. Bryant's "Save Our Children" campaign fueled the growing LGBT+ rights movement.[21]

June 14, 2021 Thousands of Hungarians protested outside parliament in Budapest against legislation that would ban discussions of homosexuality or gender change in schools. Prime Minister Viktor Orbán rallied against the LGBT+ community, constitutionally redefining marriage as a union between one man and one woman. His administration also limited gay adoption and outlawed legal status for transgender people. The bill was attached to a separate law strictly penalizing pedophilia, making it difficult for the opposition to vote against it.

Organizers of the protest argued the legislation was dividing the former Soviet bloc nation. One protester, who attended the action with his boyfriend, told *France 24*, "The law is an outrage. We live in the twenty-first century, when things like that should not be happening. We are no longer in communist times, this is the EU and everyone should be able to live freely." Hungary is a member of the European Union, and in light of this the European Commission launched legal action against Orbán's government over the law. The commission argued the law was discriminatory and violated European values of tolerance and individual freedom.

In response, Orbán argued he was seeking to safeguard traditional Christian values from Western liberalism. In a radio interview, he stated, "We are working on building an old-school Christian democracy, rooted in European traditions."[22]

15 **June 15, 1987** *The New York Times* allowed its writers to use *gay* as an adjective meaning "homosexual." Despite this win, *The New York Times* has continued to be criticized for its anti-trans coverage.[23]

16 **June 16, 1836** Mary Jones, a Black American sex worker and soldier in the 1800s, is frequently considered to be one of the first transgender people ever recorded in an official capacity in the United States.

Jones, who was assigned male at birth, reportedly presented as a man during the day and a woman at night, wearing a dress, wig, and jewelry. She used a prosthetic vagina to solicit sex from men, during which she allegedly pickpocketed their wallets.

Jones is best known for a court case in which she was charged with grand larceny as a result of this alleged theft. She was tried on June 16, 1836, five days after Robert Haslem, a white mason, discovered his wallet, which had held ninety-nine dollars, had been replaced with an empty one after he solicited Jones for sex. She appeared in court dressed as a woman and was widely ridiculed by the court and the audience. She was challenged on her attire and responded:

> I have been in the practice of waiting upon girls of ill fame and made up their beds and received the company at the door and received the money for rooms and they induced me to dress in women's clothes,

saying I looked so much better in them and I have always attended parties among the people of my own colour dressed in this way— and in New Orleans I always dressed in this way.

During the trial, Jones used her prior military service as a plea to the jury. She denied having seen Haslem, let alone stealing his wallet. Jones was found guilty and was sentenced to five years' imprisonment in New York's Sing Sing.

She was eventually arrested again for allegedly stealing money from her sex work clients. She served a six-month sentence at Blackwell's Island (now Roosevelt Island) on February 15, 1846, for the repeat offense. Little is known about the rest of Jones's life.[24]

June 16, 1951 Louis Graydon Sullivan, one of the first transgender men in the US to publicly identify as gay, was born on this day.

Sullivan grew up in Milwaukee, Wisconsin, in a very religious Catholic family. He kept a diary from the age of ten and held on to copies of those diaries. In 1973, he identified himself as a "female transvestite" and by 1975 identified himself as a "female to male transsexual." He decided to move to San Francisco to find a more understanding community, and his family was supportive of the move. They gifted him a suit—his mother told the tailor it was for her son—and his grandfather's pocket watch as going-away presents. His grandmother would later offer to pay for gender confirmation surgery.

Once he arrived in San Francisco, Sullivan lived as an out gay man. He was involved in the gay and transsexual communities. Heterosexuality was still a requirement for medical transition at the time. Medical professionals did not believe that transgender men could be homosexual. Gay men and transgender men were understood as two distinct and separate groups.

Sullivan fought for the American Psychiatric Association and the World Professional Association for Transgender Health to recognize gay trans men and to change the requirements for gender identity disorder so that they no longer included sexuality. He wrote the first guidebook for trans men, *Information for the Female to Male Cross-Dresser and Transsexual*. Sullivan edited *The Gateway*, a newsletter for trans people.

In 1979, Sullivan was finally able to find doctors and therapists who accepted his sexuality and gender identity, providing him with hormone therapy and a double mastectomy surgery a year later. In 1986, Sullivan obtained genital reconstruction surgery, and he was diagnosed as HIV positive shortly after. Sullivan wrote in his diary, "I took a certain pleasure in informing the gender clinic that even though their program told me I could not live as a Gay man, it looks like I'm going to die like one."

Before his death, Sullivan began a support group for trans men that evolved into FTM International, the largest organization of its kind still running today.[25]

June 16, 1990 Queer Nation called for a massive demonstration addressing anti-queer violence. Fifteen hundred participants crossed New York City from the West to East Villages, demanding police and government action to stop the increase of hate crimes. The group held a banner that read "Queers Take Back the Night."

The four-hour march became violent when queerphobic bystanders pelted the protesters with eggs and a beer bottle. Three youths from Brooklyn attacked a group of marchers, assaulting them with a golf club, a knife, and a baseball bat. The youths were eventually stopped by police and arrested. The violence continued, however, as a man attempted to run protesters over with his car.

Three marchers were arrested on disorderly conduct charges. Michelangelo Signorile, a Queer Nation founder, and Lori Cohen, a lawyer, were arrested after arguing with police following the violent confrontation.[26]

17 **June 17, 1926** Eve's Hangout, a New York underground queer and radical café run by Eve Adams, was raided by police.

Adams was born Chawa Zloczower in Poland to a Jewish family in 1891. Her hangout was a lesbian bar, host to a number of meetings and poetry nights, and a safe haven for radicals in Greenwich Village. The proprietor cut a scandalous figure, having open lesbian relationships and eschewing what at the time was traditional women's wear. She was a well-known associate of anarchists and had made her living in the US through collecting subscriptions to anarchist and socialist papers.

The café would be targeted by landlords and police and was eventually raided on June 17. Adams was arrested and many queer and radical texts were destroyed, including Adams's own *Lesbian Love*. She would be found guilty of "obscenity" and deported.

Adams then lived in France, where she would continue to sell radical publications and fall in love with Jewish cabaret singer Hella Olstein. Adams and Olstein were both arrested in Nice in 1943 and sent to Auschwitz, where they were murdered.[27]

June 17, 1950 Gay rights activist Thomas Lawrence Higgins was born. He attended the University of North Dakota in 1967 and studied journalism but was suspended in 1968 for his involvement in an underground student publication titled *Snow Job*. He did not return to the university and instead moved to the Twin Cities. In 1969, Higgins became the first person in Minnesota to be granted conscientious objector status from the Vietnam War.

Higgins joined Fight Repression of Erotic Expression (FREE), a gay rights organization, where he was credited with coining the term "gay pride." Higgins was fired from his job at the State Radio Services for the Blind due to his affiliation with FREE. In response, FREE picketed his former workplace, calling for antidiscrimination protections.

On October 14, 1977, Higgins along with fellow activist Bruce Brockway attended a televised press conference hosted by actress and antigay activist Anita Bryant. Bryant was answering questions about her plan to open a network of Anita Bryant Centers, which would "rehabilitate homosexuals." During the conference, Higgins pushed a banana cream pie into Bryant's face.

In 1980, Higgins and Brockway founded the Positively Gay Cuban Refugee Task Force, in response to an influx of Cuban refugees. Among the refugees were gay men who faced legal persecution in Cuba. They were unable to leave refugee camps without an American sponsor. The Positively Gay Cuban Refugee Task Force mobilized Minneapolis's gay community to sponsor refugees, in particular gay refugees, so that they could resettle.

Higgins died of AIDS in 1994.[28]

June 17, 2010 PolitiQ-queer solidaire, an activist group fighting against all forms of heterosexist and cissexist oppression and exclusion in Quebec, organized the first trans protest in the province.

Nearly two hundred people gathered for the 2010 demonstration. The protesters demanded that Quebec change existing regulations requiring people seeking gender marker changes to their civil status to undergo forced sterilization. They also called for more additional accessible ways for trans people to legally change their name.

Trans people who wanted to change their name in under five years required a psychiatric diagnosis of gender identity disorder and needed to begin medical treatments to change sexual characteristics. Trans people who were not Canadian citizens could not change their civil status documents to align with their identity. Trans people who had children before changing their sex designation could not change the gender they were assigned on their children's birth certificates.

The protest group advocated for an end to these policies and stated they were open to meeting with the Director of Civil Status, the official body responsible for managing records, to make these changes.[29]

June 17, 2017 Four organizers of a coalition of queer and trans people of color in Columbus, Ohio, were arrested. Wriply Bennet, Kendall Denton, Ashley Braxton, and DeAndre Antonio Miles-Hercules became known as the Black Pride 4. They faced charges including aggravated robbery, resisting arrest, causing harm to a police officer, failure to comply with a police officer's order, and disorderly conduct.

The arrests came after protesters disrupted the Stonewall Columbus Pride Festival and Parade to highlight the previous day's acquittal of Jeronimo Yanez, the Minnesota police officer who killed Philando Castile. The organizers, in a press release, wrote they planned the demonstration to raise awareness of the violence against and erasure of Black and Brown queer and trans people and the lack of space for Black and Brown people at Pride festivals. Additionally, they intended to highlight the numbers of trans women of color who had been murdered in 2017 up until that point, which was already fourteen people.

Bennet told *Teen Vogue* that before taking to the street, she saw a white lesbian making a derogatory comment about a Black man selling T-shirts at Pride. In a later interview about the protest itself, Bennet claimed a white woman spit on her after laughing as Bennet was arrested.

Bodycam footage from the arrest details transphobic, racist, and violent treatment of the Black Pride 4, including asking protesters about their genitals and placing them in jails that did not accord with their gender identity.[30]

18 **June 18, 1981** The US House of Representatives approved an amendment introduced by Georgia Democrat Larry McDonald, a staunchly conservative and virulently antigay legislator. The amendment targeted the Legal Services Corporation—a federally funded nonprofit established to provide civil legal aid to low-income Americans—by prohibiting it from offering assistance in "any case which seeks to promote, defend or protect homosexuality."

While this amendment was not approved in the Senate, this vote occurred during a broader right-wing backlash against LGBT+ rights in the early years of the Reagan administration, as conservative lawmakers sought to restrict federal support for legal advocacy connected to gay rights, even in matters such as housing, employment, and custody.[31]

19 **June 19, 1975** The American Medical Association approved a resolution urging the repeal of state laws that criminalize consensual same-sex acts between adults. Despite this, medicine continues to be a site of violence for queer and trans people in the US.[32]

20 **June 20, 1983** Patrisse Cullors, cofounder of the Black Lives Matter movement, artist, and writer, was born in Los Angeles. Cullors and cofounders Opal Tometi and Alicia Garza state the Black Lives Matter movement has "always recognized the need to center the leadership of women and queer and trans people." The goal of the movement, according to the founders, was to support new and emerging Black leaders and to develop a network for Black people to feel empowered "to determine our destinies in our communities."[33]

21 **June 21, 1977** Robert Hillsborough was murdered by John Cordova. Hillsborough, a thirty-three-year-old gardener at a playground near San Francisco City Hall, went to a disco club with his boyfriend, Jerry Taylor. They left after midnight and stopped at Whiz Burger. Once they left the restaurant, they were approached by a group of young men who shouted antigay slurs at them.

Hillsborough and Taylor ran to Hillsborough's car, and several of the attackers climbed onto the car's roof and hood. They drove off, but members of the group followed them in another car. Hillsborough parked four blocks away from their apartment, and once they got out of their car they were immediately attacked by the men. Taylor managed to escape. Hillsborough was beaten and stabbed fifteen times by nineteen-year-old John Cordova, who purportedly yelled, "F****t! F****t! F****t!" and "This one's for Anita!" referring to antigay activist Anita Bryant, who led a campaign fighting to overturn an antidiscrimination law in Dade County, Florida.

Neighbors called the police and an ambulance, but Hillsborough was pronounced dead shortly after. Hillsborough's family unsuccessfully sued Bryant for inciting violence against gay people.[34]

22 **June 22, 1947** Octavia Butler was born in Pasadena, California. Butler used science fiction as a genre to explore issues facing humanity.

Patternmaster, her first series, examines the questions of what it means to be human, ethical and unethical usages of power, and how power can change people. Butler published her best-selling novel *Kindred* in 1979.

Butler never spoke publicly about her sexual orientation; however, after her death in 2006, several obituaries recognized her as "both a Black and Lesbian science-fiction writer."[35]

23 **June 23, 1952** William Dale Jennings was arrested in Los Angeles in the spring of 1952 for allegedly soliciting a police officer in Westlake Park, now known as MacArthur Park. Jennings's trial drew national attention to the Mattachine Society, of which he was a part, and membership of the society increased drastically as it decided to help Jennings contest the charges. Jennings called on Harry Hay, a fellow founding member of the Mattachine Society, and together they enlisted the help of George Sibley, a member of the Citizens Committee to Outlaw Entrapment. Jennings was one of the first gay men to contest solicitation charges.

The organization raised funds to promote Jennings's case throughout the US. The trial began on June 23, 1952, and lasted ten days. Jennings confessed to being a homosexual but denied any wrongdoing. The jury voted eleven to one for acquittal on the basis of police intimidation, harassment, and entrapment of homosexuals. The case was dismissed.[36]

June 23, 1990 Queer Nation and ACT UP members organized a march before New York City's annual Pride parade in 1990. Five hundred people came together to illegally march from Central Park to Union Square in protest of the New York City Parks Department's refusal to allow the annual gay and lesbian rally to be held in Central Park.

Gay and lesbian victim assistance agencies throughout the country, including in New York City, had experienced a rise in victims of antigay violence. Additionally, the queer community was facing significant abuse and stigma due to the AIDS epidemic. Queer Nation and ACT UP's protest highlighted the increasing marginalization of the queer community.[37]

June 23, 2022 Gay Shame organized a "'Queers 4 Tents/Tents 4 Queers'" event in support of homeless people in San Francisco. With flyers and banners reading "Street Sweeps Kill Queers," the event was a protest of Mayor London Breed's policies of refusing to house people, increasing street sweeps and police presence, and using conservatorships to imprison poor people.[38]

June 23, 2023 Starbucks workers began a weeklong protest against alleged unfair labor practices. Earlier in June 2023, the conglomerate would not allow workers to put up Pride decorations or displays in its stores. Starbucks additionally threatened workers' access to existing benefits, denied new benefits to union stores, fired union leaders, and made other illegal attempts to dissuade unionization.

Starbucks Workers United stated this was an "anti-union campaign to intimidate workers and make them feel unwelcome in their workplace." The union said their ongoing "Strike with Pride" protest closed twenty-one Starbucks locations, including its Reserve Roastery in Seattle. The National Labor Relations Board prosecuted Starbucks for failing to bargain in good faith with workers. NLRB judges found that Starbucks committed 161 federal labor law violations. Moreover, the federal government prosecuted Starbucks for seventy-five complaints, alleging over 1,300 violations.

The "Strike with Pride" campaign noted that Starbucks's labor practices have a significant negative impact on its LGBT+ workforce. Starbucks has frequently touted itself as an ideal workplace for LGBT+ people due to its benefits, which cover gender-affirming care such as hair removal, facial feminization, and hair transplants, among other forms of care. In 2023, the company highly publicized the extension of its medical travel reimbursement coverage for people who travel to receive gender-affirming care. Because of these benefits, Starbucks has a relatively high number of LGBT+ workers. But as corporations have begun to withdraw support from the queer community, Starbucks has proven it is no different.[39]

24 **June 24, 1973** An arsonist set the UpStairs Lounge, a queer nightclub in New Orleans's French Quarter, on fire. Thirty-two people died and fifteen were injured. The crime was egregiously mishandled. Nobody was ever charged with a crime, even though there were several prominent suspects.

Buddy Rasmussen, UpStairs Lounge bartender and survivor, had ejected Roger Dale Nunez from the bar earlier in the evening. Nunez allegedly screamed, "I'm gonna burn you all out." After throwing Nunez out, Rasmussen attempted to convince a police officer to hold Nunez for questioning. However, the police officer ignored the original scuffle and waved off the possible conflict. Rasmussen ran into fellow survivor Courtney Craighead after the fire. They were pushed away from the scene. Craighead, a closeted church deacon, attempted to explain to the same officer why Nunez was a person of interest. Nonetheless, the officer again told them to leave.

Craighead and Rasmussen agreed, hoping to avoid any possible arrest due to New Orleans's antigay ordinances. One broadly outlawed a "crime against nature," which was a felony charge carrying a mandatory prison sentence that unscrupulous police were known to accuse people of on mere suspicion. Equally, neither Craighead nor Rasmussen was certain they could convince a reporter to cover the story without revealing their names.

Due to the stigma against queer people at the time, New Orleans and Louisiana quickly and quietly moved on from the fire.

Four bodies of the thirty-two people killed by the fire were quietly buried in unmarked graves at the Resthaven Memorial Park cemetery. There was no signage or plaque to mark their burials. The location of their remains is still unknown.

In 1974, a year after the fire, an anonymous caller told the city that one of the bodies was that of World War II veteran Ferris LeBlanc, who could be identified by a ring he was wearing at the time of his death. LeBlanc's family stated decades later that they did not know how Ferris had died until discovering it online in 2015.[40]

June 24, 1973 The parades that would come to be known as Pride were initially known as the Christopher Street Liberation Day March, frequently shortened to "Liberation Day." The parades occurred predominantly in New York, Chicago, and Los Angeles and marked the anniversary of the Stonewall riots. In 1970, during the first New York City Liberation Day, people met at Christopher Street near the Stonewall Inn and walked up Sixth Avenue to Central Park, where speeches and events spanned the rest of the day.

On this day in 1973, Sylvia Rivera, an activist in the Gay Liberation Front and a cofounder of Street Transvestite Action Revolutionaries (STAR), took the stage at Washington Square Park as people began to rally. There was a rift in the movement, and transgender women like Sylvia Rivera experienced significant violence from cisgender queer people. Lesbian feminist Jean O'Leary saw transgender women as disruptive and called Rivera a "man in women's clothing."

Rivera took the microphone and a member of the crowd told her to "shut the fuck up," at which she proceeded to point out the sacrifices she had made for the movement: "I have been beaten. I have had my nose broken. I have been thrown in jail. I have lost my job. I have lost my apartment for gay liberation and you all treat me this way?" Rivera continued to speak for the homeless and incarcerated members of the LGBT+ community. Her work with the Street Transvestite Action Revolutionaries (STAR) provided a home, meals, and clothing to struggling homeless gay and transgender youth as well as formerly incarcerated people. Despite the transphobic violence and attempts to silence Rivera, she used the stage to highlight the importance of STAR within a movement that was silencing the most marginalized members of its community in order to gain mainstream acceptance.[41]

June 24, 1978 The Gay Solidarity Group assembled for a march in Sydney, Australia. Roughly a thousand people gathered. Mark Gillespie, a participant, reported that attendees made up a diverse crowd "with transgender and Aboriginal people and people from migrant backgrounds all mixing in.... The atmosphere was more one of celebration than protest."

The march began in Taylor Square, and the reception of the march was mixed. Although many people watched and some joined the crowd, the marchers were subject to homophobic slurs. Once they arrived at Hyde Park, they were denied entry.

The police officer in charge tried to end the march. Participants quickly decided to break through the police lines and turned their route toward Kings Cross. Gillespie recounts the moment as being exhilarating: "We were sick and tired of being criminalized, pathologized, demonized, of being made to hide who were and have our rights to live as human beings denied."

That night, the police met the crowd with violence, taking advantage of darkness. Marchers fought back against the police even as they were violently beaten. Fifty-three people were arrested, and their names and occupations were subsequently published in *The Sydney Morning Herald*. Many lost their jobs as a result.

Many members of the march gathered at the police station regardless of their injuries, chanting in solidarity. One, who was a lawyer, organized the group around raising bail money for the recently incarcerated people.

The protest is recognized as one of the first Pride parades in Australia.[42]

June 24, 1994 LGBT+ labor leaders convened in New York for a meeting called "Pride at Work, the Founding Conference of the Lesbian, Gay, Bi-Sexual and Transgender People in the Labor Movement." The gathering held significance, as it coincided with the twenty-fifth anniversary of the Stonewall riots.

Nancy Wohlforth, representing the Office and Professional Employees International Union and the Lesbian-Gay Labor Alliance, cochaired a group working to create an organization uniting the different LGBT+ labor organizations into a single entity, Pride at Work. Wohlforth was elected to the position of copresident of Pride at Work with Cal Noyce in 1996, and the organization adopted a resolution in support of affiliation with the AFL-CIO as an official constituency group.

Wohlforth, an American union leader and activist, was a staunch advocate for numerous civil, labor, and LGBT+ causes over the course of her career. Her advocacy spanned diverse issues such as single-payer health care, domestic partner worker benefits, and nondiscrimination protections for LGBT+ workers. Notably, in 2005, she made history as the first openly LGBT+ member to be elected to the AFL-CIO Executive Council. She died in 2024.[43]

June 24, 2015 Jennicet Eva Gutiérrez, a transgender woman and an undocumented immigrant, disrupted a Pride reception at the White House. President Barack Obama was giving a speech about the civil rights of lesbian, gay, and transgender Americans when Gutiérrez cried out, "President Obama, stop the torture and abuse of trans women in detention centers."

Gutiérrez stated she could not celebrate Pride Month while seventy-five transgender detainees were subject to assault and abuse. As she was expelled from the White House, Obama shook his head, saying, "You're not going to get a good response from me by interrupting me like this. I'm sorry. I'm sorry.... Shame on you, you shouldn't be doing this."

After Gutiérrez was thrown out, Obama stated that discrimination against transgender Americans was an area where more progress was needed.

Gutiérrez argued that if Obama wanted to celebrate Pride, he should release LGBT+ immigrants in detention centers immediately. Notably, Obama had faced interruptions and heckling by immigration activists before but appeared to be more willing to engage with them, as opposed to his treatment of Gutiérrez.

Following the event, thirty-five members of Congress sent a letter to the secretary of the Department of Homeland Security to express concern for lesbian, gay, bisexual, and transgender detainees held by Immigration and Customs Enforcement (ICE), writing they were "extremely vulnerable to abuse, including sexual assault."[44]

25 **June 25, 2011** Jean Harris, American LGBT+ rights activist, died. Harris led the first successful campaign for lesbian and gay domestic partnership rights in the US, San Francisco's Proposition K in 1990. The measure eliminated the difference in legal rights and responsibilities between marriage and domestic partnerships. She served as the chair of the California Democratic Party's Lesbian and Gay Caucus and was the president of the Harvey Milk Lesbian, Gay, Bisexual, Transgender Democratic Club.[45]

June 25, 2022 Norway canceled the annual Pride parade in Oslo after an early-hours shooting at and around the London Pub, a popular LGBT+ bar. Two people were killed and twenty-one were injured in the attack. The forty-two-year-old shooter was charged with terrorist acts, murder, and attempted murder. In response, Norway raised its terror alert to its highest level.

The national police chief requested all Pride events be indefinitely postponed while the gathering remained a target for violence. He noted that the attack was a result of extremists who view LGBT+ as "the enemy." An Oslo police official urged people to not attend an event being held outside Oslo's city hall in remembrance of the victims of the attack.

However, thousands of people ignored the request and gathered. The group held signs reading "Sexual Freedom" and "You Can't Cancel Us." People marching chanted, "We're here, we're queer, we won't disappear!"

Activists critiqued the police chief, contending that it's the police's job to protect people from extremists. Alongside the march, people also laid flowers at the three clubs. Rain Vangen Dalberg, in an interview with the BBC, stated her reason for attending the rally: "It is to show that the fight is progressing."[46]

June 25, 2023 Turkish police arrested 133 LGBT+ protesters, activists, and journalists at Istanbul's twenty-first Pride parade, which had been banned. President Recep Tayyip Erdoğan had banned numerous Pride Month events across the country following his election in 2023.

Erdoğan pledged a new constitution would be issued that would affirm and uphold "family values." Davut Gul, the governor of Istanbul, supported Erdoğan's policy. Gul announced on Twitter, "Our national future depends on keeping the family institution alive with our national and moral values. We will not allow any activity that would weaken the family institution."

A joint press release of LGBT+ groups and organizers of the Pride parade stated, "We do not accept this policy of hatred and denial. But here we are today. You couldn't deal with us, you will not."

Despite the parade being banned, several buildings along the planned route were decorated with rainbow flags. The police blocked the road from the marchers. They also prevented journalists from covering the parade, encircling them near the route to prevent press coverage.[47]

26 **June 26, 2015** The US Supreme Court issued a landmark ruling in *Obergefell v. Hodges*, legalizing same-sex marriage nationwide and granting same-sex couples the right to marry in all fifty states.[48]

June 26, 2022 Turkish police attacked and arrested hundreds of people at Istanbul's 2022 Pride march. Journalists were arrested alongside the marchers. The arrests in 2022 numbered three times more than the total of the previous seven Istanbul Pride marches combined.

Thirty-four of those arrested were under eighteen, according to Kaos GL, a Turkish LGBT+ rights group. Prior to the arrests, local officials banned Istanbul's Pride parade, citing security concerns as well as the need to uphold the public order.

Istanbul Pride at its peak had upward of a hundred thousand participants; it has been banned since 2015. Despite this ban and consistent anti-LGBT+ violence, activists have continued to celebrate Pride. Before the march, officials shut down metro stations, ousted people from cafés, and preemptively arrested fifty-two people before the parade started. Metal barriers and police in riot gear cordoned off the streets. According to *France 24*, marchers and activists were also threatened by counterdemonstrators who claimed the LGBT+ community was a danger to "Turkish values." Various human rights organizations, including Kaos GL, reported through Twitter that activists were held for hours in vehicles without air conditioning and were denied food and water. Lawyers attempting to free arrestees were met with police aggression. Nonetheless, all detainees were released within a day due to a significant network of lawyers working with local activists.[49]

27 **June 27, 1869** Emma Goldman was born in Lithuania to an Orthodox Jewish family. As a child, Goldman consistently rebelled against her father, who wanted Goldman to marry at fifteen and have a traditional domestic life. When the family moved to St. Petersburg, then the capital of Russia, the family experienced significant poverty and the entire family was forced to work.

In her autobiography, Goldman reports begging her father to let her return to school, and he threw her French book into the fire and shouted, "Girls do not have to learn much! All a Jewish daughter needs to know is how to prepare gefilte fish, cut noodles fine, and give the man plenty of children!" She pursued an education on her own, studying the ongoing Russian politics. Goldman moved to New York City in 1885 to join her sisters.

On her first day in New York, Goldman met Alexander Berkman, who invited her to a public speech that evening. Goldman quickly became a significant figure in the anarchist movement and is a founder of anarcha-feminism, a form of anarchism that challenges patriarchy alongside state power and capitalism. She was a supporter of free love and contraception.

Alongside her feminism and belief in social liberation for women, Goldman was a staunch critic of prejudice against homosexuals and genderqueer people. She was the only figure in the left, at the time, to publicly support queer people. Goldman wrote, in a letter to Magnus Hirschfeld, "It is a tragedy, I feel, that people of a different sexual type are caught in a world which shows so little understanding for homosexuals and is so crassly indifferent to the various gradations and variations of gender and their great significance in life."

Goldman was an outspoken advocate of Oscar Wilde and decried his treatment by the British government. She regularly corresponded with Almeda Sperry, a bisexual woman, and these letters have contributed to debates over Goldman's sexuality.[50]

June 27, 1970 Notably, Chicago and San Francisco held their first Pride marches on June 27, 1970, a day earlier than the more well-known New York City procession commemorating the Stonewall Uprising. Chicago's Pride began as a spontaneous, loosely organized protest that started with a rally in Bughouse Square and turned into a bold march to the Civic Center, while in San Francisco, a small group marched down Polk Street.[51]

June 27, 2009 Karah Mathiason began planning Toronto's first Trans Pride March through a Facebook event page. In an interview, Mathiason stated she expected only ten people to be interested, but the event page quickly amassed over three hundred RSVPs. Trans people have participated in the overall Pride parade as well as the Dyke March.

According to the *Toronto Star*, trans people have largely been relegated to the sidelines in these larger parades. Mathiason and other members of the trans community developed the event to provide space specifically for trans people and to highlight the community. The march was not formally recognized by Pride Toronto as an officially programmed event.

The original route was from Church and Bloor Streets to Church and Wellesley Streets. Once they arrived at Church and Wellesley, the marchers were met with large metal barricades. They pushed through the barricades and finished the first Trans Pride March inside Toronto's downtown Gay Village.[52]

June 27, 2009 Members of the Queers Against Israeli Apartheid (QuAIA) movement marched in Toronto in response to the "pinkwashing" of Israel as a "gay mecca" in the Arab world. After QuAIA activists participated in 2008 and 2009 Pride festivals in Toronto, Israeli lobby groups B'nai Brith and the Simon Wiesenthal Center attempted to portray QuAIA as an anti-Semitic hate group, even though many of the members are Jewish and have histories of antiracist organizing. After the 2009 parade, a film against QuAIA was made and distributed to city councillors to convince them to pass a resolution that would defund Pride Toronto unless it banned QuAIA from marching in the parade in 2010.

On May 25, 2010, the board of Pride Toronto held a press conference to announce that the phrase "Israeli Apartheid" would be censored from the 2010 Pride parade. The decision sought to ban the Toronto-based activist group QuAIA from the parade, which prompted a significant backlash. Eight of the founding members of the first Toronto Pride, held in 1981, denounced the decision. However, the Toronto queer community confronted Toronto Pride about the censorship of QuAIA, and, after a monthlong effort, Toronto Pride revoked the ban.[53]

June 27, 2020 Russian police detained over thirty people, primarily women, who were conducting single-person protests in central Moscow against pornography charges that had been brought against Yulia Tsvetkova, a prominent LGBT+ activist. Tsvetkova was formally charged with illegally producing and distributing pornographic materials online, punishable by up to six years of prison.

The charges stemmed from Tsvetkova's online community, called "The Vagina Monologues," which featured abstract depictions of female genitals and sexual organs and provided educational and scientific drawings as well. Tsvetkova was also charged for depicting four adults with children in a drawing titled "Family is where this is Love," allegedly for promoting nontraditional sexual relations, under a law banning LGBT+ "propaganda." Tsvetkova's criminal investigations came at the behest of homophobic activist Timur Bulatov, who, in his own words, was waging war against LGBT+ people and their supporters by making complaints about them to law enforcement and related agencies. Bulatov published Tsvetkova's home address and called on his supporters to assassinate the activist and her mother.

The protest was organized for June 27, the national youth day in Russia. Over fifty media outlets organized a "Media Strike for Yulia." Writers, journalists, actors, influencers, and bloggers published posters with the hashtag #forYulia. Close to 233,000 people signed an online petition demanding authorities drop the case against her. Protesters in central Moscow held posters reading "Female Body Is Not Pornography" and "Free Yulia Tsvetkova."

According to Russian law, there is no requirement to notify authorities before a single-person protest. However, the charges brought against protesters included violation of public gathering regulations, including the ban on mass events introduced in response to the COVID-19 pandemic.[54]

28 **June 28, 1969** The Stonewall Inn riot began in the early hours of the morning. Solicitation of same-sex relations was illegal in New York City, and as a result LGBT+ people flocked to gay bars and clubs to be able to exist authentically. However, it was still illegal to be queer in public, whether that be holding hands, kissing, or dancing with someone of the same gender, so the New York Police Department harassed patrons of gay bars and frequently shut the establishments down.

The Stonewall Inn opened in 1967 as a gay bar and quickly became an important Greenwich Village institution (see March 18, 1967). It was large and cheap to enter, and it welcomed transgender and gender-nonconforming people, who were not always welcome at other gay bars and clubs. It was also a safe place for runaways and homeless gay youths and was one of the few gay bars to allow dancing.

When the police raided the Stonewall on June 28, it was a surprise, as the owners had not been tipped off and the bar had just been raided a few days earlier.

Outside, a butch lesbian fought against the police and shouted, "Do something!" to the forming crowd. According to some eyewitnesses, this was Stormé DeLarverie, a biracial lesbian and drag performer, who was known as a "guardian of lesbians" in Greenwich Village. However, the facts are unclear, as the only police record for a lesbian arrested that night was for Marilyn Fowler.

The crowd, which contained a significant number of Black, Latine, and white LGBT+ patrons and passersby, began to physically fight the police. Activists such as Marsha P. Johnson, Miss Major Griffin-Gracy, and John O'Brien, among others, were involved in the riot that night and the following riots over the next six days. After the riots, participants and other radicals created the Gay Liberation Front. Anniversary protests were organized on June 28, 1970, in New York and Los Angeles, among other locations, which became the annual Pride celebration.[55]

June 28, 1969 The first night of the Stonewall riots, a group of women held their own protest at the Women's House of Detention, a prison at the heart of Greenwich Village, sitting where Christopher Street met Sixth Avenue. According to Daughters of Bilitis member Arcus Flynn, the imprisoned women chanted, "Gay power!" as they set fire to their possessions and threw them out the windows in solidarity with the nearby Stonewall Inn rioters.

One of the women inside was Black Panther Party member Afeni Shakur. Shakur had been arrested as part of the "Panther 21," who were accused of conspiring to bomb numerous sites around New York City. The Gay Liberation Front (GLF), an LGBT+ organization developed by participants of the Stonewall riots and other radicals, assisted in organizing twenty-four-hour protests at the Women's House of Detention.

After the trial against the Panther 21 collapsed and the charges were dismissed, Shakur attended the Revolutionary People's Constitutional Convention in Philadelphia in September 1970. There, she participated in a workshop organized by the GLF. Shakur told the group that after seeing the GLF banners outside the House of Detention, she "began relating to the gay sisters in jail beginning to understand their oppression, their anger and the strength in them and in all gay people." Shakur partnered with other workshop members to create a list of demands to bring to the floor of the convention, and she believed Black Panther Party cofounder Huey P. Newton's speech on gay and feminist liberation would bring a more expansive view of liberation to the Black power movement.[56]

29 **June 29, 1969** The Mattachine Society began as a secret Los Angeles organization founded in the 1950s by gay men (see November 11,

1950). It acted primarily as a social group in which members could discuss the discrimination and antigay violence they experienced. The Mattachine Society believed that government, religion, and psychiatry were agents of antigay oppression. Members worked to stop police entrapment of gay men and provided legal advice to those who were arrested. The society also addressed the stigmatization and medicalization of homosexuality and used "sip-ins" to protest the prohibition of LGBT+ people meeting in bars.

Historically, the Mattachine Society preferred to advocate for change through legal and political means. In the midst of the Stonewall Uprising, the Mattachine Society's leadership met with officials in the mayor's office and New York Police Department and agreed to discourage further protests. On this day in 1969, they placed a sign on the window of the Stonewall Inn reading:

WE HOMOSEXUALS PLEAD WITH OUR PEOPLE TO PLEASE HELP MAIN-
TAIN PEACEFUL AND QUIET CONDUCT ON THE STREETS OF THE VILLAGE
—MATTACHINE

This caused a divide within the group, and members left the society to form the Mattachine Action Committee, made up of individuals who enthusiastically advocated anti-police protests.[57]

30 **June 30, 1986** The US Supreme Court decision in *Bowers v. Hardwick* was published. Michael Hardwick, who had been seen by a Georgia police officer while engaging in consensual sex with another man in his home's bedroom, was charged with violating a Georgia statute that criminalized sodomy. While Hardwick challenged the statute's constitutionality, the Supreme Court found it to be legal. Justice Byron White wrote in the majority opinion that the US Constitution did not confer "a fundamental right to engage in homosexual sodomy." Chief Justice Warren E. Burger cited "ancient roots" of prohibitions against homosexual sex as a crime of nature.

Justice Harry Blackmun, in the dissent, argued the issue was one of the right to privacy. He critiqued his fellow justices, stating the court has an "almost obsessive focus on homosexual activity." In response to *Bowers v. Hardwick*, the National Gay and Lesbian Task Force established the Privacy Project to repeal sodomy laws on a state-by-state basis. The task force was the first national LGBT+ rights organization in the US and would play a prominent role in decriminalizing homosexuality.[58]

June 30, 2023 A broad coalition of over fifty organizations based in Philadelphia, including ACT UP Philadelphia and the Philadelphia Young Communist League, signed onto statements protesting a Moms for Liberty conference to be held in the city starting on this day. The protest was diverse across race, ethnicity, gender and sexuality identities, geographic origin, and age. Parents, children, and elder members of the community joined the organizers outside the Marriott hotel hosting the conference.

Occasionally, the Moms for Liberty conference attendees would attempt to antagonize the protesters by mocking them, waving, or blowing kisses. In response, the crowd turned their backs on the attendees to demonstrate that the hate group does not deserve attention. The protesters maintained a presence outside the Marriott for twelve hours a day, playing hyperpop and dancing in the streets. Alongside the Marriott protest, organizers held rallies outside libraries to demonstrate support for public libraries, hosted a drag queen story hour for young attendees, and provided online ways to demonstrate support, such as a downloadable Grandparents for Truth poster.[59]

JULY

1 **July 1, 1943** Gay Dutch anti-Nazi resistance fighter Willem Arondeus was executed by occupation forces. His resistance group falsified identity papers for Jewish people, and in March they attacked the Amsterdam registry, destroying thousands of records against which full papers could be checked (see March 27, 1943). The unit was betrayed, and most members were arrested. Alongside Arondeus, eleven others were executed. Before his execution, Arondeus asked a friend to testify after the war that "homosexuals are not cowards."[1]

July 1, 1972 In London, seven hundred people joined the first-ever Pride march in the UK.[2]

July 1, 2018 Despite Istanbul's governor banning Pride parades for four consecutive years, Istanbul held its sixteenth annual Pride parade. Prior to the ban, Pride had taken place without incidents for over a decade. The ban cited concerns about the "security of citizens and tourists" and "public order" after the ultra-nationalist group Alperen Hearths threatened the march with violence.

Istanbul's Pride parade has historically been the largest across Muslim countries and has been a safe space for members of the queer community. Organizers argued the governor's emphasis on public safety and order contributed to a perception of the planned peaceful march as disorderly. In an online statement, they wrote, "We are marching, get used to it. We are here, not going away." The organizers went on to state, "The governor cited the excuse of security in its decision to ban the march and in one word, this is comical. Our marches went on peacefully without being banned for 13 years."

Hundreds of people took part in the Pride parade, gathering in the city center, waving flags, singing, dancing, and giving speeches for roughly forty minutes before the police arrived. Police used tear gas, dogs, and batons to push back the crowds celebrating during the parade. Amnesty Turkey, in a report, documented that several people were detained at the event. Photographers stated that police used rubber bullets against some activists.[3]

2 **July 2, 1951** Sylvia Rivera, an American gay liberation and transgender rights activist, was born. While for the majority of her life Rivera identified as a drag queen, she later identified as a transgender person.

Rivera was raised by her grandmother, and she experimented with clothing and makeup at a young age. She was physically beaten for doing so, and after being attacked on a school playground in sixth grade by another student and being suspended for the altercation, she ran away from home at ten years old.

Rivera began living on the streets of New York City, and like many other homeless youths, she engaged in survival sex as a child sex worker. She was taken in and protected by local drag queens and other trans people, including Marsha P. Johnson (see August 24, 1945).

Johnson and Rivera cofounded the Street Transvestite Action Revolutionaries (STAR), a group dedicated to helping homeless young queer people. STAR provided services and advocacy for homeless queer youth and fought for the Sexual Orientation Non-Discrimination Act in New York. The act, which finally passed in 2002, prohibits discrimination on the basis of sexual orientation in employment, housing, public accommodations, education, credit, and the exercise of civil rights.

Rivera participated in numerous actions with the Gay Liberation Front's Drag Queen Caucus, and at eighteen she formally joined the Gay Activists Alliance (GAA). However, Rivera would come to disagree with the GAA. Rivera pushed for nondiscrimination laws to address discrimination against trans people and drag queens. The GAA, and other mainstream gay movements, began to shift away from protecting trans people and drag queens. Rivera was often encouraged to be vocal during dangerous demonstrations and protests. However, when press arrived, she was pushed to the side in favor of, according to Michael Bronski, "the middle-class 'straight-appearing' leadership."

Rivera was banned from New York's Gay & Lesbian Community Center for several years in the mid-1990s because, on a particularly cold winter night, she demanded the center take care of poor and homeless queer youth. Rivera's activism and work frequently intersected with issues of poverty and discrimination faced by people of color, which raised friction between her and the GAA, as it was composed largely of white, middle-class gay people. Rivera died of liver cancer on February 19, 2002, in a hospital in Greenwich Village.[4]

July 2, 1999 India's first Pride parade, called the Kolkata Rainbow Pride Walk or the Friendship Walk, occurred on this day in Kolkata. It was the first Pride march in South Asia. It began with less than fifteen people, and participants came from other cities in India, including Mumbai and Bangalore. The participants wore bright yellow T-shirts emblazoned with footsteps and a caption reading "Walk on the Rainbow." Ashok Row Kavi, noted Indian LGBT+ rights activist, was one of the participants in this first Pride.

The march split into two groups, one going to North Kolkata and the second going to South Kolkata. On the way, the groups visited various NGOs working for the prevention of AIDS.

By the time the groups reconvened at the end of the march, all of the major regional and international newspapers and television channels had arrived to cover the event. The participants were prepared with literature and a discussion of the purpose behind the walk. The walk received support from within India as well as from other South Asian countries like Pakistan and Bangladesh.

The Kolkata Rainbow Pride Walk emerged from activists fighting to overturn Section 377 of the Indian Penal Code, based on Britain's colonial code, which criminalized homosexuality. Article 14 of the Indian Constitution promises equality for all, including homosexuals. A Delhi High Court decision overturned the section in 2009, but it was reinstated in 2013. Finally, in 2018, the Supreme Court of India ruled Section 377 unconstitutional.

The walk, which has continued annually since 1999, is a political statement for equality, tolerance, love, and solidarity, and it is in solidarity with all rights-based movements, including women's rights, Dalit rights, and rights of non-able-bodied people, among others.[5]

July 2, 2021 Workers at the Geelong Library & Heritage Centre staged the first strike in Australian history for paid gender transition leave. Following a further two strikes, including a twenty-four-hour stoppage that completely closed half of Geelong's twenty public libraries, the workers won their demand for four weeks' gender transition leave per year on full wages, along with a range of other conditions.[6]

3 **July 3, 2016** Black Lives Matter brought Toronto Pride to a standstill to address anti-Blackness, anti-Indigeneity, and anti-intersectionality at the event. Protesters sat in the parade route, pausing the event for roughly thirty minutes.

Alexandra Williams, cofounder of Black Lives Matter Toronto, shut down the Pride parade to meet with Toronto Pride organizers concerning a list of demands. The demands included increasing funding for Blockorama (see June 1, 1999) and Black Queer Youth, prioritizing hiring Black transgender women and Indigenous people, reinstating the South Asian stage, hiring more Black deaf people and ASL interpreters, and removing police floats from future Pride parades. Williams argued that Pride movements have consistently been built on the efforts of Black people and other marginalized communities, which have also consistently been forgotten.

Toronto Pride executive director Mathieu Chantelois and board cochair Alica Hall reviewed the list of demands and signed them on the spot. Chantelois told the *Toronto Star*, "Their requests were extremely reasonable. Everything was making a lot of sense."

The Toronto police union president called the Toronto Pride organizers callous. However, longtime gay rights activists praised Toronto Pride for a public increased commitment to social justice. Toronto Pride's theme was "You Can Sit with Us," and the Pride Parade was preceded by a month of film screenings, community fairs, and discussions of issues regarding the trans community, Blackness and anti-Blackness, and queer politics. Activists argued that Pride needed to reflect its basis in community and social justice as opposed to profit.[7]

4 **July 4, 1965** A small group of gay and lesbian activists affiliated with the East Coast Homophile Organizations (ECHO), a regional federation of queer organizations that included the Daughters of Bilitis of New York, the Janus Society of Philadelphia, the Mattachine Society of New York, and the Mattachine Society of Washington, DC, picketed outside Philadelphia's Independence Hall to draw attention to discrimination against the LGBT+ community. Protesters held signs reading "Homosexuals Should Be Judged as Individuals."[8]

July 4, 1973 In Seattle, the Lesbian Separatist Group, which would go on to be called the Gorgons, published *Lesbian Separatism: An Amazon Analysis*. It is recognized as the most important text emerging from the separatist movement of the 1970s. While the document was never published in its entirety, it was distributed in mimeographed form and was one of the earliest separatist works to discuss race and class divisions within the lesbian separatist movement.

Lesbian separatism emerged within the feminist movement as a response to sexism within the 1960s and 1970s New Left, which was largely dominated by men. It called for the formation of women-only political groups, as well as for lesbian separatism, which was broadly defined as a commitment to feminism that precluded intimate relationships with men. Separatists advocated for the importance of all-women spaces as sites of refuge, healing, and empowerment. Many of the originators of lesbian separatist thought tended to be white and middle class. During the development of separatist theory, many women of color critiqued the argument that gender discrimination was the fundamental form of oppression and that racism is a byproduct of sexism.

Working-class women critiqued the separatist theory as based on middle-class luxury. In the midst of this, *Lesbian Separatism* was an important touchstone to develop a broader and more nuanced vision of the future. Moreover, it contributed to debates over the place of separatism within feminism itself.[9]

July 4, 1981 Rock Against Racism (RAR) was a grassroots political movement in Britain that used music to campaign against the electoral threat of the National Front.

RAR officially began on August 5, 1976, when Eric Clapton drunkenly told an audience, "Enoch was right. I think we should send them all back." He went to on to complain that Britain was in danger of becoming a "Black colony" and they needed to vote for Enoch Powell to "keep Britain white." The National Front, a neo-Nazi political organization, had won significant votes across Britain at the time, and RAR agitated to promote antiracism through music. RAR partnered with artists such as Billy Bragg, Buzzcocks, and Joy Division. It popularized the message of antiracism and also worked with the Anti-Nazi League (ANL), which provided physical support for concerts, even sleeping on the stage in 1978 to prevent the National Front from attacking it.

July 4, 1981, marked RAR's final carnival in Leeds. The large crowd reflected RAR and ANL's organizing efforts. The organizations had specifically targeted disaffected youth, who could have been drawn to the National Front, through shared love of music and art, alongside supporting Black people, Jewish people, queer people, and other targets of white supremacist violence. Kate Webb, who ran the RAR office, stated, "Part of what RAR was doing was trying to think about racism as a white problem and the idea that we were all still living consciously or unconsciously with the legacy of colonialism." RAR and ANL identified whiteness as the problem, facilitating further engagement with antiracism and conversations pertaining to British history.[10]

5 **July 5, 1986** *The New York Times* published an article titled "Homosexuals, Upset by Ruling, Plan Drive to Abolish Anti-Sodomy Laws" in response to protests over the US Supreme Court's decision in

Bowers v. Hardwick, which held that the Constitution does not protect the right of gay adults to engage in private, consensual sodomy (see June 30, 1986).

John Wahl, a San Francisco lawyer, was interviewed for the article. He stated, "If we are going to be relegated to second-class citizenship, then we'll teach the nation we are equal and we can retaliate." Wahl was one prominent voice among gay activists advocating for an economic boycott with the goal of overturning antisodomy laws. "We're going to take whatever action is necessary, and we'll escalate that action as much as necessary until we have equal treatment in this land."

Jeff Levy, then the executive director of the National Gay and Lesbian Task Force in Washington, DC, said LGBT+ organizations were going to lobby states to overturn antisodomy laws, which then existed in twenty-four states and the District of Columbia. Queer organizations held protests, including one in New York City that drew more than a thousand people. *Bowers v. Hardwick* emerged from a Georgia antisodomy law, and activists were planning nationwide boycotts on goods from Georgia such as Coca-Cola, whose headquarters are in Atlanta.

Queer activists noted the ruling came at the same time the US Justice Department released an "opinion declaring that employers can legally discharge workers infected with AIDS if they do so to protect other employees." This nationwide protest of antisodomy laws brought together emergent AIDS activists alongside broader queer rights activists.[11]

6 **July 6, 1919** Magnus Hirschfeld, Arthur Kronfeld, and Friedrich Wertheim opened the Institute for Sexual Science. It was the first sexology research center in the world. Hirschfeld, prior to establishing the Institute for Sexual Science, had run the Scientific Humanitarian Committee, which campaigned for LGBT+ rights and tolerance. Kronfeld was a famous psychotherapist at the time. Wertheim was a dermatologist.

The Institute for Sexual Science led groundbreaking research and treatment pertaining to gender and sexuality. It provided various endocrinology and surgical services, among them early gender-affirming surgeries such as facial feminization surgery and sex reassignment surgery. Hirschfeld worked with the Berlin police department to reduce arrests of transgender people and to issue transvestite passes to individuals. Alongside this, the institute provided contraception and information about contraception, even though spreading information on birth control was illegal.

The institute held a library on gender, homosexuality, and eroticism. This was the first comprehensive collection of works about sexuality, in particular homosexuality. Hirschfeld, a gay man, published works and even a film advocating for tolerance. The institute provided homosexuals with psychological treatment to help them learn how to navigate a homophobic society and helped to provide community. It also was one of the first research and medical institutions to provide comprehensive care for and recognition of intersex people. Hirschfeld advocated for intersex people to have the right to determine if they wanted genital surgery on reaching the age of eighteen as opposed to infancy. The institute collected photographs of intersex cases to understand what Hirschfeld termed "sexual intermediacy."

The Institute for Sexual Science's significant collection of medical documentation and specimens pertaining to human sexuality and gender identity was destroyed by the Nazis in 1933.[12]

July 6, 1973 Reverend Ray Broshears, a gay Pentecostal evangelist, formed the Lavender Panthers, a group of armed street vigilantes who patrolled San Francisco to defend the gay community. The Lavender Panthers' creation was spurred by the sharp increase in violence against the LGBT+ community.

The violence included beatings, verbal harassment, and sometimes death. After the death of Robert Hillsborough in 1977 from injuries he sustained from a gay bashing in San Francisco, the queer community rallied around itself for protection.

The Lavender Panthers were the first prominent safe street patrol in the Castro and Tenderloin neighborhoods of San Francisco, which were known for their trans and gay communities. Members would patrol the streets, watching for altercations. They frequently carried shotguns and bats. A *Time* magazine article chronicling the group during the 1970s referred to the Lavender Panthers as a "stiff-wristed team of gay vigilantes." The reporter noted that Reverend Broshears himself had been the victim of a hate mob outside his mission center that served the queer community. Broshears said his goal was to put fear into the hearts of "all those young punks who have been beating up my faggots."

The Lavender Panthers held self-defense training sessions for community members. In the 1970s, San Francisco was flourishing as a space for the queer community, yet queer people were reluctant to call the police to report violence in case they were accused of propositioning their attacker for sex. Due to the city's antigay statutes, it was dangerous for gay people to come forward. The Lavender Panthers were an alternative source of safety.[13]

7 **July 7, 1979** Robert Opel, an American photographer and homoerotic art gallery owner, was with his girlfriend, Camille O'Grady, and an ex-boyfriend, Anthony Rogers, at his San Francisco gallery, Fey-Wey Studios, when two men, Robert E. Kelly and Maurice Keenan, entered the studio and promptly held Opel at gunpoint. Rogers and O'Grady interrupted Kelly and Keenan and were tied up. Opel was shot and killed. Opel had briefly shot to fame in 1974 when he streaked across the stage at the Academy Awards, flashing a peace sign behind a startled David Niven.[14]

8 **July 8, 1980** The Democratic Rules Committee declared its commitment to not discriminate against homosexuals. During the Democratic National Convention held in New York City on August 11–14, 1980, the Democrats made history as the first major political party to officially endorse a platform advocating for homosexual rights.[15]

9 **July 9, 1936** June Jordan, African American poet, educator, essayist, and bisexual activist, was born. During her life, Jordan wrote twenty-seven volumes of poems, essays, libretti, and children's works on the subjects of women's rights, civil rights, and sexual freedom. Her work frequently engages with visions of a radical globalized solidarity among the world's marginalized and oppressed. In 2019, Jordan was inducted on the National LGBTQ Wall of Honor within the Stonewall National Monument in New York City's Stonewall Inn.[16]

July 9, 1969 In the wake of the Stonewall Uprising just weeks earlier, the New York Mattachine Society organized a watershed gathering in Greenwich Village, inviting both activist and community leaders to what would be referred to as the first "gay power" meeting. This groundbreaking event was the turning point of LGBT+ organizing, breaking with cautious advocacy for a more militant, mass call for liberation and civil rights.[17]

10 **July 10, 1972** The Democratic National Convention was held in Miami, Florida, in 1972, in support of presidential candidate George McGovern. McGovern was openly supportive of the LGBT+ community and advocated for nondiscrimination on the basis of sexual orientation in his campaign. Jim Foster, a cofounder of San Francisco's Society for Individual Rights and the Alice B. Toklas Democratic Club, the nation's first registered LGBT+ Democratic group, was given permission to address the convention about gay rights. His speech was relegated to the 5:00 a.m. slot, when he said:

> Mr. Chairman, Assembled Delegates. My name is Jim Foster. I am here tonight representing the twenty million gay women and men who are looking for a political party that is responsive to our needs.... We do not come to you pleading for your understanding or begging for your tolerance. We come to you affirming our pride in our lifestyles, affirming the validity of our right to seek and maintain meaningful emotional relationships, and affirming our right to participate in the life of the country on an equal basis with every other citizen....We urge the Democratic Party to enact this gay rights plank. But, regardless of whether this convention passes this plank or not, to our millions of gay brothers and sisters as well as to the Democratic Party, we say, "We are here. We will not be stilled. We will not go away until the ultimate goal of gay liberation is realized. That goal being that *all people* can live in the peace, freedom, and dignity of what they are."

Madeline Davis, a lesbian delegate, spoke after Foster. She was a cofounder of the Mattachine Society of the Niagara Frontier and was an editor of their newspaper, *The Fifth Freedom*. She lobbied against bar raids by the Buffalo police and the publication of names of arrestees by the *Buffalo News*. She also lobbied for university classes on queer studies. Davis said:

> We have suffered the gamut of oppression, from being totally ignored or ridiculed, to having our heads smashed and our blood spilled in the street. Now we are coming out of our closets and onto the convention floor to tell you, the delegates, and to tell all gay people throughout America that we are here to put an end to our fears—our fears that people will know us for who we are—that they will shun and revile us, fire us from our jobs, reject us from our families, evict us from our homes, beat us and jail us. And for what? Because we have chosen to love each other.

McGovern lost the election and experienced significant backlash due to his support of the LGBT+ community.[18]

11 **July 11, 1966** Twenty-six Oklahoma City teachers and school administrators were forced to resign following a six-month investigation into "alleged homosexual activity" led by Oklahoma County Attorney Curtis Harris. During the investigation, Harris claimed citizens were pushing him to stop but said, "It won't work. The investigation will continue." Roughly twenty years later, the Tenth Circuit Court struck down the Oklahoma law that penalized public school teachers who participated in "public homosexual conduct."[19]

12 **July 12, 1833** Johann Baptista von Schweitzer, a German politician and dramatic poet and playwright, was born. He was drawn to the social democratic movement led by Ferdinand Lassalle in his country. Despite Schweitzer facing a morals charge for homosexual activities in 1862, Lassalle defended him, arguing that personal sexuality should be respected as long as it does not cause harm to others.[20]

July 12, 1990 Queer Nation invaded Dorrian's Red Hand, a popular straight hangout on New York City's Upper East Side, for a "Nights Out" event. Nights Out events were designed to make it clear to cisgender and heterosexual patrons that queer people would not be restricted to exclusively gay bars for socializing.[21]

13 **July 13, 1863** Mary Emma Woolley, an American educator, peace activist, and advocate for women's suffrage, was born.

Woolley served as the president of Mount Holyoke College from 1900 to 1937, held the position of vice president at the American Civil Liberties Union, and played a role in the United States' entry into the League of Nations. She also collaborated with President Herbert Hoover on women's rights and with President Franklin D. Roosevelt on pacifism.

While Woolley was teaching at Wellesley College from 1895 to 1899, she and Jeannette Augustus Marks formed a partnership that would endure for the following fifty years. Shortly after assuming the presidency of Mount Holyoke, Woolley appointed Marks as an instructor in the English department, which she would go on to chair.[22]

July 13, 1952 Marie Equi, lesbian and American political activist, died. Throughout her life, she would have relationships with numerous women, never hiding them.

She became one of the first sixty women to become a physician in Oregon. At some point between 1905 and 1915, Equi began to provide abortions for people regardless of income and social status. She never faced legal consequences for her services. Additionally, she was an active member of Portland's Birth Control League and disseminated information about birth control. Equi also worked in several campaigns for women's right to vote in Oregon.

She participated in numerous political movements, including those for the eight-hour day, the right to organize a union, and an end to child labor. Equi denounced American involvement in World War I, and for this she was convicted of sedition, spending ten months in San Quentin State Prison. She was the only known lesbian and radical to be incarcerated at San Quentin.

She died on this day in 1966 at eighty years old outside Portland, Oregon. In August 2019, she was an honoree in San Francisco's Castro neighborhood's Rainbow Honor Walk.[23]

14 **July 14, 1990** Queer Nation, an LGBT+ activist organization founded in New York City in March 1990 by AIDS activists, held a "Nights Out" event at Alcatraz, an East Village bar. These events were intended to disrupt the idea that queer individuals should limit their presence to gay bars, instead asserting their right to occupy traditionally heterosexual spaces. Alcatraz was suspected to be the hangout of several "queer bashers." Queer Nation then proceeded to King Tut's Wah-Wah Hut, another straight bar, where group members were threatened by management and patrons.[24]

15 **July 15, 1953** The right-wing dictatorship of General Francisco Franco amended Spain's 1933 vagrancy law to criminalize homosexuality. The amendment also authorized the detention of all those convicted under the law in labor and concentration camps. Over the next twenty-five years, around five thousand LGBT+ people would be imprisoned—mostly gay and bisexual men and trans women. They were housed in specialist prisons in Huelva and Badajoz and in a camp in Fuerteventura, Canary Islands, and many were subjected to brutal sexual violence, as well as medical abuse like electric shock treatment. Most of those prosecuted for breaching the law were working class, and historian Pablo Fuentes told *The Guardian* that it was "not uncommon to hear homosexuals from the upper classes and the aristocracy speak about the Franco period as a great time."

After Franco's death in 1975 and the subsequent fall of the dictatorship, political prisoners were released, but LGBT+ prisoners were not. The homophobic law was eventually overturned in 1979, although those imprisoned because of it were not recognized as victims of Francoism and awarded compensation until 2009.[25]

July 15, 1984 The group that became Lesbians and Gays Support the Miners (LGSM) held its first meeting at founding member Mark Ashton's flat on the Heygate Estate in South East London.

The meeting was advertised in the newspaper *Capital Gay* and called for lesbians and gay men "interested in solidarity work … to set up an organization" to support a nationwide strike of mine workers in opposition to a pit closure program of the Conservative government.

The meeting began at 4:00 p.m. and was attended by eleven people. The group would go on to grow significantly around the UK, raise huge amounts of money for the miners, and build lasting links between the working-class movement and the LGBT+ community in Britain.

Their work ultimately resulted in the official trade union movement (and subsequent Labour Party policy) declaring support for gay rights, and the London Pride parade in 1985 would be headed by a column of miners.[26]

July 15, 1990 Sex Garage was a Montreal warehouse party in the city's Old Montreal district. Nicolas Jenkins, filmmaker and artist, presented a series of after-hours parties that were known for being safe spaces for queer people and were openly sexual during the AIDS epidemic. For Sex Garage, held during the early hours of this day in 1990, Jenkins hired DJs to play and employed stripper contortionists and go-go dancers, while vintage porn was projected inside the warehouse.

The party attracted roughly four hundred attendees. The organizer was used to police shutting down the parties; however, this night, like that of the Stonewall Uprising, would be very different. Montreal police arrived to investigate around 4:00 a.m. The police offered several different explanations in the days that followed, including noise complaints, suspecting illegal liquor sales, and that the party's promoter had reached out for assistance.

The police forced the attendees into the street. The officers did not wear their name tags or badges, but they did have batons. They taunted the crowd with homophobic slurs and then began to attack people at random. Patrons chanted, "We're here, we're queer, and we're proud of it!"

to the gathering police. The police beat many people, some severely. Nine attendees were arrested for a variety of charges, ranging from mischief to assaulting a police officer.

Photojournalist and writer Linda Dawn Hammond had originally attended Sex Garage to document people voguing. However, as the police began to beat the crowd, she continued to take photos. Hammond reports that she was knocked to the ground by police but managed to get the camera and rolls of film to a friend, who biked away. The photos later served as evidence of police brutality and the crowd's refusal to accept police violence.[27]

16 **July 16, 1994** Prince Edward Island, Canada, held its first Pride march, called the Gay and Lesbian Pride March, on this day. The march was organized to support and push for changes in the province's Human Rights Act to include sexual orientation. Some onlookers were present to support; however, others were there to yell homophobic insults and to throw oranges at the marchers, who threw the oranges back and even gathered them up to make smoothies later.[28]

17 **July 17, 1982** Commander Michael Trestrail's sexual orientation was made public when his lover attempted to sell his story to a British newspaper, leading to Trestrail's forced resignation from the British Navy and as Queen Elizabeth II's personal bodyguard. At the time, he had been the queen's bodyguard for sixteen years. He had previously been the personal bodyguard of Prince Philip, the queen's husband.

Homosexuality was a criminal offense in the UK, and being openly queer could result in significant consequences. The revelation of Trestrail's sexuality raised a discussion about the discriminatory practices of anti-LGBT+ legislation and the impact those acts held on LGBT+ people, including those of relatively high status. The Trestrail case was the second time a senior member of the royal establishment had been connected to homosexuality, which raised questions as to whether Queen Elizabeth had been aware of Trestrail's sexuality as well as to the monarchy's stance on homosexuality. Prime Minister Margaret Thatcher aligned herself against Trestrail.[29]

18 **July 18, 1966** In 1965, a group of queer youth in San Francisco, many of whom were transgender and engaged in survival sex work, formed a social and political group called Vanguard, the first known gay youth organization in the US. Vanguard members frequented Gene Compton's Cafeteria, located in the Tenderloin district, which frequently called the police on LGBT+ customers and kicked out Vanguard members. Vanguard responded by picketing the establishment on this day in 1966 in one of the first demonstrations against police violence targeting transgender people in San Francisco. The picket eventually led to the Compton's Cafeteria riot the following month (see August 1966).[30]

19 **July 19, 1990** Queer Nation's Youth Visibility Working Group met with Dr. Marjorie Hill, New York Mayor David Dinkins's liaison to the gay and lesbian community, along with the New York City Teachers Union. The group discussed the lack of queer input into the portion of the city's existing school curriculum that examined cultural diversity.[31]

20 **July 20, 1983** Tourmaline, an American artist, filmmaker, activist, editor, and writer, was born. Tourmaline has archived histories of drag queens and transgender people connected to the Stonewall Uprising. Along with Sasha Wortzel, Tourmaline wrote, directed, and produced *Happy Birthday, Marsha!*, a short film about Marsha P. Johnson, legendary trans activist and Stonewall Uprising participant (see August 24, 1945).

Tourmaline's films focus on the voices of marginalized LGBT+ people. She worked at Queers for Economic Justice, where she directed the Welfare Organizing Project and produced *A Fabulous Attitude*, which documented low-income New Yorkers surviving inequality and thriving. She also released a short animated film, *The Personal Things*, which was based on an interview she conducted with Miss Major (see October 25, 1940), director emeritus of the Transgender, Gender Variant, and Intersex Justice Project, a program that assists incarcerated transgender people.[32]

21 **July 21, 1958** The city council in New Orleans, Louisiana, encouraged police to investigate public expressions of homosexuality in the French Quarter on this day. One council member had complained that the police were not bringing charges against men for wearing women's clothing or engaging in lewd behavior. Mayor deLesseps Story "Chep" Morrison appointed his half-brother, Jacob Morrison, to head a committee to investigate the issue.

In response to increased pressure, Police Superintendent Provost A. Dayris led raids on known "deviate [*sic*] bars."[33]

22 **July 22, 1990** Over one hundred members of ACT UP Long Island and Queer Nation, a New York–based gay and lesbian activist group, marched on New York Senator Ralph Marino's Nassau County home. The activists accused Marino of being responsible as Senate majority leader for the defeat of an anti-bias bill. The bill had been sponsored by Governor Mario Cuomo. The activists marched from downtown Syosset, Long Island, to Marino's home in Muttontown. A demonstrator called the neighborhood an enclave of "rich Republicans." The marchers held signs reading "Being Queer Is Not a Choice. Being an Asshole Is" and "Marino = Bigot."

The march route was roughly a mile long, and as individuals came out of their homes and the golf club to see what was going on, they received fliers explaining the demands and causes of the march. For homes where people did not emerge, fliers were placed in mailboxes along with a "Silence = Death" sticker. Once the marchers reached Marino's home, a line of mounted police refused to let them in. The group attempted a "die-in" on Marino's driveway but were threatened with arrest. The marchers then held a picket for roughly half an hour.

The demonstration ended with Steve Quester, member of Queer Nation, leading a vow: "In the name of James Zappalorti, Julio Rivera, and Yusuf Hawkins, we will hound every state senator who voted against this bill." All three men were murdered for being gay in Staten Island, Queens, and Brooklyn. Cuomo's bias bill would have made it a crime to assault or intimidate an individual on the basis of race, religion, ethnicity, national origin, sex, disability, age, or sexual orientation.[34]

23 **July 23, 1959** The Court of Appeals of California published its opinion in *Vallerga v. Department of Alcoholic Beverage Control*. The First and Last Chance, a lesbian bar in Oakland, was accused of violating a law that bars could not serve alcohol to "illegal possessors or users of narcotics, prostitutes, pimps, panderers, or sexual perverts." The accusation alleged that during the investigation of the bar "the portions of the premises of the licensees, where the activities permitted by the license are conducted, have been and still are a resort for sexual perverts, to wit: Homosexuals." The decision overturned a previous case, *Stoumen v. Reilly*, which held that a bar cannot be closed simply for having gay patrons.

Vallerga v. Department of Alcoholic Beverage Control held that if gay people were found to publicly "demonstrate" their sexuality, the bar could have its license retracted. The police accused patrons of numerous crimes, such as women dressing in men's clothing, men dressing in women's cloth-ing, and gay people kissing and dancing together:

> During the period of surveillance police officers testified that they observed women dancing with other women, and women kissing other women.... A police officer testified that he observed a male patron and a grey-haired man approach, embrace each other at the bar, put their foreheads together while they carried on a whispered conversation, and that the grey-haired man then kissed the other and stated to the bartender: "Arley and I are going steady." This officer also testified that he observed a person dressed and made up as a man and who appeared to be a man, but who, the witness was informed, was in fact a woman, making use of the women's restroom.[35]

24 **July 24, 1969** The Gay Liberation Front (GLF) was founded. It had developed out of the Mattachine Society of New York, which had adopted very respectable and legal techniques to advance equality for gay men and lesbians. After the Stonewall riots, a group of gay men and lesbi-ans who were tired of police abuse and frustrated with the Mattachine Society's tactics formed the Gay Liberation Front.

One of the GLF's first acts was to organize a march in response to Stonewall and demand an end to the persecution of gay men and lesbians, which became New York's first Pride parade, held on June 28, 1970.

The GLF had an expansive leftist political platform. They denounced racism and supported various anti-imperialist causes and the Black Panther Party. They were publicly anticapitalist and attacked the nuclear family as well as gender roles. Nonetheless, their focus was solidly on gay rights. The members fought against mainstream attitudes and values, in direct contrast to the Mattachine Society.

GLF members also openly claimed the word *gay*, which had previ-ously been avoided by generations of gay and lesbian activists. Previous activist organizations used names such as the Mattachine Society and the Daughters of Bilitis. The GLF contended that they would demand rights as gay men and lesbians first and foremost.

They called for LGBT+ people to come "out of the closet and into the streets," while fighting against assimilation as the answer for anti-queer violence. In 1970, Sylvia Rivera and Marsha P. Johnson would join the GLF. The Gay Liberation Front sought to create a society free not only from sexism and homophobia but also from sexual labels entirely.[36]

25 **July 25–27, 1969** The First International Symposium on Gender Identity, with the title "Aims, Functions, and Clinical Problems of a Gender Identity Unit," took place at the Piccadilly Hotel in London. According to the symposium's pamphlet, it was brought together to address the "problem of gender identity disorientation, not only as a psychiatric entity but as an area requiring specialized medical study and treatment as well as social understanding."

The organizers argued that significant knowledge needed to be developed across all aspects of the "transsexual phenomenon" so that trans people's mental and physical health needs would be met.

At the time of the conference, there were few medical practices that focused on gender identity, and this had the possibility to negatively impact trans people. The pamphlet notes that lack of care, or forced care, could possibly lead a person to die by suicide. It was thus imperative for researchers and professionals to learn more about the "transsexual phenomenon" and to teach the public.[37]

July 25, 2015 The first Newfoundland and Labrador Trans March took place in St. Johns, Canada, aiming to draw attention to issues specifically faced by transgender people, such as access to health care, education, and discrimination. Protesters chanted, "Hey ho! Hey ho! Transphobia has got to go!" and were joined by supportive car horns. Roughly seventy-five people, both transgender people as well as supportive community members, gathered, making the march the largest stand-alone Trans March in the province's history.

Daze Jeffries, in an interview with *The Independent*, stated, "We have to claim our own space. It's no new thing that the trans movement has always kind of fought on their own, in part with a larger gay and lesbian liberation movement, but you know there's always been some kind of distinction."[38]

26 **July 26, 1989** Following public controversy over a retrospective of the photographs of Robert Mapplethorpe that featured explicit images of queer intimacy and BDSM subcultures, Senator Jesse Helms launched a campaign in the US Senate to curtail public funding of "obscene or indecent art."

He introduced an amendment to restrict the National Endowment for the Arts (NEA) from supporting works that included depictions of "sadomasochism, homoeroticism … or individuals engaged in sex acts."

The Senate voted for the measure by voice vote, a reflection of its broad political support in the midst of a conservative cultural backlash. Activists and artists immediately warned of the amendment's vague and expansive language. Anne Murphy, the American Arts Alliance executive director at the time, warned that under those criteria, even the majority of Shakespeare's plays would be off-limits—deadpanning, "Certainly not *Richard III*."

The amendment also singled out two arts organizations that had supported the Mapplethorpe exhibition, excluding them from NEA support for five years. The measure marked a watershed moment in the late twentieth-century culture wars, as it signaled that public arts institutions could be punished for supporting work that questioned current moral norms.[39]

27 **July 27, 1969** The Gay Liberation Front (GLF) organized multiple neighborhood protests and began the structure of marches that would become the contemporary Pride parade. The Gay Power March, held on this day in 1969, was one such event. The GLF organized over five hundred people to march from the Washington Square Arch to the Stonewall Inn to mark the one-month anniversary of the uprising. Marchers were given lavender ribbons and lavender arm bands.

Village Voice reporter Jonathan Black covered the story in his article "Gay Power Hits Back," published July 31, 1969. Black noted the chants began suddenly, with a young man yelling, "Give me a *G*! Give me an *A*! Give me a *Y*! Give me a *P*! ... an *R*! What does it spell?" The other protesters shouted, "Gay power!"

The crowd continued to chant, "Gay, gay power to the gay, gay people. Gay, gay power to the gay, gay people." Black wrote that individuals on the tourists' buses were confused by the event, at first thinking the marchers were shouting, "Play power." Martha Shelley from the Daughters of Bilitis and Marty Robinson from the Mattachine Society spoke to the crowd about the importance of gay rights.

Black wrote, "As the traffic up Sixth Avenue ground to a halt, the marchers gathered confidence. The chants and the cheers rang out more defiantly. Maybe it wasn't just a joke. Maybe there really was a gay power." As the marchers advanced to Sheridan Square, the members clapped and cheered, shouting chants of gay power. According to Black, residents looked shocked, and he concluded the article with, "A mild protest, to be sure, but apparently only the beginning."[40]

28 **July 28, 1990** Queer Nation began a series of visits to LIFE Ministry, a New York group that held (and still holds) weekly prayer meetings to change "confused" queer people's sexuality, in order to provide queer individuals with positive role models.[41]

29 **July 29, 2020** Queer Palestinians gathered in a demonstration organized by alQaws, a queer Palestinian organization. One hundred fifty protesters gathered in Haifa to decry violence against LGBT+ Palestinians after an Arab transgender teen was stabbed to death in Tel Aviv.

The protest may have been sparked by the death of the transgender teenager; however, frustration had been steadily growing. Palestinian organizers pointed to the death by suicide of Sara Hegazy, an LGBT+ rights advocate from Egypt. She had received asylum in Canada after being tortured and imprisoned by Egyptian authorities for flying a rainbow flag at a Mashrou' Leila concert in Cairo. In 2019, the Palestinian Authority began to explicitly target alQaws, banning the organization from operating in the West Bank, much to the anger of queer Palestinians.

Rauda Morcos, a human rights lawyer who founded Aswat, the first Palestinian organization for queer Palestinian women, pointed to the funerals of queer women in the year leading up to the demonstration as moments when it was possible to see positive shifts in Palestinian communities' treatment of its LGBT+ members. However, in the weeks before the event, the dialogue became increasingly heated as Julia Zaher, the owner of the Alarz tahini company, made a donation to the Aguda, the association for LGBT+ equality in Israel. The reactions were complex. Conservative members of the Palestinian community boycotted Alarz. Some queer Palestinian organizations saw the donation as a public relations stunt, while others supported Zaher. Alongside this debate, the Knesset, Israel's parliament, held its own fight over anticonversion laws, and other nations utilized LGBT+ communities as political ammunition.

The protest emerged from the increasing presence of LGBT+ discourse and the need to address and redress harms against LGBT+ Palestinian people.[42]

30 **July 30, 1960** Paul Mirguet introduced homosexuality as a category of "social scourge" to the French Penal Code. The Mirguet Amendment classified homosexuality as a "scourge" alongside alcoholism, tuberculosis, drug addiction, and prostitution. Mirguet stated homosexuality is "a social scourge … a scourge against which we have a duty to protect our children." The French parliament passed the amendment on this day in 1960.[43]

31 **July 31, 1932** Barbara Gittings, founder of the New York chapter of the Daughters of Bilitis, was born. Gittings served as editor of the national Daughters of Bilitis magazine from 1963 to 1966 and collaborated closely with Frank Kameny in the 1960s on the initial picket lines that drew attention to the ban on the employment of gay individuals by the largest US employer at the time: the US government.

Gittings was also heavily involved in the American Library Association and advocated for the inclusion of positive literature about homosexuality in libraries. She also played a significant role in the movement to convince the American Psychiatric Association to declassify homosexuality as a mental illness in 1973. Gittings described her life's mission as dismantling the "shroud of invisibility" surrounding homosexuality, which had previously been associated with crime and mental illness.[44]

AUGUST

August 1966 While San Francisco's Tenderloin district was one of the few places open to transgender people in the 1960s, the LGBT+ community was still subject to improper arrest and police violence. Specifically, transgender women were often targeted for "crimes" that included "female impersonation" and "obstructing the sidewalk."

In August 1966, the cops arrived at Gene Compton's Cafeteria in the Tenderloin and arrested drag queens, trans women, and gay men who had been sitting, eating, and gossiping as they drank their coffees. Even though Compton's was known as a safe place, workers would sometimes call the police to clear the diner of its queer clientele. When a police officer placed his hand on a woman at Compton's, she threw a cup of coffee in his face. The cafeteria then erupted. People began to flip the tables and throw cutlery at the officers. Sugar shakers were thrown through the restaurant's windows and doors. Drag queens used their heavy purses to beat the police. Outside on the street, dozens of people fought back as police forced them into paddy wagons. The crowd destroyed a police car and set a newsstand on fire.

The Tenderloin uprising occurred three years before the famous Stonewall riots in New York City. According to historian Susan Stryker, "It was the first known instance of collective militant queer resistance to police harassment in United States history."[1]

August 1, 2019 The queer Palestinian community gathered in Haifa for an unprecedented protest. Roughly two hundred people arrived at the German Colony, a central site in Haifa, to protest anti-LGBT+ violence. The protest was organized in response to the stabbing of a transgender teen from Tamra, a Palestinian city in northern Israel. They were stabbed outside a shelter for LGBT+ youth in Tel Aviv the week prior to the protest.

The protest was organized by over thirty groups, including alQaws, an organization advocating for sexual and gender diversity in Palestinian society; Aswat, a feminist queer organization for sex and gender freedom for Palestinian women; and Adalah, a legal center for the protection of Palestinian rights in Israel.

According to 972 *Magazine*, the organizations released a statement prior to the protest saying, "We reject and condemn the stabbing of the Tamra teen on the basis of sexual and gender orientation."

Protesters waved pride flags alongside transgender pride flags and Palestinian flags. They held signs reading "Queers Against Violence and

Sexual Harassment" and "Silence Kills. It's Time We Raise Our Voices." Rula Khalaileh, an organizer with Women Against Violence, noted this was the first protest based on the principles of "an intersectional struggle between queer-Palestinian struggles and struggles against the occupation." Aida Touma-Sliman was the only member of the Knesset, Israel's parliament, to join the protest, emphasizing its importance as the first public protest in support of transgender people.[2]

2 **August 2, 1924** Queer author James Baldwin was born in Harlem, New York. Baldwin was neither in nor out of the closet. He wrote *Giovanni's Room* (1956) and *Just Above My Head* (1979), two seminal queer texts. However, he never openly stated his sexuality. This may be one reason why Baldwin was not pushed out of the civil rights movement, unlike Bayard Rustin (see March 17, 1912), who was out as a gay man.[3]

3 **August 3, 1990** Queer Nation marched on the Quebec Government House in Manhattan to protest police brutality against queer people in Montreal. The group received a letter of concern from a governmental delegate, but its demands were ignored.[4]

4 **August 4, 1990** The term *Two-Spirit* was proposed and adopted at the Third Annual Gathering of Native American Gays and Lesbians held near Beausejour, Manitoba. According to Harlan Pruden, managing editor of *Two Spirit Journal*, Two-Spirit (2S) is an Indigenous identity for individuals "who embody diverse (or non-normative) sexualities, genders, gender roles, and/or gender expressions." The term itself is a translation of the Ojibwe *niizh manidoowag*, or "two spirits." For early adopters, the intent was to deliberately differentiate themselves from non-Native gays and lesbians as well as the non-Native terminology *gay*, *lesbian*, and *transgender*. Additionally, the term was a purposeful replacement for the offensive anthropological term *berdache*, which had been preferred among non-Native anthropologists for describing Indigenous people who did not conform to European and American gender roles and gender presentations. Journalist Mary Annette Pember, Red Cliff Ojibwe, notes that replacing the offensive term was a strong driver in adopting the term *Two-Spirit*.

Even so, the ceremonial roles traditionally embodied by Two-Spirit people vary widely across Indigenous cultures. The Indigenous Foundation notes, "Notions, ideas, and identities should not be generalized to *all*

Indigenous peoples and cultures. Due to the diverse and culturally specific nature of these traditions and understandings, it is crucial to recognize that the concept of 2S folks is not universal to all Indigenous worldviews."[5]

August 4, 2004 The Warehouse Spa and Bath, a bathhouse in Hamilton, Ontario, was raided by police as a part of the city's Multi-Agency Task Force (MATF). MATF was a team of three police officers, two health inspectors, two city bylaw officials, and two fire inspectors. They visited the Warehouse to investigate hygiene and bylaw issues.

Jamie Bursey, co-owner of the Warehouse, was charged with three fire regulation violations, five city licensing and standard violations, serving food, and two provincial health violations for smoking infractions. The Warehouse was a meeting spot predominantly for closeted gay men. Police raided the space after using the cruising website Squir.org to gather information about the Warehouse. Although the majority of the comments were about sexual activity and not bylaw infractions, one commenter wrote, "Went to the Warehouse Saturday and only half the hydro was working, and a lot of the furniture/pool table, etc. was moved out. The hot tub was drained as well." In less than three hours after the comment was posted, police were arresting patrons.

Police stated they arrested patrons having sex; however, Bursey said an anonymous witness reported the men were standing, fully clothed in towels, and speaking to one another when police entered. These men were given a conviction that could result in a criminal record as well as jail time.

Out of fourteen businesses visited by MATF that night, three were queer. One was Show World, a peepshow known as a cruising spot for gay and bisexual men. The third was the Windsor Bar. However, the day after the raid, police spokesperson Sergeant Glenn Bullock told *Xtra* magazine the Warehouse was the only gay establishment on that evening's list. The raid roused outrage among the queer community for the criminalization of consensual sex.[6]

5 **August 5, 1969** A little over a month after the raid of the Stonewall Inn and the following weeks of resistance, Atlanta experienced its own Stonewall. Seventy people went to Ansley Mall Mini-Cinema to watch *Lonesome Cowboys*, a homoerotic underground comedy directed by Andy Warhol.

The *Atlanta Constitution* described the film as "not the kind of movie where you send the kids on a Saturday afternoon." Fifteen minutes into the film, it was shut off, the house lights were turned on, and Atlanta police officers rushed into the theater's aisles. The raid had begun.

The police had selected the theater to enforce obscenity laws. Many of the audience members were targeted for being "known homosexuals." They were harassed, photographed, and arrested.

Abby Drue, an attendee of the movie and LGBT+ activist, stated in an interview, "They had everybody get up and line up. We had popcorn in our mouths. I think I had a submarine sandwich I was in the middle of eating. That's how absurd it was."

After the raid, protesters at the local alternative newspaper, *Great Speckled Bird*, were confronted by police and sprayed with Mace, and many were arrested. This response by police further inflamed the rage against antigay discrimination and motivated greater organization by queer people.

After the raid, members of Atlanta's queer community met at the New Morning Café in Emory Village, forming the Georgia Gay Liberation Front. They registered LGBT+ people to vote, protested antigay laws, and in 1971 organized the first Atlanta Pride event. Gay nightclubs and bars began to open. One such club was Backstreet, which Madonna and Elton John visited in disguise. The gay community began to come out of secrecy and established a public presence in Atlanta.[7]

6 **August 6, 1945** Gloria Allen, a transgender activist who ran a charm school in Chicago for at-risk transgender youth, was born. Allen transitioned before the Stonewall riots with the support of her mother and her grandmother, Mildred, who was a seamstress for drag queens.

Allen, also known as "Mama Gloria," ran her charm school out of the Center on Halstead, a community center for LGBT+ people in Chicago's Lakeview neighborhood. The school was free and informal. According to *The New York Times*, Allen often paid for students' meals out of her own budget.

Attendees were usually transgender people in their teens or early twenties who were economically impoverished. Allen's lessons covered table manners, dating etiquette, and job interview skills. She also provided tips on hygiene, dressing, and makeup. In addition to etiquette, Allen taught her students queer and trans history. The school did not last long; after opening in 2012, it operated for less than a decade.

In the 2020 documentary film *Mama Gloria*, Allen said, "Back then, we were brutally murdered or beaten up, and I just couldn't understand why they were doing this to me and my sisters. But I got by. I made it through by the grace of God."[8]

7 **August 7, 1987** In London, over one hundred lesbians and gay men held a "kiss-in" at Piccadilly Circus in defiance of the Sexual Offences Act. The act had decriminalized private sex acts between consenting adults; however, it kept public displays of same-sex affection a misdemeanor.[9]

August 7, 2020 The "Rainbow Night," also dubbed a "Polish Stonewall" by some outlets, occurred in reaction to the arrest of LGBT+ activist Margo, who was accused of causing damage in June 2020 to a truck that was covered with anti-LGBT+ slurs and had loudspeakers projecting slurs against queer people. Hundreds of protesters in Warsaw gathered outside the offices of the Campaign Against Homophobia, an LGBT+ rights organization, to protest her arrest.[10]

8 **August 8, 1978** The International Lesbian and Gay Association (ILGA) was founded on this day in 1978 by activists from the UK, Ireland, Australia, Denmark, France, Italy, the Netherlands, and the US. Homosexuality was criminalized based on the common law tradition, which activists found exceedingly difficult to overturn. The activists adopted a human rights–based framing, focusing on international courts, specifically the European Court of Human Rights. ILGA was involved in *Dudgeon v. United Kingdom* (1981) and *Norris v. Ireland* (1988), two cases that led to the repeal of laws criminalizing homosexuality in Northern Ireland and the Republic of Ireland.

ILGA also worked on cases related to unequal ages of consent, military service, transgender rights, and asylum and housing rights. However, those projects were unsuccessful. The organization gained consultative status as an NGO at the United Nations Economic and Social Council (ECOSOC) in 1993. It represents more than two thousand member organizations from over 170 countries.[11]

9 **August 9, 1967** Queer theorist José Esteban Muñoz was born in Havana, Cuba. Muñoz is best known for his highly influential books *Disidentifications* and *Cruising Utopia: The Then and There of Queer Futurity.* His work combines performance studies and queer studies and frequently focused on queer futurity. He wrote, "Queerness is not yet here."

Muñoz proposed disidentificatory performance (hijacking cultural norms to undermine and reimagine them) as acts of transgression and creation by which racial and sexual minorities articulate truths of cultural hegemony. He developed a critical methodology of hope to question the present and open up the future as queer. Muñoz worked on the initial Crossing Borders Conference in 1996, which focused on Latin American and Latine queer sexualities. He was a board member of the City University of New York's Center for LGBTQ Studies (CLAGS).

Muñoz died in New York City in 2013 while working on what would have been his third book, *The Sense of Brown: Ethnicity, Affect and Performance*. Shortly after his death, CLAGS created an award in his honor to be given to LGBT+ activists who integrate queer studies into their work.[12]

10 **August 10, 1969** In June 1969, a week before the Stonewall Uprising, thirty to forty residents of Kew Gardens in Queens, New York, formed a "vigilante committee" to harass gay men cruising in a local park. Initially they used flashlights and patrols to harass the men, claiming they were "concerned for the safety of the women and children." In mid-June, however, gay men insisted they had a right to be on public land. The vigilantes chopped down at least thirty trees. Eyewitnesses contacted the police to report the vigilantes. Police officers visited the park, talked with the men cutting down the trees, and left without making any arrests.

According to *The New York Times* and *New York Post*, neighborhood residents did not support the vigilantes. One woman argued that cutting down trees late at night did not help any mother or child. Another resident stated the actions were an infringement on the gay men's rights.

The Parks Department commissioner disparaged the acts, estimating the cost of replacing the trees to be roughly $15,000 and promising a further investigation. The American Civil Liberties Union called on the mayor and police commissioner to communicate to police that gay men have as much a right to the park as heterosexuals and are entitled to protections from antigay harassment and violence. The Mattachine Society of New York began a "Trees for Queens" fundraising drive to replace the trees.

On this day in 1969, the Mattachine Society partnered with the Daughters of Bilitis and other groups to protest the vigilantes' actions at the site, which became recognized as the earliest known public demonstration for LGBT+ rights.[13]

August 10, 1981 Fumino Sugiyama, a Japanese transgender activist, former fencer, and co-representative director of Tokyo Rainbow Pride, was born. Sugiyama went into fencing at the age of ten and joined Japan's national women's fencing team in 2004. He left the team in 2006, the year in which he published *Double Happiness*, an autobiography in which he discusses gender dysphoria. In 2012, Sugiyama retired from fencing altogether, stating that he did so after deciding to come out as transgender and being unsure if he would be accepted by his team. In 2021, Sugiyama was appointed as a member of the Japanese Fencing Federation and Japanese Olympic Committee; he is the first openly transgender board member.[14]

11 **August 11, 1992** One of the first protests against India's government repression of the LGBT+ community was held outside police head-quarters in New Delhi on this day. The protest was triggered by police officers picking up men from Connaught Place on suspicion of homosexual activity. At the time, Section 377 of the Indian Penal Code was still in effect. The law, which dated to 1862 and came into being under Britain's colonial rule, established homosexuality as a criminal offense.[15]

12 **August 12, 1907** Gladys Bentley was born in Philadelphia. At a young age, she realized she was a lesbian and that she felt more comfortable in masculine clothing. Her parents disapproved of her sexuality and gender presentation, taking her to several doctors to "cure" her. At the age of sixteen, Bentley ran away to Harlem, New York, as the Harlem Renaissance was reaching its height.

Bentley began to play piano at all-night parties and became well known for her deep voice and masculine clothing and for performing songs with an "unladylike" twist. She moved from these parties to the Mad House, a club located in "Jungle Alley," a street known for numerous speakeasies as well as the intermingling of Black people, other people of color, and white people. Bentley quickly rose to notoriety and became a headliner in numerous clubs. She performed in a signature tuxedo and top hat, openly flirting with women during her performances.[16]

13 **August 13, 2016** *Trans Hirstory in 99 Objects* was made public on this day in 2016. The multimedia project brings together a selection of archival materials and work by contemporary artists to provide an expansive and critical history of trans communities. It focuses on trans lives and experiences in the Pacific Northwest. The project seeks to blur "the line between the real and the imaginary, the known and the unknowable, giving visibility to actual people and events that remain foundational for transgender history while embracing partial facts, rumors, and maybes."

Trans Hirstory in 99 Objects was inspired by the Smithsonian's *American History in 101 Objects*. It includes objects such as the first transgender pride flag, designed by Monica Helms. The project was organized by Chris E. Vargas, executive director of the Museum of Transgender History & Art. Vargas commissioned transgender artists to fabricate missing objects, which appear with accompanying text to explore the reasons for their absence. The project takes the form of exhibitions online and in gallery spaces, a book, and a touring multimedia presentation.[17]

14 **August 14, 1988** French libertarian communist theorist, historian, gay liberation activist, and staunch opponent of colonialism Daniel Guérin died at the age of eighty-three. Initially drawn toward syndicalism and then Trotskyism, Guérin would eventually move in a libertarian direction. After studying the works of classic anarchist theorists like Mikhail Bakunin and Peter Kropotkin, while not abandoning elements of Marxism, he began to argue for the synthesis of the best elements of anarchism and Marxism. He was one of the first major leftist intellectuals in the twentieth century to openly articulate the necessity of integrating queer liberation with broader anticapitalist, anticolonial, and antifascist struggles. His work helped carve out space for a radical, queer left politics at a time when homosexuality was often marginalized—even within revolutionary movements.[18]

15 **August 15, 1971** The Homosexuelle Aktion Westberlin (HAW) was formed in Berlin. It came into being after the premiere of *It Is Not the Homosexual Who Is Perverse, but Rather the Situation in Which He Lives* at the International Forum for New Film at the Berlin International Film Festival. The film was the work of director Rosa von Praunheim and sociologist Martin Dannecker. It argued that Germany's reforms to legalize homosexuality had not brought about liberation. Instead, gay people oppressed themselves through focusing largely on sex and not on solidarity, which would develop political power.

The film was divisive, but it advanced discourses of gay power and the idea that the personal is political. It contended that gay people should accept their status as "the other" to exercise social and political power.

HAW began several weeks after the showing of the film. It was a new gay liberation group that rejected social prejudices as well as the tactics of previous gay activist groups. It argued that the problem was one of solidarity: "Discrimination ... generates a kind of communal spirit. Transforming this phony solidarity into real solidarity would be a precondition for the emancipation of homosexuals." Founders hoped to get gay people to "mediate existence as homosexual with their economic-political existence." HAW stated it would "support them in their conflict with society." HAW hoped gay men and lesbians would recognize themselves as a social minority and begin to politically organize in ways that furthered their interests as gay people.[19]

16 **August 16, 1946** David Benjamin Mixner, an antiwar and gay rights advocate, was born. He grew up in Elmer, New Jersey. In 1964, Mixner enrolled in Arizona State University, and while there he became involved in civil rights and antiwar activism.

In the 1970s, Mixner came out of the closet, and his activism began to involve the LGBT+ community. He led a pushback against Proposition 6, also known as the Briggs Initiative, a 1978 California ballot measure that sought to make it illegal for queer people to be teachers in public schools. Mixner worked with Harvey Milk and numerous other gay activists to vote against the proposition, making it the first of its kind to be defeated. Mixner would later protest nuclear weapons proliferation and fight a California act of legislation that would have required people with AIDS to be quarantined. Mixner's long-term lover and business partner, Peter Scott, died from AIDS-related illnesses in 1989. Mixner would go on to assist his friend Bill Clinton in getting elected president and would later chain himself to the fence outside the White House to protest the "Don't Ask, Don't Tell" policy for gays in the military.

Mixner was recognized by Washington College for his "lifetime in the forefront of American politics and international human rights, championing LGBT equality, wildlife conservation and progressive political causes." He died in 2024.[20]

17 **August 17, 1885** Kurt Hiller, a German essayist, lawyer, and expressionist poet, was born. Hiller played a significant part in the early German gay rights movement during the first two decades of the twentieth century.

Hiller was outspoken in his support for sexual minorities at a time when homosexuality was criminalized under Paragraph 175 of the German Penal Code. He became involved with the Scientific-Humanitarian Committee, the world's first homosexual rights organization. In 1929, he was elected vice-chairman and later that same year succeeded fellow gay activist Magnus Hirschfeld as chairman.[21]

August 17, 1968 The Patch Bar, owned and managed by Lee Glaze, was raided in Wilmington, California, a neighborhood of Los Angeles. It operated during a time when California law strictly discriminated against queer people. Homosexuality was illegal, as was dressing in a way that did not match one's legally assigned gender.

Glaze had been warned by LAPD repeatedly that to legally remain in business, he needed to prohibit drag queens, prevent men from dancing together, and refuse to allow more than one person at a time to enter the bar's bathrooms.

Instead of complying, Glaze developed a warning system where he would play "God Save the Queen" on the jukebox and patrons would then comply with all legal restrictions. On this day in 1968, frustrations about police discrimination and harassment came to a head.

Accounts vary as to the specifics. Some stated that undercover officers witnessed a man flirtatiously touching another man. Others said Glaze singled out the police officers from onstage and taunted them, chiding LAPD for sending "homely" cops. The undercover cops left but returned around midnight with five to six uniformed officers as backups. The police began to demand IDs. Two men were arrested on charges of lewd conduct.

During the raid, Glaze jumped onto the stage and addressed the patrons, yelling, "It's not against the law to be a homosexual, and it's not a crime to be in a gay bar!" He successfully rallied the crowd to chant, "We're American too!" After the arrests, he then led them to a flower shop owned by one of the customers, and together they bought massive amounts of carnations, roses, daisies, gladioli, and mums. They continued on to the Harbor Division Police Station. They stayed in the police station waiting room, waiting for bail to be posted for their friends. This came to be known as the "Flower Power" protest. People continued to be peaceful even as officers reportedly threatened the crowd with arrests if flowers touched any police officer.

Customers returned to the bar, which survived the police raid. Numerous queer activist organizations were founded in the Los Angeles area following the raid and protest.[22]

18 **August 18, 1936** This is the most likely date on which the gay socialist poet Federico García Lorca was taken from his jail cell in Spain and executed on the order of right-wing General Francisco Franco's military forces. The exact circumstances of his death are unclear, but after being arrested on August 16, he was probably killed on August 18 in the early hours of the morning.

The Spanish Civil War, which pitted workers and peasants against the military, nationalists, and fascists, had broken out one month previously. And it was clear on what side Lorca's sympathies lay: "I will always be on the side of those who have nothing and who are not even allowed to enjoy the nothing they have in peace."

To date, his remains have still not been found.[23]

August 18, 1970 Angela Davis was put on the FBI's Ten Most Wanted Fugitives list for her supposed involvement in kidnapping and murder growing out of an armed seizure of a Marin County courthouse in Northern California. She was listed as "armed and dangerous." On August 7, Jonathan Jackson, brother of George Jackson, one of the Soledad Brothers, used weapons allegedly purchased by Davis to arm the defendant and two prisoners in the courtroom and hold Judge Harold Haley and four other people as hostages. Jonathan wanted to trade the hostages for the release of the Soledad prisoners, who had been accused of killing a prison guard (the death of whom had occurred three days after another guard had shot and killed three Black prisoners during a riot). However, during the escape from the courtroom, a firefight broke out and the judge was killed, as well as Jonathan and two of the men who had joined him.

Davis was arrested on October 13, and her subsequent sixteen-month incarceration while awaiting trial was a formative period for developing her prison abolition work. Prior to the courthouse shooting, Davis had gained notoriety for being fired by the philosophy department at the University of California, Los Angeles for her political activism and affiliation with the Communist Party. She sued UCLA and got her position back, but she left in 1970 once her contract expired. Davis disclosed her sexuality as a lesbian in 1997.[24]

August 18, 2004 ACT UP held a naked protest outside the Republican National Convention in New York City. The protest was developed as a peaceful, provocative, and visual message against the Bush administration's policies regarding debt repayment in poor nations experiencing significant rates of HIV/AIDS. The administration had stated they would contribute to the Global Fund to Fight AIDS; however, there had been a significant lack of movement. A dozen members blocked traffic on Eighth Avenue in New York City. The first arrests were outside Madison Square Garden.

Robert Dabney kept his clothing on to speak with reporters and stated, "This protest is to tell the naked truth to President George W. Bush and the Republican Party. Our protesters are demanding number one that the president support full debt cancellation for the poorest nations in the world." Protesters chanted, "Drop the debt. Stop AIDS." They painted their bodies with various slogans such as "STOP AIDS." Two members of ACT UP are reported to have climbed on top of a rig on West 33rd Street opposite Madison Square Garden, holding a sign reading "W: Drop the Debt. Stop AIDS."

Eustacia Smith, an organizer, articulated the rationale behind their argument: "Countries are spending all the money they have on paying off debt … when they could be spending that money on prevention of HIV." The protesters were able to bring traffic to a halt for fifteen minutes. ACT UP staged the protest four days before the Republican Party's convention so that their message was not overshadowed by other protests.[25]

19 **August 19, 1999** Monica Helms designed the first transgender flag as a symbol of trans diversity on this day. The pink and blue stripes represent colors that have traditionally been associated with femininity and masculinity, and the white stripe represents people who are intersex, transitioning, or do not have a defined gender. Helms is a trans activist who grew up in Arizona and served in the US Navy. She debuted the flag at a Pride parade in Phoenix.[26]

20 **August 20, 1943** Sir Lady Java, an American transgender rights activist, dancer, comedian, and actress, was born in New Orleans, Louisiana. She transitioned at a young age with the support and love of her mother. After graduating high school, Java became a part of Los Angeles's Black performance art scene. She performed stand-up comedy and also was a go-go dancer at nightclubs across the city.

Even as Java was featured in magazines such as *Jet, Ebony*, and *Sepia*, she became increasingly targeted by the LAPD. The local municipal code's Rule 9 dictated that no bar owner could employ someone who performed as the opposite sex to the one they were assigned at birth.

In October 1967, Java was performing at the Redd Foxx, a Black-owned nightclub. The police attempted to close the club and took photographs of Java in her go-go dancing outfits.

John Elroy Sanford, the club's owner, applied for a permit that would allow her to perform, but the LAPD denied the request. Java organized a protest for her right to work and was supported by the American Civil Liberties Union. However, California's state supreme court refused to hear the case, stating that only club owners could sue. Even so, Java's case highlighted the discrimination transgender people, specifically Black and Brown transgender women, experienced.

In June 2016, she was a guest of honor at the annual Trans Pride LA festival. In 2022, she was the community grand marshal at the Los Angeles Pride Parade.[27]

21 **August 21, 1970** *The Black Panther* newspaper published a letter from cofounder Huey P. Newton. The letter, coming one year after the Stonewall Rebellion and the subsequent founding of the Gay Liberation Front (GLF), which actively supported the Black Panthers, criticized homophobia and sexism within the Black Panthers. Newton called for solidarity with women and gay liberation movements, stating that all radical events should include "full participation of the gay liberation movement and the women's liberation movement." He pointedly spoke to the oppression of gay people, writing, "Homosexuals ... might be the most oppressed people in ... society," and called on the left to decry homophobic language and sentiments:

> We should be careful about using those terms that might turn our friends off. The terms "f****t" and "punk" should be deleted from our vocabulary, and especially we should not attach names normally designed for homosexuals to men who are enemies of the people, such as [President Richard] Nixon or [Attorney General John] Mitchell. Homosexuals are not enemies of the people.

Newton delved into internal biases, noting that members of the Black Panther Party ought to be open to speak about insecurities surrounding homosexuality and to grapple with biases. He consistently returned to embracing gay liberation and accepting that "a person should have the freedom to use his body in whatever way he wants." Newton's speech brought the Black Panther Party and the GLF together as allies, all the while welcoming complex discussions.[28]

August 21, 2006 A Camp Trans press release was published to announce the Michigan Womyn's Music Festival ending their policy of discriminating against transgender women. The festival's policy against trans women was first enforced in 1991, when security escorted Nancy Burkholder from the festival's grounds. The Michigan Womyn's Music Festival was the largest women-only festival of its kind, and the last remaining women's event to openly discriminate against trans women. The festival was widely criticized for this policy. In 2004, a group of attendees dropped a twenty-five-foot banner opposing the policy during the headlining act.

Camp Trans was the name of an annual protest that occurred across the road from the festival. Organizers stated that at least once a year, a trans woman from Camp Trans would attempt to buy a ticket to the Michigan Womyn's Music Festival and be turned away. Organizers from Camp Trans worked with the festival to conduct a workshop discussion on the retired policy, and trans women were included.

Emilia Lombardi, a Camp Trans organizer and trans woman, stated, "We didn't expect to change anyone's minds in the workshop—but in the end we didn't need to. The support we found was overwhelming."[29]

22 **August 22, 1983** Organizers of a Washington march commemorating the twentieth anniversary of Dr. Martin Luther King Jr.'s "I Have a Dream" speech announced that representatives from gay and lesbian rights groups would not be permitted to speak. In response, a group of four gay men, including three Black men, staged a sit-in at the office of the event's national director. The four activists were arrested.[30]

23 **August 23, 1851** A violent riot broke out in Sydney, Australia, when police tried to arrest Michael Knight, a sailor who was wearing women's clothing. A police constable had arrived on the scene to quell the supposed "disorder" and intercepted Michael at a pub. To the cheers of the other patrons, Knight decked the officer and fled.

While the officer called for reinforcements, Knight proceeded to St. Philip's Church and began heckling the parishioners until subdued, arrested, and dragged to a watchhouse by seven police officers.

On hearing of the arrest, sailors from two military ships formed a crowd, who then marched on several watchhouses, attacking police and succeeding in freeing many prisoners, although not Knight, who was later fined.[31]

24 **August 24, 1945** Marsha P. Johnson was born in Elizabeth, New Jersey. In language typical of that used by queer communities at the time, she described herself variously as gay, a transvestite, and a drag queen, and expressed her desire to seek gender affirmation surgery in Sweden, once she had saved up enough money to pay for it. Having difficulty finding employment, Johnson turned to sex work.

Johnson's life changed drastically on June 28, 1969, the night of the Stonewall Uprising. Johnson arrived at around 2:00 a.m., and in an interview she stated, "The place was already on fire, and there was a raid already. The riots had already started." Johnson took a prominent role at the Uprising; according to numerous accounts, she was at the forefront of the crowd's resistance to the police. In the wake of the raid, Johnson, along with Sylvia Rivera (see July 2, 1951), led a series of protests.

Together they formed the Street Transvestite Action Revolutionaries (STAR), an organization dedicated to helping homeless transgender youth. Johnson was vocal about the exclusion of transgender women and people of color from the growing mainstream LGBT+ movement. She turned her attention, along with Rivera, to assisting transgender youth. They began a STAR House, a safe space for the youth to stay. The first STAR House was in the back of an abandoned truck in Greenwich Village. STAR House then shifted locations to a dilapidated building, which the group tried to repair, but they were evicted after eight months.

Throughout the 1970s, Johnson became a more visible and prominent member of the gay rights movement. She frequently performed with drag groups and was included in a series of paintings by Andy Warhol titled *Ladies and Gentlemen, 1975*. In an interview, Johnson said her goal was "to see gay people liberated and free and to have equal rights that other people have in America" and to see "her gay brothers and sisters out of jail and on the streets again." In 1980, Johnson was invited to ride in the lead car in New York City's Pride parade.

On July 6, 1992, Johnson's body was found in the Hudson River. She was forty-six. Initially, her death was ruled a suicide, but many friends suspected foul play. Police reclassified the case as drowning from undetermined cause, but the LGBT+ community was furious that they refused to investigate further and that numerous press outlets did not cover her death. Hundreds of people attended her funeral; the church was so crowded people stood on the street.

In 2019, New York City announced Marsha P. Johnson and Sylvia

Rivera would be the subjects of a monument commissioned by the Public Arts Campaign, titled "She Built NYC." The monument is the first in New York City to honor transgender women. In 2020, New York State named a Brooklyn waterfront park after Johnson.[32]

25 **August 25, 1918** Leonard Bernstein, an American conductor, composer, pianist, author, and humanitarian, was born. Bernstein was also a public activist and protested the Vietnam War, advocated for nuclear disarmament, and raised money for HIV/AIDS research.

Bernstein married actress Felicia Montealegre Cohn in 1951. During their marriage, they hosted an event at their Manhattan apartment to raise awareness and funds for the Black Panther Party, which was criticized heavily by *The New York Times*. Their apartment was picketed by the Jewish Defense League. Alongside this, Bernstein robustly supported artists of color in classical music, holding blind auditions. He participated in the Stars for Freedom Rally, which supported the marchers from Selma to Montgomery in demand of voting rights. The FBI had a decades-long investigation of Bernstein, but he was never asked to testify before the House Un-American Activities Committee.

Throughout his life, Bernstein had affairs with both men and women. In April 1943, he approached fellow composer Aaron Copland, who was gay, about how to live as a queer man while in the public eye. In a private letter, Felicia acknowledged Bernstein's sexual orientation, writing, "You are a homosexual and may never change—you don't admit to the possibility of a double life, but if your peace of mind, your health, your whole nervous system depends on a certain sexual pattern what can you do?"[33]

26 **August 26, 1969** Bill C-150, a Canadian bill decriminalizing homosexual acts, went into effect. Despite this, gay men continued to be targeted by police for "gross indecency" charges. From 1968 to 2004, over 1,300 men across Canada were prosecuted under the "bawdy house" law for visiting gay bars or bathhouses.[34]

27 **August 27, 2008** Dorothy Louise Taliaferro "Del" Martin died, just weeks after she and her partner, Phyllis Lyon, got married in California's first legal gay wedding. Martin and Lyon founded the Daughters of Bilitis with six other lesbians in 1955 and worked together to address the homophobia within the feminist movement.[35]

28 **August 28, 1963** Bayard Rustin, a leader in the movements for civil rights, socialism, and gay rights, helped organize the March on Washington for Jobs and Freedom. Rustin trained off-duty police as marshals, helped bus captains become traffic directors, and scheduled speakers.

Despite Dr. Martin Luther King Jr.'s support of Rustin, NAACP chairman Roy Wilkins did not want Rustin to receive public recognition for his role in organizing the march, due to his sexuality. Because of these concerns, Rustin was relegated to acting as A. Philip Randolph's deputy rather than a co-organizer. Even so, *Life* magazine featured a picture of Rustin and Randolph on its September 6, 1963, cover, identifying them as "the leaders" of the march.[36]

August 28, 1971 Approximately two hundred activists gathered in Ottawa for the first large-scale gay rights demonstration in Canada. It would become known as the "We Demand Rally." The demonstrators had created a thirteen-page document that contained a list of ten demands for gay and lesbian rights and intended to present it to Parliament.

One of the catalysts for organizing was police discrimination against homosexuals and legal attempts to drive out queer people working in the civil service, government, and military. Discrimination against sexuality was not legally prohibited, and there were no avenues for queer people to mobilize.

Toronto Gay Action and the Community Homophile Association of Toronto organized the rally. The groups had collaborated with twelve other organizations from across Canada to draft the demands:

1. Removal and replacement of "gross indecency" and "indecent acts" in the Criminal Code; defining "in private" in the Criminal Code to mean "a condition of privacy."
2. Removal of "gross indecency" and "buggery" as grounds for indictment as a "dangerous sexual offender."
3. A uniform age of consent for all female and male homosexual and heterosexual acts.
4. Amending the Immigration Act so that it does not reference homosexuals or "homosexualism."
5. The right of equal employment and promotion at all government levels for homosexuals.

6. Amending the Divorce Act so that homosexual acts cannot be used as grounds for divorce; allowing equal right of child custody to both parents, regardless of sexual orientation.
7. The right of homosexuals to serve in the Armed Forces without being convicted of misconduct or illegal acts.
8. To know whether the RCMP has a practice of targeting homosexual individuals working in public service in order to let them go, and if so, to end the practice and destroy any records that were collected.
9. Equal legal rights for homosexuals and heterosexuals.
10. All public officials and law enforcement agents to do everything they can to address negative attitudes and discrimination against homosexuals.

As a direct result of the rally, the Immigration Act was amended and removed the ban on gay men from traveling and immigrating to Canada.[37]

29 **August 29, 1867** Karl Heinrich Ulrichs became the first self-proclaimed homosexual to speak out publicly for gay rights when he pleaded at the Congress of German Jurists in Munich for a resolution urging the repeal of antihomosexual laws.[38]

August 29, 1970 In 1970, after the first Christopher Street Day, which would go on to become the modern-day Pride parade, gay residents of New York City's Greenwich Village noticed increased police harassment, especially toward the end of August. The Gay Liberation Front's newsletter, *Come Out!*, reported that one man was looking at a display window when a police officer came up to him, asking, "Were you ever arrested?" The young man said, "No." To which the police officer replied, "There's always a first time," and arrested him. Queer women also began to face increasing harassment, which was new to police harassment of queer people.

Local activists became frustrated with the discrimination and lack of action. On this day in 1970, the Gay Liberation Front (GLF), Gay Activists Alliance (GAA), Radical Lesbians, and other women's groups organized a demonstration. Roughly 250 people showed up at Eighth Avenue and West 42nd Street near Times Square. They proceeded to march down Seventh Avenue to Sheridan Square in Greenwich Village.

The demonstration ended around midnight, but some protesters continued to march around the Women's House of Detention at Greenwich

Avenue and Sixth Avenue. Police arrived to break the group up, and demonstrators ran toward Christopher Street, whereupon they saw a bar called the Haven being raided by police.

As the crowd arrived, police called for reinforcements. A police bus came and protesters threw bottles at it. For two hours, crowds participated in what has been known as the "Forgotten Riot," setting trash cans on fire and overturning a car. Eight people were injured and fifteen were arrested. The following day, the GLF and GAA held a news conference at the Episcopal Church of the Holy Apostles, accusing the police of harassment. They also decried police inaction against gay bashings and antigay harassment.[39]

August 29, 1979 During Gay Liberation Week, the Swedish Federation for Lesbian, Gay, Bisexual, and Transgender Rights (RFSL) occupied the Stockholm headquarters of the National Board of Health and Welfare, demanding that it no longer classify homosexuality as a mental illness.

Around forty protesters entered the building, in small groups of twos and threes to avoid suspicion. They gathered on the main stairwell, unfolding banners and chanting. Police were called, but before they arrived, the protesters met with Barbro Westerholm, the new director general of Social Security. Westerholm let the protesters know she agreed with them and advocated for the declassification of homosexuality. Her efforts were met with resistance by the National Board of Health and Welfare, but it eventually agreed to change the diagnosis registry and remove homosexuality from the list of illnesses. The change took effect on October 19, 1979.[40]

30 **August 30, 1958** Daniel Sotomayor, the first openly gay political cartoonist in the US, was born in Chicago.

In 1988, at thirty years old, he was diagnosed with AIDS. He joined the organization Chicagoans for AIDS Rights, which led to his involvement in ACT UP. Sotomayor was the cofounder of the Chicago branch of ACT UP. During his time at ACT UP, he organized "zaps," highly visible protest actions in which he would call out public officials as well as advocate for safer sex education. Sotomayor quit ACT UP in 1990 due to the group's movement away from AIDS activism.

Throughout his time as an organizer, Sotomayor continued to draw. He became a cartoonist for *Windy City Times* and was given featured spots in gay news sources in New York and California. His work routinely critiqued health departments, the law, insurance companies, and in-fighting within the LGBT+ community. In 1989, he drew a cartoon of President George H.W. Bush reading a newspaper with the headline "100,000 Diagnosed with AIDS in the US." Barbara Bush, the First Lady, asks if there is anything important in the paper, to which Bush responds, "Nope." This cartoon propelled Sotomayor into the limelight as a queer political cartoonist.

Sotomayor died in 1992 due to AIDS-related complications. He was posthumously recognized in the AIDS Memorial Quilt and in the Smithsonian's exhibition *Presente! A Latino History of the United States*, as well as being inducted into the Chicago Hall of Fame.[41]

31 **August 31, 1979** During Labor Day weekend, early gay rights advocates Harry Hay and Don Kilhefner organized the Spiritual Conference for Radical Fairies. Over two hundred participants gathered at the Sri Ram Ashram near Benson, Arizona, to explore how to merge spirituality with gay liberation.

The conference emerged from discussions of Edward Carpenter, Arthur Evans, Jungian psychology, and Hay's studies of Indigenous spirituality. Hay and Kilhefner integrated these discussions into workshops on topics ranging from gay consciousness and gay mythos to the evolving nature of gay subculture. "We didn't want people to be spectators," Kilhefner said. "We wanted people to explore, bring their gifts and share their gifts with the other gay men there."

The Radical Faeries (the spelling change would come within a year), grounded in the counterculture antiestablishment and community-focused beliefs of the 1960s, challenged the commercialization of the gay rights movement.[42]

SEPTEMBER

1 **September 1, 1949** Leslie Feinberg, author of *Stone Butch Blues* and *Transgender Warriors*, was born. Feinberg was the first theorist to develop a Marxist conception of "transgender liberation."

Ze described hirself as an "anti-racist white, working class, secular Jewish, transgender, lesbian, female, revolutionary communist." Feinberg frequented gay bars in Buffalo, New York, and worked in low-wage temporary jobs after dropping out of high school. These jobs included washing dishes, cleaning cargo ships, acting as an American Sign Language interpreter, inputting medical data, and working at a PVC pipe factory.

In hir early twenties, Feinberg met Workers World Party members at a demonstration for Palestinian land rights and self-determination. Ze quickly joined the group and founded the Buffalo branch. Eventually, Feinberg moved to New York City, where ze continued to participate in numerous mass mobilizations. Ze was a key organizer in the December 1974 March Against Racism in Boston, which was a campaign against white supremacist attacks on Black people in the city. Ze led a group of ten lesbian-identified people on an all-night "paste up" to cover every visible racist epithet in South Boston.

Feinberg's activism extended into reproductive rights as well. Throughout the 1990s, ze worked with Buffalo United for Choice and the Rainbow Peacekeepers, which organized community self-defense training for local queer bars and the women's clinic. Ze was also a journalist for the *Workers World* newspaper and eventually became its managing editor.

Feinberg's work on gender was instrumental to the development of queer and gender studies. In *Transgender Warriors*, ze defines *transgender* as a broad term including all people who cross cultural gender boundaries, such as butch dykes, drag queens, and women who passed as men to find work or survive. Hir work frequently appeared in *Workers World*, examining the intersections of queerness and socialism.

In June 2019, Feinberg was inducted on the National LGBTQ Wall of Honor within the Stonewall National Monument.[1]

September 1, 1959 A chain of events began in Paraguay that would result in the persecution of gay men and would become known as the "Case of the 108." At 2:00 a.m., police found the body of dancer and radio announcer Bernardo Aranda, who had been killed in a fire. The right-wing military authorities, which were backed by the US, decided that since gay men visited Aranda's house, one of them must be responsible. So police began rounding up and torturing gay men, arresting 108 over the course of the investigation. To this day, the number 108 is used as a pejorative term referring to LGBT+ people, although some in the community have reclaimed the term and proudly use it to self-identify.[2]

September 1, 1991 Fifteen hundred ACT UP demonstrators marched to President George H.W. Bush's seaside home in Kennebunkport, Maine, to demand more action addressing the AIDS epidemic. President Bush was preparing to begin formally running for a second presidential term.

The marchers held a "die-in" on Ocean Avenue. There were no reported arrests.

Demonstrators shouted, "Shame!" and, "How many more have to die?" Jon Greenberg, a participant of the protest, accused Bush of "murderous, deliberative negligence.... We with this disease, we are all innocent. The real guilt lies with [Bush] ... who sat by and watched while innocent people die needlessly."[3]

2 **September 2, 1967** Dick Michaels, Bill Rand, and Sam Winston published the first issue of *The Los Angeles Advocate*, the forerunner of *The Advocate*. It emerged from a local newsletter that was inspired by a police raid on the Black Cat Tavern, a noted Los Angeles gay bar, and the following demonstrations against police brutality. The first issue of *The Los Angeles Advocate* was sold primarily in gay bars. After it transformed into *The Advocate* in 1969, it reached national distribution. It is now the largest LGBT+ publication.[4]

3 **September 3, 1791** Postrevolutionary France completed its new penal code, becoming the first Western European country to decriminalize homosexuality, as it no longer made any mention of prohibitions against sodomy in private.[5]

September 3, 2016 Indigenous women and LGBT+ people, ranging from grassroots activists to tribal government leaders, led protests over the Dakota Access Pipeline, crossing a perimeter fence to stop bulldozers that had just demolished a contested area containing sacred sites and Native artifacts.

The protest movement began with a few individuals at the encampment on the Standing Rock Sioux reservation in North Dakota and had grown to thousands in the summer of 2016. It was the largest Indigenous protest of the twenty-first century. Although the pipeline was built, it brought together over eighty-seven tribes, and the call to stop construction of the pipeline reached the United Nations.

In October, the Two Spirit Nation was formally honored in a traditional entry into the main campgrounds at Sacred Stone Camp, the site of the resistance.[6]

4 **September 4, 2007** American lesbian activist Cheryl Ann Spector died. Spector sat on the board of directors for the Rainbow History Project and was also involved with the Human Rights Campaign, Servicemembers Legal Defense Network, Queer Nation, and the Mautner Project. She was a key member of the LGBT+ community in Washington, DC.[7]

5 **September 5, 1987** The Homomonument, the first monument in the world to commemorate the gays and lesbians who were killed by the Nazis, was opened in Amsterdam. The monument uses the pink triangle symbol sewn onto the uniforms of gay men in concentration camps as the basis for its design.

The monument consists of three large pink triangles that together compose a larger triangle. The triangles are strategically positioned: one points to the headquarters of COC Nederland, the oldest continuously operating gay rights organization in the world, one points to the memorial in Dam Square, and the third points to Anne Frank's house and includes an inscription from a poem by a gay Jewish poet Jacob Israel de Haan: "*Naar Vriendschap Zulk een Mateloos Verlangen*" ("Such an endless desire for friendship").

On May 4, during the Netherlands' annual Remembrance Day ceremony, wreaths are laid on the monument to commemorate gay and lesbian victims of persecution. A day later, on Liberation Day, the Homomonument becomes the site of a street party.[8]

September 5, 2018 On this day, the Yellow Finch tree sit was established in the path of the Mountain Valley Pipeline near Elliston, Virginia. The tree sit lasted for 932 days (until 2021), making it one of the longest aerial blockades in US history. A twenty-seven-year-old activist named Gator fondly called the camp's occupants "a bunch of badass queer anarchists that held it down for a long period of time."[9]

6 **September 6, 1850** Laura Jane Addams, who established the Hull House, one of first settlement houses in the US, was born. Established in urban settings during the late 19th and early 20th centuries, settlement houses served as community centers that provided social services, educational resources, and support for poor and immigrant neighbors.

Addams's work addressed critical issues such as child labor, public health reform, garbage collection, labor laws, and race relations and made Addams one of the legendary social reformers of Chicago. In 1931, Addams became the first American woman to receive the Nobel Peace Prize, acknowledging her relentless activism against war and violence. Biographer Louise Knight has noted the "long silence about the historical significance of Addams's intimate love life," and historian Lillian Faderman observes that Addams "spent her adult years, almost until her death, with other women, in long-term relationships that we would describe as lesbian today."

Addams shared enduring relationships with at least two women, including Mary Rozet Smith, with whom she had a forty-year partnership. Traveling together, sharing living spaces, and jointly owning property, Addams and Smith's intimacy was evident to their close associates. Historian John D'Emilio has said, "No matter how you cut it, these are all marks that we use to understand women and men as lesbian or gay."[10]

September 6, 1947 Sylvester James Jr. (known simply as "Sylvester") was born. Sylvester was an American singer-songwriter primarily active in disco, rhythm and blues, and soul who was known for his flamboyant and androgynous appearance. In San Francisco, he found friendship among a group of Black cross-dressers and transgender women who called themselves the Disquotays. Sylvester was part of the avant-garde drag troupe the Cockettes and produced solo segments for their shows that were heavily influenced by Billie Holiday and Josephine Baker.

Sylvester's biographer Joshua Gamson has said that for Sylvester, "Gender was an everyday choice." Sylvester was an openly gay man throughout his career and came to be seen as a spokesperson for the gay community. Sylvester once told a journalist, "I realize that gay people have put me on a pedestal and I love it. After all, of all the oppressed minorities, they just have to be the most oppressed. They have all the hassles of finding something or someone to identify with—and they chose me. I like being around gay people and they've proven to be some of my closest friends and most loyal audiences."[11]

September 6, 2019 Alejandra Barrera, a transgender asylum seeker who had fled violence in El Salvador and faced deportation after twenty months in the Cibola County Correctional Center, a for-profit Immigration and Customs Enforcement (ICE) detention center in New Mexico, was freed.

Her release from the ICE detention center was made possible because of an intense and sustained campaign by her attorney Rebekah Wolf from Equal Justice Works, Bamby Salcedo's TransLatin@ Coalition, Amnesty International, and ordinary citizens. Salcedo said:

> It was because of all of your calls, because of all of you signing petitions, showing up to the rallies, showing up the press conferences, her lawyers—everyone—all of you who wrote letters to Alejandra, everyone who participated in la campaigna de #FreeAlejandra—should be very proud because this is one more victory and we should be able to celebrate.[12]

7 **September 7, 1976** Ian Davies, a gay social worker in London, won his original job back after being demoted, following a strike by his colleagues.

Davies was employed by Tower Hamlets Council until he was convicted of a "gross indecency" charge for cottaging (a British slang term used to describe men meeting for anonymous sex in public restrooms) and fined twenty-five pounds. A workplace disciplinary panel initially dismissed him, but following the intervention of his union, Nalgo, he was instead redeployed into a lower-ranked job in a different department.

Davies and Nalgo took the council to an industrial tribunal, which determined that he was unfairly dismissed and requested his reinstatement. However, on August 9, the council decided it would not reinstate him. According to the union, council officials saw homosexuality as being comparable with pedophilia.

On hearing the news, twenty-five of Davies's colleagues immediately walked out on a wildcat strike, a move that was later approved by the local Nalgo branch. Three of the seven social work teams also began a rolling campaign of one-day protest strikes. The national union agreed to back the action, but only on the basis of the council not respecting the request of the tribunal. The local union rep, Derek Ralph, wrote in *Socialist Worker* that the "equally important issue of discrimination against homosexuals has been ignored."

Eventually, the entire Nalgo branch of around 1,300 members announced that they had determined to stage a one-day all-out strike on September 10, after which more key departments would begin rotating sectional strikes.

A few days prior to this action taking place, the council relented and agreed to reinstate Davies to his original job.[13]

September 7, 2011 The US Department of Health and Human Services issued a memorandum establishing an enforcement mechanism for a policy introduced by the Obama administration the previous year. This policy mandated that hospitals receiving Medicare and Medicaid funding must permit patients to designate their preferred visitors during inpatient stays, including same-sex partners.[14]

8 **September 8, 1954** Following a police raid on San Francisco lesbian bars 12 Adler and Tommy's Place, the two owners, Grace Miller and Joyce Van de Veer, were arrested and charged with contributing to the delinquency of minors. Miller was sentenced to six months in jail. Both establishments permanently closed their doors.[15]

9 **September 9, 1992** The Lesbian Avengers, a direct-action group in New York City, conducted their first action, targeting right-wing attempts to suppress a multicultural "Children of the Rainbow" curriculum for elementary schoolchildren.

The group was founded by Ana Maria Simo, Anne Maguire, Anne-Christine D'Adesky, Marie Honan, Maxine Wolfe, and Sarah Schulman. The Avengers believed that this right-wing tactic to suppress multicultural curriculum was not only homophobic but also had a racist agenda.

On this day in 1992, the Avengers paraded through Queens School District 24, where the opposition to the "Rainbow Curriculum" was strongest, leading an all-lesbian marching band to a local elementary school. The Avengers wore T-shirts reading "I Was a Lesbian Child" and gave out lavender balloons to children and their parents. The Avengers demonstrated without permits, refusing to ask the state for permission to exist.[16]

10 **September 10, 1996** The US Senate passed the Defense of Marriage Act (DOMA) with a vote of 85–14. This legislation defined marriage at the federal level as a union between one man and one woman and permitted states to refuse recognition of same-sex marriages performed in other jurisdictions.

The enactment of DOMA represented a significant setback for gay rights activists in the US, as it barred federal recognition of same-sex marriages and allowed states to deny recognition of such marriages performed elsewhere. This legislative move was largely a reaction to a 1993 Hawaii Supreme Court decision that suggested the state's prohibition of same-sex marriage might be unconstitutional, raising concerns that other states would be compelled to recognize same-sex marriages from Hawaii.[17]

11 **September 11, 1948** Jewelle Lydia Gomez, an American author, poet, critic, and playwright, was born. For twenty-two years, she resided in New York City, where she was involved in public television, theater, and philanthropy before moving to the West Coast. Gomez's writing spans fiction, poetry, essays, and cultural criticism, in which she focused on women's experiences, particularly those of LGBT+ women of color. She is best known for the double Lambda Literary Award–winning *The Gilda Stories*, a Black lesbian vampire novel. Gomez has been featured in several documentaries exploring LGBT+ rights and culture.[18]

12 **September 12, 1969** The Gay Liberation Front (GLF) protested against *The Village Voice* newspaper in New York City for its homophobic advertising policy.

In the August 7 issue of the *Voice*, members of the GLF placed an ad in the classified section requesting material for its own newspaper, *Come Out!* The ad was headed by the phrase "Gay Power to Gay People." In response, the *Voice*, which considered the word *gay* to be obscene, deleted the phrase, censoring the ad without asking or telling the GLF.

On September 12, GLF members organized a chanting picket line outside the *Voice* and passed out thousands of leaflets. During the peak of the demonstration, a member of GLF submitted a classified ad saying, "The Gay Liberation Front sends love to all Gay men and women in the homosexual community."

Because of the protest, the *Voice* agreed to no longer alter ads after payment, such as removing the words *gay* or *homosexual* in the classified ads section.[19]

13 **September 13, 1879** Annie Kenney, cotton mill worker and pioneering direct-action suffragette, was born in Springhead, a suburban area of Manchester, England. She came to prominence in 1905 when she and her friend Christabel Pankhurst, who some historians have speculated was possibly her lover, were imprisoned for assault and obstruction after heckling the foreign secretary and spitting on a police officer at a Liberal rally.[20]

14 **September 14, 1961** At 3:15 a.m., police barged in and raided the Tay-Bush Inn, herding the over one hundred patrons onto the sidewalk and arresting them as "visitors to a disorderly house." Robert Johnson, the twenty-seven-year-old bar owner, was booked on four counts, including "lewd and indecent acts" and "keeping a disorderly house." Luckily, charges against all but two of those arrested were later dropped.

The Tay-Bush Inn raid is credited as having helped to create a political consciousness in San Francisco's gay community. Additionally, LGBT+ groups such as the Mattachine Society used the incident to advocate for gay civil rights.[21]

September 14, 2000 Six male Toronto police officers raided Club Toronto during an all-female queer and transgender event known as the "Pussy Palace." That night, there were around 350 women in attendance, many of whom were nude or partially clothed. No charges were made that night, but weeks later two volunteers were charged with Liquor License Act violations. However, those charges were dismissed in 2002, as the Ontario Court of Justice held that the raid had been carried out in an unreasonable manner.

Protests and pickets took place outside of the Toronto Police Service's 52 Division after the raid, and the Women's Bathhouse Committee filed a complaint to the Ontario Human Rights Commission. A 2005 class-action lawsuit on behalf of the patrons resulted in a $350,000 settlement and a formal apology in writing by the police division.[22]

15 **September 15, 1969** *Gay Power*, New York City's first homosexual newspaper, published its first issue. (Although *The Advocate* began publishing two years earlier, it was not readily available on the East Coast.) *Gay Power* covered the culture and politics of the New York gay scene and included columns from all the active gay activist groups, including the Mattachine Society and the Gay Liberation Front.[23]

September 15, 1988 ACT UP protested Nicholas Nixon's photography exhibit, *Pictures of People*, at New York's Museum of Modern Art. Nixon, who was neither gay nor afflicted by AIDS, exhibited a series of portraits of Tom Moran that documented his physical deterioration from AIDS-related illness from August 1987 until a few days before his death in February 1988.

Nixon's exhibit was criticized by art critics. Art historian Douglas Crimp found fault with the photographs' lack of social context and their perpetuation of stereotypes about people with AIDS, and Michael Kimmelman, a *New York Times* critic, wrote, "The artist makes people with AIDS look like freaks, like sickly, helpless 'victims,' in the most fatalistic sense of the word."

ACT UP activists distributed fliers that called for "no more pictures without context," reminding exhibition-goers that Moran was a human being "whose health has deteriorated not simply due to a virus, but due to government inaction and institutionalized neglect in the forms of heterosexism, racism, and sexism." Activists also sat in the gallery with photographs of people captioned with the phrase "Living with"—not dying of—"AIDS" and fliers reading "Stop looking at us, start listening to us."[24]

16 **September 16, 1919** Marusya Nikiforova, Ukrainian revolutionary fighter, was put on trial by counterrevolutionary authorities and later executed.

She had become an anarchist communist while a young factory worker, then began undertaking robberies and attacks on tsarist authorities until she was jailed in Moscow. Nikiforova escaped, traveled around Europe, and returned to Ukraine at the height of the Russian Revolution, where she became a fierce and effective military leader in the Revolutionary Insurrectionary Army of Ukraine, fighting against White forces and being jailed by the Bolsheviks, before eventually being shot alongside her husband. Sources conflict, but some sources report that Nikiforova was intersex, and others that she was lesbian or bisexual.[25]

September 16, 2017 Scout Schultz, a twenty-one-year-old student and president of Pride Alliance on campus at Atlanta's Georgia Institute of Technology, was shot and killed by Georgia Tech police. Schultz was bisexual, nonbinary, and intersex and used singular they/them pronouns.

Vigils and protests erupted after their death. On September 18, fifty protesters marched through campus while carrying a banner that read "Protect LGBTQ" and chanting, "Justice now." Demonstrators set a police car ablaze in the protest. On September 22, students and staff organized a teach-in and protest.

In 2018, in response to Schultz's death, queer student leaders including Collin Spencer established the Mental Health Joint Allocations Committee, a million-dollar fund to improve mental health at Georgia Tech. The fund has been directed toward various projects, including the development of a new LGBT+ center, the provision of telemental health services, advancements in therapeutic biotechnologies, and research into health systems.[26]

17 **September 17, 2019** Dozens of people protested outside the Congress of the Republic of Guatemala to reject legislation that would increase the penalties for abortion and prohibit gay marriage. Protesters condemned the measure as being motivated by "persecution and violence."

"We need abortion to be free, legal and safe," a transgender protester said. "We need a trans law because we exist."[27]

18 **September 18, 1977** Leading members of the Mississippi Gay Alliance (MGA) and the NAACP partnered to protest police brutality, harassment, and entrapment of LGBT+ and low-income people in Jackson, Mississippi.

MGA organized "pink triangle patrols" to monitor the park where the protest was held. "All the monitors wear a pink triangle, the symbol homosexuals were forced to wear by the gestapo in Nazi Germany. We wear the pink triangle in solidarity with resistance to gay oppression," an MGA organizer told *Workers World*.

The American Civil Liberties Union and MGA filed complaints with the police department after police began threatening the monitors with arrest for "interfering with officers in the line of duty and disturbing the peace."[28]

September 18, 1980 The Toronto Board of Education voted to change its antidiscrimination policy, now prohibiting discrimination based on sexual orientation. However, it also added a clause explicitly prohibiting the "proselytizing of homosexuality in schools."[29]

19 **September 19, 1964** Randy Wicker of the Homosexual League of New York (HLNY) and the New York City League for Sexual Freedom led one of the first public demonstrations for gay rights in the United States in front of the US Army Building in Lower Manhattan. The demonstrators expressed their discontent with the military's handling of LGBT+ individuals, which included issues such as dismissal, dishonorable discharges, and the breach of privacy by forwarding records of gay men to their current and prospective employers.[30]

20 **September 20, 2011** The enforcement of the "Don't Ask, Don't Tell" policy, which had been repealed in December 2010, ended. This policy, which was established by the Clinton administration on February 28, 1994, under Department of Defense Directive 1304.26, governed military service by individuals who identified as gay, bisexual, or lesbian. Under this policy, military personnel were prohibited from discriminating against or harassing closeted gay or bisexual service members or applicants, yet the policy also simultaneously prohibited openly gay, lesbian, or bisexual individuals from serving in the military. Repealing a policy that targets queer people is a key historical moment, but it raised an important question for queer radicals: Is the military-industrial complex really something we want to be a part of?[31]

21 **September 21, 1955** Four lesbian couples, including Phyllis Lyon and Del Martin, held the founding meeting of the Daughters of Bilitis, the first lesbian civil and political rights organization in the US. A Filipina woman, Rosalie "Rose" Bamberger, hosted the meeting in the San Francisco house she shared with her partner, Rosemary Sliepen. The organization advertised itself as "A Woman's Organization for the Purpose of Promoting the Integration of the Homosexual into Society."[32]

22 **September 22, 1962** Italian director Pier Paolo Pasolini punched a young fascist who tried to confront him outside the premiere for his film *Mamma Roma*. Pasolini's radical politics and openness about his homosexuality made him a frequent target of the right. Meanwhile, right-wing newspapers reporting on the scuffle wrote misleading headlines about what took place, about which Pasolini later wrote, "The newspapers that reported the episode switched it around [illustrating it with misleading photographs] so that it looked like I was the one beaten up."[33]

23 **September 23, 1984** The inaugural Folsom Street Fair, called "Megahood," was held in San Francisco, establishing itself as the world's premier leather event and a platform for showcasing BDSM products and culture.[34]

24 **September 24, 1982** The Centers for Disease Control and Prevention officially used the term *AIDS* for the first time. Before this, the US government had largely ignored the disease and its effects on the LGBT+ community.[35]

25 **September 25, 1952** Queer writer, teacher, and cultural critic bell hooks was born on September 25, 1952, in Hopkinsville, Kentucky. The trailblazing author of over thirty books described being queer as "not who you're having sex with, but about being at odds with everything around it."[36]

September 25, 1970 LGBT+ activists in the Gay Liberation Front (GLF) launched a sit-in at Weinstein Hall, part of New York University (NYU). The action came after the university suddenly banned queer dances regularly put on by the GLF, which had up to four hundred attendees; the group was seeking alternative venues to gay bars run by the Mafia. Trans activist Sylvia Rivera, who took part in the occupation, explained, "It happened when there had been several gay dances there and all of a sudden the plug was pulled because the rich families were offended that queers and d*kes were having dances and their impressionable children were going to be harmed."

The occupiers demanded the reinstatement of the contractually agreed dances, as well as an end to homophobic teaching and free tuition for gay people and other oppressed minorities. Rather than agree to the demands, NYU had security guards lock the doors of the hall, then let in dozens of police officers with helmets and clubs to evict the protesters. Rivera and her friend, Marsha P. Johnson, who took part in the occupation, subsequently founded Street Transvestite Action Revolutionaries (STAR) to provide housing and support for homeless gay and gender-nonconforming youth. Rivera recounted, "STAR House was born out of the Weinstein Hall demonstration because there were so many of us living together."

The following excerpt is from a statement read at the occupation, titled "Gay Power—When Do We Want It? Or Do We?":

> This is the question that is running through our minds. Do you really want Gay Power or are you looking for a few laughs or maybe a little excitement. We are not quite sure what you people really want. If you want Gay Liberation then you are going to have to fight for it.

We don't mean tomorrow or the next day, we are talking about today. We can never possibly win by saying "Wait for a better day" or "We're not ready yet." If you're ready to tell people that you want to be free, then your [sic] ready to fight. And if your [sic] not, then shut up and crawl back into your closets. But let us ask you this, Can you really live in a closet? We can't.[37]

September 25, 2017 Seven people were arrested in Cairo at a concert by the Lebanese band Mashrou' Leila for raising rainbow flags. Mashrou' Leila's singer is openly gay. The band said the Cairo concert was "one of the best shows we've ever played."

While homosexuality was not explicitly criminalized under Egyptian law, authorities routinely arrested people suspected of engaging in consensual homosexual conduct on charges of "debauchery," "immorality," or "blasphemy." Between 2013 and 2016, the advocacy group Solidarity with Egypt LGBTQ+ said that it had recorded 114 criminal investigations involving 274 lesbian, gay, bisexual, and transgender individuals.[38]

26 **September 26, 1945** Gloria Evangelina Anzaldúa, an American scholar of Chicana feminism, cultural theory, and queer theory, was born in Texas. Anzaldúa wrote extensively about her queer identity and the marginalization of queer people, particularly in communities of color. One of Anzaldúa's most influential works is the semiautobiographical *Borderlands/La Frontera: The New Mestiza*, which was published in 1987.

While she identified as a lesbian in most of her writing and had always experienced attraction to women, she also wrote that *lesbian* was "not an adequate term" to describe herself. Anzaldúa said that she "became a lesbian in my head first, the ideology, the politics, the aesthetics" and that the "touching, kissing, hugging, and all came later."[39]

27 **September 27, 1961** Samson Chan was born. In 1980, he came to the US, and in 1984, at the age of twenty-three, he cofounded and assumed the role of the first president of Asians and Friends–Chicago, a group dedicated to providing support for gay Asians and non-Asians. After facing challenges obtaining permanent US residency, Chan returned to Hong Kong in 1991, where he became a pioneering figure in gay rights and AIDS activism.[40]

28 **September 28, 2022** High school students organized a walkout in Morgantown, West Virginia, to protest a board of education policy that prohibited pride flags in classrooms. "[The pride flag] means everything to me," junior Olivia Krech said. "I resonate a lot with it. I've been bullied most of my life. My parents are very kind to me, but their family does not agree with me so I have to pretend to be someone I'm not around them and it hurts. So, when I just see these [pride flags] it just makes me really happy."[41]

29 **September 29, 1991** California Governor Pete Wilson vetoed AB 101, a gay and lesbian employment rights bill, inciting what some called "Stonewall II," a month of marches and angry protests across the state. Wilson had originally promised during an electoral campaign to sign the bill into law, but he ultimately vetoed it in a move that was widely condemned as dishonest by the California LGBT+ community. Many gay organizations, including ACT UP, had worked hard to get AB 101 through the legislature, with some activists even participating in a hunger strike to get it passed.

On September 30, eight to ten thousand people took part in a demonstration on Castro Street in San Francisco to protest Wilson's veto. Protesters marched to the Old State Office Building, smashing windows and lighting a corner of the building on fire. A year after the protest, AB 101 was passed again by the state legislature and signed into law by Wilson.[42]

September 29, 2023 More than a hundred students at Hamilton High School in Chandler, Arizona, staged a walkout to protest two laws that took effect in the state on September 24 that targeted LGBT+ youth. The laws, HB 2495 and HB 2161, banned books in public schools with "sexual conduct" and required that parents have access to all health, counseling, and electronic records of their children, which could out LGBT+ children.

"These bills are killing us," junior Dawn Shim said. "We aren't out here missing our school day and interrupting our education because we want to. We have been forced into it."

The students marched, some with bullhorns, to the Chandler Public Library next door and gathered on the lawn.

"It is embarrassing that we live in both a state and a country where people are at risk simply for being who they are and loving who they want," Blues Patrick, another Hamilton student and the president of the school's

Gender Sexuality Alliance, told the crowd to cheers. "We should not have to live in this pseudo-apocalyptic bullshit that we're dealing with right now."[43]

30 **September 30, 2008** Ecuador granted legal recognition to same-sex civil unions through the enactment of its new constitution, approved by voters in a referendum. However, gay and lesbian couples remained unable to adopt children.[44]

OCTOBER

1 **October 1, 1867** George Cecil Ives was born in Germany. Ives was a poet, writer, and early gay rights activist who in 1897 formed the first British gay rights organization: the secret Order of Chaeronea, which included gay men and lesbians. The manifesto of the Order of Chaeronea read: "We believe in the glory of passion / We believe in the inspiration of emotion / We believe in the holiness of love." While no membership lists survive, it is very likely that Ives's friend, libertarian socialist author and poet Oscar Wilde, was a member.

In 1914, Ives, together with Magnus Hirschfeld, Edward Carpenter, and others, founded the British Society for the Study of Sex Psychology, which became the British Sexological Society in 1931.[1]

October 1, 2020 Players for the San Diego Loyal soccer team walked off the pitch and forfeited the final game of the season in solidarity with a gay player, Collin Martin, who was subjected to homophobic abuse by a member of the opposing team.[2]

2 **October 2, 1999** Governor Gray Davis of California signed AB 26, the state's first domestic partnership legislation, which officially recognized same-sex domestic partnerships. This step still marked out certain kinds of relationships as fundamentally different, and it encouraged queer people to participate in the heteronormative institution of marriage.[3]

3 **October 3, 1993** Katerina Gogou, Greek poet, author, and actor, died by suicide at fifty-three. Under the right-wing military dictatorship in Greece, Gogou could only make a living as an actor portraying sexist stereotypes of women, like "housewife" or "love interest" in comedies that reinforced the ideology of the dictatorship, so Gogou expressed her feminist and revolutionary ideas in her poetry.

After the fall of the dictatorship, she was a key figure in the early Athens anarchist scene and a vigorous proponent of LGBT+ rights.[4]

4 **October 4, 1908** Eleanor Flexner, left-wing American independent scholar who was instrumental in laying the foundation for the emerging field of women's studies, was born. Flexner had been a member of the Communist Party from 1936 to 1956 and witnessed the careers of some of her closest friends and associates ruined by the House Un-American Activities Committee. In the late 1940s, she forged a romantic bond with Helen Terry, who supported Flexner during the McCarthy era.[5]

5 **October 5, 2013** Juan Andrés Benítez, founder of the Catalan Gay and Lesbian Association of Companies, died after being beaten for twelve minutes by Catalan police agents after he was reported arguing with a neighbor in Barcelona. In May 2016, six officers were sentenced to two years in prison and suspension of employment and salary. However, they never served any time.

On October 5, 2014, neighbors occupied a space on the same street on which Juan lived and was beaten to death. Originally destined to become a luxury hotel, the space on Calle Aurora del Raval was occupied in memory of the first anniversary of his death and as a protest against the increased real estate speculation in the neighborhood. Now named Àgora Juan Andrés Benítez, it became a self-managed common space, operated through weekly assemblies that address the social needs, support, and activities of the locals with a strict antimachismo and antiracist culture.[6]

6 **October 6, 1971** Thirty people held a sit-in at the Chepstow pub in London in a protest organized by the Gay Liberation Front, in response to the landlord refusing to serve LGBT+ people. The protesters were forcibly evicted by police, after which some were strip-searched and sexually assaulted by officers. However, in the wake of the action, the landlord relented and agreed to stop the discrimination.[7]

October 6, 1989 Two hundred fifty protesters gathered at the Federal Building Plaza in San Francisco for ACT UP's National Day of Action. At 5:00 p.m., demonstrators started to march toward San Francisco City Hall and were met with "a colossal and incomprehensible show of force" by the San Francisco Police Department.

Despite the police harassment, protesters continued to march and, at twilight, approximately fifty protesters engaged in a "die-in" on Castro Street. The police arrested the protesters and then moved to arrest the five hundred or so people in the crowd cheering on the activists. This became known as the "Castro Sweep." Fifty-three people were arrested, and fourteen were injured. In the aftermath of the sweep, LGBT+ media compared the event to the Stonewall riots.

"If the SFPD's crackdown was designed to silence AIDS activists and to reimpose police power in the public space of the Castro, the effort backfired spectacularly," wrote historian Gerard Koskovich, who was part of the sweep. "The evening of October 7, 1989, brought some 2,000 people to the Castro for a protest against the attack."

Multiple cultural and political actions were organized after the sweep to "reclaim" Castro for the LGBT+ community. San Franciso activists began to organize "permit-free street parties" in reaction to the police violence, which combined protest with festivity. An LGBT+ Halloween street party that month brought tens of thousands of people to the neighborhood, and in late June 1990 a street party organized by ACT UP began the "Pink Saturday" celebrations that became an official event during San Francisco's Pride weekend.[8]

7 **October 7, 2020** Five members of Pussy Riot, the feminist punk collective, were detained in Moscow after affixing rainbow flags to government buildings on the birthday of President Vladimir Putin. The activists hung rainbow flags on the Federal Security Service and the Ministry of Culture buildings, along with three other locations, to protest against homophobia in Russia. The rainbow flags were "our gift to Putin as a symbol of missing love and freedom" for the LGBT+ community in Russia, the collective said.

A manifesto published on Pussy Riot's social media said that while Putin promised that "there will never be any restrictions on the basis of orientation in Russia," in fact "the government was killing gay people in Chechnya, passing transphobic laws (for [the purpose of] 'strengthening the institution of the family'), persecuting fathers of children born from surrogate mothers."

Pussy Riot also made a list of demands to the Putin government, including to investigate the "killings and kidnapping of gay, lesbian, transgender and queer people in Chechnya," to end "the harassment of activists and organizations that help the LGBTQ community," to legalize same-sex partnerships, and to stop taking away children from such families.[9]

8 **October 8, 1826** Emily Blackwell, the second woman to attain a medical degree from what is now Case Western Reserve University, was born in Bristol, England. Blackwell played a key role in founding the New York Infirmary for Indigent Women and Children and in establishing the Women's Central Association of Relief. Alongside her sister Elizabeth Blackwell, Emily also founded the Women's Medical College in New York City.

Blackwell and Elizabeth Cushier, a professor of medicine at the college, were life partners for twenty-eight years. Reflecting on their relationship, Dr. Cushier wrote, "Thus the years happily passed" until 1910, when "a sad blow came in the death of Dr. Blackwell, making an irreparable break in my life."[10]

October 8, 1970 In New York City, two police officers forcefully entered a private club, disrupting an organizing meeting of the Daughters of Bilitis. The aggressive and intrusive behavior of the police officers convinced many members of this previously low-key group of the importance of adopting a more assertive and militant stance.[11]

October 8, 1972 Protesters at the annual convention of the Association for the Advancement of Behavioral Therapy voiced their objections to the ongoing practice of "aversion therapy" as a supposed "treatment" for homosexuality.[12]

9 **October 9, 1970** Members from fourteen cities and sixteen organizations—GLF of Washington, DC; GLF of New York; Chicago Gay Liberation; GLF at the University of Iowa; Gay Women of Iowa City; GLF and Gay Sunshine of San Francisco; GLF at Mankato State in Minnesota; GLF of Philadelphia; ONE of Chicago; GLF of Lawrence, Kansas; GLF of Northern Illinois University; GLF of Milwaukee; GLF of Ann Arbor; and GLF of Washington University in St. Louis—arrived in Minneapolis for the first national gay liberation convention. In all, over 110 men and over 35 women met in sessions over the weekend to discuss the activities of gay liberation as carried on at local levels, to reexamine the questions of sexism and racism, and to prepare for the second meeting of the Revolutionary People's Constitutional Convention.[13]

10 **October 10, 1973** The Toronto City Council approved a resolution prohibiting discrimination based on sexual orientation in civic hiring practices. For the first time in Canadian history, a legislative entity acknowledged gay individuals as a legitimate minority, granting them the right to equal employment opportunities.[14]

October 10, 1987 At a mass wedding behind the National Museum of Natural History and in front of the Internal Revenue Service building in Washington, DC, two thousand same-sex couples exchanged vows. The choice of location enabled the group to protest against the absence of recognition for same-sex domestic partners in the US tax code. Organizers acknowledged that securing a permit to gather was only feasible in this particular area. Nearly five thousand protesters crowded the streets to witness or take part in the mass wedding, officiated by minister Dina Bachelor. This event, known as "The Wedding," was one component of a larger six-day demonstration called the Second National March on Washington for Lesbian and Gay Rights.[15]

11 **October 11, 1941** Elana Dykewomon, an American lesbian activist, author, editor, and teacher, was born. After Dykewomon graduated from the California Institute of Art, she moved to Northampton, Massachusetts, where she was involved with the Valley Women's Center and lesbian separatist projects. There she helped found Megaera Press, a lesbian publishing house, as well as the Women's Film Coop. In the 1980s, she moved to Oakland, California, where she helped organize the San Francisco Dyke March.[16]

October 11, 1987 In Washington, DC, during the Second National March on Washington for Lesbian and Gay Rights, ACT UP called on the Reagan administration to take action against the HIV/AIDS epidemic.

Also on this day, the AIDS Memorial Quilt made its first appearance on the National Mall in Washington. This massive quilt, which commemorated those who had succumbed to AIDS, covered an area larger than a football field and comprised a total of 1,920 panels. Over the weekend, half a million people visited the quilt.[17]

October 11, 1988 ACT UP protested the FDA, decrying that its slow drug-approval procedures had led to the unnecessary loss of thousands of lives due to limited access to life-saving medications. Remarkably, within a year, significant strides were made in expediting this process.[18]

October 11, 1992 At 1:00 p.m., activists affiliated with ACT UP New York staged a political funeral at the White House, now recognized as the "Ashes Action," in which activists scattered the ashes of their loved ones who had succumbed to AIDS on the White House lawn. In unison, they chanted, "150,000 dead! Where was George?" Their act was a powerful rebuke. After dispersing the ashes over the White House fence, these ACT UP activists seized bullhorns to deliver heartfelt eulogies for those whose remains they had dispersed as a form of protest.

The inspiration for this action largely stemmed from David Robinson, an ACT UP member who had contemplated sending his lover's ashes to

President George H.W. Bush, and a passage from artist David Wojnarowicz's 1991 memoir *Close to the Knives*, in which he wrote:

> I imagine what it would be like if friends had a demonstration each time a lover or a friend or a stranger died of AIDS. I imagine what it would be like if, each time a lover, friend or stranger died of this disease, their friends, lovers or neighbors would take the dead body and drive with it in a car a hundred miles an hour to Washington D.C. and blast through the gates of the white house and come to a screeching halt before the entrance and dump their lifeless form on the front steps.... It would be comforting to see those friends, neighbors, lovers and strangers mark time and place and history in such a public way.[19]

12 **October 12, 1911** Betty Millard, a writer, artist, political activist, philanthropist, and feminist, was born. She is notably recognized for her feminist pamphlet *Woman Against Myth* and her affiliation with the Communist Party USA during the 1940s and 1950s.

Despite documenting her struggles with her sexual orientation in private journals, Millard refrained from publicly coming out as gay until her late eighties, confiding only in close family and friends. She frequently noted her infatuations with classmates in her journals and identified her younger self as bisexual.

Faced with societal pressures and the Communist Party's overt homophobia, Millard sought to suppress this aspect of her identity, undergoing conversion therapy from 1942 to 1948. In 1956, she experienced a breakdown related to her sexuality and was hospitalized. Nevertheless, Millard engaged in significant long-term relationships with women both before and after coming out.[20]

October 12–15, 1979 The inaugural National Conference of Third World Lesbians and Gays, hosted by the National Coalition of Black Gays, took place in Washington, DC.

Represented organizations spanned a broad spectrum, including the Combahee River Collective, a Black feminist group hailing from Boston (see April 1977); Salsa Soul Sisters from New York City; the Bay Area Gay Alliance of Latin Americans; and Lambda of Mexico. The 450 participants broke free from centuries-old invisibility and courageously asserted their prominent role in the various struggles encompassing race, gender, sexuality, and the working class. This conference stood out for its remarkable levels of feminism, radicalism, class awareness, internationalism, and invigorating enthusiasm.

"Our struggle consists of the subversion of all concepts and practices which have defamed lesbians and gay men, and subjugated women in general," Claudia Hinojosa and Max Mejia of Lambda said during the opening night's general session. "The struggle against sexism, racism, imperialism, and class oppression is integral to gay liberation. We wish to leave no aspect of daily life unchallenged."[21]

13 **October 13, 1917** Reed Erickson, an American transgender man renowned for his philanthropic endeavors, was born. In 1964, he established the Erickson Educational Foundation (EEF), a nonprofit organization whose mission was to "offer aid and support in areas where human potential faced constraints due to adverse physical, mental, or social circumstances, or where research ventures were too novel, contentious, or imaginative to secure conventional forms of backing."

From 1964 to 1984, Erickson channeled millions of dollars through the EEF to bolster the early growth of LGBT+ movements. Beyond philanthropy, the EEF also served as an informational and counseling resource for transgender people. It established a network of referrals to medical and psychological professionals, published educational materials for transgender individuals and their families, and engaged in outreach efforts targeting medical practitioners, clergy, law enforcement personnel, and academics.[22]

October 13, 1970 Famous Black activist Angela Davis was arrested by the FBI in New York City at the age of twenty-six. She had fled California after a warrant for her arrest was issued in August in connection with an attempted jailbreak (see August 18, 1970). Notorious FBI director J. Edgar Hoover had listed Davis on the FBI's Ten Most Wanted Fugitives list, and with her arrest President Richard Nixon congratulated the FBI on its "capture of the dangerous terrorist." Following a sensational trial in front of an all-white jury, Davis was acquitted of all charges.[23]

October 13, 1987 In the largest civil disobedience protest in the history of the gay and lesbian rights movement, more than six hundred lesbians, gay men, and their supporters were arrested on the steps of the US Supreme Court for protesting the court's decision upholding an antisodomy statute. During the hours-long protest that marked the culmination of a week of gay rights activities in the nation's capital, protesters chanted, "Shame, shame, shame," at the marble edifice. They also scattered pink paper triangles like confetti while crossing police lines in waves.

"This is not the first time gays have done civil disobedience," Pat Norman, a San Francisco lesbian who helped coordinate the march, told *The Washington Post*. "Every day we commit an act of civil disobedience by loving each other."[24]

October 13, 1990 The first South African Pride parade was held near the end of the apartheid era in Johannesburg. It is considered the first Pride event on the continent. Organized by the Gay and Lesbian Organization of the Witwatersrand (GLOW), eight hundred people attended, and they were addressed by multiple speakers. One such speaker was gay anti-apartheid activist Simon Tseko Nkoli (see November 26, 1957), who said in his speech, "I'm fighting for the abolition of apartheid. And I fight for the right of freedom of sexual orientation. These are inextricably linked with each other. I cannot be free as a Black man if I am not free as a gay man."[25]

14 **October 14, 1979** Between 75,000 and 125,000 people participated in the first March on Washington for Lesbian and Gay Rights.

In the introduction to the march's official souvenir program, Alan Young wrote:

> Today in the capital of America, we are all here, the almost liberated and the slightly repressed; the butch, the femme and everything in-between; the androgynous; the monogamous and the promiscuous; the masturbators and the fellators and the tribadists; men in dresses and women in neckties; those who bite and those who cuddle; celebates [sic] and pederasts; diesel dykes and nelly queens; amazons and size queens, Yellow, Black, Brown, White, and Red; the shorthaired and the long, the fat and the thin; the nude and the prude; the beauties and the beasts; the studs and the duds; the communes, the couples, and the singles; pubescents and the octogenarians. Yes, we are all here! We are everywhere! Welcome to the March on Washington for Lesbian and Gay Rights![26]

October 14, 1977 Minneapolis gay rights activist Thom Higgins (see June 17, 1950) threw a pie into the face of Anita Bryant during a news conference in Des Moines, Iowa, in which she was answering questions about her plan to open a network of Anita Bryant Centers where "homosexuals could go for rehabilitation." After being pied, Bryant burst into tears and began praying.

Bryant, who was already well known as a singer, led Save Our Children, a homophobic campaigning group that successfully overturned legal protections for LGBT+ people in Dade County, Florida. Bryant had declared about homosexuality, "I will lead such a crusade to stop it as this country has not seen before."

Bryant was also brand ambassador for Florida orange juice, which then became subjected to a mass boycott campaign. Gay bars replaced screwdrivers (vodka and orange juice cocktails) with "Anita Bryants"—made with vodka and apple juice—with the profits donated to the campaign.[27]

15 **October 15, 1926** Michel Foucault, a French philosopher and social theorist, was born. Foucault's work during the latter half of the twentieth century transformed the way society perceived sexuality and was instrumental in the emergence of queer theory. Building on his ideas, queer theory expanded its focus to examine the intersections of sexuality with other identity categories, such as gender, race, and class.

Foucault died in Paris in 1984 from complications of HIV/AIDS, and he became the first public figure in France to die from the disease. His partner, Daniel Defert, founded the AIDES charity in his memory.[28]

October 15, 1952 In Los Angeles, W. Dorr Legg and a group of six people all affiliated with the Mattachine Society convened to explore the possibility of establishing an organization dedicated to advancing educational and research endeavors that would benefit the gay and lesbian community. This meeting would ultimately give rise to the formation of ONE, Inc., one of the first gay rights organizations in the US.[29]

October 15, 1973 The first LGBT+ organization that was truly national in scope, the National Gay Task Force, was founded. (The words "and Lesbian" would be added later, and today the organization is known as the National LGBTQ Task Force.) The original founders included Dr. Bruce Voeller, Barbara Gittings, Frank Kameny, Dr. Howard Brown, Arthur Bell, Ron Gold, Nathalie Rockhill, and Martin Duberman. Only a few months after the task force's founding, it succeeded in getting homosexuality removed from the American Psychiatric Association's list of mental disorders.[30]

16 **October 16, 1854** Oscar Fingal O'Flahertie Wills Wilde was born in Dublin. Wilde was a leading proponent of aestheticism and became famous as the author of *The Importance of Being Earnest* and *The Picture of Dorian Gray*. At the height of his fame, Wilde was convicted of gross indecency after unsuccessfully prosecuting his male lover's father for libel. He was sentenced to two years' hard labor (see May 25, 1895), and his experiences in prison inspired his final work, *The Ballad of Reading Gaol*. He lived his final years in exile and poverty and died of meningitis at the age of forty-six.[31]

17 **October 17, 1981** Lesbians Against the Right organized a "Dykes in the Streets" march in Toronto, centered around the themes of lesbian empowerment, pride, and visibility. At least 350 women participated in this demonstration.[32]

October 17, 1995 The United Nations addressed instances of violations of lesbian and gay rights for the first time at its International Tribunal on Human Rights Violations Against Sexual Minorities. After hearing testimonies from numerous individuals who had experienced a spectrum of abuses, from torture to involuntary institutionalization, the tribunal urged the UN to actively document global issues related to sexual orientation and gender identity and include them in the organization's broader human rights agenda.[33]

18 **October 18, 1887** Pauline M. Newman, renowned as an American labor activist, was born. Newman was the first female general organizer of the International Ladies' Garment Workers' Union (ILGWU) and dedicated six decades to serving as the education director of the ILGWU Health Center.

In 1917, the Women's Trade Union League assigned Newman to establish a new branch in Philadelphia. It was there that she crossed paths with Frieda S. Miller, a young economics instructor at Bryn Mawr College. Miller, disillusioned with academia, eagerly joined Newman in her organizing efforts. Their collaboration soon evolved into a close personal relationship.[34]

19 **October 19, 1991** At least nine lesbian and gay employees of Cracker Barrel Old Country Stores were fired as a result of the company's policy of supporting "heterosexual values." Queer Nation and other activist groups mounted a series of protests across the southeast US in response.

While many gay rights advocates organized protests and sit-ins at Cracker Barrel restaurants throughout the South, Carl Owens, an activist with Queer Nation Atlanta, took a different approach: the "Buy One" campaign. His idea was strategic: encourage people to purchase a single share of Cracker Barrel stock, then use their status as shareholders to demand workplace protections for gay employees. Owens described it as a "vivid example of our presence and power."

The campaign was notably bold for its time. With no federal protections and only two states offering legal safeguards against discrimination based on sexual orientation, Owens's initiative managed to gain significant traction. He also built unexpected alliances, including from religious communities. To spread the word, Owens reached out to ninety-one publications, but his message traveled further, appearing in smaller newsletters and local bulletins not originally targeted. The campaign eventually began to influence Cracker Barrel's shareholder structure. In a report to Lambda Legal, Owens noted that the company had 4,500 shareholders in 1991. By 1993, that number had jumped to 11,500. He estimated that more than half of those investors owned just one share and identified as lesbian, gay, or allies of the community.[35]

October 19, 1998 Following the brutal antigay hate crime that led to Matthew Shepard's death on October 12, 1998—after he was beaten and left tied to a fence near Laramie, Wyoming—a "political funeral" was held in his honor in New York City. Nearly five thousand people marched down Fifth Avenue in Manhattan to pay their respects and protest the violence faced by LGBT+ people. Police disrupted the demonstration and arrested several participants, including activist Sylvia Rivera. Shepard's death became a national symbol of anti-LGBT+ violence and helped mobilize efforts toward federal hate crime legislation.[36]

October 19, 2008 The Russian LGBT Network, which had been founded in 2006, was re-formed into the first Russian interregional LGBT+ rights organization. The organization, as well as being a social movement, is the largest human rights organization in Russia that deals with the rights of LGBT+ people. It is a member of the International Lesbian and Gay Association.[37]

20 **October 20, 1873** Frances Alice Kellor, an American social reformer and researcher, was born. In 1909, she became the secretary and treasurer of the New York State Immigration Commission, and she served as chief investigator for the Bureau of Industries and Immigration of New York State from 1910 to 1913. Kellor was in a lasting partnership with Mary Dreier, and they resided together from 1905 until Kellor's passing in 1952.[38]

21 **October 21, 1917** William Dale Jennings, an American author, playwright, and activist, was born. Jennings was one of the founders of the Mattachine Society, one of the earliest LGBT+ rights organizations in the United States.

In the spring of 1952, Jennings was arrested for allegedly soliciting an undercover police officer in a toilet in a park in Los Angeles. During the trial, Jennings admitted to his homosexuality but vehemently denied any wrongdoing. He was acquitted of the charges, and the case was dismissed.[39]

22 **October 22, 1977** Montreal police conducted a forceful raid on Truxx and Le Mystique, two gay bars located on Stanley Street. A contingent of fifty police officers clad in bulletproof vests and brandishing firearms, including machine guns, executed the raid. In an unprecedented move, they apprehended 146 patrons, all of whom were gay men. Following the arrests, the detained men endured over eight hours in cramped holding cells, where they were subjected to mandatory venereal disease tests and denied the right to contact lawyers.

The next day, two thousand people took to the streets and blocked the intersection of Saint-Catherine Street West and Stanley Street in protest of the raid. Law enforcement responded by riding motorcycles into the assembly and clubbing the protesters.[40]

23 **October 23, 1965** The East Coast Homophile Organizations (ECHO) organized its second and last White House picket. The FBI reported thirty-five demonstrators.[41]

24 **October 24, 1981** The inaugural National Conference on Lesbians and Gay Aging took place. This two-day conference took place at California State University, Dominguez Hills in Carson, California, and was supported by the National Association of Lesbian and Gay Gerontologists. The conference aimed to honor the experiences of elderly gays and lesbians and featured peer group panels, discussion groups, and a noteworthy slide presentation by the San Francisco Gay History Project.[42]

25 **October 25, 1929** Democratic socialist, lifelong pacifist, and activist David Ernest McReynolds was born in Los Angeles. He went on to become a leading voice in American left and antiwar movements. He was a steadfast organizer and worked nearly four decades with the War Resisters League and remained committed to nonviolence, civil disobedience, and socialism. McReynolds was the first openly gay presidential candidate in the US, when he ran for the Socialist Party USA in 1980, and again in 2000. His campaigns and his entire body of work were marked by a commitment to contesting not only capitalism but militarism and institutional oppression in all its forms. As he said well one time, "Revolutions are not tidy things"—a warning that freedom is messy, communal, and never simple. His legacy embodies the interwoven struggles for peace, queer freedom, and economic justice and offers a vision of radical solidarity that resonates deeply with this work.[43]

October 25, 1940 Miss Major Griffin-Gracy, a Black transgender activist who has tirelessly advocated for her transgender and gender-nonconforming community for more than five decades, was born in Chicago.

Miss Major participated in the historic Stonewall riots, was a sex worker, and is a survivor of both Dannemora prison and the notorious "queen tank" at Bellevue Hospital. Her global legacy of activism is deeply rooted in her personal experiences, and she continues her advocacy work with a focus on uplifting transgender women of color, particularly those who have endured incarceration and police brutality.

In the early 1980s, Miss Major's unwavering commitment and intersectional approach to justice led her to provide direct care for people with HIV/AIDS in New York. Later, she played a crucial role in establishing San Francisco's first mobile needle exchange. As the director of the Transgender, Gender-Variant, and Intersex (TGI) Justice Project, she returned to prisons as a mentor for incarcerated transgender individuals. Now, she oversees the House of GG-TILIFI, a retreat center in Little Rock, Arkansas, catering to trans and gender-nonconforming leaders from the southern US.

Miss Major's recent endeavors include serving as executive producer of the series *Trans in Trumpland* and the release of *Miss Major Speaks*, a book coauthored with Toshio Meronek (host of the podcast *Sad Francisco*) that details her life's activism.[44]

26 **October 26, 2022** *Truthout* reported that for the first time in US history, out LGBT+ political candidates were on the ballot in every

US state. According to a report by the LGBTQ Victory Fund, there were at least 678 LGBT+ candidates on the ballot for the general election, an increase of 18 percent from the 574 candidates in 2020. Coming alongside this representational milestone were drastic, concerted efforts to eliminate queer and trans people from public life—a contradiction that has led to many of these queer and trans representatives being recorded in this book.[45]

27 **October 27, 1970** In response to the September 1970 *Harper's* cover story titled "The Struggle for Sexual Identity," wherein editor Joseph Epstein disparaged homosexuals as "an affront to our rationality" and homosexuality as "anathema," Pete Fisher, a graduate student at Columbia, organized a sit-in at the magazine's Park Avenue offices alongside forty other members of the Gay Activists Alliance (GAA).

While the sit-in did not prompt an official response from the magazine, it resulted in GAA's national television debut and significantly influenced subsequent media coverage of lesbian and gay issues.[46]

October 27, 2016 Hundreds of law enforcement officers converged on a small resistance camp obstructing the route of the Dakota Access Pipeline, forcibly removing residents and detaining 142 people— marking the highest number of arrests on any day during the eleven-month-long opposition on the Standing Rock Sioux reservation. Seven Indigenous people were hit with unusual federal charges.

Protests against the Dakota Access Pipeline were spearheaded by Indigenous women and LGBT+ individuals, ranging from grassroots activists to leaders within tribal governments.

"Standing Rock was a chance to go back to our own roots in terms of gender and sexuality," Layha Spoonhunter, a Wyoming resident and member of the Eastern Shoshone and Northern Arapaho tribes, said. "Being at Standing Rock and being around LGBT youth who, for maybe the first time, weren't afraid to express themselves and be in this community where you were actually welcomed, was a huge difference."[47]

28 **October 28, 2009** US President Barack Obama enacted the Matthew Shepard and James Byrd Jr. Hate Crimes Prevention Act, which extended hate crime protections to include acts based on sexual orientation. The bill was named after Matthew Shepard, an openly gay college student who was brutally beaten and left on the side of a road in Wyoming to die in 1998, and James Byrd Jr., who was murdered in 1998 by white supremacist extremists in Texas by being dragged behind a car for miles. These hate crime protections have increased the length of sentences after violence has occurred, under certain conditions, but this has also funneled those who commit anti-queer and anti-trans violence into a prison system that only intensifies rather than addresses the underlying causes of queer- and transphobia.[48]

29 **October 29, 2019** Transgender rights activists, including poet and essayist Gwen Benaway, gathered in front of the Toronto Public Library's Palmerston branch to protest a talk by writer and speaker Meghan Murphy. Murphy, the founder of Feminist Currents, self-billed as "Canada's leading feminist website," was scheduled to speak at the library by Radical Feminists Unite, who noted on its website that "Biological sex is innate (male/female/intersex)" and that the organization was "critical of the politics of transgenderism."

Beneway said, "Having a transphobic speaker at the library endangers me because among other things they advocate ... that I'm a threat to other women. These statements cause people to fear trans women and act violently toward us in public spaces."

Beneway and Ceilidh Wood, an activist with Artists for Climate & Migrant Justice and Indigenous Sovereignty, along with other activists, decided that instead of having the protest be about blocking Murphy from speaking, they would instead use the space to hold a "read-in" and "celebrate trans, nonbinary, and Two-Spirit voices."

In the aftermath of the protest, many authors and queer organizers reduced events or engagements at the library. The Canadian Association of Professional Academic Librarians also subsequently issued a statement asserting that the Toronto Public Library failed to adequately consider the impact the decision to let Murphy rent the space for her event would have in perpetuating discrimination against the transgender community.[49]

30 **October 30, 1987** Police raided a lesbian bar in Lima, Peru, and arrested about seventy women. Television reporters, who were notified by police about the raid, filmed the arrested women for local news reports. As a result, many of the women lost their jobs, some were beaten by their families, and at least two were sexually assaulted on their way home from the police station.[50]

31 **October 31, 1940** Craig Rodwell was born. Rodwell took part in the Mattachine Society's historic "sip-in" at the New York City bar Julius' in 1966 and participated in the iconic Fourth of July Annual Reminder pickets from 1965 to 1969 at Philadelphia's Independence Hall. Rodwell also owned and operated the Oscar Wilde Memorial Bookshop in New York City's Greenwich Village, the first bookstore in the US dedicated to LGBT+ literature.[51]

October 31, 1969 San Francisco's LGBT+ activists responded to a hostile *San Francisco Examiner* article with the infamous "Purple Hands" protest, leaving handprints on the Examiner building's walls.[52] After failed attempts to engage with the newspaper, between fifty and a hundred activists picketed outside the newspaper's headquarters but were attacked by the police. Someone from the *Examiner* threw printer ink on the protesters, which splattered the walls of the building. Activists responded by placing handprints on the walls and windows of the building and writing phrases in the ink.

"Suddenly a plastic bag full of printers' ink was thrown from a second-floor *Examiner* office, soaking the pickets and splattering the walls of the building," a member of the Committee for Homosexual Freedom, a radical gay liberation group, later described. "Someone wiped his hands on the wall. In a few seconds, inked handprints covered the wall and windows. 'Fuck the *Examiner*,' was written by a finger dripping with ink. 'Gay is,' wrote a handsome young man just before he was dragged by the hair into the waiting police van."

After police broke up the demonstration outside the Examiner building, LGBT+ activists decided to march on city hall to protest police brutality. Fifteen to twenty-five activists formed a picket line outside the building, and a handful of protesters conducted a sit-in in the offices of the mayor. Three activists who refused to leave the mayor's office were arrested and charged with trespassing, unlawful assembly, and remaining at the site of a riot.[53]

October 31, 1969 The Queens Liberation Front (QLF) was founded in New York City. The QLF, initially called Queens, was a prominent trans liberation group created by Barbara de Lamere (then known as Bunny Eisenhower), Lee Brewster, Bebe Scarpinato, Vicky West, and Chris Moore.

De Lamere and the others first met in the gay rights advocacy group the Mattachine Society. Queens was formed following the

Stonewall Rebellion, due to the lack of interest the Mattachine Society had in gender-nonconforming people, trans people, and self-identified drag queens and their issues. And while Stonewall had been a violent, anti-police riot, the Mattachine Society was aiming for mainstream respectability.

The Queens issued two important goals in a prospectus: "Rights to Congregate" and "Rights to Dress as We See Fit." After these goals were declared, they became known as the Queens Liberation Front.

While acting as an activist group, they worked to achieve social liberation and acceptance for drag queens and gender-nonconforming people. In this, they created a magazine called *Drag* that reached over 3,500 readers. Before this, they participated in and financially supported the first Pride march: the Christopher Street Liberation Day March on June 28, 1970. Later that year on Halloween, the first anniversary of the QLF, then–Executive Director Lee Brewster announced the victory of their first goal, after New York City scrapped its ban on cross dressing, and they held the first legal drag ball in the city's history.

As their activist work continued, they supported attempts to pass a bill in 1973 banning discrimination based on sexuality in employment, housing, and public accommodation—even though in this bill nothing was explicit in support of those who were trans, and it was subsequently passed without this.

The final ball thrown by QLF took place at the Hotel Diplomat on West 43rd Street in 1973. While the group eventually disbanded, *Drag* magazine continued into the 1980s.[54]

October 31, 1992 In honor of Hattie Mae Cohens and Brian Mock, a lesbian and gay man who were burned to death in their own home during the last days of a heated campaign to pass a statewide ballot measure in Oregon, the Lesbian Avengers literally ate fire on the streets of Greenwich Village in New York City.

The New York Times described the protest: "They ate fire, chanting, as they still do: 'The fire will not consume us. We take it and make it our own.'" During the demonstration, the Avengers also marched with torches and burned signs with the names of anti-lesbian and antigay propositions blamed for the homophobic violence.

The Oregon measure would have classified homosexuality as "abnormal, wrong, unnatural and perverse" and required the state government to be assertive in discouraging homosexuality, teaching that it is a moral offense similar to pedophilia, sadism, and masochism. It was defeated that November, albeit narrowly, in part due to the public horror over the hate crime against Cohen and Mock, which many blamed on the toxic environment created by the campaign to pass the ballot measure.[55]

NOVEMBER

November 1970 Transgender sex workers and activists Sylvia Rivera and Marsha P. Johnson set up a house for Street Transvestite Action Revolutionaries (STAR), providing safe accommodation for working-class and poor LGBT+ youth. It was known as the STAR House. Initially the two had provided safe haven for homeless LGBT+ young people in a parked trailer truck in Greenwich Village, but using their earnings from sex work they were able to secure a building at 213 East Second Street. STAR House has been described as the first LGBT+ youth shelter in the United States.[1]

November 1, 1999 *The Trouble with Normal*, by Michael Warner, was published. The book challenged the prevailing emphasis on same-sex marriage within the gay rights movement, proposing a broader focus on equal benefits for unconventional families. *The Trouble with Normal* contends that institutional approval of specific relationship types perpetuates inequality and shame, advocating for a shift from the pursuit of normality to the recognition of varied sexual expressions as dignified. Warner explores the negative consequences of societal norms, including an increased risk of violence and disease, urging a more inclusive approach in the pursuit of queer rights.[2]

November 2, 1977 José Jaime Parada Hoyl, a prominent advocate for gay rights and a politician, was born in Santiago, Chile. He made history in 2012 by becoming the first openly gay person elected to public office in Chile. Parada also served as the spokesperson for Movimiento de Integración y Liberación Homosexual, the foremost gay rights organization in Chile.[3]

November 2, 2012 Sherri Lou "Dusty" Ellis died. Ellis was a participant in the Kerr-McGee plutonium plant criminal trial of the 1970s. She and her roommate Karen Silkwood became nuclear whistleblowers and activists when both women tested positive for plutonium contamination within their own bodies while working at a Kerr-McGee facility in Oklahoma.

Though little known in popular narratives, Ellis has recently come to be an influential, though forgotten, queer and labor historian. Her close relationship with Silkwood—more frequently read by queer historians as potentially erotic—paralleled the deep emotional and political bonds between women who resisted corporate and state violence. At Silkwood's untimely passing in a car accident in 1974, Ellis became increasingly militant, engaging in acts of resistance that led to her criminalization and social ostracism. She was defined consistently as "unstable," echoing centuries of pathologization of women—and queer women, and gender-nonconforming folk—who subvert power structures.

Where chivalrous martyrdom became exemplified by Silkwood, Ellis embodied another heritage: one of unyielding resistance, mourning, and resilience. Her history speaks to us today of rich, queer past centuries in which not only love and communion but also messy, oftentimes unruly borders of resistances persist.[4]

3 **November 3, 1889** Amelio Robles Ávila was born. Robles, assigned female at birth, was a colonel during the Mexican Revolution with the Zapatista military organization El Ejército Liberación del Sur, and he lived openly as a man from twenty-four until his death at ninety-five (see December 9, 1984). Robles's male identity was accepted by family, society, and the Mexican government, and according to a former neighbor, if anyone called Robles a woman, he would threaten them with a pistol. Robles married, adopted children, and retired with military honors.[5]

4 **November 4, 2008** California voters passed Proposition 8, a voter initiative that took the right to marry away from same-sex couples. The initiative amended the state constitution to restrict marriage to opposite-sex couples and passed with 52 percent of the voters in favor and 47 percent opposed.

The vote came just months after the California Supreme Court had ruled in May 2008 that withholding marriage rights from gay and lesbian couples was unconstitutional under state law. The ruling briefly made same-sex marriage legal in California, permitting thousands of couples to wed. But Proposition 8 effectively reversed the court's decision, the first time an American state revoked the right to same-sex marriage after it had been established. The move prompted instant lawsuits and protests and became a lightning rod for the broader struggle for LGBT+ rights nationwide.[6]

5 **November 5, 1974** Elaine Noble made history as the first openly gay or lesbian person elected to a state legislature in the US when she won a seat in the Massachusetts House of Representatives.[7]

6 **November 6, 1903** German antifascist, feminist, lesbian, postal worker, and communist activist Hilde Radusch was born. Radusch was jailed by the Nazis in 1933, then released under the supervision of the

Gestapo. They tried to arrest her again in the 1940s, but she went underground and evaded capture until the end of the war.

Following the war, Radusch worked for the Department for the Victims of Fascism, and she began to question some of the practices of the Communist Party, for example asking, "Can the goal of socialism be achieved via a bad, totalitarian path?" These concerns eventually led her to decide to resign from the party, but before she could, they expelled her for being a lesbian, while other Communist Party officials denounced her to her employer, leading to her dismissal. She later recalled that this incident "was really the end of all my illusions.... A piece of my life's dream was destroyed." However, Radusch remained politically active, later setting up Germany's first lesbian newspaper as well as a group of lesbian elders in West Berlin called L74.[8]

November 6, 2012 In Maine, voters approved the legalization of same-sex marriages, while in Washington state, Minnesota, and Maryland, voters upheld existing statutes allowing same-sex marriage.[9]

7 **November 7, 2017** In a historic election, Virginia voters chose Danica Roem as the first openly transgender candidate to serve in the Virginia House of Delegates. This was part of what became known as the "trans tipping point," a reference to increased visibility and representation for trans people. Since Roem's election, concerted efforts have been made to target this "newly visible" population.[10]

8 **November 8, 1997** Three activists affiliated with ACT UP New York disrupted President Bill Clinton's speech at a Washington, DC, hotel to the Human Rights Campaign, which had been a major financial supporter of Clinton's 1996 reelection campaign. The protesters questioned the administration's stance on the federal ban on funding for needle-exchange programs. Acting in rapid succession, they called on President Clinton to clarify the refusal to allocate funds for initiatives aimed at providing drug users with clean needles to combat the HIV/AIDS epidemic.[11]

9 **November 9, 1960** A new Massachusetts law enacted on this day excluded people convicted of sodomy from early release from parole. The previous year, the Massachusetts Supreme Court's unanimous ruling in *Commonwealth v. Marshall* had allowed sodomy convictions based on mostly circumstantial evidence.[12]

10 **November 10, 1881** Toni Ebel, a German painter, was born. Ebel was employed in housekeeping at the Institute for Sexual Science and was one of the pioneering trans women to undergo sex reassignment surgery, likely predating Lili Elbe, who was known as one of the first recipients of the gender-affirming surgery.

Around 1928, Ebel met Charlotte Charlaque, who was also in the process of transitioning. Seeking a formal name change, she applied for the name Annie in 1929, but this request was denied. However, her subsequent name change to Toni was approved in 1930. With the backing of Magnus Hirschfeld, Ebel underwent five sex reassignment surgeries.

In 1933, Ebel adopted Judaism, the religion of Charlaque, her Jewish partner. The couple faced persecution under the Nazi regime: Charlaque was deported to the United States, and Ebel was prohibited from leaving Europe. Despite the forced separation, Ebel survived the war and later lived in East Germany, where she received a modest pension as a victim of Nazi racial prejudice and continued her work as a painter.

Specializing in landscapes and portraits, she gained recognition in East Germany starting from the 1950s. Ebel was affiliated with the Association of Visual Artists of East Germany and participated in German art exhibitions in Dresden during the 1950s and early 1960s.[13]

November 10, 1973 Lambda Legal, a pioneering LGBT+ advocacy organization, was founded. Throughout its history, Lambda Legal has been at the forefront of landmark cases, addressing issues such as job discrimination, police harassment, and the broader challenges encountered by LGBT+ people. From its involvement in *Bowers v. Hardwick* (see June 30, 1986) to overturning antisodomy laws in the landmark 2003 case *Lawrence v. Texas* (see November 20, 1998), Lambda Legal has significantly shaped legal precedents that expanded LGBT+ rights.[14]

November 10, 1984 A thousand people protested in Rugby, England, against the local council removing LGBT+ people from its equal opportunities policy. To critics, it seemed clear that the council intended to actively discriminate against LGBT+ people, with the leader of the council stating, "We're not having men turn up for work in dresses and earrings." Other councilors denigrated "all queers and perverts" and declared "all homosexuals to be vile and perverted people."

The Sun, owned by media mogul Rupert Murdoch, supported the "brave" Conservative local authority in its war against the "sick nonsense" of LGBT+ rights and called on its readers to "ALL follow Rugby in fighting back!" Sandwell Council then followed suit, trying to ban lesbians and gay men from caring roles. While local public opinion was divided, with around 46 percent of people agreeing with the council as opposed to 54 percent disagreeing, months of protests were organized by council workers, LGBT+ rights groups, and others.

On November 10, police arrested eighteen people for unfurling banners in the town center, and in January tomatoes and smoke flares were thrown at councillors in the town hall. By mid-February, the council had been forced to backtrack and amend its policy to state that it would not discriminate against employees on the basis of sexual orientation.[15]

November 10, 2014 The first Hijra Pride took place in Bangladesh. *Hijra* is a term used in South Asia to describe a diverse group of people who don't conform to traditional male or female gender roles. Hijras may be intersex or transgender, or they may simply not adhere strictly to the binary understanding of gender. The hijra community has a long history in South Asia and has faced both societal discrimination and legal challenges.

Hijra Pride began with the Dhaka Declaration, a statement to the government demanding that persistent challenges experienced by the transgender community in Bangladesh be addressed.[16]

11 **November 11, 1950** The Mattachine Society—originally called the Society of Fools—was founded in Los Angeles by a group of leftist gay men that consisted of Harry Hay (see April 7, 1912), Rudi Gernreich, Dale Jennings, Bob Hull, and Chuck Rowland. It was the first durable gay rights group in the US. The name "Mattachine" was taken from a medieval French troupe whose actors used masks to satirize societal norms, as the group was founded on the belief that queers had to wear metaphorical masks in order to survive in society.[17]

12 **November 12, 1963** Michael Rogers was born on this day. In 1989, after moving to New York City, Rogers joined ACT UP and participated in the "Stop the Church" demonstration, in which seven thousand demonstrators gathered outside St. Patrick's Cathedral and hundreds of protesters entered the church to protest the Catholic Church's policies perpetuating homophobia, misogyny, fear of AIDS, and abortion restrictions.

In 2002, Rogers founded Stop the Box to oppose an automated convenience store in Washington, DC. Rogers's activism also targeted Subway in

2008 in response to its donation to Proposition 8, a ballot measure that temporarily repealed same-sex marriage rights in California before ultimately being ruled unconstitutional in 2010. The boycott threat led by Rogers prompted Subway to add sexual orientation and gender identity to its nondiscrimination policies.[18]

13 **November 13, 1970** The UK branch of the Gay Liberation Front held its first-ever public demonstration by lesbians and gay men at Highbury Fields in London, protesting against police use of agents provocateurs to entrap gay men. It was a standard police practice at the time to use "pretty policemen" to entrap gay men into attempting acts of gross indecency in order to increase the figures for crime detection and prosecution.[19]

November 13, 1970 Amid the turmoil of the Vietnam War, a group of five individuals affiliated with the Gay Liberation Front of New York embarked on a winding journey through the southern US in a maroon-and-white Volkswagen bus. Their objective was to motivate the LGBT+ community to participate in the second meeting of the Revolutionary People's Constitutional Convention, organized by the Black Panthers, in Washington, DC. There, they aimed to unite with fellow liberationists from across the nation in the collective endeavor of drafting a new constitution for America.

According to a government memorandum, the FBI was watching them closely and was worried about "a connection between the homosexual movement and the Black Panther Party."[20]

14 **November 14, 1969** The Gay Liberation Front published the first issue of *Come Out!*, a newspaper crafted "By and for the Gay Community."[21] The first paragraph read:

COME OUT FOR FREEDOM! COME OUT NOW! POWER TO THE PEOPLE! GAY POWER TO GAY PEOPLE! COME OUT OF THE CLOSET BEFORE THE DOOR IS NAILED SHUT!

The cost was thirty-five cents, or fifty cents outside New York City.[22]

November 14, 1985 In response to the *New York Post*'s highly criticized and sensationalized coverage of HIV and AIDS, a modest group composed of journalists and writers coalesced to form Gay and Lesbian Alliance Against

Defamation, or GLAAD. Later that year, an assembly of nearly a thousand people protested outside the headquarters of the *New York Post*.[23]

November 14, 2012 Radical American gay trade union activist Howard Wallace died. He served on the NAACP Denver and Colorado executive boards, advocated for the passage of Colorado's Fair Employment Practices and Anti-Discrimination law in 1957, and cofounded the Denver Friends of the Student Nonviolent Coordinating Committee.

In 1962, Wallace played a role in organizing the Denver Fair Play for Cuba Committee. Around this time, he joined the Denver branch of the Socialist Workers Party (SWP) and became the party's candidate for the Denver School Board in 1965. However, he parted ways with the SWP in 1972 due to a disagreement over the party's reluctance to address LGBT+ issues. In 1975, he established Bay Area Gay Liberation and collaborated with Harvey Milk in a labor strike at Coors Brewing Company to denounce the company's discriminatory practices against the LGBT+ community.

In the mid-1980s, Wallace, alongside Nancy Wohlforth (see June 24, 1994), who served as the international secretary treasurer of the Office and Professional Employees International Union, established the Lesbian-Gay Labor Alliance. This organization later transformed into Pride at Work, an LGBT+ labor association affiliated with the AFL-CIO.[24]

15 **November 15, 1963** In pursuit of discrediting and undermining the civil rights movement, the FBI installed a wiretap on the phone of Bayard Rustin at his home in Harlem, New York. On the first day of surveillance, an FBI agent documented a conversation, noting, "Engaged in a conversation with an unidentified male … propositions of a homosexual nature were made."[25]

November 15, 1997 Journalist, author, historian, and archivist Jim Kepner died on this day. He became a member of the Communist Party USA and contributed to a Communist newspaper in New York City, *The Daily Worker*, but was expelled from the party because of his homosexuality.[26]

16 **November 16, 1946** Barbara Smith, lesbian, Black feminist, author, and cofounder of the Combahee River Collective, was born in Cleveland, Ohio. She and her twin sister, Beverly Smith, along with Demita Frazier, coauthored "The Combahee River Collective Statement" (see April 1977).

In 1980, together with Cherríe Moraga and Audre Lorde (see February 18, 1934), she founded Kitchen Table: Women of Color Press, the first publisher for women of color in the United States.[27]

17 **November 17, 1962** James Baldwin (see August 2, 1924) published "Letter from a Region in My Mind" in *The New Yorker*. This was the first of two essays that would become his book *The Fire Next Time*.

In this book, Baldwin integrates personal memoir and philosophical examination, intertwining his own coming of age in Harlem with broader commentary on the institutionalization of racism, the role of Christianity in Black life, and the attraction of Marxism within the Nation of Islam. With prophetic brashness, Baldwin warns that if America is not to destroy itself, it must confront the "racial nightmare" that it has unleashed. It will be destroyed, he says, not by water, but by fire. His prose insists on white America's acknowledgment of Black humanity and on reckoning.

The essays, particularly "Letter from a Region in My Mind," further solidified Baldwin as a moral voice of the civil rights movement, though withering critiques of his work always placed him at odds with white liberals and traditional Black leadership.[28]

18 **November 18, 2001** In Vancouver, over three thousand protesters marched and held a vigil for Aaron Webster, a gay man who was beaten to death in Stanley Park in 2001 in what was one of Canada's most horrific antigay hate crimes. Webster's death marked a turning point, sparking widespread outrage and grief after a troubling rise in violence targeting queer people. The event was not only an act of memory but also a public protest against the then-dominating dangers inflicted on LGBT+ communities.[29]

19 **November 19, 1980** Ex-transit cop Ronald K. Crumpley unleashed a submachine gun on patrons of the Ramrod, a gay leather bar situated at 394–395 West Street in New York City's Greenwich Village, resulting in the death of two people and injuries to three others. This act of antigay violence led to the permanent closure of the bar.[30]

20 **November 20, 1910** Pauli Murray was born. Murray was the first Black person to earn a JSD (Doctor of the Science of Law) degree from Yale Law School, a founder of the National Organization for Women (NOW), and the first Black person perceived as a woman to be ordained an Episcopal priest. Pauli Murray's legal arguments and interpretation of the US Constitution were winning strategies for public school desegregation, women's rights in the workplace, and an extension of rights to LGBT+ people based on Title VII of the 1964 Civil Rights Act.

In *The Activist History Review*, philosopher Naomi Simmons-Thorne writes, "From *Brown v. Board of Education* and *Reed v. Reed*, the protected legal classes enshrined in the 1964 Civil Rights Act, down to the very concept of intersectionality, much of our modern legal and sociopolitical discourse is directly indebted to the intellectual futurity of a scantly known figure, the 'pseudo-hermaphrodite' Pauli Murray."

Historians believe that Murray, who identified as part male and part female, was also an early transgender figure in American history because of vast personal documentation of his perennial battle with gender dysphoria.

"What we do know is that Pauli Murray suffered lifelong battles with gender dysphoria as a result of biological essentialism, transphobia as a result of his gender identity, discrimination and criminalization of his gender expression, queerphobia as a result of his attraction to women in a body assigned female, sexism having been perceived as a cisgender woman, and racism having been a person of color in Jim Crow America," Simmons-Thorne explains. "These are not the experiences of a cisgender woman, nor a stealth transgender person who consistently performed their gender as the opposite sex. These are the experiences of a man of color who publicly identified as a woman, privately identified with masculinity, whose body made them queer."[31]

November 20, 1998 John Lawrence and Tyrone Garner were fined $125 each following their arrest for engaging in consensual sexual activity in their own home in Texas. Their refusal to pay the fine triggered a legal challenge against the Texas sodomy law that culminated in the landmark 2003 case *Lawrence v. Texas*, resulting in the nationwide repeal of sodomy laws.[32]

November 20, 1999 The first Transgender Day of Remembrance was organized by transgender activist Gwendolyn Ann Smith after Rita Hester, a transgender woman, was murdered on November 28, 1998, in Boston.[33]

November 20, 2019 The Transgender Persons (Protection of Rights) Bill 2019 was tabled in the Rajya Sabha, the upper house of the Indian parliament. Four days later, members of India's transgender community marched in

Delhi's Queer Pride Parade to voice their concerns about the proposed legislation. Though claiming to protect transgender rights, the bill was regressive, requiring individuals to register with the government if they wanted to be recognized officially as "transgender," as well as requiring proof of gender confirmation surgery in order to be legally recognized as a trans man or trans woman.[34]

November 20, 2022 Hundreds of transgender activists gathered at Frere Hall in Karachi to raise awareness of discrimination and demand equal rights and civil rights protection in Pakistan's first transgender rights march. The organizers demanded that the federal government criminalize transphobic hate speech, protect the right to self-perceived gender identity, and enact antidiscrimination laws to address the transgender community's housing crisis.[35]

21 **November 21, 2007** Governor Jennifer Granholm of Michigan signed an executive order banning employment discrimination in the public sector on the basis of gender identity or expression. The order, which was proactive rather than prompted by specific examples of discrimination, stated, "To build a more inclusive Michigan our state government must be a model of tolerance, accessibility, equal opportunity—reaching out to people, knocking down barriers, and dispelling prejudices which hold Michigan back."[36]

November 21, 1870 Russian American anarchist and author Alexander Berkman was born in Vilnius, now part of Lithuania. In 1892, Berkman attempted to assassinate businessman Henry Clay Frick during the Homestead steel strike. His unsuccessful endeavor resulted in a fourteen-year prison sentence. During his incarceration, Berkman was intimately involved with other incarcerated men and wrote his renowned autobiographical narrative of prison life, *Prison Memoirs of an Anarchist*.[38]

22 **November 22, 1958** Nathan Phelps, an American-born Canadian author, LGBT+ rights activist, and public speaker on the topics of religion and child abuse, was born. Phelps ran away from his family home when he turned eighteen, and four years later he permanently left the famously homophobic Westboro Baptist Church, which was founded and headed by his father, Pastor Fred Phelps. The church is notorious for its hate-filled rhetoric, including the slogan "God hates f**s," and for staging protests against LGBT+ people, funerals, and other events. Nathan Phelps has since become a powerful voice against religious extremism and abuse.[37]

23 **November 23, 1973** Over three hundred people attended the first conference of the Gay Academic Union (GAU) in New York City. The GAU was organized with the goal of making academia more hospitable to the LGBT+ community in the US. The pioneering lesbian and gay studies group, which was founded the previous March, included Martin Duberman, John D'Emilio, Jonathan Ned Katz, and Joan Nestle among its members.[39]

24 **November 24, 1886** Margaret Caroline Anderson was born. Anderson was the American founder, editor, and publisher of the art and literary magazine *The Little Review*. In 1913, Anderson wrote the first published defense of homosexuality in the US, which appeared in the magazine.[40]

November 24, 1967 Gay rights activist Craig Rodwell opened the Oscar Wilde Memorial Bookshop at 291 Mercer Street in New York City's Greenwich Village neighborhood. It was the first bookstore in the US dedicated to LGBT+ literature, providing not only access to queer books and periodicals at a time when such material was scarce, but also serving as a crucial community space for connection, education, and resistance. In tandem with the bookstore, Rodwell launched the Homophile Youth Movement in Neighborhoods (HYMN), along with a newsletter, *HYMNAL*, that circulated news and ideas across the burgeoning gay rights movement, reflecting the radical potential of print culture as a form of organizing and visibility.[41]

25 **November 25, 1950** Aiyyana Maracle was born on the Six Nations territory on the Grand River near Ohsweken in southern Ontario. Maracle was a multidisciplinary artist, scholar, educator, story-crafter, and storyteller who described herself as a "transformed woman who loves women."

In her work, she argued that gender identifications in most traditional Indigenous cultures do not conform strictly to the Western gender binary, recognizing them as socially and spiritually integral to the culture. Her solo show, *Chronicle of a Transformed Woman*, vividly depicted her journey through traditional medicine rituals for gender transition amid the challenges of colonial rule.[42]

26 **November 26, 1957** Simon Tseko Nkoli, a South African anti-apartheid, gay rights, and AIDS activist, was born. Nkoli is revered as the founder of South Africa's Black gay movement and was an integral participant in the anti-apartheid struggle for Black freedom. His association with that movement's leaders was instrumental in gaining recognition for gay rights in his country.

Nkoli's involvement in anti-apartheid activism took root during the student rebellions of 1976, when he was arrested four times. Joining the Congress of South African Students in 1979, he became the secretary for the Transvaal region, though his homosexuality became a subject of debate within the organization. Despite the discussions, he retained his post.

Nkoli encountered a lack of resources for gay people of color after the end of his first relationship. The majority of gay venues were segregated, to be found only in districts reserved for whites. In 1983, he formed a significant intersection of his racial and sexual identity politics by publicly coming out in an interview with the *City Press*, a Black newspaper, and simultaneously joining the predominantly white Gay Association of South Africa (GASA), which maintained a politically neutral stance in the anti-apartheid struggle. Dissatisfied with GASA's reluctance to shift social activities away from whites-only facilities, Nkoli founded the Saturday Group in May 1984, marking South Africa's first gay Black organization.

Throughout the 1980s, Nkoli's activism extended to the African National Congress and the United Democratic Front (UDF). In 1984, he played a role in establishing the Vaal Civic Association for tenant organizing in Delmas township. Nkoli and twenty-one fellow UDF members were arrested during a march protesting government-imposed rent hikes, facing charges of "subversion, conspiracy, and treason," which carried the death penalty.

The "Delmas Treason Trial" spanned four years, during which Nkoli came out to his comrades in Pretoria Central Prison, sparking debates on homophobia as a form of oppression. His proof of having attended a GASA meeting became a crucial point in countering prosecution attempts to place him at a murder scene. This defense, doubling as a public coming out, garnered international attention from the gay rights movement. Acquitted in 1988, Nkoli and the rest of the "Vaal 22" were released.

On his release, Nkoli cofounded the Gay and Lesbian Organization of Witwatersrand (GLOW), the first major, Black-based LGBT+ organization in South Africa. Starting in 1990, GLOW organized the country's initial three Pride marches and served as a model for several other gay groups in the country's Black townships.[43]

November 26, 2022 Community members convened for a candlelight vigil to pay tribute to the victims of the Club Q shooting on November 19 in Colorado Springs. The tragic incident claimed the lives of five people— Daniel Aston, Raymond Green Vance, Kelly Loving, Ashley Paugh, and Derrick Rump.[44]

27 **November 27, 1835** James Pratt and John Smith, a groom and laborer, respectively, were executed in London for having sex. They were the last men executed in Britain for homosexuality.

However, while after this the death penalty was no longer used as a punishment for homosexuality in Britain itself, it was elsewhere in much of the British Empire for many years. Britain outlawed homosexuality in all of its colonies, and as of 2019, of the seventy-two countries that still criminalized same-sex relationships, thirty-eight of them were previously under British rule.[45]

November 27, 2012 In Washington, DC, shortly before World AIDS Day, a group of seven AIDS activists representing QUEEROCRACY, ACT UP New York, and ACT UP Philadelphia took a bold stand by entering House Speaker John Boehner's office and disrobing, demanding a meeting with the Congress member. Instead of traditional signs, the activists painted slogans on their bodies, such as "AIDS Cuts Kill," "Fund PEPFAR," "Fund Ryan White," "Fund Global Fund," "Fund Medicaid," and "Fund HOPWA."

Cassidy Gardner from QUEEROCRACY said, "When you strip away the rhetoric of the fiscal cliff and the grand bargain, you see that these terms are a way to thinly veil draconian budget cuts that will leave millions around the world with absolutely nothing."

The police arrested three women who took part in the action, charging them with indecent exposure.[46]

November 27, 2016 Hundreds of gay rights activists marched in Delhi's ninth annual Pride parade to celebrate their sexuality and to draw attention to the continuing discrimination faced by India's LGBT+ community. LGBT+ activists marching in the parade demanded that a colonial-era antisodomy law be repealed. The law had been deemed unconstitutional in 2009 but had recently been reinstated.[47]

28 **November 28, 1971** Members of the Gay Liberation Front picketed outside of the headquarters of the San Diego Police Department to "protest the department's treatment of gays, lesbians, and drag queens." The demonstration garnered TV news coverage and brought local attention to the violence of policing.[48]

29 **November 29, 2007** Uruguay became the first Latin American country to pass a national civil union law. The new law allowed both gay and straight couples to form civil unions after living together for five years. These unions granted them rights similar to those of married couples, including inheritance, pensions, and child custody.[49]

30 **November 30, 1999** Forty thousand antiglobalization demonstrators protested the World Trade Organization (WTO) Ministerial Conference in Seattle. Seattle and the WTO conference were effectively shut down; every entrance to the Washington State Convention and Trade Center was successfully blocked and held.

Seattle Mayor Paul Schell imposed a 7:00 p.m. curfew and declared a state of civil emergency. Simultaneously, an unconstitutional "no-protest zone" was established, accessible exclusively to WTO delegates and business owners.

At around 5:30 p.m., an aggressive offensive was launched by the police units against the remaining protesters, forcibly ejecting them from the no-protest zone well before the curfew took effect. The pursuit involved the use of concussion grenades, rubber bullets, and tear gas, stretching from downtown to the residential Capitol Hill district. This decision proved to be a significant misstep.

Capitol Hill was known as Seattle's primary gay community and one of the most liberal neighborhoods in the city, and its residents viewed the police units' intrusion as an invasion of their homes. Commissioner Ken Schulman, representing the Seattle Commission on Sexual Minorities and a Capitol Hill resident, asserted that the only destruction witnessed in Capitol Hill was caused by the police.

Police units fired rubber bullets at close range, clubbing, kicking, and beating immobilized, handcuffed protesters. A particularly haunting image featured a motorcycle police unit running over a locked-down protester, then reversing and repeating the action.

Notably absent from the news coverage was the homophobic violence inflicted by some police units on Capitol Hill residents. Numerous reports detailed instances of police units beating gay residents while uttering derogatory slurs. Many of these victims had no connection to the WTO protests; they were merely going about daily activities such as grocery shopping, having dinner, or renting a movie. The police units' pursuit beyond the "no-protest zone" into Seattle's residential communities lacked any justifiable reason, causing significant concern and condemnation.[50]

DECEMBER

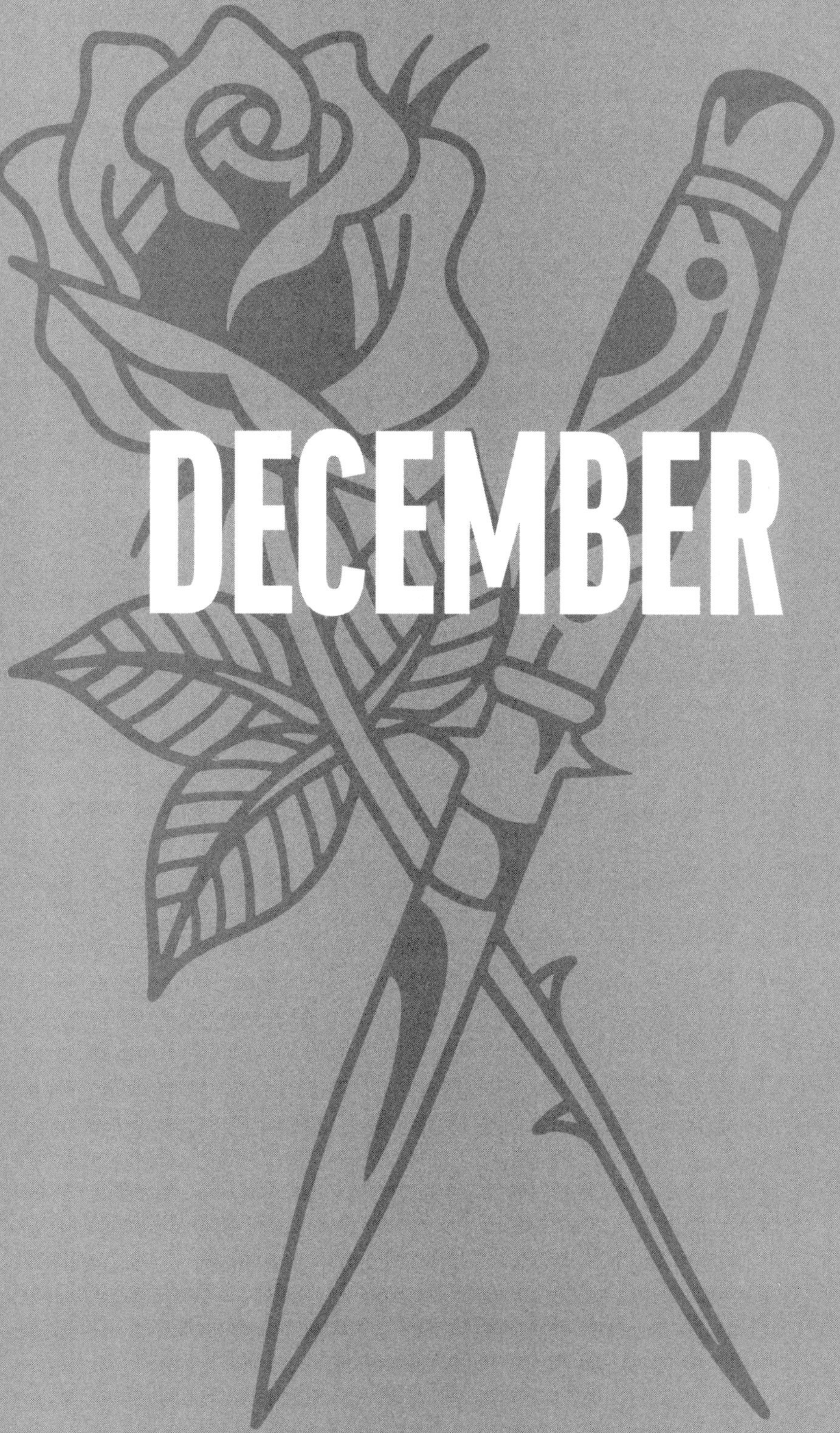

1 **December 1, 1989** Amid the escalating AIDS crisis and in conjunction with the World Health Organization's second annual World AIDS Day, Visual AIDS organized the first Day Without Art to commemorate the lives and accomplishments of those lost to AIDS. Over eight hundred arts organizations, museums, and galleries across the US symbolically draped artworks with shrouds and replaced them with information about HIV and safer sex. Some institutions chose to lock their doors or dim their lights, while others organized exhibitions, programs, readings, memorials, rituals, and performances.[1]

December 1, 1998 A few seconds after midnight on World AIDS Day, Fed Up Queers protested outside of New York State Assemblywoman Nettie Mayersohn's house in Queens to condemn her stance on partner notification, which protesters held criminalizes HIV.[2]

December 1, 2017 Jaime Harker, a lesbian English professor at the University of Mississippi, opened a queer feminist bookstore named Violet Valley Bookstore in Water Valley, Mississippi.

"Stories were spreading that we were selling porn, that we'd be teaching children to be queer," Harker told *VICE*. "A group of my students came once on a Saturday to unpack books, and a rumor started flying that we were organizing a lesbian takeover of the town. A group organized a prayer meeting in a park across the street from the store for weeks in a row."

The store's mission statement reads:

> Violet Valley Bookstore makes feminist, queer, and multicultural books available to the Water Valley community, the state of Mississippi, and the South. The bookstore provides a series of readings and other programs to support diverse voices in Mississippi. It features new and used books so that everyone, no matter their income bracket, can afford to have books.[3]

2 **December 2, 1964** The second-ever public demonstration supporting gay rights in the US, and the first effort to challenge the psychiatric profession, unfolded outside the Great Hall at Cooper Union in New York City. Randy Wicker organized the protest, in which three gay men and a lesbian distributed homophile literature while protesting against a psychiatrist presenting a lecture titled "Homosexuality: A Disease."[4]

3 **December 3, 1946** Allan Bérubé, an American historian, activist, and independent scholar, was born. He described himself as a "community-based" researcher who focused on the experiences of gay men and lesbians in the US armed forces during World War II. His research also explored the intersections of class and race within gay culture. His book on the subject, *Coming Out Under Fire*, was published in 1990.[5]

4 **December 4, 1920** Jeanne Sobelson Manford, educator and trailblazing LGBT+ ally, is most known for cofounding Parents, Families, and Friends of Lesbians and Gays (PFLAG), one of the most powerful and longest-running LGBT+ activist organizations in the United States.

In April 1972, when Jeanne and her husband, Jules, were at their Queens residence, they received a chilling phone call from a hospital: their gay activist son, Morty, had been physically assaulted while handing out leaflets at the Inner Circle dinner, a visible political event in New York City. Morty was "kicked and stomped" and taken away by police, who did nothing to intervene. Angered, Jeanne published an open letter in the *New York Post*, announcing to the public that she was the mother of a gay man and condemning the authorities for failing to protect him.

In later weeks, she did both radio and TV interviews, always with her husband or son for company to bear witness against injustice. On June 25 the same year, she marched at the New York Pride March beside Morty, carrying a homemade sign that read "Parents of Gays Unite in Support for Our Children."

Her public stance came during a period in which homosexuality was criminalized and pathologized. As California Senator Mark Leno later described, for a mother to so openly declare support for her gay son in such a culture was radical and deeply loving: "No small act," he said, "but it was what a mother's love does."[6]

5 **December 5, 1642** The first recorded legal prosecution of lesbians in America took place with the case of servant Elizabeth Johnson in 1642. On this day, she was sentenced to a fine, as well as to be "severely whipped," for engaging in unspecified "unseemly practices betwixt her and another maid."[7]

6 **December 6, 2011** Elio Di Rupo became prime minister of Belgium, making him the first full-time openly gay male head of a nation. When asked directly whether he was homosexual in an interview, Di Rupo replied simply, "Yes. So what?"—a disarmingly forthright statement that underscored both his refusal to be defined by his identity and his stance that sexual orientation is irrelevant to political leadership.[8]

7 **December 7, 1896** Japanese translator, feminist, socialist, and lesbian Yuasa Yoshiko was born in Kyoto. She was an early supporter of the women's rights movement in the country and became involved in the left-wing Tyrian literature movement. With the leading woman proletarian author Chūjō Yuriko, she traveled to the Soviet Union for three years, studying Russian language and literature, and developed a friendship with film director Sergei Eisenstein (see January 22, 1898). She translated a significant number of Russian works into Japanese.[9]

December 7, 1984 Lesbians and Gays Support the Miners (LGSM) held a fundraising benefit disco for striking UK miners at the Northbridge pub in Leicester, England. The event ran from 8:00 p.m. until late, with the cost of admission beginning at 75 pence, featuring a breakdance crew known as Electro Force. LGSM groups around the country raised significant amounts of money to support the miners' strike against Margaret Thatcher's Conservative government.[10]

8 **December 8, 1986** Canadian customs seized over five hundred books and magazines intended for Little Sister's Book & Art Emporium in Vancouver (see June 7, 1990), invoking the 1847 Customs Act, which prohibited the importation of publications deemed to have an "immoral or indecent character." This provision granted customs officials the authority to confiscate shipments of allegedly "obscene" titles at their discretion.

Tensions escalated when customs deemed *The Advocate* magazine inadmissible, leading the store to pursue legal action. It took two years and $5,000 in legal fees for the store to compel the government to acknowledge that the magazines should never have been confiscated. Unfortunately, by then, the magazines had already been burned and destroyed.[11]

9 **December 9, 1984** Mexican revolutionary fighter Amelio Robles Ávila died in his hometown of Xochipala, Guerrero, at ninety-five years old. Assigned female at birth (see November 3, 1889), Robles joined the turbulent events of the Mexican Revolution in 1912, and his first mission was to extort funds from oil companies to fund the revolutionary movement. He fought in the army of Emiliano Zapata and reached the rank of colonel. He was famous for shooting his pistol with his right hand while holding a cigar in his left, and he was himself shot at least six times.

In 1924, Robles declared his identity as male and was recognized as such by the military, and he was later recognized as the first transgender veteran of the Mexican army. He forged a male birth certificate and insisted he be recognized as male for his next seven decades. Mexican historian Gabriela Cano explains that Robles's gender identity "must be distinguished from the strategic cross-dressing—the adoption of masculine outfits to pass as a man—that some women employed in periods of war to protect themselves from sexual violence that is usually more acute during armed conflict, to access military leadership positions or simply to fight as soldiers and not as *soldaderas*, that is to say, without the social gender restrictions that usually weigh on women in the military."

According to rumor, on one occasion Robles was assaulted by men who tried to inspect his anatomy, and in defending himself two of the attackers were killed. A neighbor later recounted how Robles would challenge anyone who misgendered him: "I always called him Mr. Robles, because he'd pull out his gun if someone called him a woman or Mrs."

After his death, Mexican institutions began to undermine his identity. A rumor began that he had requested to be buried in women's clothes, and a school and museum was named after his dead name.[12]

10   **December 10, 1924** Henry Gerber, an immigrant from Germany, secured a charter from the state of Illinois to establish a nonprofit corporation in Chicago known as the Society for Human Rights. This marked the earliest documented gay rights organization in the United States.

Despite its initial purpose to mirror contemporary German LGBT+ emancipation groups, Gerber and other members faced criminal charges shortly after it incorporated for their involvement in the group, leading to the dissolution of the society in 1925.

Gerber sustained connections within the emerging homophile movement of the 1950s and continued to advocate for the rights of homosexuals after the society's abrupt end.[13]

December 10, 1984 "Pits and Perverts," a benefit concert, was held by the London Lesbian and Gays Support the Miners group to support striking miners in the UK.

The concert proved to be a significant financial triumph, generating £5,650 (equivalent to over £20,000 in today's currency) for striking miners and their families in South Wales. Moreover, it marked a historic political milestone, as a representative from the National Union of Mineworkers took the stage before the audience of 1,500 to say:

> You have worn our badge, "Coal Not Dole," and you know what harassment means, as we do. Now we will pin your badge on us; we will support you. It won't change overnight, but now 140,000 miners know that there are other causes and other problems. We know about blacks, and gays and nuclear disarmament, and will never be the same.

The miners stayed true to their commitment. Not only did they proudly display their trade union banners at the 1985 Gay and Lesbian Pride Rally in London, but they also played a crucial role in advancing gay rights policies at the 1985 Labour Party Conference, despite facing opposition from the party's national executive.[14]

December 10, 1989 Over seven thousand protesters affiliated with ACT UP and WHAM! (Women's Health and Action Mobilization) gathered in the bitter cold outside St. Patrick's Cathedral in New York for the "Stop the Church" action to protest the AIDS-phobic, homophobic, misogynistic, and anti-abortion policies of the Catholic Church and John Cardinal O'Connor, archbishop of New York. Several hundred protesters peacefully entered the church, and 111 were arrested for disrupting Mass.[15]

December 11, 1948 American photographer Alvin Baltrop was born. Baltrop's work focused on New York City's abandoned, dilapidated Hudson River piers and the gay men who gathered there during the 1970s and 1980s prior to the AIDS crisis. During the 1970s and '80s, the piers drew an ever-shifting population of homeless people, teenage runaways, artists, and sexual adventurers. One of Baltrop's photographs was a portrait of drag queen and activist Marsha P. Johnson, who was a famous waterfront habitué.[16]

December 11, 1973 Mark Segal, a twenty-three-year-old Gay Raiders member, managed to enter CBS News studios in New York by posing as a student journalist. While Walter Cronkite was reporting a story about the Middle East, Segal jumped in front of the camera, displaying a sign that read "Gays Protest CBS Prejudice," causing the network feed to go black for several seconds. Technicians subdued Segal, wrapping him up with cable wire as they awaited the arrival of the police. Segal and his accomplice were charged with trespassing.

At the trial's conclusion, Segal was fined $450, a penalty he deemed "the happiest check I ever wrote." This direct action not only garnered significant media attention but also got Segal a private meeting with Cronkite, who sought a better understanding of how CBS could cover gay pride events.

"Walter Cronkite was my friend and mentor," Segal recounted. "Following that incident, CBS News agreed to investigate the 'possibility' of censoring or displaying bias in news reporting. Walter, on the *Evening News*, presented a map of the US, highlighting cities that had passed gay rights legislation. Network news was never the same after that."[17]

December 11, 2023 Hundreds of people took part in a "Queers for Palestine" demonstration, obstructing the Manhattan Bridge in New York City. The pro-Palestinian marchers, originating from the Barclays Center in Brooklyn, proceeded across the bridge into Manhattan, advocating for a free Palestine and chanting, "Queer, trans, no peace on stolen land."[18]

12 **December 12, 1969** Police arrested three patrons and three employees at the Continental Baths, a gay bathhouse in the basement of the Ansonia Hotel in New York City. Established a year prior to the Stonewall riots, the bathhouse experienced approximately two hundred police raids. The patrons were charged with lewd and lascivious acts, and the employees were charged with criminal mischief. This raid marked the first incident in a series of actions targeting the Continental over the subsequent weeks.[19]

13 **December 13, 1922** José Julio Sarria, also known as the Grand Mere, Absolute Empress I de San Francisco, and the Widow Norton, was born in San Francisco. In 1961, Sarria became the first openly gay candidate for public office in the US, running for the San Francisco Board of Supervisors. He was also celebrated for his performances as a drag queen at the Black Cat Cafe and for founding the Imperial Court System, a charitable organization of drag performers.[20]

14 **December 14, 1974** Michael Fesco opened the Flamingo, New York City's first exclusively gay disco. The club was situated on the second floor of a building at the intersection of Houston Street and Broadway.

Due to the persistent threat of police raids, the club had to take precautions. It employed two women to operate the door, and it maintained an unlisted telephone number, although those in the know could discover it under "Gallery for the Promotion of People, Places, and Events" at 599 Broadway.[21]

15 **December 15, 1961** Jack Halberstam, an American cultural critic, gender theorist, and professor known for his work in the fields of queer studies, gender studies, and cultural studies, was born. His celebrated 1998 book *Female Masculinity* explores alternative masculinities outside of cis male bodies, including his own experiences growing up as someone assigned female at birth. The book has become a foundational text in queer theory and gender studies.[22]

16 **December 16, 1988** Disco superstar Sylvester passed away from AIDS-related complications in his Castro area home in San Francisco. Maintaining openness about his sexuality throughout his career, Sylvester came to be regarded as a spokesperson for the gay community (see September 6, 1947).

Reflecting on his musical work in an interview, he expressed that he believed his career had "transcended the gay movement." He went on to say, "I mean, my sexuality has nothing to do with my music. When I'm fucking I'm not thinking about singing and vice versa."[23]

17 **December 17, 1933** Sexual contact between men was recriminalized in the USSR after it had been decriminalized in 1922 in the wake of the 1917 Russian Revolution.

Authorities claimed that homosexuality was the result of bourgeois Western and German fascist influence, and the official Soviet newspaper *Pravda* published an article that ended with the slogan: "Destroy homosexuality and fascism will disappear!"

From the beginning of 1934, gay men began to be arrested in large numbers in major Russian cities and sent to the gulags. One prisoner, Valery Klimov, wrote about the treatment gay detainees received:

> There were about 10 occasions when gays were murdered before my eyes. One was beaten to death in a prison in Sverdlovsk. There were 100 men in our cell; three or four raped him every day and then chucked him under the bunks. It was bestial, a nightmare. Once 10 of them raped him and then jumped on his head. I nearly went mad

there; my hair turned grey. That's how people lose their sanity; many never recover even after they leave.

While lesbianism was never prohibited, and some masculine lesbians were valued in the military, many lesbians did still suffer persecution, such as termination of studies or jobs, bullying, threats to remove custody of their children, or being committed to psychiatric facilities.[24]

December 17, 1970 Nine prominent figures in the women's liberation movement, among them Gloria Steinem and Susan Brownmiller, convened for a press conference in New York City to convey their "support for the efforts of homosexuals to achieve liberation within a sexist society."[25]

18 **December 18, 1980** The New York State Court of Appeals struck down the state's sodomy law as unconstitutional. Judge Hugh Jones found in *People v. Onofre* that the law violated both privacy and equal protection rights. Jones emphasized the right to privacy as essential for making important decisions independently. He noted that the legislature's retention of criminal penalties for sodomy in the 1965 penal code was primarily based on moral considerations. Jones contended that the state failed to demonstrate any credible threat stemming from private, consensual sodomy and lacked a rational basis for the marital exemption.[26]

19 **December 19, 1908** Photographer, socialist, and antifascist Gisèle Freund was born to a Jewish family in Germany. She photographed the German antifascist movement until one of her friends was jailed and murdered, after which she went to France, where she began a relationship with avant-garde poet Adrienne Monnier, who arranged for her to marry a male friend to remain in the country.

Following the Nazi invasion of France, Freund fled to Argentina, where she worked for Magnum Photos until forced to break ties following the American Red Scare. After the publication of photographs she took of Eva Perón wearing lavish jewelry, she was forced to leave the country, as it contradicted the Peronist propaganda about austerity. Freund eventually returned to France, where she lived until her death in 2000.[27]

20 **December 20, 1957** Frank Kameny (see May 21, 1925) was dismissed from his US government position due to his sexual orientation during what is known as the "Lavender Scare." Just five months into his job with the Army Map Service, Kameny received orders to return to Washington, DC, while on assignment in Hawaii in 1957. On his return, investigators from the Civil Service Commission interrogated him about a 1955 arrest in San Francisco. In August of that year, Kameny had been arrested in a known "gay cruising area" and charged with lewd and indecent conduct. The resulting termination prompted him to embark on "a Herculean struggle with the American establishment," leading to "a new period of militancy in the homosexual rights movement of the early 1960s."

Kameny formally contested his dismissal. While unsuccessful, this proceeding marked the first documented civil rights claim based on sexual orientation pursued in a US court.[28]

21 **December 21, 1866** A coalition of Lakota, Cheyenne, and Arapaho warriors, commanded by Maȟpíya Lúta ("Red Cloud") and Tȟašúŋke Witkó ("Crazy Horse"), achieved victory over the US Army in the Battle of the Hundred-in-the-Hands near Fort Kearny, Wyoming. The successful winter solstice battle strategy was notably prophesied by a *winkte*, a revered Two-Spirit individual who served as an adviser to Red Cloud and Crazy Horse.[29]

December 21, 1969 The Gay Activists Alliance (GAA) split from the more radical Gay Liberation Front (GLF). While the GLF saw itself as part of a revolutionary movement of all oppressed people that sought to overturn capitalism, imperialism, and racism, the GAA was formed by more moderate members who wished to focus on the single issue of gay and lesbian rights within the current system. One of the GAA's primary tactics was the use of "zaps"—noisy but nonviolent confrontations with homophobic public officials designed to generate media attention. The group eventually disbanded in 1981.[30]

22 **December 22, 1946** Bisexual Black liberation activist Kuwasi Balagoon was born in Maryland. He joined the military and faced violent racism both from officers and his fellow servicemen, and as a result Balagoon and some Black comrades formed a collective called De Legislators. In the collective autobiography of the Panther 21, *Look for Me in the Whirlwind*, Balagoon writes:

> From then on, every time a racial situation appeared, we did. Every time white G.I.s ganged a black G.I., we moved to more than even the

score. One at a time we would catch up with them and beat and stomp them so bad that helicopters would have to be used to take them to better hospitals than the ones in the area. We were not playing. We would plan things so that we could kick something off inside a club that would instantly turn into a riotous condition—once everything was in chaos it was impossible to pick us out. We then broke faces and bodies of whoever we planned to get and made our escape. Afterward we would have critiques, just like in the end of war games; get our alibis together; and keep the whole thing under our hats.

Later returning to civilian life, Balagoon moved to New York City and got involved in grassroots tenant organizing. He soon became involved in the Black Panther Party and was subsequently arrested and put on trial as part of the notorious Panther 21 case, the defendants in which were all later acquitted. Balagoon then joined the urban guerrilla group the Black Liberation Army and was imprisoned and escaped various times. He was eventually convicted and jailed for life for participation in the $1.6 million robbery of a Brink's armored car. Balagoon kept up his radical activity in prison, authoring a number of texts, until his death from AIDS-related illness in 1986.[31]

23 **December 23, 1954** Danny Nicoletta, a photographer, photojournalist, and advocate for gay rights, was born. In 1974, at the age of nineteen, Nicoletta met Harvey Milk and Scott Smith at Castro Camera, their camera shop located on Castro Street. The following year, they offered him a position at the store, which Nicoletta accepted; he would also work on Milk's political campaigns. During this period, Nicoletta captured numerous iconic photographs of Milk.[32]

24 **December 24, 1920** Stormé DeLarverie, pioneering drag performer who may have thrown the first punch at the Stonewall Uprising (see June 28, 1969), was born.

"Nobody knows who threw the first punch, but it's rumored that she did, and she said she did," her friend and legal guardian Lisa Cannistraci, owner of a Greenwich Village lesbian bar, told *The New York Times* upon her death in 2014. "She told me she did."[33]

25 **December 25, 1908** Quentin Crisp was born. Crisp was an English raconteur whose work in the public eye included a memoir of his life and various media appearances. At the age of ninety, Crisp wrote that they had "accepted" that they were transgender:

> Having labelled myself homosexual and having been labelled as such by the wider world, I have effectively lived a "gay" life for most of my years. Consequently, I can relate to gay men because I have more or less been one for so long in spite of my actual fate being that of a woman trapped in a man's body. I refer to myself as homosexual without thinking because of how I have lived my life. If you are reading this and are gay, think of me as one of your own even though you now know the truth. If it's confusing for you, think how confusing it has been for me these past ninety years.[34]

26 **December 26, 1960** Stuart Milk, the nephew of civil rights leader Harvey Milk, was born. He cofounded the Harvey Milk Foundation in 2009. Engaging in both domestic and international activism, he has worked extensively with LGBT+ movements in Latin America, Europe, Asia, and the Middle East.[35]

27 **December 27, 1943** Martha Shelley, an American activist, writer, and poet best known for her involvement in lesbian feminist activism, was born. Shelley was involved with the New York City chapter of the Daughters of Bilitis and the Student Homophile League at Barnard College and was one of the twenty or so women and men who formed the Gay Liberation Front after the Stonewall Uprising.

In 1970, the group known as Lavender Menace, later rebranded as Radicalesbians, orchestrated the Lavender Menace "zap" during the Second Congress to Unite Women. Seventeen women with matching T-shirts emblazoned with "LAVENDER MENACE" surrounded the audience, holding signs and yelling, while others planted in the crowd rose to join them. The group then stormed the stage and shared thoughts and questions about lesbianism with the crowd for two hours. Shelley played a pivotal role in the zap itself, and some assert her involvement in crafting the Radicalesbians manifesto, "The Woman-Identified Woman," which introduced the terms *women-identified* and *male-identified* to the lexicon of the lesbian feminist discourse community. During the same year, Shelley authored "Subversion in the Women's Movement," a piece published in both *Come Out!* and *off our backs*, a feminist publication.[36]

28 **December 28, 2009** Alex Freyre and José María di Bello exchanged vows at the southern tip of Argentina, marking the first same-sex marriage in Latin America.

"This marriage is bigger than José María and I," Freyre said in an interview. "It is a victory for all who face prejudice and discrimination across Latin America and the Caribbean. It is proof that at last the grip of the Catholic church is slipping across Latin America, the system that has kept gay communities silent and fearful is crumbling. What is happening on Tuesday is a strike against those attitudes that have repressed sexual rights across this continent for too long."[37]

29 **December 29, 2018** The first Transgender Pride march in Pakistan took place. Demonstrators called for the enforcement of a trans rights bill that had been passed but not effectively implemented. This legislation, enacted in May 2018, granted individuals the right to self-identify their gender on official documentation, including for nonbinary people.

Elements of the law, including self-identification and inheritance rights, were overturned in 2023 by the Federal Shariat Court. Pakistan also still maintains laws prohibiting homosexuality, which were previously implemented by British colonial authorities.[38]

30 **December 30, 1977** Members of the metropolitan Toronto police and the Ontario provincial police raided the offices of the Canadian Gay Archive and activism-based queer magazine *The Body Politic*, seizing over twelve crates of material deemed "pornographic," along with the list of the magazine's subscribers.[39]

31 **December 31, 1918** Radical labor activist, lesbian, and abortion provider Marie Equi (see April 7, 1872) was found guilty of sedition in the United States under a newly amended Espionage Act after she unfurled a large banner during a rally reading "Prepare to die, workingmen, J.P. Morgan & Co. want preparedness for profit." The law "forbade criticism of the U.S. government, the constitution, the military, the flag, navy or uniform." After a long trial, Equi, a supporter of the Industrial Workers of the World union, was sent to San Quentin State Prison to serve a three-year term, which was later commuted to a year and a half.[40]

Acknowledgments

We would like to thank the queer activists, historians, and archivists who made this work possible: Donn Teal, Hugh Ryan, Riley Snorton, Susan Stryker, Michael Bronski, Ryan Conrad, Mattilda Sycamore, John D'Emilio, Eric Marcus, Marc Stein, Ronni Sanlo, Jonathan Katz, Urvashi Vaid, John O'Brien, Josephine Donovan, Back2Stonewall, the Lavender Effect, OutHistory, and Making Queer History. We would also like to thank our stakeholders in this process who supported this project: Emily K. Hobson, Karma Chávez, Eric Stanley, Evelyn Blackwood, Shuli Branson, and Jack Halberstam. Lastly, we would like to thank Steven, Wade, and PM Press for their guidance and Working Class History for recognizing the importance of queer radical history.

Notes

Introduction

1   "George Floyd Murdered," Working Class History, last edited July 19, 2022, https://
    stories.workingclasshistory.com/article/9773/george-floyd-murdered.

2   "E25-26: The Stonewall Riots and Pride at 50," *Working Class History*, podcast
    transcript, May 13, 2019, https://workingclasshistory.com/podcast/e25-the-stonewall-
    riots-and-pride-at-50/.

3   Oliver Pieper, "LGBTQ Rights Under Legal Attack Around the World," *DW*, August 27,
    2023, https://www.dw.com/en/lgbtq-rights-worldwide-report-2023/a-66601820.

4   Conor Payne, "Transphobia and the Left: Bogus Science and Bogus Marxism,"
    Socialist Alternative, May 12, 2020, https://www.socialistalternative.org/2020/05/12/
    transphobia-and-the-left-bogus-science-and-bogus-marxism/.

5   Jarred Keller, "HRC Foundation Report: Epidemic of Violence Continues; Transgender
    and Gender Nonconforming People Still Killed at Disproportionate Rates in 2023,"
    Human Rights Campaign, press release, November 20, 2023, https://www.hrc.org/
    press-releases/hrc-foundation-report-epidemic-of-violence-continues-transgender-
    and-gender-nonconforming-people-still-killed-at-disproportionate-rates-in-2023;
    Jacqueline Teschon, "Data Reveals New Insights on Transgender Workplace
    Experiences," Columbia University Teachers College, April 15, 2024, https://www.
    tc.columbia.edu/articles/2024/april/data-reveals-new-insights-on-transgender-
    workplace-experiences/; Owen Jones, "Transphobia Was Always Going to End Up
    as Crude, Old-Fashioned Homophobia," *Medium*, April 5, 2021, https://owenjones84.
    medium.com/transphobia-was-always-going-to-end-up-as-crude-old-fashioned-
    homophobia-a98af68b3a73.

6   Angelica Stabile, "Exposing the Trans Agenda Aimed at Our Kids: Faith Leader
    Reveals How Parents Can Keep Children Safe," *Fox News*, April 6, 2023, https://www.
    foxnews.com/lifestyle/exposing-trans-agenda-aimed-kids-faith-leader-reveals-how-
    parents-can-keep-children-safe; Achilles Fergus Seastrom, "Far from Protecting
    Women, New Law Poses Silent Threats to Transgender Kansans," *Kansas Reflector*,
    June 8, 2023, https://kansasreflector.com/2023/06/08/far-from-protecting-women-
    new-law-poses-silent-threats-to-transgender-kansans/.

7   Aryn Fields, "Human Rights Campaign Condemns X, Elon Musk for Accepting
    Timeline Takeover of Transphobic, Fact-Free 'Documentary,'" Human Rights Campaign,
    press release, November 2, 2023, https://www.hrc.org/press-releases/human-rights-
    campaign-condemns-x-elon-musk-for-accepting-timeline-takeover-of-transphobic-

fact-free-documentary; James Factora, "Elon Musk Has Spent Pride Month Liking Transphobic Tweets," *Them*, June 7, 2023, https://www.them.us/story/elon-musk-pride-month-tweet-likes-anti-trans; Samantha Riedel, "Twitter Has Removed Its Ban on Misgendering and Deadnaming Trans People," *Them*, April 18, 2023, https://www.them.us/story/elon-musk-twitter-transphobic-harassment-deadnaming-misgendering; Laurie Penny, "Moving Towards Solidarity," *The F-Word*, December 6, 2009, https://thefword.org.uk/2009/12/cis_feminists_s.

8   Annette Choi, "Record Number of Anti-LGBTQ Bills Were Introduced in 2023," *CNN*, January 3, 2024, https://www.cnn.com/politics/anti-lgbtq-plus-state-bill-rights-dg/index.html.

9   Bill Barrow and Marc Levy, "Trump Hammered Democrats on Transgender Issues. Now the Party Is at Odds on a Response," *AP*, November 14, 2024, https://www.ap.org/news-highlights/spotlights/2024/trump-hammered-democrats-on-transgender-issues-now-the-party-is-at-odds-on-a-response/.

10   Geoff Mulvihill, "6 Ways Trump's Executive Orders Are Targeting Transgender People," *PBS News*, February 1, 2025, https://www.pbs.org/newshour/politics/6-ways-trumps-executive-orders-are-targeting-transgender-people.

11   "Defending Women from Gender Ideology Extremism and Restoring Biological Truth to the Federal Government," The White House, January 21, 2025, https://www.whitehouse.gov/presidential-actions/2025/01/defending-women-from-gender-ideology-extremism-and-restoring-biological-truth-to-the-federal-government/.

12   Tara Copp, Lolita C. Baldor, and Kevin Vineys, "War Heroes and Military Firsts Are Among 26,000 Images Flagged for Removal in Pentagon's DEI Purge," *AP*, March 7, 2025, https://apnews.com/article/dei-purge-images-pentagon-diversity-women-black-8efcfaec909954f4a24bad0d49c78074.

13   Brajesh Upadhyay, "Transgender References Removed from Stonewall Monument Website," *BBC*, February 14, 2025, https://www.bbc.com/news/articles/cglywwn29n6o.

14   Ben Quinn and Peter Walker, "Wes Streeting Expected to Tell Parliament Why He Backs Puberty Blockers Ban," *Guardian*, July 15, 2024, https://www.theguardian.com/politics/article/2024/jul/15/wes-streeting-defends-puberty-blocker-ban-decision-after-labour-criticism; Andrew Gregory, "Puberty Blockers to Be Banned Indefinitely for Under-18s Across UK," *Guardian*, December 11, 2024, https://www.theguardian.com/society/2024/dec/11/puberty-blockers-to-be-banned-indefinitely-for-under-18s-across-uk.

15   Amy Sedghi, Severin Carrell, and Libby Brooks, "UK Supreme Court Ruling on Legal Definition of Woman 'Brings Clarity and Confidence,' Says Government—As It Happened," *Guardian*, April 16, 2025, https://www.theguardian.com/law/live/2025/apr/16/uk-supreme-court-to-rule-on-legal-definition-of-a-woman-gender-recognition-certificates.

16   Pieper, "LGBTQ Rights."

17   Martin Luther King Jr., "Remaining Awake Through a Great Revolution," speech given at the National Cathedral on March 31, 1968, Smithsonian, accessed October 23, 2024, https://www.si.edu/spotlight/mlk?page=4&iframe=true.

January

1   **January 1, 1962** "Getting Rid of Sodomy Laws: History and Strategy That Led to the Lawrence Decision," American Civil Liberties Union, June 26, 2003, https://www.aclu.org/documents/getting-rid-sodomy-laws-history-and-strategy-led-lawrence-decision.

2   **January 1, 1965** Amanda Harbrecht, "New Year's Eve Jan 1. 1965: A Night for Gay Rights," FoundSF: The San Francisco Digital History Archive, accessed November 10, 2023, https://www.foundsf.org/index.php?title=New_Year%27s_Eve_Jan._1_1965:_A_Night_for_Gay_Rights.

3   **January 1, 1967** "Police Raid Black Cat," Working Class History, last edited July 19, 2022, https://stories.workingclasshistory.com/article/8071/police-raid-black-cat.

4   **January 2, 1971** "Timeline: African American LGBTQ+ U.S. History, 1912–2009,"

OutHistory, accessed November 10, 2023, https://outhistory.org/exhibits/show/afam-timeline/timeline; John Goins, "Forging a Community: The Rise of Gay Political Activism in Houston," *Houston History* 7, no. 2 (Spring 2010), https://www.houstonlgbthistory.org/Houston80s/Goins-Gay-Political-Activism-Dec2010.pdf.

5   **January 3, 1990** "ACT UP Accomplishments 1987–2012," ACT UP, accessed June 15, 2023, https://actupny.com/actions/.

6   **January 4, 1982** "Gay History—January 4, 1982: NYC's Gay Men's Health Crisis Founded in Response to AIDS Epidemic," Back2Stonewall, January 4, 2023, archived at https://web.archive.org/web/20230128003424/http://www.back2stonewall.com/2023/01/gay-history-january-4-1982-nycs-gay-mens-health-crisis-founded-in-response-to-aids-epidemic.html.

7   **January 5, 1974** "The Tipping Point: Four Key Protests in Canadian LGBT2Q+ History," Queer Events, November 25, 2019, https://www.queerevents.ca/queer-history/articles/tipping-points/key-protest-lgbt-history.

8   **January 6, 1863** Harper-Hugo Darling, "Emma Trosse," Making Queer History, January 25, 2024, https://www.makingqueerhistory.com/articles/2024/1/25/emma-trosse.

9   **January 6, 1967** Michael Annetta, "January 6 in LGBTQ History," Lavender Effect, January 6, 2013, https://thelavendereffect.org/2013/01/06/january-6-in-lgbtq-history; Gregory B. Lewis, "Lifting the Ban on Gays in the Civil Service: Federal Policy Toward Gay and Lesbian Employees Since the Cold War," *Public Administration Review* 57, no. 5 (1997): 387–95, https://doi.org/10.2307/3109985.

10   **January 7, 1949** "Gay History—January 7, 1949: 4 Men Plead Guilty to 'Homosexual Offenses' After Gay Witch Hunt at University of Missouri," Back2Stonewall, January 7, 2023, archived at https://web.archive.org/web/20230128004826/http://www.back2stonewall.com/2023/01/lgbt-history-january-7-1949.html.

11   **January 8, 1962** "Gay History—January 8, 1962: Two Men Arrested for 'Abominable Act and Detestable Crime Against Nature' in North Carolina Under 429-Year-Old Law," Back2Stonewall, January 8, 2023, archived at https://web.archive.org/web/20230128005801/http://www.back2stonewall.com/2023/01/gay-history-january-8-1962-two-men-arrested-for-abominable-act-and-detestable-crime-against-nature-in-north-carolina-under-429-year-old-law.html.

12   **January 9, 1946** "Countee Cullen," National Museum of African American History and Culture, accessed February 6, 2025, https://nmaahc.si.edu/countee-cullen.

13   **January 9, 1978** CNN Editorial Research, "LGBTQ Rights Milestones Fast Facts," *CNN*, August 21, 2023, https://www.cnn.com/2015/06/19/us/lgbt-rights-milestones-fast-facts/index.html.

14   **January 10, 1982** "The Sexes: The Lavender Panthers," *Time*, October 8, 1973, https://content.time.com/time/magazine/article/0,9171,908008,00.html; Eric Markowitz, "The Most Dangerous Gay Man in America Fought Violence with Violence," *Newsweek*, January 25, 2018, https://www.newsweek.com/2018/02/02/most-dangerous-gay-man-america-789402.html; "Interview with Rev. Ray Broshears," video, KPIX News footage from July 6, 1973, Bay Area Television Archive, 1 min., 50 sec., accessed December 5, 2023, https://diva.sfsu.edu/collections/sfbatv/bundles/232644.

15   **January 11, 2007** "Mexican State Approves Gay Civil Unions," *Mail & Guardian*, January 13, 2007, https://mg.co.za/article/2007-01-13-mexican-state-approves-gay-civil-unions/.

16   **January 12, 1977** Michael Annetta, "January 12 in LGBTQ History," Lavender Effect, January 12, 2013, https://thelavendereffect.org/2013/01/12/january-12-in-lgbtq-history.

17   **January 13, 1958** Michael Annetta, "January 13 in LGBTQ History," Lavender Effect, January 13, 2013, https://thelavendereffect.org/2013/01/13/january-13-in-lgbtq-history.

18   **January 13, 2014** "CeCe McDonald Released from Prison," National LGBTQ Task Force, press release, January 13, 2014, https://www.thetaskforce.org/news/cece-mcdonald-released-from-prison/.

19   **January 14, 1975** Bella Abzug, Civil Rights Amendments, H.R. 166, 94th Cong. (1975), https://www.congress.gov/bill/94th-congress/house-bill/166/all-info.

20 **January 15, 1909** Michael Rosenfeld, "Les réseaux queer d'Akademos," *Sextant*, no. 40 (2023), http://journals.openedition.org/sextant/2379.

21 **January 16, 1956** "Carlos Mock," Chicago Gay History, accessed July 11, 2024, http://www.chicagogayhistory.com/biography.html?id=771; Carlos T. Mock, "The New Faces of Puerto Rican Lesbian Activism," *Windy City Times*, September 1, 2005, https://www.windycitytimes.com/lgbt/The-New-Faces-of-Puerto-Rican-Lesbian-Activism/9342.html; "Carlos T. Mock," Chicago LGBT Hall of Fame, accessed February 7, 2025, https://chicagolgbthalloffame.org/mock-carlos/.

22 **January 17, 1969** Stefanie Dazio and Haven Daley, "Meet D'Arcy Drollinger, a Drag Queen Who's Now the First Drag Laureate in the US," *AP*, May 18, 2023, https://apnews.com/article/san-francisco-first-drag-queen-ambassador-c97a296e3895f86b21c0562e6e92656d; "About D'Arcy," D'Arcy Drollinger official website, accessed February 7, 2025, https://www.darcydrollinger.com.

23 **January 18, 1928** "Gay History—January 18: The Gay King of America, Anita Bryant Wants to 'Save the Children' and an American Family," Back2Stonewall, January 18, 2023, archived at https://web.archive.org/web/20230127235804/http://www.back2stonewall.com/2023/01/lgbt-gay-history-january-18-gay-king-america-betty-berzon-american-family-anita-bryant-l-word.html.

24 **January 18, 2023** James Factora, "Queer 'Cop City' Protestor Tortuguita Fatally Shot by Law Enforcement in Atlanta," *Them*, January 23, 2023, https://www.them.us/story/tortuguita-shot-killed-atlanta-police-cop-city.

25 **January 19–20, 2017** Kim Kelly, "DisruptJ20 Protests Should Be Remembered as Part of the Anti-Trump Resistance," *Teen Vogue*, January 21, 2020, https://www.teenvogue.com/story/j20-protest-trump-anniversary.

26 **January 20, 1857** Harper-Hugo Darling, "Charlotte Payne-Townshend," Making Queer History, April 5, 2023, https://www.makingqueerhistory.com/articles/2021/5/25/charlotte-payne-townshend-part-i.

27 **January 20, 1944** Dianca Potts, "The Radical Poetry of Audre Lorde's Confidante, Pat Parker," *VICE*, March 20, 2018, https://www.vice.com/en/article/9kgw57/pat-parker-audre-lorde-black-lesbian-revolutionary-poetry; Rae Alexandra, "The Oakland Poet Who Brought Lesbian Feminism to the Fore," KQED, April 30, 2018, https://www.kqed.org/pop/102855/rebel-girls-from-bay-area-history-pat-parker-lesbian-feminist-poet-and-activist; "Pat Parker," *prosa caótica* (blog), August 24, 2017, archived at https://web.archive.org/web/20200316092009/https://prosacaotica.blogspot.com/2017/08/pat-parker.html.

28 **January 21, 1966** "Forest Town Raid," Working Class History, last edited July 19, 2022, https://stories.workingclasshistory.com/article/7847/forest-town-raid.

29 **January 22, 1898** Sergey Yuryev, "'интеллектуальная Ориентация'. Закадровая Жизнь Сергея Эйзенштейна" ("Intellectual Orientation": The Behind-the-Screen Life of Sergei Eisenstein), *AiF*, January 22, 2018, https://aif.ru/culture/person/intellektualnaya_orientaciya_zakadrovaya_zhizn_sergeya_eyzenshteyna.

30 **January 22, 1953** "Timeline: African American LGBTQ+ U.S. History, 1912–2009," OutHistory, accessed November 10, 2023, https://outhistory.org/exhibits/show/afam-timeline/timeline; John D'Emilio, *The Lost Prophet: The Life and Times of Bayard Rustin* (Free Press, 2003).

31 **January 22–23, 1991** "ACT UP Accomplishments 1987–2012," ACT UP, accessed June 15, 2023, https://actupny.com/actions/.

32 **January 23, 1882** Judit Takács, "The Double Life of Kertbeny," in *Past and Present of Radical Sexual Politics: Working Papers, Fifth Meeting of the Seminar "Socialism and Sexuality," Amsterdam, October 3–4, 2003*, ed. Gert Hekma (Mosse Foundation, 2004); Robert Beachy, "The German Invention of Homosexuality," *The Journal of Modern History* 82, no. 4 (December 2010): 801–38.

33 **January 24, 1915** "Documenting Nazi Persecution of Gays: The Josef Kohout/Wilhelm Kroepfl Collection," United States Holocaust Memorial Museum, accessed January 5,

2024, https://www.ushmm.org/collections/the-museums-collections/curators-corner/documenting-nazi-persecution-of-gays-the-josef-kohout-wilhelm-kroepfl-collection.

34 **January 25, 1962** Maggie Kerins, "Local LGBTQ Legend: Aaron Fricke," *Newport OUT*, March 8, 2020, https://www.newportout.com/post/local-lgbtq-legend-aaron-fricke.

35 **January 26, 2011** "Obituary: Uganda Gay Activist David Kato," *BBC*, January 27, 2011, https://www.bbc.com/news/world-africa-12299786; Start to WISH, "WISH interview with David Kato," posted April 3, 2010, by starttowish, YouTube, 9 min., 51 sec., http://www.youtube.com/watch?v=jdLdsCwGPbo; "Gay History—January 26: Nikola Tesla Was Hot, the First Gay Wedding License, and RENT Opens off B'Way," Back2Stonewall, January 26, 2023, archived at https://web.archive.org/web/20230322232218/http://www.back2stonewall.com/2023/01/gay-lgbt-history-january-26.html.

36 **January 27, 2025** Zane McNeill, "Incarcerated Trans Woman Sues Trump over Anti-Trans Order Redefining 'Sex,'" *Truthout*, January 28, 2025, https://truthout.org/articles/incarcerated-trans-woman-sues-trump-over-anti-trans-order-redefining-sex/. Reprinted in modified form under Creative Commons (CC BY-NC-ND 4.0).

37 **January 28, 1961** "Gay History—July 28, 1961: Illinois Becomes First State to Rescind Sodomy Law by Mistake," Back2Stonewall, July 28, 2023, archived at https://web.archive.org/web/20230928052047/http://www.back2stonewall.com/2023/07/gay-history-july-28th-1961-illinois.html.

38 **January 28, 2024** James Factora, "After Two Seattle Gay Bars Received 'Lewd Conduct' Citations, Owners Demand Answers," *Them*, January 30, 2024, https://www.them.us/story/two-seattle-gay-bars-received-lewd-conduct-citations-owners-demand-answers.

39 **January 29, 2017** Isabela Vieira, "Protest Held on Copacabana Beach in Memory of Trans People Murdered," *Agência Brasil*, January 30, 2017, https://agenciabrasil.ebc.com.br/en/direitos-humanos/noticia/2017-01/protest-held-copacabana-beach-memory-trans-people-murdered.

40 **January 30, 1997** Abby Johnston, "There's a March Against Revenge Porn in NYC," *Bustle*, March 25, 2017, https://www.bustle.com/p/theres-a-march-against-revenge-porn-coming-up-in-nyc-46944; Elly Belle, "GLAAD Names 3 LGBTQ Activists as This Year's 'Rising Stars,'" *Teen Vogue*, April 4, 2018, https://www.teenvogue.com/story/glaad-names-3-lgbtq-activists-as-this-years-rising-stars; "Leah Juliett," March Against Revenge Porn, archived October 22, 2023, at https://web.archive.org/web/20231022005455/https://marchagainstrevengeporn.org/leahjuliett.

41 **January 31, 1989** "State: AIDS Protest Closes Golden Gate," *Los Angeles Times*, January 31, 1989, https://www.latimes.com/archives/la-xpm-1989-01-31-mn-1493-story.html.

February

1 **February 1, 1901** "Langston Hughes," National Museum of African American History and Culture, accessed February 7, 2025, https://nmaahc.si.edu/langston-hughes.

2 **February 1, 1950** Jason Okundaye, "Ted Brown: The Man Who Held a Mass Kiss-In and Made History," *Guardian*, April 8, 2021, https://www.theguardian.com/society/2021/apr/08/ted-brown-the-man-who-held-a-mass-kiss-in-and-made-history; Thomas Stichbury, "Gay Liberation Front's Ted Brown Recalls Laying the Foundations for the Fight for LGBTQ Rights," *attitude*, July 8, 2020, https://www.attitude.co.uk/culture/sexuality/gay-liberation-fronts-ted-brown-recalls-laying-the-foundations-for-the-fight-for-lgbtq-rights-301417.

3 **February 2, 1988** "Lesbians Protest Against Section 28," Working Class History, last edited July 19, 2022, https://stories.workingclasshistory.com/article/9181/lesbians-protest-against-section-28.

4 **February 3, 1975** Josephine Donovan, *The Lexington Six: Lesbian and Gay Resistance in 1970s America* (University of Massachusetts Press, 2020).

5 **February 4, 2004** Rose Arce, "Massachusetts Court Upholds Same-Sex Marriage," *CNN*, February 6, 2004, archived at https://web.archive.org/web/20040622232846/https://www.cnn.com/2004/LAW/02/04/gay.marriage/.

6   **February 5, 1981** Jamie Bradburn, "Toronto Bathhouse Raids (1981)," *Canadian Encyclopedia*, April 17, 2018, https://www.thecanadianencyclopedia.ca/en/article/toronto-feature-bathhouse-raids.

7   **February 6, 1936** Neal Broverman, "Dancer, Professor, Queer Activist Angela Bowen Dead at 82," *Advocate*, July 22, 2018, https://www.advocate.com/people/2018/7/22/dancer-professor-queer-activist-angela-bowen-dead-82.

8   **February 7, 1970** Paulo Murillo, "'Fagots Stay Out': Protest at Barney's Beanery 53 Years Ago Today," *Los Angeles Blade*, February 7, 2023, https://www.losangelesblade.com/2023/02/07/fagots-stay-out-protest-at-barneys-beanery-53-years-ago-today/.

9   **February 8, 1917** Robin Washington, "Remembering the Only Jew on the First Freedom Ride—75 Years Ago," *Forward*, April 21, 2022, https://forward.com/culture/500331/remembering-the-only-jew-on-the-first-freedom-ride-75-years-ago/.

10 **February 9, 1874** Diane Ellen Hamer, "Amy Lowell Wasn't Writing About Flowers," *Gay & Lesbian Review Worldwide*, July–August 2004, https://glreview.org/article/article-1347/.

11 **February 10, 1990** Benjamin Lee, "'There Was a Lot of Panic': Behind the First Movies to Tackle the Aids Crisis," *Guardian*, June 21, 2018, https://www.theguardian.com/film/2018/jun/21/there-was-a-lot-of-panic-behind-the-first-movies-to-tackle-the-aids-crisis.

12 **February 11, 1916** Andrew Glass, "Emma Goldman Snubs Comstock law, Feb. 11, 1916," *Politico*, February 2, 2009, https://www.politico.com/story/2009/02/emma-goldman-snubs-comstock-law-feb-11-1916-018679; Amanda Davis, "Emma Goldman Residence & Mother Earth Office," NYC LGBT Historic Sites Project, May 2018, https://www.nyclgbtsites.org/site/emma-goldman-residence-mother-earth-office/.

13 **February 11, 1954** "Tefía Concentration Camp Opened," Working Class History, last edited July 19, 2022, https://stories.workingclasshistory.com/article/8291/tef%C3%ADa-concentration-camp-opened.

14 **February 11, 1967** "Black Cat Protest," Working Class History, last edited July 19, 2022, https://stories.workingclasshistory.com/article/8292/black-cat-protest.

15 **February 12, 1928** "2013 Leather Hall of Fame Inductee—The Mayor of Folsom Street: The Life and Times of Alan Selby, aka Mr. S.," Leather Hall of Fame, accessed February 7, 2025, https://www.leatherhalloffame.com/inductees-list/18-alan-selby.

16 **February 13, 2025** Zane McNeill, "Stonewall Monument's Transgender History Scrubbed by Trump Administration," *Truthout*, February 14, 2025, https://truthout.org/articles/stonewall-monuments-transgender-history-scrubbed-by-trump-administration/. Reprinted in modified form under Creative Commons (CC BY-NC-ND 4.0).

17 **February 14, 1991** Charles E. Brown, "Telling Students It's Okay to Be Gay—Queer Nation Protests on Valentine's Day," *Seattle Times*, February 15, 1991, https://archive.seattletimes.com/archive/?date=19910215&slug=1266422.

18 **February 15, 1820** Lillian Faderman, *To Believe in Women: What Lesbians Have Done for America; A History* (Harper, 2000).

19 **February 16, 2020** "Black & Pink Officially Opens Lydon House," *KMTV 3 News Now*, February 17, 2020, https://www.3newsnow.com/news/local-news/black-pink-officially-opens-lydon-house.

20 **February 17, 1977** "Pickets Against CBC Halifax," Queer Events, accessed December 5, 2023, https://www.queerevents.ca/queer-history/canadian-history-timeline.

21 **February 17, 1994** "Montreal's Katakombes Bar Raids," Queer Events, accessed December 5, 2023, https://www.queerevents.ca/queer-history/canadian-history-timeline.

22 **February 18, 1934** "Audre Lorde Born," Working Class History, last edited July 19, 2022, https://stories.workingclasshistory.com/article/8968/audre-lorde-born.

23 **February 18, 1966** Michael Annetta, "February 18 in LGBTQ History," Lavender Effect, February 18, 2013, https://thelavendereffect.org/2013/02/18/february-18-in-lgbtq-history.

24 **February 19, 2002** "Sylvia Rivera Dies," Working Class History, last edited October 31, 2022, https://stories.workingclasshistory.com/article/11069/sylvia-rivera-dies.

25 **February 20, 1988** "Demonstration Against Section 28," Working Class History, last edited July 19, 2022, https://stories.workingclasshistory.com/article/9263/demonstration-against-section-28.

26 **February 20, 2023** CC23 Trans Active Collective, "CC23 Trans Action Collective Demands," press release, accessed July 11, 2024, https://docs.google.com/document/d/e/2PACX-1vSdtwQZg3lQC4LbZM7JR_lrKx6oLA7CQRhyUqLnXHUve5GWTArg-Hk4hUgeX7hoI-FbnhXwG6YjsZKF/pub; Heather Cassell, "Protest and Resolve Mark Creating Change 35 in San Francisco," *Gay City News*, February 23, 2023, https://gaycitynews.com/protest-resolve-mark-creating-change-35-in-san-francisco/.

27 **February 21, 1903** Michael Annetta, "February 21 in LGBTQ History," Lavender Effect, February 21, 2013, https://thelavendereffect.org/2013/02/21/february-21-in-lgbtq-history.

28 **February 21, 1933** Chardine Taylor-Stone, "The Radical Politics of Nina Simone," *Tribune*, April 21, 2021, https://tribunemag.co.uk/2021/04/the-radical-politics-of-nina-simone.

29 **February 22, 1943** "Feb. 22, 1943: White Rose Members Executed," Zinn Education Project, accessed July 11, 2024, https://www.zinnedproject.org/news/tdih/white-rose-members-executed; "Hans Scholl—Nominee," Legacy Project, accessed March 22, 2025, https://legacyprojectchicago.org/person/hans-scholl.

30 **February 23, 1943** Tom Hayden and Carl Wittman, An Interracial Movement of the Poor? (Students for a Democratic Society, 1963), http://www.sds-1960s.org/Interracial-Movement-Poor.pdf; Carl Wittman, *A Gay Manifesto* (Red Butterfly, 1970); Liz Highleyman, "Who Was Carl Wittman?," *Seattle Gay News*, May 5, 2006, https://archive.ph/20170422030509/http://www.sgn.org/sgnnews34_18/page30.cfm; "Carl Whittman—Nominee," Legacy Project, accessed February 7, 2025, https://legacyprojectchicago.org/person/carl-wittman.

31 **February 24, 2025** Joseph Gedeon, "US Threatens Permanent Visa Bans on Trans Athletes Based on Sex Markers," *Guardian*, February 25, 2025, https://www.theguardian.com/us-news/2025/feb/25/visa-ban-transgender-athletes.

32 **February 25, 1982** "First in the Nation—Wisconsin's Gay Rights Law," *Now@MPL* (Milwaukee Public Library blog), June 18, 2015, https://www.mpl.org/blog/now/first-in-the-nation-wisconsin-s-gay-rights-law.

33 **February 26, 1960** "February," SF Gay History, accessed February 11, 2025, https://www.sfgayhistory.com/timeline/this-month/february; Craig Scott, "The Great SF 'Gayola' Scandal," *Bay Area Reporter*, March 10, 2010, https://www.ebar.com/story.php?ch=opinion&sc=guest_opinion&id=235818.

34 **February 26, 2024** Jo Yurcaba, "Oklahoma Students Walk Out After Trans Student's Death to Protest Bullying Policies," *NBC News*, February 26, 2024, https://www.nbcnews.com/nbc-out/out-news/nex-benedict-death-protest-bullying-owasso-oklahoma-rcna140501.

35 **February 27, 2004** Jonathan Wald, "New York Town's Mayor Marries Same-Sex Couples," *CNN*, February 28, 2004, archived at https://web.archive.org/web/20040405075259/http://www.cnn.com/2004/US/Northeast/02/27/ny.samesex.marriage/; "February in LGBT History," *Hotspots!*, February 14, 2024, https://hotspotsmagazine.com/2024/02/14/february-in-lgbt-history/.

36 **February 28, 1994** "February," SF Gay History.

37 **February 29, 1940** "Hattie McDaniel Segregated Oscars," Working Class History, last edited November 28, 2023, https://stories.workingclasshistory.com/article/12527/hattie-mcdaniel-segregated-oscars; Mikelle Street, "These Are the Queer Folk Netflix's 'Hollywood' Is Based On," *Out*, May 1, 2020, https://www.out.com/television/2020/5/01/these-are-queer-folk-netflixs-hollywoods-based#rebelltitem1.

March

1   **March 1, 1990** "NY Disaster Zone in Albany," ACT UP Oral History Project, accessed February 11, 2025, https://www.actuporalhistory.org/lc-archive/day-of-desperation-in-albany.

2   **March 1, 2023** James Factora, "Hundreds of Iowa Students Staged a 'We Say Gay' School Walkout," *Them*, March 3, 2023, https://www.them.us/story/iowa-we-say-gay-student-walkout.

3   **March 2, 1982** "March," SF Gay History, accessed February 11, 2025, https://www.sfgayhistory.com/timeline/this-month/march.

4   **March 3, 1973** "March," SF Gay History; David-Elijah Nahmod, "Before Staying at Home, LGBTs Recalled Castro Businesses," *Bay Area Reporter*, April 1, 2020, https://www.ebar.com/story/290140/redirect/News/News/.

5   **March 3, 1970** Craig Jennex and Nisha Eswaran, *Out North: An Archive of Queer Activism and Kinship in Canada* (Figure 1 Publishing, 2020); Ron Levy, "Jearld Moldenhauer," *Canadian Encyclopedia*, last edited September 24, 2024, https://www.thecanadianencyclopedia.ca/en/article/jearld-moldenhauer.

6   **March 4, 1948** "Jean O'Leary, 57, Former Nun Who Became a Lesbian Activist, Dies," *New York Times*, June 7, 2005, https://www.nytimes.com/2005/06/07/us/jean-oleary-57-former-nun-who-became-a-lesbian-activist-dies.html.

7   **March 4, 2023** "'Stop Cop City' Week of Action Begins in Atlanta," *Unicorn Riot*, March 4, 2023, https://unicornriot.ninja/2023/stop-cop-city-week-of-action-begins-in-atlanta/.

8   **March 5, 1971** Michael Sibalis, "Gay Liberation Comes to France: The *Front Homosexuel d'Action Révolutionnaire*," in *French History and Civilization*, vol. 1 (George Rudé Society, 2005), https://h-france.net/rude/wp-content/uploads/2017/08/vol1_Sibalis2.pdf.

9   **March 6, 1987** "20 Years Later, GLAA Remembers Mel Boozer," Gay and Lesbian Activist Alliance, accessed July 11, 2024, http://www.glaa.org/archive/2000/boozer0816.shtml.

10 **March 6, 2023** Samantha Riedel, "Four Florida College Students Were Arrested at a Protest Against Ron DeSantis," *Them*, March 8, 2023, https://www.them.us/story/florida-college-students-arrested-ron-desantis-protest; Mark Schreiner, "Protestors Accuse USF Police of Abuse as Four Are Arrested," *WUSF*, March 7, 2023, https://www.wusf.org/university-beat/2023-03-07/protestors-accuse-usf-police-abuse-four-arrested.

11 **March 7, 2023** Orion Rummler, "Oklahoma Legislature Censures Nonbinary Lawmaker as Proposed Gender-Affirming Care Bans Move Forward," *19th*, March 8, 2023, https://19thnews.org/2023/03/oklahoma-censures-nonbinary-lawmaker-mauree-turner; "Rep. Mauree Turner Censured After Hiding Fugitive Wanted for Alleged Assault at State Capitol," *KOCO 5 News*, March 7, 2023, https://www.koco.com/article/oklahoma-state-representative-mauree-turner-censure-harboring-fugitive/43235638.

12 **March 8, 1970** "Diego Viñales Injured," Working Class History, last edited July 20, 2022, https://stories.workingclasshistory.com/article/10730/diego-vi%C3%B1ales-injured; Erin Blakemore, "Zapping: The Boisterous Protest Tactic That Ignited Early LGBTQ Activism," *National Geographic*, June 9, 2021, archived at https://web.archive.org/web/20210609195315/https://www.nationalgeographic.com/history/article/zapping-the-boisterous-protest-tactic-that-ignited-early-lgbtq-activism; Jay Shockley, "The Snake Pit," NYC LGBT Historic Sites Project, March 2017, https://www.nyclgbtsites.org/site/the-snake-pit/.

13 **March 9, 1969** "Dover Hotel," Queer Maps, accessed September 1, 2024, https://www.queermaps.org/place/dover-hotel.

14 **March 10, 1867** "Lillian Wald House," US National Park Service, accessed March 21, 2024, https://www.nps.gov/places/lillian-wald-house.htm.

15 **March 10, 1971** Guy Hocquenghem, *Gay Liberation After May '68* (Duke University Press, 2022); Sibalis, "Gay Liberation."

16 **March 11, 2004** "March," SF Gay History; "Marriage Equality at the U.S. Supreme Court," Center for American Progress, March 20, 2013, https://www.americanprogress.org/article/marriage-equality-at-the-u-s-supreme-court/.

17 **March 12, 2020** Brakkton Booker, "Judge Orders Chelsea Manning Released from Jail," *NPR*, March 12, 2020, https://www.npr.org/2020/03/12/814974205/chelsea-manning-recovering-after-suicide-attempt-in-jail-lawyers-say.

18   **March 13, 1990** "'Paris Is Burning' Premieres in New York," History.com, last updated March 10, 2024, https://www.history.com/this-day-in-history/paris-is-burning-documentary-premieres-in-theaters.

19   **March 14, 1868** "Magnus Hirschfeld," Holocaust Encyclopedia, United States Holocaust Memorial Museum, accessed January 2, 2024, https://encyclopedia.ushmm.org/content/en/article/magnus-hirschfeld-2; Laurie Marhoefer, *Racism and the Making of Gay Rights: A Sexologist, His Student, and the Empire of Queer Love* (University of Toronto Press, 2023).

20   **March 14, 1971** "March on Albany: Gay Liberation Takes Its Fight to New York's State Capital," The Center: The Lesbian, Gay, Bisexual, and Transgender Community Center, on the Google Arts & Culture website, accessed February 11, 2025, https://artsandculture.google.com/story/march-on-albany-the-new-york-gay-and-lesbian-community-center/zAWxc6rL3sUqJg?hl=en.

21   **March 14, 2024** Matt Tracy, "Joan Gibbs, Renowned Lesbian Activist and Attorney, Dies at 71," *Gay City News*, March 25, 2024, https://gaycitynews.com/joan-gibbs-act-up-activist-attorney-dies-71/.

22   **March 15, 1942** Jonathan Ned Katz, "Envisioning the World We Make, Social-Historical Construction, a Model, a Manifesto," OutHistory, accessed February 11, 2025, https://outhistory.org/exhibits/show/katz-writing-work/katz-vision-model.

23   **March 16, 1987** Young Joon Kwak, "Mark Aguhar," *Brooklyn Rail*, July–August 2016, https://brooklynrail.org/2016/07/criticspage/mark-aguhar; Roy Pérez, "Proximity: On the Work of Mark Aguhar," in *Trap Door: Trans Cultural Production and the Politics of Visibility*, ed. Reina Gossett, Eric A. Stanley, and Johanna Burton (MIT Press, 2017), 283–93; see Mark Aguhar's blog, *Blogging for Brown Gurls*, at https://calloutqueen-blog.tumblr.com.

24   **March 17, 1912** "Bayard Rustin," Martin Luther King Jr. Research and Education Institute, accessed December 14, 2023, https://kinginstitute.stanford.edu/encyclopedia/rustin-bayard.

25   **March 18, 1967** "Stonewall: The Basics," fact sheet, Stonewall 50 Consortium, 2019, https://stonewall50consortium.org/stonewallfactsheet.pdf.

26   **March 19, 1983** Patrick Freyne and Una Mullally, "Ireland's First Pride Parade, 40 Years Ago: 'We Had to Suffer the Beatings, the Spittings, the Jeerings, Just for the Right to Walk Down the Street Holding Hands,'" *Irish Times*, June 23, 2023, https://www.irishtimes.com/life-style/people/2023/06/24/40-years-of-pride-we-had-to-suffer-the-beatings-the-spittings-the-jeerings-just-for-the-right-to-walk-down-the-street-holding-hands/.

27   **March 20, 1990** "Queer Nation NY History," Queer Nation NY, accessed April 7, 2024, https://queernationny.org/history.

28   **March 21, 2025** Joe Kottke, "University of Maine Complies with Policies Restricting Trans Sports Participation," *NBC News*, March 21, 2025, https://www.nbcnews.com/nbc-out/out-politics-and-policy/university-maine-complies-policies-restricting-trans-sports-participat-rcna197536.

29   **March 22, 1972** Michael Annetta, "March 22 in LGBTQ History," Lavender Effect, March 22, 2013, https://thelavendereffect.org/2013/03/22/march-22-in-lgbtq-history.

30   **March 23, 2011** Tim Murphy, "Remembering Actress and AIDS Activist Elizabeth Taylor," *POZ*, March 23, 2024, https://www.poz.com/article/remembering-actress-aids-activist-elizabeth-taylor.

31   **March 24, 1987** "ACT UP Wall St Protest," Working Class History, last edited July 19, 2022, https://stories.workingclasshistory.com/article/9675/act-up-wall-st-protest.

32   **March 24, 2018** Jackson Howard, "How Queer Activists Rose Up at New York City's March for Our Lives," *Them*, March 25, 2018, https://www.them.us/story/queer-activists-at-march-for-our-lives-nyc.

33   **March 25, 1998** "Our Team," Trevor Project, accessed November 2, 2023, https://www.thetrevorproject.org/our-team/.

34   **March 26, 1977** "March," SF Gay History; Trudy Ring, "Jimmy Carter, First President to Meet with Gay Rights Activists, Dead at 100," *Advocate*, February 18, 2024, https://www.advocate.com/politics/jimmy-carter-dead-100.

35   **March 27, 1943** "Amsterdam Population Registry Destroyed," Working Class History, last edited July 20, 2022, https://stories.workingclasshistory.com/article/9931/amsterdam-population-registry-destroyed.

36   **March 27, 2023** Bryan Hughes, Act Relating to Restricting Certain Sexually Oriented Performances on Public Property, on the Premises of a Commercial Enterprise, or in the Presence of a Child, S.B. 12, Texas Senate (2023), https://capitol.texas.gov/tlodocs/88R/billtext/pdf/SB00012I.pdf#navpanes=0; Candice Bernd, "Texas Pushes Draconian Drag Ban Bills Amid Unprecedented Assault on Trans Rights," *Truthout*, March 31, 2023, https://truthout.org/articles/texas-pushes-draconian-drag-ban-bills-amid-unprecedented-assault-on-trans-rights/.

37   **March 28, 1969** Bill Brent, "Society for Individual Rights (SIR)," FoundSF: The San Francisco Digital History Archive, originally published in *Black Sheets* magazine, 1998, accessed February 11, 2025, https://www.foundsf.org/index.php?title=Society_for_Individual_Rights_(SIR); Michael Annetta, "March 28 in LGBTQ History," Lavender Effect, March 28, 2013, https://thelavendereffect.org/2013/03/28/march-28-in-lgbtq-history.

38   **March 29, 1932** Terry Gross, "This Forgotten Women's Prison Helped Cement Greenwich Village's Queer Identity," interview with Hugh Ryan, *NPR*, May 16, 2022, https://www.npr.org/2022/05/16/1098786259/hugh-ryan-queer-history-womens-house-of-detention. Ryan's book on prison is *The Women's House of Detention: A Queer History of a Forgotten Prison* (Bold Type Books, 2022).

39   **March 29, 1973** Jill Johnston, "Was Lesbian Separatism Inevitable?," *Gay and Lesbian Review Worldwide*, March–April 2006, archived August 13, 2007, at https://web.archive.org/web/20070813001841/http://glreview.com/issues/13.2/13.2-johnston.php.

40   **March 30, 1964** Jennex and Eswaran, *Out North*.

41   **March 31, 2022** Shah Meer Baloch, "Pakistan's Transgender Women Protest Against Rising Tide of Violence," *Guardian*, April 1, 2022, https://www.theguardian.com/global-development/2022/apr/01/pakistan-transgender-women-protest-against-rising-tide-of-violence.

42   **March 31, 2023** Jessie Pang, "Hong Kong Transgender Protestors Say Government Not Abiding by Landmark Ruling," *Reuters*, March 31, 2023, https://www.reuters.com/world/china/hong-kong-transgender-protesters-say-government-is-not-abiding-by-landmark-2023-03-31/.

43   **March 31, 2024** "Latest," QUIT!: Queers Undermining Israeli Terrorism!, accessed April 7, 2024, https://quitpalestine.org/latest/.

April

1   **April 1977** Combahee River Collective, "The Combahee River Collective Statement," Black Past, accessed February 12, 2025, https://www.blackpast.org/african-american-history/combahee-river-collective-statement-1977.

2   **April 1, 1969** "Homepage of Homosexuals Intransigent!," *Mr. Gay Pride* (blog), accessed February 11, 2025, https://mrgaypride.tripod.com.

3   **April 1, 1998** Dale Evva Gelfand, *Coretta Scott King: Civil Rights Activist* (Chelsea House, 2007); "Gay Group Honors Coretta Scott King," *Advocate*, November 22, 2002, https://www.advocate.com/news/2002/11/26/gay-group-honors-coretta-scott-king-7048.

4   **April 2, 1974** Julie Compton, "Meet the Lesbian Who Made Political History Years Before Harvey Milk," *NBC News*, April 2, 2020, https://www.nbcnews.com/feature/nbc-out/meet-lesbian-who-made-political-history-years-harvey-milk-n1174941.

5   **April 3, 1942** "April," SF Gay History, accessed February 11, 2025, https://www.sfgayhistory.com/timeline/this-month/april.

6   **April 4, 1928** "LGBTQ+ History Month Profile: Maya Angelou," Falmouth & Exeter

Students' Union, accessed April 7, 2024, https://www.thesu.org.uk/news/article/6013/LGBTQ-History-Month-profile-Maya-Angelou.

7   **April 4, 1981** Michael Annetta, "April 4 in LGBTQ History," Lavender Effect, April 4, 2013, https://thelavendereffect.org/2013/04/04/april-4-in-lgbtq-history; Safe Space Alliance (@safe_space_alliance), "On April 4, 1981, the first national march for gay rights in France took place in Paris led by CUARH (Comité d'urgence anti-répression homosexuelle)," Instagram, April 4, 2024, https://www.instagram.com/safe_space_alliance/p/C5VCeGWuKLz/.

8   **April 5, 1997** "Allen Ginsberg Dies," Working Class History, last edited July 20, 2022, https://stories.workingclasshistory.com/article/10488/allen-ginsberg-dies.

9   **April 6** "International Asexuality Day (IAD)," International Asexuality Day, accessed February 11, 2025, https://internationalasexualityday.org/en/.

10   **April 6, 2001** "Robert Sloane Basker," Chicago LGBT Hall of Fame, accessed February 11, 2025, https://chicagolgbthalloffame.org/basker-robert/.

11   **April 7, 1872** Nadine Jelsing, "Physician, Lesbian, Radical Labor Activist—The Passions of Portland's Dr. Marie Equi," *OPB*, March 13, 2023, https://www.opb.org/article/2023/03/13/portland-oregon-history-dr-marie-equi-lesbian-labor-activist/.

12   **April 7, 1891** Bert Hansen, "Public Careers and Private Sexuality: Some Gay and Lesbian Lives in the History of Medicine and Public Health," *American Journal of Public Health* 92, no. 1 (January 2002): 36–44, https://doi.org/10.2105/AJPH.92.1.36.

13   **April 7, 1912** "Radically Gay: The Life of Harry Hay," San Francisco Public Library, accessed February 11, 2025, https://sfpl.org/locations/main-library/lgbtqia-center/radically-gay; Dudley Clendinen, "Harry Hay, Early Proponent of Gay Rights, Dies at 90," *New York Times*, October 25, 2002, https://www.nytimes.com/2002/10/25/us/harry-hay-early-proponent-of-gay-rights-dies-at-90.html.

14   **April 7, 2018** "Russian Police Break Up Gay Pride Protest in St. Petersburg," *Reuters*, April 8, 2018, https://www.euronews.com/2018/08/04/russian-police-break-up-gay-pride-protest-in-st-petersburg.

15   **April 7, 2023** Amanda Friedman, "UF 'Inject-In' Protest Shows Support for Gender-Affirming Care," *Alligator*, April 10, 2023, https://www.alligator.org/article/2023/04/gender-affirming-care-protest.

16   **April 8, 1974** "April in LGBT History," *Hotspots! Magazine*, April 9, 2024, https://hotspotsmagazine.com/2024/04/09/april-in-lgbt-history; "Discrimination Against Homosexuals," policy adopted by the APA Council of Representatives on January 24–26, 1975, American Psychological Association, accessed March 27, 2025, https://www.apa.org/about/policy/discrimination.

17   **April 9, 1936** Mackenzie Martin, "Before Stonewall, This Kansas City Activist Helped Unite the National Gay Rights Movement," *KCUR*, June 1, 2022, https://www.kcur.org/arts-life/2022-06-01/before-stonewall-this-kansas-city-activist-helped-unite-the-national-gay-rights-movement.

18   **April 9, 2020** "April," SF Gay History; "Phyllis Lyon & Del Martin," California Museum, accessed February 11, 2025, https://californiamuseum.org/inductee/phyllis-lyon-del-martin/.

19   **April 10, 1880** "LGBT History Month—Frances Perkins—U.S. Cabinet Member," *Erie Gay News*, n.d., accessed March 15, 2024, https://www.eriegaynews.com/news/article.php?recordid=201510francesperkins.

20   **April 11, 1964** Craig Jennex and Nisha Eswaran, *Out North: An Archive of Queer Activism and Kinship in Canada* (Figure 1 Publishing, 2020).

21   **April 11, 1978** "April," SF Gay History.

22   **April 12, 1888** Kittredge Cherry, "William Dorsey Swann: Former Slave Celebrated as First Drag Queen," Q Spirit, last updated April 8, 2024, https://qspirit.net/william-dorsey-swann-queer; Marjorie Morgan, "From Slavery to Voguing: The House of Swann," National Museums Liverpool, accessed February 11, 2025, https://www.liverpoolmuseums.org.uk/stories/slavery-voguing-house-of-swann.

23 **April 13, 1970** Jay Shockley, "Gay Activists Alliance Zap at the Metropolitan Museum of Art," NYC LGBT Historic Sites Project, August 2020, https://www.nyclgbtsites.org/site/gay-activists-alliance-zap-at-the-metropolitan-museum-of-art/.

24 **April 13, 1990** "Queer Nation NY History," Queer Nation NY, accessed April 7, 2024, https://queernationny.org/history.

25 **April 14, 1954** Michael Annetta, "April 14 in LGBTQ History," Lavender Effect, April 14, 2013, https://thelavendereffect.org/2013/04/14/april-14-in-lgbtq-history.

26 **April 14, 1964** Mac Glackin, "Pride Profile: Rachel Carson—Queer Marine Biologist, Author, and Environmentalist," Clean Water Action, June 20, 2023, https://cleanwater.org/2023/06/20/pride-profile-rachel-carson-queer-marine-biologist-author-and-environmentalist.

27 **April 15–16, 2000** "ACT UP Accomplishments 1987–2012," ACT UP, accessed June 15, 2023, https://actupny.com/actions/.

28 **April 15, 2014** Ryan Conrad, ed., *Against Equality: Queer Revolution, Not Mere Inclusion* (AK Press, 2014). More information on the book can be found at https://www.akpress.org/againstequality.html.

29 **April 16, 1882** Andrew S. Dolkart, "Rose Schneiderman Residence," NYC LGBT Historic Sites Project, September 2022, https://www.nyclgbtsites.org/site/rose-schneiderman-residence/; Annelise Orleck, "Rose Schneiderman," Jewish Women's Archive, accessed March 15, 2024, https://jwa.org/encyclopedia/article/schneiderman-rose#pid-1600.

30 **April 16, 1892** Von Oliver Noffke, "Was wurde aus Dora?," *RBB24*, January 6, 2023, https://www.rbb24.de/panorama/beitrag/2023/05/dora-richter-magnus-hirschfeld-berlin-transsexualitaet-institut-fuer-sexualwissenschaft.html.

31 **April 16, 1967** "Essex Hemphill," Poetry Foundation, accessed April 7, 2024, https://www.poetryfoundation.org/poets/essex-hemphill.

32 **April 16, 1977** Neil Amdur, "Renee Richards Ruled Eligible for U.S. Open," *New York Times*, August 17, 1977, https://www.nytimes.com/1977/08/17/archives/renee-richards-ruled-eligible-for-us-open-ruling-makes-renee.html.

33 **April 17, 1943** "Little Palace Cafeteria Sit-In," Working Class History, last edited July 19, 2022, https://stories.workingclasshistory.com/article/8851/little-palace-cafeteria-sit-in.

34 **April 17, 1965** "What It Was Like at the First Gay Rights Demonstration Outside White House 50 Years Ago," *ABC News*, April 17, 2015, https://abcnews.go.com/Politics/gay-rights-demonstration-white-house-50-years-ago/story?id=30379792.

35 **April 18, 1970** Trudy Ring, "Legendary 1970 Gay Dance Party Honored by Chicago Pride Concert," *Advocate*, June 26, 2019, https://www.advocate.com/pride/2019/6/26/legendary-1970-gay-dance-party-honored-chicago-pride-concert.

36 **April 18, 2010** Editors of *The Black Agenda Review*, "Manifesto: African LGBTI Manifesto/Declaration, April 18, 2010," *Black Agenda Report*, March 10, 2021, https://www.blackagendareport.com/manifesto-african-lgbti-manifestodeclaration-april-18-2010.

37 **April 19, 1978** Michael Annetta, "April 19 in LGBTQ History," Lavender Effect, April 19, 2013, https://thelavendereffect.org/2013/04/19/april-19-in-lgbtq-history; Sally Jo Sorensen, "Crabby Old Chapter in MN's March Toward LGBTQ Rights: 1978 St. Paul Ordinance Vote," *Twin Cities Daily Planet*, January 3, 2013, https://www.tcdailyplanet.net/crabby-old-chapter-mns-march-toward-lgbtq-rights-1978-st-paul-ordinance-vote/.

38 **April 20, 1990** "Queer Nation NY History."

39 **April 21, 1966** Andrew S. Dolkart, "Julius'," NYC LGBT Historic Sites Project, March 2017, last revised December 2022, https://www.nyclgbtsites.org/site/julius/.

40 **April 21, 1982** "Glad Day Bookshop Raid," Queer Events, accessed April 7, 2024, https://www.queerevents.ca/queer-history/canadian-history-timeline; Marcus McCann, "Fifty Years of Defending Queer Expression," Freedom to Read, February 27, 2019, https://www.freedomtoread.ca/articles/fifty-years-of-defending-queer-expression/.

41 **April 22, 1944** "Thompson's Cafeteria Sit-In," Working Class History, last edited July 19, 2022, https://stories.workingclasshistory.com/article/9444/thompson's-cafeteria-sit-in.

42   **April 22, 1973** "Chile's First LGBT+ Protest," Working Class History, last edited April 22, 2023, https://stories.workingclasshistory.com/article/11256/chile's-first-lgbt+-protest.

43   **April 23, 1946** "Passages Activist Arthur Gursch Dies at 72," *Windy City Times*, July 4, 2018, https://www.windycitytimes.com/lgbt/PASSAGES-Activist-Arthur-Gursch-dies-at-72/63423.html.

44   **April 23, 1967** Michael Annetta, "April 23 in LGBTQ History," Lavender Effect, April 23, 2013, https://thelavendereffect.org/2013/04/23/april-23-in-lgbtq-history; Dina Mazina and Rebecca DiBrienza, "Student Homophile League/Gay Liberation Front," OutHistory, accessed March 22, 2025, https://outhistory.org/exhibits/show/queer-youth-campus-media/on-college-campuses/glf; Andrew S. Dolkart, "Student Homophile League at Earl Hall, Columbia University," NYC LGBT Historic Sites Project, last revised March 2018, https://www.nyclgbtsites.org/site/columbia-university/.

45   **April 24, 1941** Victoria A. Brownworth, "Black History Month: Ernestine Eckstein," *Philadelphia Gay News*, February 9, 2022, https://epgn.com/2022/02/09/black-history-month-ernestine-eckstein/.

46   **April 24, 1993** "History of the Dyke March," NYC Dyke March, accessed February 27, 2025, https://www.nycdykemarch.com/history; amy c. branner, Laura Butterbaugh, and April Jackson, "There Was a Dyke March?" *Off Our Backs* 24, no. 8 (1994): 1–20, http://www.jstor.org/stable/20834872.

47   **April 25, 1965** Susan Ferentinos, "Dewey's Lunch Counter Sit-In," Encyclopedia of Greater Philadelphia, March 16, 2022, https://philadelphiaencyclopedia.org/essays/deweys-lunch-counter-sit-in/.

48   **April 25, 1993** "LGBTQ March on Washington," Working Class History, last edited July 19, 2022, https://stories.workingclasshistory.com/article/9709/lgbtq-march-on-washington.

49   **April 25, 2016** Euan McKirdy, "Protesters Arrested During North Carolina 'Bathroom Bill' Demonstrations," *CNN*, April 26, 2016, https://www.cnn.com/2016/04/26/us/north-carolina-transgender-protest-arrests/index.html.

50   **April 25, 2023** Meredith Deliso, "Drag Queens Protest Against Florida Law LGBTQ Advocates Say Targets Drag Shows," *ABC News*, April 25, 2023, https://abcnews.go.com/US/protest-held-florida-law-lgbtq-advocates-targets-drag/story?id=98830404.

51   **April 26, 1968** "April 26, 1968: Kiyoshi Kuromiya Led Protest of Vietnam War Napalm," Zinn Education Project, accessed February 27, 2025, https://www.zinnedproject.org/news/tdih/kiyoshi-kuromiya-protests-napalm.

52   **April 27, 1953** "LGBTQIA+ Federal Employment in the Records at the National Archives," US National Archives and Records Administration, accessed April 7, 2024, https://www.archives.gov/research/lgbt/federal-employment.

53   **April 28, 1990** "Queer Nation NY History."

54   **April 29, 1945** "Liberation of Dachau," Working Class History, last edited July 20, 2022, https://stories.workingclasshistory.com/article/10070/liberation-of-dachau.

55   **April 30, 1989** Michael Annetta, "April 30 in LGBTQ History," Lavender Effect, April 30, 2013, https://thelavendereffect.org/2013/04/30/april-30-in-lgbtq-history.

May

1   **May 1, 1996** Urvashi Vaid, *Virtual Equality: The Mainstreaming of Gay and Lesbian Liberation* (Penguin Random House, 1995).

2   **May 1, 1997** Cathy Cohen, "Punks, Bulldaggers, and Welfare Queens: The Radical Potential of Queer Politics?," *GLQ* 3, no. 4 (1997): 437–65, https://doi.org/10.1215/9780822387220-003.

3   **May 1, 2016** L. Leigh Ann van der Merwe, "African Trans Feminist Charter," *TSQ: Transgender Studies Quarterly* 3, nos. 1–2 (2016): 272–75, https://doi.org/10.1215/23289252-3334511.

4   **May 2, 2023** Dade Phelan (@DadePhelan), "Rules matter in the TX House. Today's outbursts in the gallery were a breach of decorum & continued after I warned that such behaviors would not be tolerated. There will always be differing perspectives, but in

our chamber, we will debate those differences w/ respect," X, May 2, 2023, https://twitter.com/DadePhelan/status/1653565723116032000; Samantha Riedel, "Texas Police Forcibly Detained LGBTQ+ Protestors During a Debate Over Anti-Trans Law," *Them*, May 3, 2023, https://www.them.us/story/texas-anti-trans-law-police-clear-house-gallery.

5   **May 3, 1879** Andrew S. Dolkart, "Rose Schneiderman Residence," NYC LGBT Historic Sites Project, September 2022, https://www.nyclgbtsites.org/site/rose-schneiderman-residence/; "Maud Swartz Obituary," Newspapers.com, from *The Brooklyn Eagle*, February 23, 1937, accessed February 11, 2025, https://www.newspapers.com/article/the-brooklyn-daily-eagle-maud-swartz-obi/17905969/.

6   **May 3, 2023** Samantha Riedel, "Police Arrested 14 Protestors Who Occupied Florida Governor Ron DeSantis' Office," *Them*, May 5, 2023, https://www.them.us/story/ron-de-santis-office-protestors-arrested-anti-lgbtq-legislation.

7   **May 4, 1958** "LGBT+ History Month—Meet Keith Haring, Pop Artist and AIDS Awareness Advocate," Open Table, February 2, 2022, https://opentable.lgbt/our-blog/2022/2/2/lgbt-history-month-meet-keith-haring-pop-artist-and-aids-awareness-advocate.

8   **May 5, 1725** "Leendert Hasenbosch Marooned," Working Class History, last edited July 19, 2022, https://stories.workingclasshistory.com/article/7963/leendert-hasenbosch-marooned.

9   **May 6, 1933** "6 May 1933: Looting of the Institute of Sexology," Holocaust Memorial Day Trust, accessed February 11, 2025, https://www.hmd.org.uk/resource/6-may-1933-looting-of-the-institute-of-sexology/.

10   **May 7, 1365** "Gay History—May 7, 1365: 15 Year Old Giovanni di Giovanni Tortured and Killed for the Crime of Sodomy in Italy," Back2Stonewall, May 7, 2023, archived at https://web.archive.org/web/20230529082633/http://www.back2stonewall.com/2023/05/lgbt-history-may-7-1365-15-year-giovanni-di-giovanni-tortured-killed-sodomy.html.

11   **May 8, 1920** "Happy Tom of Finland Day! May 8, 1920: Iconic Gay Artist Tom of Finland (Touko Laaksonen) Born," Back2Stonewall, May 8 2023, archived at https://web.archive.org/web/20230528232436/http://www.back2stonewall.com/2023/05/gay-history-may-8-1920-iconic-gay-artist-tom-of-finland-touko-laaksonen-born.html.

12   **May 9, 1943** ACT UP Philadelphia, *HIV Adult Standard of Care* (Critical Path AIDS Project, 1996); Pamela Mendels, "AIDS Activist's Dilemma Proved Decisive in Decency Act Case," *New York Times*, June 18, 1996.

13   **May 9, 1968** "Where Perversion Is Taught," from the collection "The Untold History of a Gay Rights Demonstration at Bucks County Community College, May 9, 1968, by Marc Stein," OutHistory, April 13 2021, last edited February 8, 2023, https://outhistory.org/exhibits/show/wh/whe.

14   **May 10, 1904** Hannah Wilson, "The Life and Legacy of Frieda Belinfante," Music and the Holocaust, accessed February 11, 2025, https://holocaustmusic.ort.org/resistance-and-exile/frieda-belinfante; "Frieda Belinfante," Holocaust Encyclopedia, United States Holocaust Memorial Museum, accessed February 11, 2025, https://encyclopedia.ushmm.org/content/en/photo/frieda-belinfante.

15   **May 10, 1933** "Nazi Book Burning," Working Class History, last edited May 11, 2023, https://stories.workingclasshistory.com/article/11315/nazi-book-burning.

16   **May 10, 2000** "Stagecoach Vandalism," Working Class History, last edited July 19, 2022, https://stories.workingclasshistory.com/article/8229/stagecoach-vandalism; Gerard Seenan, "Call to Boycott Stagecoach Over 'Anti-Gay' Donation," *Guardian*, January 14, 2000, https://www.theguardian.com/world/2000/jan/15/transport.uk2; "Boycott Call in Stagecoach 'Anti-Gay' Row," *BBC News*, January 14, 2000, http://news.bbc.co.uk/2/hi/uk_news/scotland/604015.stm.

17   **May 11, 1935** Dick Leitsch, "Police Raid on N.Y. Club Sets Off First Gay Riot," *Advocate*, September 1969, https://www.advocate.com/society/activism/2012/06/29/our-archives-1969-advocate-article-stonewall-riots?pg=1#article-content.

18   **May 12, 1990** "Queer Nation NY History," Queer Nation NY, accessed April 7, 2024, https://queernationny.org/history.

19   **May 13–14, 1976** Richard "Bugs" Burnett, "Canada Pride Ideal Time to Apologize for Anti-Gay Montreal Police Raids," Three Dollar Bill, August 12, 2017, https://bugsburnett. blogspot.com/2017/08/canada-pride-ideal-time-to-apologize.html; Ronni Sanlo, "This Day in LGBTQ History," on Ronni Sanlo's blog, February 9, 2024, https://ronnisanlo. com/this-day-in-lgbtq-history.

20   **May 14, 1974** Bella Abzug, Equality Act, H.R. 14752, 93rd Cong. (1973–74), https://www. congress.gov/bill/93rd-congress/house-bill/14752. See also Jeffry J. Iovannone, "'Battling Bella' Abzug and the Equality Act," *Medium*, January 14, 2018, https://medium.com/ queer-history-for-the-people/battling-bella-abzug-and-the-equality-act-859663317f9f.

21   **May 15, 1897** "First LGBT+ Rights Group Formed," Working Class History, last edited July 19, 2022, https://stories.workingclasshistory.com/article/8710/first-lgbt+-rights-group-formed; "The Scientific-Humanitarian Committee," Legacy Project Chicago, accessed February 12, 2025, https://legacyprojectchicago.org/milestone/scientific-humanitarian-committee; "Lost in History: The Scientific-Humanitarian Committee," *Lesbian News*, August 31, 2017, archived at https://web.archive.org/web/20230804222053/ https://lesbiannews.com/history-scientific-humanitarian-committee/.

22   **May 16, 1981** Michael Annetta, "May 16 in LGBTQ History," Lavender Effect, May 16, 2013, https://thelavendereffect.org/2013/05/16/may-16-in-lgbtq-history; "Finland's Queer History Timeline," Sateenkaarihistorian ystävät, accessed February 28, 2025, https:// sateenkaarihistoria.fi/en/finlands-queer-history-timeline/.

23   **May 17, 2004** Victoria Whitley-Berry, "The 1st Legally Married Same-Sex Couple Wanted to Lead by Example," *NPR*, May 17, 2019, https://www.npr.org/2019/05/17/723649385/ the-1st-legally-married-same-sex-couple-wanted-to-lead-by-example.

24   **May 18, 2023** Kory Grow, "San Francisco Names Nation's First 'Drag Laureate': D'Arcy Drollinger," *Rolling Stone*, May 18, 2023, https://www.rollingstone.com/culture/ culture-news/san-francisco-drag-laureate-darcy-drollinger-1234737585/.

25   **May 19, 1904** Ian Birchall, "Daniel Guérin Showed Us What a Socialist Writer Should Be," *Jacobin*, August 7, 2022, https://jacobin.com/2022/08/daniel-guerin-socialist-anarchism-anti-colonialism-gay-liberation; Cole Stangler, "The Red and the Rainbow: The Life and Work of Daniel Guérin," *Dissent*, Spring 2017, https://www.dissentmagazine.org/ article/red-rainbow-life-work-daniel-guerin-french/.

26   **May 19, 1930** Melissa Anderson, "Lorraine Hansberry's Letters Reveal the Playwright's Private Struggle," *Village Voice*, February 26, 2014, https://www.villagevoice.com/ lorraine-hansberrys-letters-reveal-the-playwrights-private-struggle; Natalie, "The Quiet Lesbian Biography of Lorraine Hansberry," *Autostraddle*, February 25, 2020, https://www.autostraddle.com/the-lesbian-biography-of-lorraine-hansberry; Kaitlyn Greenidge, "What I Love, What I Hate, What I Should Like," OutHistory, accessed February 12, 2025, https://outhistory.org/exhibits/show/lorraine-hansberry/ what-i-love; Lorraine Hansberry, "In Her Own Words," Lorraine Hansberry Literary Trust, accessed February 12, 2025, https://www.lhlt.org/quotes?tid=16; Elisa Harris, "The Double Life of Lorraine Hansberry," *Out Magazine*, September 1999, reprinted in *Medium*, September 26, 2018, and archived October 30, 2020, at https://web.archive.org/web/20201030115552/https://girlsinmitsouko.medium.com/ the-double-life-of-lorraine-hansberry-out-magazine-september-1999-a60c1d471d49.

27   **May 20, 1885** Although Baer underwent gender-affirming surgery in 1906, the exact details of the medical procedures remain unknown, as his medical records were destroyed during the Nazi book-burning campaign of the 1930s, which specifically targeted Hirschfeld's studies (see May 10, 1933). Harper-Hugo Darling, "Karl M. Baer," Making Queer History, December 11, 2022, https://www.makingqueerhistory.com/ articles/2022/12/11/karl-m-baer.

28   **May 20, 1936** "Mujeres Libres First Published," Working Class History, last edited July 19, 2022, https://stories.workingclasshistory.com/article/9305/mujeres-libres-first-published.

29   **May 21, 1925** Caleb Crain, "Frank Kameny's Orderly, Square Gay-Rights Activism,"

New Yorker, June 22 2020, https://www.newyorker.com/magazine/2020/06/29/frank-kamenys-orderly-square-gay-rights-activism; Franklin E. Kameny to John F. Kennedy, May 15, 1961, Papers of John F. Kennedy, Presidential Papers, White House Central Name File, John F. Kennedy Presidential Library and Museum, JFKWHCNF-1418-002.

30 **May 21, 1990** Diane Bernard, "Three Decades Before Coronavirus, Anthony Fauci Took Heat from AIDS Activists," *Washington Post*, May 20 2002, https://www.washingtonpost.com/history/2020/05/20/fauci-aids-nih-coronavirus; Hugh Ryan, "When Queers Fought the State and Won," *Boston Review*, May 11 2021, https://www.bostonreview.net/articles/when-queers-fought-the-state-and-won/.

31 **May 22, 1930** "Harvey Milk," Legacy Project, accessed February 12, 2025, https://legacyprojectchicago.org/person/harvey-milk; "The Official Harvey Milk Biography," Harvey Milk Foundation, accessed February 12, 2025, https://milkfoundation.org/about/harvey-milk-biography.

32 **May 23, 1908** "Annemarie Schwarzenbach Born," Working Class History, last edited July 19, 2022, https://stories.workingclasshistory.com/article/9587/annemarie-schwarzenbach-born.

33 **May 24, 2008** "A Project History," Firestorm, accessed February 12, 2025, https://firestorm.coop/history.html.

34 **May 24, 2023** Victor R. Caivano, "Transgender March in Argentina Highlights Abuses," *AP*, May 25 2023, video, 1 min., 12 sec., https://www.yahoo.com/lifestyle/transgender-march-argentina-highlights-abuses-113326550.html; Mariana Carbajal, "What the World Has to Learn from Argentina About Trans Rights," *openDemocracy*, June 19 2023, https://www.opendemocracy.net/en/5050/argentina-trans-rights-luana-self-id-gabriela-mansilla-healthcare; "Argentina Establishes 1% Quota for Trans Workers in Civil Service Jobs," *Buenos Aires Times*, September 4, 2020, https://www.batimes.com.ar/news/argentina/argentina-establishes-1-quota-for-trans-workers-in-civil-service-jobs.phtml.

35 **May 25, 1895** "Oscar Wilde Imprisoned," Working Class History, last edited July 19, 2022, https://stories.workingclasshistory.com/article/9769/oscar-wilde-imprisoned.

36 **May 26, 1989** Nicole Pasulka, "The Case of CeCe McDonald: Murder—Or Self-Defense Against a Hate Crime?" *Mother Jones*, May 22 2012, https://www.motherjones.com/politics/2012/05/cece-mcdonald-transgender-hate-crime-murder; Russell Goldman, "Transgender Activist CeCe McDonald Released from Prison," *ABC News*, January 13 2014, https://abcnews.go.com/blogs/headlines/2014/01/transgender-activist-cece-mcdonald-released-early-from-prison; Sabrina Rubin Erdely, "The Transgender Crucible," *Rolling Stone*, July 30, 2014, https://www.rollingstone.com/culture/culture-news/the-transgender-crucible-114095/; "CeCe McDonald Released from Prison," National LGBTQ Task Force, January 13 2014, https://www.thetaskforce.org/news/cece-mcdonald-released-from-prison/.

37 **May 26, 2019** Shane Gibson, "University of Winnipeg Two-Spirit Archives a First in Canada," *CBC News*, May 26, 2019, https://www.cbc.ca/news/canada/manitoba/two-spirit-archives-university-winnipeg-1.5150759; "Two-Spirit Archives," University of Winnipeg website, accessed February 12, 2025, https://archives.uwinnipeg.ca/our-collections/two-spirit-archives.html.

38 **May 27, 1960** Helen Sanders, "Impressions," *The Ladder* 4, no.9 (1960): 24.

39 **May 28, 2004** Mattilda Bernstein Sycamore, "That's Revolting! Queer Strategies for Resisting Assimilation," book product page on Mattilda Bernstein Sycamore's blog, accessed February 12, 2025, https://www.mattildabernsteinsycamore.com/thats-revolting.

40 **May 29, 1979** Michael Annetta, "May 29 in LGBTQ History," Lavender Effect, May 29, 2013, https://thelavendereffect.org/2013/05/29/may-29-in-lgbtq-history.

41 **May 30, 1926** "From GI Joe to GI Jane: Christine Jorgensen's Story," National WWII Museum, June 30, 2020, https://www.nationalww2museum.org/war/articles/christine-jorgensen.

42   **May 31, 1975** Daniel Lindsley, "A Glance at the George Jackson Brigade and Its Legacy of Prison Activism," *SGN*, June 23, 2023, https://www.sgn.org/story.php?326385; Feliks Banel, "George Jackson Brigade Terrorize the Northwest in the 1970s," *My Northwest*, December 21 2022, https://mynorthwest.com/780193/george-jackson-brigade-terrorized-the-northwest-in-the-1970s/.

June

1   **June 1, 1987** G. Boodman and Michael Specter, "64 Demonstrators Arrested in Protest of U.S. AIDS Policy," *Washington Post*, June 2, 1987, https://www.washingtonpost.com/archive/politics/1987/06/02/64-demonstrators-arrested-in-protest-of-us-aids-policy/cc77861f-8086-4c4c-8bac-857bc1c108ab/.

2   **June 1, 1999** "Blockorama," Queer Events, accessed February 12, 2025, https://www.queerevents.ca/queer/spaces/blockorama; Joey Viola, "Blockorama's Nik Red Talks 20 Years at Pride, 'Black Is Magic,' and SWV," *Buzz*, June 2018, https://thebuzzmag.ca/2018/06/blockoramas-nik-red-talks-20-years-at-pride-black-is-magic-and-swv/.

3   **June 2, 1990** "Queer Nation NY History," Queer Nation NY, accessed April 7, 2024, https://queernationny.org/history.

4   **June 3, 1906** Elyssa Goodman, "Remembering Josephine Baker, a Radical Bisexual Performer and Activist," *Them*, October 21, 2019, https://www.them.us/story/josephine-baker-activism-history; "1952 Josephine Baker Event," St. Louis LGBT History Project, accessed February 12, 2025, http://www.stlouislgbthistory.com/timeline/1900-1960s/1952-josephine-baker-event.html.

5   **June 3, 1926** Amanda Davis, "Allen Ginsberg and Peter Orlovsky Residence," NYC LGBT Historic Sites Project, May 2018, https://www.nyclgbtsites.org/site/allen-ginsberg-peter-orlovsky-residence/.

6   **June 4, 2016** "Swakopmund First Pride," Working Class History, last edited December 20, 2023, https://stories.workingclasshistory.com/article/12677/swakopmund-first-pride.

7   **June 5, 1994** Micco Caporale, "How Homocore Chicago Propped Open the Gate for Queer Punks," *Chicago Reader*, June 19, 2019, https://chicagoreader.com/music/how-homocore-chicago-propped-open-the-gate-for-queer-punks/.

8   **June 6, 1976** Jack Ryan Wampler, "The Death of Richard Heakin," Pima County Democratic Party, June 8, 2021, https://pimadems.org/2021/06/the-death-of-richard-heakin.

9   **June 6, 1990** "Queer Nation NY History."

10   **June 6, 1991** "Assassination of Sònia Rescalvo Zafra," Working Class History, last edited July 19, 2022, https://stories.workingclasshistory.com/article/8004/assassination-of-s%C3%B2nia-rescalvo-zafra.

11   **June 7, 1954** "Alan Turing Dies," Working Class History, last edited July 20, 2022, https://stories.workingclasshistory.com/article/10718/alan-turing-dies.

12   **June 7, 1990** Maryse Zeidler, "25 Years Ago, This LGBT Landmark in Vancouver Took on 'Big Brother' and Won," *CBC News*, October 20 2019, https://www.cbc.ca/news/canada/british-columbia/little-sisters-cbsa-challenge-1.5325456; "Little Sister's Bookstore Constitutional Challenge," Queer Events, accessed February 12, 2025, https://www.queerevents.ca/queer-history/canadian-history-timeline.

13   **June 8, 1974** "PRIDE Month + Gay History—June 8: The First Gay Activist Priest, Lambda Rising Bookstore, and So Much More!" Back2Stonewall, June 8, 2022, archived at https://web.archive.org/web/20221006102337/http://www.back2stonewall.com/2022/06/lgbt-gay-history-pride-june-8.html.

14   **June 9, 2019** Scott Rodd, "Sacramento Pride Reversed a Ban on Uniformed Policy from Its Parade. Now, Key Organizers Are Demanding Its President Resign," *CapRadio*, June 7 2019, https://www.capradio.org/articles/2019/06/07/sacramento-pride-reversed-a-ban-on-uniformed-police-from-its-parade-now-key-organizers-are-demanding-its-chairmans-resignation; Eric Escalante and Mayde Gomez, "Protest at Sacramento Pride Criticizes Inclusion of Police of Uniform at Event," *ABC10*, June

9, 2019, https://www.abc10.com/article/news/protest-at-sacramento-pride-blocks-people-from-event-entrance/103-b57df9bc-fda1-47c7-9e00-b7333abde214.

15 **June 10, 2017** Rachel Kurzius, "Capital Pride Producer Resigns amid Outcry over Bathroom Article," *dcist*, April 28, 2017, https://dcist.com/story/17/04/28/capital-pride-1; Rachel Sadon, "'No Justice, No Pride' Protesters Block Capital Pride Route," *dcist*, June 10, 2017, https://dcist.com/story/17/06/10/no-justice-no-pride-protesters-bloc/.

16 **June 11, 1943** "Karl Gorath Deported to Auschwitz," Working Class History, last edited July 19, 2022, https://stories.workingclasshistory.com/article/8323/karl-gorath-deported-to-auschwitz.

17 **June 11, 2013** Thomas Grove, "Russian Gay Rights Activists Detained After 'Kissing Protest,'" *Reuters*, June 11, 2013, https://www.reuters.com/article/russia-gay/russian-gay-rights-activists-detained-after-kissing-protest-idINDEE95A09L20130611/.

18 **June 12, 2018** Caroline Simon and Christal Hayes, "Two Years After the Orlando Shooting, Young Activists Hold a Die-In on the Capitol Lawn," *USA Today*, June 12, 2018, https://www.usatoday.com/story/news/2018/06/12/two-years-after-orlando-young-activists-protest-gun-violence-capitol/695132002; Jacob Ogles, "Two Years After Pulse Massacre, National Die-In Planned for D.C.," *Advocate*, May 26 2018, https://www.advocate.com/crime/2018/5/26/two-years-after-pulse-massacre-national-die-planned-dc.

19 **June 13, 2022** Jennicet Eva Gutiérrez, "White House Pride Reception," *Washington Blade*, June 13, 2022, https://www.washingtonblade.com/content/files/2022/06/White-House-Pride-reception.pdf; Josh Milton, "Trans Immigrant Activist Emphatically Turns Down White House Invite over Biden's LGBTQ+ Failures," *Pink News*, June 15, 2022, https://www.thepinknews.com/2022/06/15/joe-biden-white-house-pride-jennicet-gutierrez; Amy Goodman, "Trans Activist Skips White House Event in Protest of LGBTQ Asylum Seeker Policy," *Truthout*, June 16, 2022, https://truthout.org/video/trans-activist-skips-white-house-event-in-protest-of-lgbtq-asylum-seeker-policy/.

20 **June 14, 1974** Harper-Hugo Darling, "FannyAnn Viola Eddy," Making Queer History, April 28, 2023, https://www.makingqueerhistory.com/articles/2016/12/20/fannyann-viola-eddy-speaking-against-silence.

21 **June 14, 1977** Albert Williams, "On June 14, 1977 Chicago Had Its First Big Gay-Rights Protest," *Chicago Reader*, June 14 2016, https://chicagoreader.com/blogs/on-june-14-1977-chicago-had-its-first-big-gay-rights-protest; Meredith Francis, "How Chicago's Pride Parade Grew from a Small March to a Big Event," *WTTW*, June 28, 2019, https://interactive.wttw.com/playlist/2019/06/28/chicago-pride-parade.

22 **June 14, 2021** Marton Dunai, "Hungarians Protest Against PM Orban's LGBTQ Rights Crackdown," *Reuters*, June 15, 2021, https://www.reuters.com/world/europe/hungarians-protest-against-pm-orbans-lgbtq-rights-crackdown-2021-06-14; "Thousands Join Budapest Pride March to Protest Anti-LGBTQ Education Law in Hungary," *France 24*, June 24 2021, https://www.france24.com/en/europe/20210724-thousands-join-budapest-pride-march-to-protest-anti-lgbtq-education-law-in-hungary; "PM Orban Vows to Preserve Hungary's Christian Culture," *Reuters*, March 7, 2018, https://www.reuters.com/article/us-hungary-orban/pm-orban-vows-to-preserve-hungarys-christian-culture-idUSKBN1I80NC.

23 **June 15, 1987** Michael Annetta, "June 15 in LGBTQ History," Lavender Effect, June 15, 2013, https://thelavendereffect.org/2013/06/15/june-15-in-lgbtq-history; "The New York Times' Bias Continues to Endanger Transgender People," GLAAD, February 16, 2024, https://glaad.org/the-new-york-times-bias-continues-to-endanger-transgender-people/.

24 **June 16, 1836** Jorie McKibbin, "Trans Is Not a Trend: 4 Gender-Nonconforming Historical Figures Who Dared to Be Themselves," *LGBTQ Nation*, October 2, 2023, https://www.lgbtqnation.com/2023/10/trans-is-not-a-trend-4-gender-nonconforming-historical-figures-who-dared-to-be-themselves/.

25 **June 16, 1951** Liz Highleyman, "Who Was Lou Sullivan?," *Seattle Gay News*, February 22, 2008, archived at https://web.archive.org/web/20080906123232/http://www.sgn.org/sgnnews36_08/page30.cfm; Dean Strauss, "Lou Sullivan," Making Queer History,

accessed February 12, 2025, https://www.makingqueerhistory.com/articles/2018/5/21/lou-sullivan.

26 **June 16, 1990** "Queer Nation NY History"; "Gay History—June 16, 1990: Queer Nations 'Take Back the Night' Michelangelo Signorile Arrested," Back2Stonewall, June 16, 2023, archived at https://web.archive.org/web/20230618212657/http://www.back2stonewall.com/2023/06/history-june-16th-queer-nation-signorile-arrested.html.

27 **June 17, 1926** "Eve's Hangout Raided," Working Class History, last edited July 19, 2022, https://stories.workingclasshistory.com/article/7789/eve%27s-hangout-raided.

28 **June 17, 1950** Thom Higgins Papers, 1967–77, Elwyn B. Robinson Department of Special Collections, accessed September 1, 2024, https://apps.library.und.edu/archon/?p=collections%2Ffindingaid&id=3&q=; Britt Aamodt, "Positively Gay Cuban Refugee Task Force," Mnopedia, last modified June 21, 2023, https://www.mnopedia.org/group/positively-gay-cuban-refugee-task-force.

29 **June 17, 2010** "First Trans Protest in Quebec," Queer Events, accessed February 12, 2025, https://www.queerevents.ca/queer-history/resistance; "Upcoming Trans ID Protest in Quebec," *TransGriot* (blog), June 13 2010, https://transgriot.blogspot.com/2010/06/upcoming-trans-id-protest-in-quebec.html.

30 **June 17, 2017** Prince Shakur, "Ohio's Black Pride 4 Were Arrested at the Stonewall Columbus Pride Festival and Parade," *Teen Vogue*, December 6, 2017, https://www.teenvogue.com/story/ohios-black-pride-4-were-arrested-at-the-stonewall-columbus-pride-festival-and-parade; "BQIC Statement on the 5 Year Anniversary of the #BlackPride4 Arrests During the Stonewall Parade and Festival on June 17th, 2017," Black Queer & Intersectional Collective, June 18, 2022, https://bqic.net/2022/06/18/bqic-statement-on-the-5-year-anniversary-of-the-blackpride4-arrests-during-the-stonewall-parade-and-festival-on-june-17th-2017.

31 **June 18, 1981** Michael Annetta, "June 18 in LGBTQ History," Lavender Effect, June 18, 2013, https://thelavendereffect.org/2013/06/18/june-18-in-lgbtq-history.

32 **June 19, 1975** Michael Annetta, "June 19 in LGBTQ History," Lavender Effect, June 19, 2013, https://thelavendereffect.org/2013/06/19/june-19-in-lgbtq-history.

33 **June 20, 1983** "Herstory," Black Lives Matter, July 7, 2017, https://blacklivesmatter.com/herstory/; Sony Salzman, "From the Start, Black Lives Matter Has Been About LGBTQ Lives," *ABC News*, June 21 2020, https://abcnews.go.com/US/start-black-lives-matter-lgbtq-lives/story?id=71320450.

34 **June 21, 1977** "San Francisco—June 21, 1977: The Brutal Gay Hate Murder of Robert Hillsborough Rocks the Nation," Back2Stonewall, June 21, 2023, archived at https://web.archive.org/web/20230621145537/http://www.back2stonewall.com/2023/06/june21-brutal-murder-of-robert-hillsborough.html.

35 **June 22, 1947** Terrance Health, "This Black Lesbian Became a Giant in Her Field No Matter What Her Critics Threw at Her," LGBTQ History Month, February 20, 2019, https://www.lgbtqnation.com/2019/02/overcame-dyslexia-become-award-winning-sci-fi-author/.

36 **June 23, 1952** Michael Annetta, "June 23 in LGBTQ History," Lavender Effect, June 22, 2013, https://thelavendereffect.org/2013/06/23/june-23-in-lgbtq-history.

37 **June 23, 1990** *Anti-Gay/Lesbian Violence, Victimization & Defamation in 1990* (National Gay & Lesbian Task Force Policy Institute, 1991), https://digitallibrary.usc.edu/asset-management/2A3BF1KTP8LY; "Queer Nation NY History," Queer Nation NY, accessed April 7, 2024, https://queernationny.org/history.

38 **June 23, 2022** "Street Sweeps Kill Queers, 2022–Ongoing," Gay Shame, accessed April 7, 2024, https://gayshame.net/index.php/street-sweeps-kill-queers.

39 **June 23, 2023** "Strike with Pride," SB Workers United, archived July 5, 2023, at https://web.archive.org/web/20230705021151/https://sbworkersunited.org/strike-with-pride; "Addressing Misinformation: Access to Gender-Affirming Care for All Partners," One Starbucks, May 19, 2023, https://one.starbucks.com/get-the-facts/access-to-gender-affirming-care; Jelisa Castrodale, "Starbucks Union Workers Are on Strike over an

Alleged Pride Decoration Ban," *Food & Wine*, June 27, 2023, https://www.foodandwine.com/starbucks-workers-union-strike-pride-decorations-7553801.

40 **June 24, 1973** Robert W. Fieseler, "A Deadly Fire, an Indifferent Cop, and an Escaped Arsonist," *CrimeReads*, February 11, 2019, https://crimereads.com/a-deadly-fire-an-indifferent-cop-and-an-escaped-arsonist; Andrew Sciallo, "50 Years Later, the UpStairs Lounge Fire Is More Important to Remember than Ever," *The Nation*, June 22, 2023, https://www.thenation.com/article/society/upstairs-lounge-anniversary/.

41 **June 24, 1973** "Sylvia Rivera Speaking at the Fourth Annual Christopher Street Liberation Day Rally, 1973," Stonewall Forever, accessed February 12, 2025, https://stonewallforever.org/monument/sylvia-rivera-speaking-at-the-fourth-annual-christopher-street-liberation-day-rally-1973; "Christopher St. Liberation Day, 1973," Whose Streets Our Streets, December 24, 2012, https://whosestreetsourstreets.org/washington-square-park/.

42 **June 24, 1978** Mark Gillespie, "The Sydney Mardi Gras March of 1978," University of Sydney website, February 19, 2016, https://www.sydney.edu.au/news-opinion/news/2016/02/19/the-sydney-mardi-gras-march-of-1978.html.

43 **June 24, 1994** "Program for the Pride at Work Founding Conference of the Lesbian, Gay, Bi-Sexual, and Transgender People in the Labor Movement," June 24, 1994, Digital Collections at University of Maryland Libraries, accessed February 12, 2025, https://digital.lib.umd.edu/result/id/0d4b5d91-624a-4dbb-97f5-fbe8aa756431?relpath=dc/2023/1; Stefen Styrsky, "Lesbian Assumes a Top AFL-CIO Role," *Gay City News*, September 21, 2005, https://www.gaycitynews.nyc/stories/2005/19/lesbian-assumes-a-top-2005-09-21.html.

44 **June 24, 2015** Matthew Weaver, "Transgender Woman Heckles Barack Obama at White House Gay Pride Event," *Guardian*, June 25, 2015, https://www.theguardian.com/us-news/2015/jun/25/barack-obama-heckled-transgender-woman-gay-pride-white-house; Liam Stack, "Activist Removed After Heckling Obama at L.G.B.T Event at White House," *New York Times*, June 24, 2015, https://www.nytimes.com/2015/06/25/us/politics/activist-removed-after-heckling-obama-at-lgbt-event.html.

45 **June 25, 2011** Trudy Ring, "Activist Jean Harris Dies," *Advocate*, July 2, 2015, https://www.advocate.com/news/daily-news/2011/07/02/activist-jean-harris-dies.

46 **June 25, 2022** "Oslo Shooting: Norway Attack Being Treated as Islamist Terrorism, Police Say," *BBC*, June 25, 2022, https://www.bbc.com/news/world-europe-61933817; Malu Cursino, "Oslo Shooting: Memorial Service Takes Place at Oslo Cathedral," *BBC*, June 26, 2022, https://www.bbc.com/news/world-europe-61941172; Leo Sands, "Oslo Attacks: Pride Protesters Defy Norway Police Warnings," *BBC*, June 28, 2022, https://www.bbc.com/news/world-61961211.

47 **June 25, 2023** Umut Colak and Ezel Sahinkaya, "Turkey Detains Dozen of LGBTQ Activists During Pride March," *VOA*, June 27, 2023, https://www.voanews.com/a/turkey-detains-dozens-of-lgbtq-activists-during-pride-march/7154381.html; Hamdi First Buyuk, "Turkish Police Detain 113 at Istanbul's Banned Pride Parade," *Balkan Insight*, June 26 2023, https://balkaninsight.com/2023/06/26/turkish-police-detain-113-at-istanbuls-banned-pride-parade/.

48 **June 26, 2015** NCC Staff, "Why June 26 Is Already a Landmark Day for Gays and the Supreme Court," *Constitution Daily* (blog), National Constitution Center, June 26, 2015, https://constitutioncenter.org/blog/why-june-26-is-already-a-landmark-day-for-gays-and-the-supreme-court.

49 **June 26, 2022** Dilara Senkaya, "Turkey: Mass Arrests, Anti-LGBT Violence at Pride," *Human Rights Watch*, June 30, 2022, https://www.hrw.org/news/2022/06/30/turkey-mass-arrests-anti-lgbt-violence-pride; "Turkish Authorities Arrest More than 200 at Banned Pride March in Istanbul," *France 24*, June 26, 2022, https://www.france24.com/en/middle-east/20220626-turkish-authorities-arrest-dozens-in-istanbul-over-banned-pride-march.

50 **June 27, 1869** Emma Goldman, *Living My Life* (Knopf, 1931), available at https://

theanarchistlibrary.org/library/emma-goldman-living-my-life; Amanda Davis, "Emma Goldman Residence & 'Mother Earth' Office," NYC LGBT Historic Sites Project, May 2018, https://www.nyclgbtsites.org/site/emma-goldman-residence-mother-earth-office/.

51   **June 27, 1970** Erin Blakemore, "Inside the First Pride Parade: A Raucous Protest for Gay Liberation," *National Geographic*, June 28, 2020, https://www.nationalgeographic. com/history/article/inside-the-first-pride-parade-a-raucous-protest-for-gay -liberation-lgbtq.

52   **June 27, 2009** Paul Gallant, "Trans March 'Overdue,'" *Toronto Star*, June 18, 2009, https:// www.thestar.com/news/gta/trans-march-overdue/article_8dc91c23-6c46-5ed3-a6f4- f18003a7a77d.html; "Toronto's First Trans March," Queer Events, accessed February 12, 2025, https://www.queerevents.ca/queer-history/canadian-history-timeline.

53   **June 27, 2009** Savannah Garmon, "Queers Against Israeli Apartheid Refuse to be Silenced," *Electronic Intifada*, July 1, 2010, https://electronicintifada.net/content/ queers-against-israeli-apartheid-refuse-be-silenced/8905.

54   **June 27, 2020** "Pornography Charges Target Feminist Artist," Free Yulia Tsvetkova, accessed February 12, 2025, https://www.freetsvet.net; "Police Detains over 30 Protesting LGBT Activists in Moscow—Monitoring Group," *Reuters*, June 27, 2020, https://www.reuters.com/article/russia-lgbt-arrests/police-detains-over-30- protesting-lgbt-activists-in-moscow-monitoring-group-idUSL8N2E40DB; Anastasiia Kruope, "Dozens Detained in Russia for Protesting Prosecution of Feminist Activist," *Human Rights Watch*, June 30, 2020, https://www.hrw.org/news/2020/06/30/ dozens-detained-russia-protesting-prosecution-feminist-activist.

55   **June 28, 1969** "Stonewall Rebellion," Working Class History, last edited July 20, 2022, https://stories.workingclasshistory.com/article/10029/stonewall-rebellion.

56   **June 28, 1969** Hugh Ryan, "The Queer History of the Women's House of Detention," *Activist History Review*, May 31, 2019, https://activisthistory.com/2019/05/31/ the-queer-history-of-the-womens-house-of-detention/.

57   **June 29, 1969** Ariel Kates, "The Mattachine Society, and the Post-Stonewall Shift," *Off the Grid* (Village Preservation blog), July 16, 2021, https://www.villagepreservation. org/2021/07/16/the-mattachine-society-and-the-post-stonewall-shift; "Mattachine Society," National Park Service, accessed February 12, 2025, https://www.nps.gov/ articles/000/mattachine-society.htm.

58   **June 30, 1986** Bowers v. Hardwick, 478 U.S. 186 (1986), https://supreme.justia.com/cases/ federal/us/478/186/#tab-opinion-1956747; Elizabeth Sheyn, "The Shot Heard Around the LGBT World: *Bowers v. Hardwick* as a Mobilizing Force for the National Gay and Lesbian Task Force," *Journal of Race, Gender and Ethnicity* 4, no. 1 (May 2009); "Our History and Timeline," National LGBTQ Task Force, accessed February 12, 2025, https:// www.thetaskforce.org/about/history/.

59   **June 30, 2023** Lexi McMenamin, "Moms for Liberty Protests: How Philly Got Creative with Its Resistance at the Sold-Out Conference," *Teen Vogue*, July 1, 2023, https://www. teenvogue.com/story/moms-for-liberty-protest-signs-philly; Home page for Stand Up to Moms for Liberty in Philly!, accessed February 12, 2025, https://sites.google.com/ view/stand-up-to-moms-for-liberty/home.

July

1   **July 1, 1943** "Willem Arondeus Executed," Working Class History, last edited July 19, 2022, https://stories.workingclasshistory.com/article/8082/willem-arondeus-executed.

2   **July 1, 1972** "London First Pride," Working Class History, last edited July 19, 2022, https:// stories.workingclasshistory.com/article/8084/london-first-pride.

3   **July 1, 2018** "Istanbul Bans LGBT Parade," *DW*, July 24, 2017, https://www.dw.com/ en/istanbul-bans-lgbt-parade-citing-public-safety-concerns/a-39402000; Agence France-Presse, "Police Use Rubber Bullets as Gay Groups Defy Ban, March in Istanbul Pride Parade," *Times of Israel*, July 1, 2018, https://www.timesofisrael.com/police-use- rubber-bullets-as-gay-groups-march-in-istanbul-pride-despite-ban; Sheena McKenzie,

"Hundreds of LGBTI+ Campaigners March in Banned Istanbul Pride Parade," *CNN*, July 2, 2018, https://www.cnn.com/2018/07/02/europe/istanbul-pride-parade-intl/index.html.

4   **July 2, 1951** Michael Bronski, "Sylvia Rivera: 1951–2002," *Z*, April 1, 2002, https://znetwork.org/zmagazine/sylvia-rivera-1951-2002-by-michael-bronski; David W. Dunlap, "Sylvia Rivera, 50, Figure in Birth of the Gay Liberation Movement," *New York Times*, February 20, 2002, https://www.nytimes.com/2002/02/20/nyregion/sylvia-rivera-50-figure-in-birth-of-the-gay-liberation-movement.html.

5   **July 2, 1999** "Looking Back at the History of the Pride Movement," *Outlook Traveller*, June 8, 2022, https://www.outlooktraveller.com/explore/inspiration/looking-back-at-the-history-of-the-pride-movement; Stuti Agrawal, "Somewhere over the Rainbow," *Times of India*, July 17, 2012, https://timesofindia.indiatimes.com/life-style/spotlight/Somewhere-over-the-rainbow/articleshow/15016989.cms.

6   **July 2, 2021** "Geelong Regional Libraries Strike," Working Class History, last edited April 25, 2023, https://stories.workingclasshistory.com/article/11259/geelong-regional-libraries-strike.

7   **July 3, 2016** Sarah Joyce Battersby, "Black Lives Matter Protest Scores Victory After Putting Pride Parade on Pause," *Toronto Star*, July 3, 2016, https://www.thestar.com/news/gta/black-lives-matter-protest-scores-victory-after-putting-pride-parade-on-pause/article_22b52c19-dc98-5008-8fa2-1deaa4748193.html; "Black Lives Matter Toronto Stall Pride Parade," *CBC News*, July 3, 2016, https://www.cbc.ca/news/canada/toronto/pride-parade-toronto-1.3662823.

8   **July 4, 1965** Marc Stein, "Annual Reminders in Philadelphia, July 4, 1965–July 4, 1969," OutHistory, accessed February 12, 2025, https://outhistory.org/exhibits/show/50th-ann/intro; Bobby Allyn, "Remember 1965 Philly March That Helped Spark Gay Rights Movement," *WHYY*, March 10, 2015, https://whyy.org/articles/remembering-and-the-philly-lgbt-march-that-led-the-way-photos/.

9   **July 4, 1973** Greta Rensenbrink, "Parthenogenesis and Lesbian Separatism: Regenerating Women's Community Through Virgin Birth in the United States in the 1970s and 1980s," *Journal of the History of Sexuality* 19, no. 2 (May 2010): 288–316, https://doi.org/10.1353/sex.0.0102.

10   **July 4, 1981** Sarfraz Manzoor, "The Year Rock Found the Power to Unite," *Guardian*, April 20, 2008, https://www.theguardian.com/music/2008/apr/20/popandrock.race; Stephanie Phillips, "The Punks That Took on Prejudice: White Riot and the 1970s Rock Against Racism Movement," British Film Institute, September 17, 2020, https://www.bfi.org.uk/features/white-riot-rock-against-racism.

11   **July 5, 1986** "Homosexuals, Upset by Ruling, Plan Drive to Abolish Anti-Sodomy Laws," *New York Times*, July 5, 1986, https://www.nytimes.com/1986/07/05/us/homosexuals-upset-by-ruling-plan-drive-to-abolish-anti-sodomy-laws.html.

12   **July 6, 1919** "Magnus Hirschfeld and HKW," Haus der Kulturen der Welt, September 23, 2022, https://archiv.hkw.de/en/hkw/geschichte/ort_geschichte/magnus_hirschfeld.php.

13   **July 6, 1973** "The Sexes: The Lavender Panthers," *Time*, October 8, 1973, https://content.time.com/time/magazine/article/0,9171,908008,00.html; Michael Annetta, "July 6 in LGBTQ History," Lavender Effect, July 6, 2013, https://thelavendereffect.org/2013/07/06/july-6-in-lgbtq-history.

14   **July 7, 1979** Kevin O'Keeffe, "The Life, Death and Legacy of Robert Opel, the Bisexual Oscar Streaker," *Advocate*, February 23, 2019, https://www.advocate.com/arts-entertainment/art/2014/03/26/life-death-and-legacy-robert-opel-oscar-streaker; Michael Schulman, "What Became of the Oscar Streaker?," *New Yorker*, February 6, 2023, https://www.newyorker.com/magazine/2023/02/06/what-became-of-the-oscar-streaker.

15   **July 8, 1980** Ronni Sanlo, "This Day in LGBTQ History—July," on Ronni Sanlo's blog, February 9, 2024, https://ronnisanlo.com/this-day-in-lgbtq-history-july-2/.

16   **July 9, 1936** Stephanie Farnsworth, "Queeroes: June Jordan," *Queerness*, February 3, 2016, https://thequeerness.com/2016/02/03/queeroes-june-jordan/.

17   **July 9, 1969** Michael Annetta, "July 9 in LGBTQ History," Lavender Effect, July 9, 2013, https://thelavendereffect.org/2013/07/09/july-9-in-lgbtq-history.

18   **July 10, 1972** Michael Bedwell, "In 1972, Gay People Spoke at the Democratic National Convention for the First Time," *LGBTQ Nation*, October 10, 2019, https://www.lgbtqnation.com/2019/10/in-1972-gay-people-spoke-at-the-democratic-national-convention-for-the-first-time.

19   **July 11, 1966** "Gay History—July 11, 1966: Twenty-Six Oklahoma City Teachers Forced to Resign for Being Gay," Back2Stonewall, July 11, 2023, archived at https://web.archive.org/web/20230714184828/http://www.back2stonewall.com/2023/07/gay-history-july-11-1966-twenty-six-oklahoma-city-teachers-forced-resign-gay.html.

20   **July 12, 1833** Hubert Kennedy, "Johann Baptist von Schweitzer," *Journal of Homosexuality* 29, nos. 2–3 (February 1995): 69–96, https://doi.org/10.1300/j082v29n02_03.

21   **July 12, 1990** "Queer Nation NY History," Queer Nation NY, accessed April 7, 2024, https://queernationny.org/history.

22   **July 13, 1863** "Mary and Jeannette," Mary Woolley & Jeannette Marks: Life, Love, & Letters, accessed March 20, 2024, https://commons.mtholyoke.edu/marywooleyjeannettemarks/mary-and-jeannette/.

23   **July 13, 1952** Mark Krone, "Marie Equi: Her Fights for Women's Equality," History Project, March 1, 2019, https://historyproject.org/news/2019-03/marie-equi-her-fight-womens-equality.

24   **July 14, 1990** "Queer Nation NY History."

25   **July 15, 1953** Giles Tremlett, "Gays Persecuted by Franco Lose Criminal Status at Last," *Guardian*, December 13, 2001, https://www.theguardian.com/world/2001/dec/13/gayrights.gilestremlett; "Franco Criminalises Homosexuality," Working Class History, last edited July 19, 2022, https://stories.workingclasshistory.com/article/8682/franco-criminalises-homosexuality.

26   **July 15, 1984** "First LGSM Meeting," Working Class History, last edited April 18, 2023, https://stories.workingclasshistory.com/article/11247/first-lgsm-meeting.

27   **July 15, 1990** Taylor C. Noakes, "Sex Garage Raid," *Canadian Encyclopedia*, November 26, 2020, https://www.thecanadianencyclopedia.ca/en/article/sex-garage-raid; Denis Benson, "Montreal's Stonewall: How the Sex Garage Raid Mobilized a Generation of LGBT Activists," *VICE*, March 13, 2017, https://www.vice.com/en/article/4x8pjq/montreal-sex-garage-raid-feature.

28   **July 16, 1994** "This Is Where You Come From," Pride PEI, accessed February 12, 2025, https://www.pridepei.ca/our-vision; Jane Roberston, "Reflections on P.E.I.'s First Pride March—25 Years Later," *CBC News*, July 23, 2019, https://www.cbc.ca/news/canada/prince-edward-island/pei-pride-march-human-rights-1994-1.5214615.

29   **July 17, 1982** Barry James, "Royal Bodyguard Confesses to Homosexual Relationship," *UPI*, July 19, 1982, https://www.upi.com/Archives/1982/07/19/Royal-bodyguard-confesses-to-homosexual-relationship/3144395899200; "Gay History—July 17, 1982: The Scandal of Commander Michael Trestrail. The Queen's Gay Bodyguard," Back2Stonewall, July 17, 2023, http://www.back2stonewall.com/2023/07/gay-history-july-17-1982-the-scandal-of-commander-michael-trestrail-the-queens-gay-bodyguard.html (archive not available).

30   **July 18, 1966** Nicole Pasulka, "Ladies in the Streets: Before Stonewall, Transgender Uprising Changed Lives," *NPR*, May 5, 2015, https://www.npr.org/sections/codeswitch/2015/05/05/404459634/ladies-in-the-streets-before-stonewall-transgender-uprising-changed-lives.

31   **July 19, 1990** "Queer Nation NY History."

32   **July 20, 1983** "Queer Art Prize 2017 Recent Work Finalist: 'The Personal Things' (2016) by Tourmaline," Queer Art, accessed February 12, 2025, https://www.queer-art.org/tourmaline-2.

33   **July 21, 1958** "Gay History—July 21, 1958: New Orleans Launches Raids Against French Quarter Gay Bars and 'Deviants,'" Back2Stonewall, July 21, 2023, archived at https://

web.archive.org/web/20231129023848/http://www.back2stonewall.com/2023/07/lgbt-gay-history-july-21-1958.html.

34 **July 22, 1990** Duncan Osborne, "What Will the Neighbors Think?" *Out Week*, August 8, 1990, 24–25.

35 **July 23, 1959** "Vallerga v. Department of Alcoholic Beverage Control," S.F. No. 20285. In Bank. (December 23, 1959), https://law.justia.com/cases/california/supreme-court/2d/53/313.html.

36 **July 24, 1969** "Gay History—July 24, 1969: The Gay Liberation Front Is Founded," Back2Stonewall, July 24, 2023, archived at https://web.archive.org/web/20230929070419/http://www.back2stonewall.com/2023/07/gay-history-july-24-1969-gay-liberation-front-founded.html.

37 **July 25–27, 1969** "Trans Pioneers," Historic England, accessed February 12, 2025, https://historicengland.org.uk/research/inclusive-heritage/lgbtq-heritage-project/trans-and-gender-nonconforming-histories/trans-pioneers; Program for "First International Symposium on Gender Identity: Aims, Function and Clinical Problems of a Gender Identity Unit," accessed February 12, 2025, https://wpath.org/wp-content/uploads/2024/11/1st-hbigda-symposium.pdf. See more from the World Professional Association for Transgender Health at https://wpath.org/about/history/international-symposia/.

38 **July 25, 2015** "First-Ever St. John's Trans March a Success, Organizers Say," *CBC News*, July 26, 2015, https://www.cbc.ca/news/canada/newfoundland-labrador/first-ever-st-john-s-trans-march-a-success-organizers-say-1.3168197; Rhea Rollmann, "Trans March in St. John's 'An Important Radical Act,'" *Independent*, July 26, 2015, https://theindependent.ca/news/trans-march-in-st-johns-an-important-radical-act/.

39 **July 26, 1989** Michael Annetta, "July 26 in LGBTQ History," Lavender Effect, July 26, 2013, accessed March 29, 2025, https://thelavendereffect.org/2013/07/26/july-26-in-lgbtq-history.

40 **July 27, 1969** Hew Evan, "June Is Gay Pride; But July Is Gay Liberation," *Off the Grid* (Village Preservation blog), July 23, 2022, https://www.villagepreservation.org/2022/07/27/gay-liberation; Jonathan Black, "In the Wake of Stonewall: Gay Power Hits Back," *Village Voice*, July 31, 1969, https://www.villagevoice.com/in-the-wake-of-stonewall-gay-power-hits-back.

41 **July 28, 1990** "Queer Nation NY History."

42 **July 29, 2020** Lilach Ben David, "'A Queer Cry for Freedom': Meet the LGBTQ Palestinians Demanding Liberation," *972 Magazine*, August 2, 2020, https://www.972mag.com/lgbtq-palestinians-haifa-queer.

43 **July 30, 1960** Assemblée Nationale, 2nd Séance du Lundi, "Full Report of the Discussion," July 18, 1960, https://archives.assemblee-nationale.fr/1/cri/1959-1960-ordinaire2/060.pdf; Alexandre Marchant, "Daniel Guérin and the Militant Discourse on Male Homosexuality in France (1950s–1980s)," *Modern and Contemporary History Review* 4, nos. 53–55 (2006): 175–90.

44 **July 31, 1932** Ronni Sanlo, "This Day in LGBTQ History—July," on Ronni Sanlo's blog, February 9, 2024, https://ronnisanlo.com/this-day-in-lgbtq-history-july-2/.

August

1 **August 1966** Nicole Pasulka, "Ladies in the Streets: Before Stonewall, Transgender Uprising Changed Lives," *NPR Code Switch*, May 5 2015, https://www.npr.org/sections/codeswitch/2015/05/05/404459634/ladies-in-the-streets-before-stonewall-transgender-uprising-changed-lives.

2 **August 1, 2019** Oren Ziv, "Queer Palestinian Community Holds 'Historic' Protest Against LGBT Violence," *972 Magazine*, August 2, 2019, https://www.972mag.com/queer-palestinian-protest-lgbt-violence.

3 **August 2, 1924** "An Introduction to James Baldwin," National Museum of African

American History and Culture, accessed February 12, 2025, https://nmaahc.si.edu/explore/stories/introduction-james-baldwin.

4 **August 3, 1990** "Queer Nation NY History," Queer Nation NY, accessed April 7, 2024, https://queernationny.org/history.

5 **August 4, 1990** "Two-Spirit Adopted by Indigenous LGBT+ People," Working Class History, last edited July 20, 2022, https://stories.workingclasshistory.com/article/10407/two-spirit-adopted-by-indigenous-lgbt+-people; Isabella Thurston, "The History of Two-Spirit Folks," Indigenous Foundation, accessed February 12, 2025, https://www.theindigenousfoundation.org/articles/the-history-of-two-spirit-folks.

6 **August 4, 2004** Tanya Gulliver, "Charged for Bathhouse Sex: Hamilton Cops Go After Gay Businesses, Play Dumb," *Xtra*, August 18, 2004, https://xtramagazine.com/power/charged-for-bathhouse-sex-41175.

7 **August 5, 1969** Will Butler, "Atlanta's Stonewall: The Lonesome Cowboys Raid at Ansley Mall," Atlanta History Center, September 22, 2021, https://www.atlantahistorycenter.com/blog/atlantas-stonewall-the-lonesome-cowboys-raid-at-ansley-mall.

8 **August 6, 1945** Alex Williams, "Gloria Allen, Transgender Activist Who Ran a Charm School, Dies at 76," *New York Times*, June 24, 2022, https://www.nytimes.com/2022/06/24/us/gloria-allen-dead.html.

9 **August 7, 1987** Michael Annetta, "Today in LGBTQ History," Lavender Effect, August 7, 2013, https://thelavendereffect.org/category/lgbtq-history/today-in-lgbtq-history/page/15/.

10 **August 7, 2020** "Poland: Crackdown on LGBT Activists," *Human Rights Watch*, August 7, 2020, https://www.hrw.org/news/2020/08/07/poland-crackdown-lgbt-activists.

11 **August 8, 1978** SILGA, "The History of ILGA: 1978/2012," ILGA World, August 7, 2012, https://ilga.org/news/ilga-history; "Member Organisations," ILGA World, accessed March 6, 2025, https://ilga.org/member-organisations.

12 **August 9, 1967** Jennifer Doyle and Tavia Nyong'o, "José Esteban Muñoz (1967–2013)," *Artforum*, March 14, 2014, https://www.artforum.com/columns/jennifer-doyle-and-tavia-nyongo-on-jose-esteban-munoz-1967-2013-219565/.

13 **August 10, 1969** Marc Stein, "Stonewall and Queens," *From the Square* (NYU Press blog), August 9, 2019, https://www.fromthesquare.org/stonewall-and-queens; Amanda Davis, "Demonstration Against LGBT Harassment in Flushing Meadows-Corona Park Tree Grove," NYC LGBT Historic Sites Project, April 2021, https://www.nyclgbtsites.org/site/demonstration-against-lgbt-harassment-in-flushing-meadows-corona-park-tree-grove.

14 **August 10, 1981** "Fumino Sugiyama," International House of Japan, accessed September 1, 2024, https://ihj.global/en/leadership/leadership-5235/.

15 **August 11, 1992** "Tracing the History of Pride Month," *Outlook*, June 1, 2023, https://www.outlookindia.com/national/tracing-the-history-of-pride-month-news-291095; Eshna Benegal, "When Did the LGBTQIA+ Movement Begin in India?" *Fifty Two*, July 29, 2022, https://fiftytwo.in/blog/when-did-the-lgbtqia-movement-begin-in-india.

16 **August 12, 1907** "Gladys Bentley," Unladylike 2020, accessed February 12, 2025, https://unladylike2020.com/profile/gladys-bentley.

17 **August 13, 2016** "Trans Hirstory in 99 Objects," Museum of Transgender Hirstory and Art, accessed February 12, 2025, https://www.motha.net/transhirstory-in-99-objects; "Transgender Hirstory in 99 Objects," Creative Capital, accessed February 12, 2025, https://creative-capital.org/projects/transgender-hirstory-in-99-objects/.

18 **August 14, 1988** "Daniel Guérin Died," Working Class History, last edited July 19, 2022, https://stories.workingclasshistory.com/article/8539/daniel-gu%C3%A9rin-died.

19 **August 15, 1971** Samuel Clowes Huneke, "The Beginnings of Queer Citizenship," *Boston Review*, February 23, 2022, https://www.bostonreview.net/articles/the-beginnings-of-queer-citizenship.

20 **August 16, 1946** Washington College, "Social Activist David Mixner to Address

Washington College Class of 2015," *News Wise*, April 16, 2015, https://www.newswise.com/articles/social-activist-david-mixner-to-address-washington-college-class-of-2015.

21 **August 17, 1885** Hubert Kennedy, "Kurt Hiller: Sexual Reform," glbtq Archives, accessed March 22, 2025, http://www.glbtqarchive.com/ssh/hiller_k_S.pdf; Laurie Marhoefer, *Sex and the Weimar Republic: German Homosexual Emancipation and the Rise of the Nazis* (University of Toronto Press, 2015).

22 **August 17, 1968** "The Patch Bar Flower Power Protest," ONE National Gay & Lesbian Archives at the USC Libraries, August 16, 2018, https://one.usc.edu/story/patch-bar-flower-power-protest.

23 **August 18, 1936** "Frederica García Lorca Executed," Working Class History, last edited July 20, 2022, https://stories.workingclasshistory.com/article/10961/federico-garcia-lorca-executed.

24 **August 18, 1970** Antonio Mejías-Rentas, "How Angela Davis Ended Up on the FBI Most Wanted List," History.com, last updated January 3, 2024, https://www.history.com/news/angela-davis-fbi-most-wanted-list; Colin Evans, "Angela Davis Trial: 1972," Encyclopedia.com, accessed February 26, 2025, https://www.encyclopedia.com/law/law-magazines/angela-davis-trial-1972.

25 **August 18, 2004** "Republican National Convention Protest 2004," ACT UP, historical archive, accessed February 12, 2025, https://actupny.org/reports/rnc_nyc.html.

26 **August 19, 1999** "Who Designed the Transgender Flag?" Smithsonian, March 29, 2022, https://www.si.edu/stories/who-designed-transgender-flag.

27 **August 20, 1943** Suyin Haynes, "How One Drag Performer's Overlooked Activism Helped Lay the Groundwork for Today's Fight for Transgender Rights," *Time*, June 25, 2021, https://time.com/6074496/sir-lady-java-trans-rights-history.

28 **August 21, 1970** Huey P. Newton, "Huey P. Newton on Gay Liberation," *Workers World*, May 16, 2012, https://www.workers.org/2012/us/huey_p_newton_0524; "Huey Newton Intersectional Letter," Working Class History, last edited July 19, 2022, https://stories.workingclasshistory.com/article/8650/huey-newton-intersectional-speech.

29 **August 21, 2006** "Michigan Women's Music Festival Ends Policy of Discrimination Against Trans Women," Camp Trans press release, August 21, 2006, https://www.transadvocate.com/wp-content/uploads/2014/08/CampTransPressRelease_Michigan WomynsMusicFestivalEndsPolicyOfDiscriminationAgainstTransWomen _082106.pdf.

30 **August 22, 1983** Michael Annetta, "August 22 in LGBTQ History," Lavender Effect, August 22, 2013, https://thelavendereffect.org/2013/08/22/august-22-in-lgbtq-history; Colin Clews, "1983: Fighting to Share Martin Luther King's Dream," Gay in the 80s, January 5, 2016, https://www.gayinthe80s.com/2016/01/1983-fighting-to-share-martin-luther-kings-dream/.

31 **August 23, 1851** "Sydney Sailors Riot," Working Class History, last edited July 19, 2022, https://stories.workingclasshistory.com/article/9540/sydney-sailors-riot.

32 **August 24, 1945** Emma Rothberg, "Marsha P. Johnson," National Women's History Museum, accessed February 12, 2025, https://www.womenshistory.org/education-resources/biographies/marsha-p-johnson; Marsha P. Johnson, "Rapping with a Street Transvestite Revolutionary: An Interview with Marsha P. Johnson," in *Street Transvestite Action Revolutionaries: Survival, Revolt, and Queer Antagonist Struggle* (Untorelli Press, 2013), available at https://theanarchistlibrary.org/library/ehn-nothing-untorelli-press-street-transvestite-action-revolutionaries#toc14.

33 **August 25, 1918** Felicia Bernstein to Leonard Bernstein, n.d., Leonard Bernstein Collection, circa 1900–1995, Library of Congress, accessed February 12, 2025, https://www.loc.gov/resource/music.musbernstein-100060233/?st=gallery.

34 **August 26, 1969** "Homosexuality Decriminalized: Parliament Passes Bill C-150, yet Homophobia Persists," British Columbia: An Untold History, accessed August 26, 2024, https://bcanuntoldhistory.knowledge.ca/1960/homosexuality-decriminalized.

35 **August 27, 2008** Guy Adams, "Pioneering Lesbian Rights Activist Dies Just Weeks After

Wedding," *Independent*, August 28, 2008, https://www.independent.co.uk/news/world/americas/pioneering-lesbian-rights-activist-dies-just-weeks-after-wedding-911906.html.

36 **August 28, 1963** Cheryl Corley, "Bayard Rustin: The Man Who Organized the March on Washington," *NPR*, August 15, 2013, https://www.npr.org/sections/codeswitch/2013/08/15/212338844/bayard-rustin-the-man-who-organized-the-march-on-washington; Peter Dreier, "The Life and Legacy of Bayard Rustin," *The Progressive*, December 15, 2023, https://progressive.org/latest/the-life-and-legacy-of-bayard-rustin-dreier-20231215/.

37 **August 28, 1971** Peter Knegt, "We Demand: 50 Years After Our First Major Rights Rally, This Is What Queer Canadians Say We Need Today," *CBC Arts*, August 27, 2021, https://www.cbc.ca/arts/we-demand-50-years-after-our-first-major-rights-rally-this-is-what-queer-canadians-say-we-need-today-1.6152754; see the original list of demands at https://digitalexhibitions.arquives.ca/exhibits/show/1971-we-demand-march/item/1196.

38 **August 29, 1867** "First Openly Gay Appeal for Gay Rights," Working Class History, last edited July 20, 2022, https://stories.workingclasshistory.com/article/10074/first-openly-gay-appeal-for-gay-rights.

39 **August 29, 1970** "Gay History—August 1970: The Gay Activist Alliance and Gay Liberation Front Battle the NYPD in the 'Forgotten Riot,'" August 1, 2022, Back2Stonewall, archived at https://web.archive.org/web/20230604175744/http://www.back2stonewall.com/2022/08/august-29-1970-gaa-glf-protest-riot-nypd-harassment.html.

40 **August 29, 1979** Steven Johns, "The Occupation of the Swedish National Board of Health and Welfare, 1979," libcom, August 27, 2014, https://libcom.org/article/occupation-swedish-national-board-health-and-welfare-1979-steven-johns.

41 **August 30, 1958** Gerber Hart Library and Archives, "1989 cartoon by Chicago cartoonist Daniel Sotomayor criticizing President George H.W. Bush and his lack of response to the AIDS pandemic," Facebook, March 26, 2020, https://www.facebook.com/photo.php?fbid=10157886928266352&id=115146166351&set=a.22808083635l; "Daniel Sotomayor," Chicago LGBT Hall of Fame, accessed September 1, 2024, https://chicagolgbthalloffame.org/sotomayor-daniel/.

42 **August 31, 1979** "Don Kilhefner: The Radical Faeries: Interview," LGBTQ History Project, October 20, 2023, https://www.lgbtqhp.org/post/radical-faeries.

September

1 **September 1, 1949** "Leslie Feinberg Born," Working Class History, last edited July 19, 2022, https://stories.workingclasshistory.com/article/8159/leslie-feinberg-born; Minnie Bruce Pratt, "Leslie Feinberg—A Communist Who Revolutionised Transgender Rights," *Workers World*, November 18, 2014, https://www.workers.org/2014/11/16937/.

2 **September 1, 1959** "Case of the 108," Working Class History, last edited July 19, 2022, https://stories.workingclasshistory.com/article/8160/case-of-the-108.

3 **September 1, 1991** Associated Press, "AIDS Protest Brings Issue to Bush's Door," *Los Angeles Times*, September 2, 1991, https://www.latimes.com/archives/la-xpm-1991-09-02-mn-1142-story.html.

4 **September 2, 1967** Michael Annetta, "September 2 in LGBTQ History," Lavender Effect, September 2, 2013, https://thelavendereffect.org/2013/09/02/september-2-in-lgbtq-history.

5 **September 3, 1791** "Revolutionary France Decriminalises Homosexuality," Working Class History, last edited July 20, 2022, https://stories.workingclasshistory.com/article/10252/revolutionary-france-decriminalises-homosexuality.

6 **September 3, 2016** Zaria Howell, "Indigenous Women and LGBTQ+ People Led Dakota Access Pipeline Protests. Five Years Later, They Reflect on Standing Rock," *19th*, May 20, 2021, https://19thnews.org/2021/05/indigenous-women-and-lgbtq-people-led-

dakota-access-pipeline-protests-five-years-later-they-reflect-on-standing-rock/; Rebecca Hersher, "Key Moments in the Dakota Access Pipeline Fight," *NPR*, February 22, 2017, https://www.npr.org/sections/thetwo-way/2017/02/22/514988040/key-moments-in-the-dakota-access-pipeline-fight; Samuel White Swan-Perkins, "Two Spirit Nation to Hold Grand Entry at Standing Rock," *HuffPost*, October 14, 2016, https://www.huffpost.com/entry/two-spirit-nation-to-hold-grand-entry-at-standing-rock_b_580 off8be4b0f42ad3d25ffc.

7   **September 4, 2007** Yusef Najafi, "Saying Goodbye to Cheryl," *Metro Weekly*, September 5, 2007, https://www.metroweekly.com/2007/09/saying-goodbye-to-cheryl/.

8   **September 5, 1987** Aaron Netsky, "Homomonument," Atlas Obscura, July 31, 2017, https://www.atlasobscura.com/places/homomonument.

9   **September 5, 2018** Mason Adams, "How a 'Bunch of Badass Queer Anarchists' Are Teaming Up with Locals to Block a Pipeline Through Appalachia," *Mother Jones*, May 25, 2020, https://www.motherjones.com/politics/2020/05/yellow-finch-mountain-valley-pipeline-appalachia.

10   **September 6, 1850** "Jane Addams," Chicago LGBT Hall of Fame, accessed March 20, 2024, https://chicagolgbthalloffame.org/addams-jane/.

11   **September 6, 1947** Joshua Gamson, *The Fabulous Sylvester: The Legend, the Music, the Seventies in San Francisco* (Picador, 2006); Sharon Davis, *Mighty Real: Sharon Davis Remembers Sylvester* (Bank House Books, 2015).

12   **September 6, 2019** Karen Ocamb, "Alejandra Is Free! Trans Asylum Seeker out of ICE Detention After 20 Months," *Los Angeles Blade*, September 7, 2019, https://www.losangelesblade.com/2019/09/07/alejandra-is-free-trans-asylum-seeker-out-of-ice-detention-after-20-months/.

13   **September 7, 1976** "Gay Social Worker Reinstated," Working Class History, last edited February 21, 2025, https://stories.workingclasshistory.com/article/13671/gay-social-worker-reinstated.

14   **September 7, 2011** Michael Annetta, "September 7 in LGBTQ History," Lavender Effect, September 7, 2013, https://thelavendereffect.org/2013/09/07/september-7-in-lgbtq-history.

15   **September 8, 1954** Malinda Lo, "The True Story of the Raid on Tommy's Place," on Malinda Lo's blog, June 22, 2021, https://www.malindalo.com/blog/2021/6/22/the-raid-on-tommys.

16   **September 9, 1992** Steven Lee Myers, "How a 'Rainbow Curriculum' Turned into Fighting Words," *New York Times*, December 13, 1992, https://www.nytimes.com/1992/12/13/weekinreview/ideas-trends-how-a-rainbow-curriculum-turned-into-fighting-words.html; Cassidy George, "An Oral History of the Lesbian Avengers," *The Cut*, June 25, 2021, https://www.thecut.com/2021/06/lesbian-avengers-and-the-dyke-march.html.

17   **September 10, 1996** Molly Ball, "How Gay Marriage Became a Constitutional Right," *Atlantic*, July 1, 2015, https://www.theatlantic.com/politics/archive/2015/07/gay-marriage-supreme-court-politics-activism/397052; John F. Kowal, "An Improbable Victory for Marriage Equality," Brennan Center for Justice, September 29, 2015, https://www.brennancenter.org/our-work/analysis-opinion/improbable-victory-marriage-equality.

18   **September 11, 1948** John Howard, "Selected Strands of Identity," *Callaloo* 17, no. 4 (1994): 1276–78, https://doi.org/10.2307/2932202.

19   **September 12, 1969** "The First Gay Liberation Front Demonstration—John Lauritsen," libcom, July 4, 2016, https://libcom.org/article/first-gay-liberation-front-demonstration-john-lauritsen.

20   **September 13, 1879** "Annie Kenney Born," Working Class History, last edited July 19, 2022, https://stories.workingclasshistory.com/article/8531/annie-kenney-born.

21   **September 14, 1961** Gary Kamiya, "1961 Police Raid Pivotal for Gay Rights in S.F.,"

SFGate, June 21, 2013, https://www.sfgate.com/bayarea/article/1961-police-raid-pivotal-for-gay-rights-in-s-f-4615713.php.

22 **September 14, 2000** "Tipping Point: Pussy Palace Raids," Queer Events, accessed December 5, 2023, https://www.queerevents.ca/queer-history/canadian-history-timeline.

23 **September 15, 1969** Will Kohler, "Gay History—September 15, 1969: 'Gay Power' New York City's First 'Homosexual' Newspaper Published," Back2Stonewall, September 15, 2021, archived at https://web.archive.org/web/20210916114430/http://www.back2stonewall.com/2021/09/september-15-1969-gay-power-nyc-newspaper-published.html.

24 **September 15, 1988** Michael Annetta, "September 15 in LGBTQ History," Lavender Effect, September 15, 2013, https://thelavendereffect.org/2013/09/15/september-15-in-lgbtq-history; Bethany Ogdon, "Through the Image: Nicholas Nixon's 'People with AIDS,'" *Discourse* 23, no. 3 (2001): 75–105, https://dx.doi.org/10.1353/dis.2001.0023; "ACT UP—Nicholas Nixon Action," T.L. Litt Photography, accessed August 15, 2023, https://www.tllittphotography.com/image/I00002n7pvsDJ1kY.

25 **September 16, 1919** "Trial of Marusya Nikiforova," Working Class History, last edited July 19, 2022, https://stories.workingclasshistory.com/article/8839/trial-of-marusya-nikiforova.

26 **September 16, 2017** "Scout Schultz: Protests After Police Shoot LGBT Student," *BBC*, September 19, 2023, https://www.bbc.com/news/world-us-canada-41323175.

27 **September 17, 2019** "Guatemala: Protest Against Project That Criminalizes Abortion and Gay Marriage," *Equal Eyes*, September 19, 2019, https://equal-eyes.org/database/2019/9/19/guatemala-protest-against-project-that-criminalizes-abortion-and-gay-marriage.

28 **September 18, 1977** Invisible Histories Project (@iHPSouth), "Check out this source from Mississippi in 1977!! This source is an example of radical solidarity between southern civil rights activists and queer rights activists in Mississippi in the 1970s. We can learn a lot from studying this history today!," X, July 12, 2023, https://twitter.com/iHPSouth/status/1679189224409673730.

29 **September 18, 1980** "September 9," Lesbian and Gay Liberation in Canada, accessed February 12, 2025, https://lglc.ca/event/n80.262.

30 **September 19, 1964** Jay Shockley, "Picket in Front of U.S. Army Building, First-Ever U.S. Gay Rights Protest," NYC LGBT Historic Sites Project, July 2018, https://www.nyclgbtsites.org/site/picket-in-front-of-u-s-army-building-first-ever-u-s-gay-rights-protest/.

31 **September 20, 2011** "Repeal of 'Don't Ask, Don't Tell,'" Human Rights Campaign, press release, accessed August 26, 2024, https://www.hrc.org/our-work/stories/repeal-of-dont-ask-dont-tell.

32 **September 21, 1955** Michael Annetta, "September 21 in LGBTQ History," Lavender Effect, September 21, 2013, https://thelavendereffect.org/2013/09/21/september-21-in-lgbtq-history.

33 **September 22, 1962** "Pasolini Punches Fascist," Working Class History, last edited July 19, 2022, https://stories.workingclasshistory.com/article/9526/pasolini-punches-fascist.

34 **September 23, 1984** Kathleen Connell and Paul Gabriel, "The Power of Broken Hearts," Folsom Street, accessed February 12, 2025, https://www.folsomstreet.org/history.

35 **September 24, 1982** "HOPWA 30th Anniversary," US Department of Housing and Urban Development, archived September 27, 2024, at https://web.archive.org/web/20221028202920/https://www.hud.gov/program_offices/comm_planning/hopwa/30th_anniversary.

36 **September 25, 1952** bell hooks, "Are You Still a Slave? Liberating the Black Female Body," conversation with bell hooks, Marci Blackman, Shola Lynch, and Janet Mock, May 6, 2014, posted May 7, 2014, by The New School, YouTube, 1 hour, 55 min., 32 sec., https://www.youtube.com/watch?v=rJk0hNROvzs&ab_channel=TheNewSchool.

37 **September 25, 1970** "Weinstein Hall Occupation," Working Class History, last edited July 19, 2022, https://stories.workingclasshistory.com/article/9790/weinstein-

hall-occupation; STAR (Street Transvestite Action Revolutionaries), "Gay Power—When Do We Want It? Or Do We?," statement read on September 14, 1970, contained on the webpage "STAR Occupation at Weinstein Hall, 1970," Whose Streets Our Streets, January 15, 2013, https://whosestreetsourstreets.org/5-11-university-place-weinstein-hall/.

38   **September 25, 2017** "Seven Arrested in Egypt After Raising Rainbow Flag at Concert," *BBC*, September 26, 2017, https://www.bbc.com/news/world-middle-east-41398193; Colin Stewart, "More than 274 LGBTQ Victims of Egypt's Ongoing Repression," *Erasing 76 Crimes*, November 17, 2016, https://76crimes.com/2016/11/17/more-than-274-lgbtq-victims-of-egypts-ongoing-repression/.

39   **September 26, 1945** Gloria E. Anzaldúa, *Interviews/Entrevistas*, ed. AnaLouise Keating (Routledge, 2000); Tace Hedrick, "Queering the Cosmic Race: Esotericism, Mestizaje, and Sexuality in the Work of Gabriela Mistral and Gloria Anzaldúa," *Aztlán: A Journal of Chicano Studies* 34, no. 2 (September 2009): 67–98, https://doi.org/10.1525/azt.2009.34.2.67.

40   **September 27, 1961** "Samson Chan," Chicago LGBT Hall of Fame, accessed September 1, 2024, https://chicagolgbthalloffame.org/chan-samson/.

41   **September 28, 2022** Riley Holsinger, "Morgantown High School Walkout: What Participants Had to Say," *WBOY*, September 28, 2022, https://www.wboy.com/news/monongalia/morgantown-high-school-walkout-what-participants-had-to-say/.

42   **September 29, 1991** Jane Gross, "California Governor, in Reversal, Signs a Bill on Gay Rights in Jobs," *New York Times*, September 26, 1992, https://www.nytimes.com/1992/09/26/us/california-governor-in-reversal-signs-a-bill-on-gay-rights-in-jobs.html; "The AB 101 Veto Riot Remembered @ GLBT History Museum (San Francisco)," on Candela Films' blog, October 3, 2011, https://candelafilms.wordpress.com/2011/10/03/the-ab101-veto-riot-remebered-glbt-history-museum-san-francisco/.

43   **September 29, 2023** Katya Schwenk, "'Pseudo-Apocalyptic Bullshit': Arizona Students Walk Out over Anti-LGBTQ Laws," *Phoenix New Times*, September 30, 2022, https://www.phoenixnewtimes.com/news/arizona-high-school-students-walk-out-over-anti-lgbtq-laws-14573631.

44   **September 30, 2008** Constitution of Ecuador, 2008, archived August 20, 2008, at https://web.archive.org/web/20080820044218/http://asambleaconstituyente.gov.ec/documentos/Nueva_Constitucion_del_Ecuador.pdf, available in English from Georgetown University's Political Database of the Americas, https://pdba.georgetown.edu/Constitutions/Ecuador/english08.html; Michael K. Lavers, "Ecuadorian Lawmakers Approve Civil Unions Bill," *Washington Blade*, April 23, 2015, http://washingtonblade.com/2015/04/23/ecuadorian-lawmakers-approve-civil-unions-bill/.

October

1   **October 1, 1867** "George Ives," LGBT Archive, last edited July 24, 2019, https://lgbthistoryuk.org/wiki/George_Ives.

2   **October 1, 2020** "San Diego Loyal Players Strike," Working Class History, last edited July 19, 2022, https://stories.workingclasshistory.com/article/8153/san-diego-loyal-players-strike.

3   **October 2, 1999** Carl Ingram, "Davis Signs 3 Bills Supporting Domestic Partners, Gay Rights," *Los Angeles Times*, October 3, 1999, https://www.latimes.com/archives/la-xpm-1999-oct-03-mn-18264-story.html.

4   **October 3, 1993** "Katerina Gogou Dies," Working Class History, last edited July 20, 2022, https://stories.workingclasshistory.com/article/10250/katerina-gogou-dies; "Gogou, Katerina: Athens' Anarchist Poetess, 1940–1993," libcom, April 9, 2010, https://libcom.org/article/gogou-katerina-athens-anarchist-poetess-1940-1993.

5   **October 4, 1908** Ellen Carol Dubois, "Overlooked No More: Eleanor Flexner, Pioneering Feminist in an Anti-Feminist Age," *New York Times*, October 16, 2020, https://www.nytimes.com/2020/10/16/obituaries/eleanor-flexner-overlooked.html; Eric A. Gordon,

"Despite the Ban, Queers Made Important Contributions to U.S. Communist Movement," *People's World*, December 1, 2022, https://peoplesworld.org/article/despite-the-ban-queers-made-important-contributions-to-u-s-communist-movement.

6   **October 5, 2013** "Ágora Juan Andrés Benítez," Working Class History, last edited July 19, 2022, https://stories.workingclasshistory.com/article/8011/%C3%A1gora-juan-andr%C3%A9s-ben%C3%ADtez.

7   **October 6, 1971** "Chepstow Pub Sit-In," Working Class History, last edited September 19, 2023, https://stories.workingclasshistory.com/article/11403/chepstow-pub-sit-in.

8   **October 6, 1989** Gerard Koskovich, "Remembering a Police Riot: The Castro Sweep of October 6, 1989," FoundSF: The San Francisco Digital History Archive, originally published 2002, accessed February 11, 2025, https://www.foundsf.org/index.php?title=Remembering_A_Police_Riot:_The_Castro_Sweep_of_October_6,_1989.

9   **October 7, 2020** Sophia Kishkovsky, "For Putin's Birthday, Pussy Riot Hangs Rainbow Flags on Moscow's Government Buildings," *Art Newspaper*, October 8, 2020, https://www.theartnewspaper.com/2020/10/08/for-putins-birthday-pussy-riot-hangs-rainbow-flags-on-moscows-government-buildings.

10   **October 8, 1826** "Emily Blackwell," History of American Women, May 31, 2020, https://www.womenhistoryblog.com/2012/02/emily-blackwell.html; "Emily Blackwell and Elizabeth Cushier," from the collection "Aspects of Queer Existence in 19th-Century America, by Rich Wilson," OutHistory, originally published 2012, accessed March 20, 2024, https://outhistory.org/exhibits/show/aspectsofqueerexistence/aspectsofqueerexistenceemilybl.

11   **October 8, 1970** Michael Annetta, "October 8 in LGBTQ History," Lavender Effect, October 8, 2013, https://thelavendereffect.org/2013/10/08/october-8-in-lgbtq-history.

12   **October 8, 1972** Annetta, "October 8."

13   **October 9, 1970** Ken Bronson, *A Quest for Full Equality* (Qlibrary, May 18, 2004), https://qlibrary.org/wp-content/uploads/2019/12/JACKBAKERQuest.pdf.

14   **October 10, 1973** "October 10," Lesbian and Gay Liberation in Canada, accessed February 12, 2025, https://lglc.ca/event/n73.116.

15   **October 10, 1987** "The Wedding," Histories of the National Mall, accessed September 1, 2024, https://mallhistory.org/items/show/532.

16   **October 11, 1941** Judith Katz, "Remembrance: Elana Dykewomon, Jewish Lesbian Poet, Novelist, Agitator," *Lambda Literary Review*, August 12, 2022, https://lambdaliteraryreview.org/2022/08/remembrance-elana-dykewomon-jewish-lesbian-poet-novelist-agitator; Elana Dykewomon, "Elana Dykewomon," interview by Betsy Kalin, Oakland, CA, April 8, 2022, Outwords, 1 hour, 45 min., 21 sec., https://theoutwordsarchive.org/interview/elana-dykewomon; Jenna Mandarano, "SF State Remembers Educator and Influential Writer Elana Dykewomon," *Golden Gate Xpress*, September 15, 2022, https://goldengatexpress.org/99901/campus-original/sf-state-remembers-educator-and-influential-writer-elana-dykewomon/.

17   **October 11, 1987** "ACT UP Accomplishments 1987–2012," ACT UP, accessed June 15, 2023, https://actupny.com/actions/.

18   **October 11, 1988** "ACT UP Accomplishments."

19   **October 11, 1992** Jeffry Iovannone, "George H.W. Bush and the ACT UP Ashes Action," *Medium*, December 8, 2018, https://medium.com/queer-history-for-the-people/george-h-w-bush-and-the-act-up-ashes-action-eb9e5e4c7779; David Wojnarowicz, *Close to the Knives: A Memoir of Disintegration* (Vintage, 1991).

20   **October 12, 1911** Eric A. Gordon, "Despite the Ban, Queers Made Important Contributions to U.S. Communist Movement," *People's World*, December 1, 2022, https://peoplesworld.org/article/despite-the-ban-queers-made-important-contributions-to-u-s-communist-movement; Betty Millard Papers, 1911–2010, Smith College Finding Aids, Sophia Smith Collection of Women's History, Smith College, accessed March 16, 2024, https://findingaids.smith.edu/repositories/2/resources/1179.

21   **October 12–15, 1979** Robert Crisman, "History Made: First Lesbians/Gays of Color

Conference," Freedom Socialist Party, originally published Winter 1979, accessed July 20, 2023, https://socialism.com/fs-article/history-made-first-lesbiansgays-of-color-conference/.

22   **October 13, 1917** Aaron H. Devor, "Reed Erickson and the Erickson Educational Foundation," personal website of Aaron H. Devor, accessed July 23, 2023, https://onlineacademiccommunity.uvic.ca/ahdevor/publications/erickson/.

23   **October 13, 1970** "Angela Davis Arrested by FBI," Working Class History, last edited July 19, 2022, https://stories.workingclasshistory.com/article/8527/angela-davis-arrested-by-fbi.

24   **October 13, 1987** Michael Annetta, "October 13 in LGBTQ History," Lavender Effect, October 13, 2013, https://thelavendereffect.org/2013/10/13/october-13-in-lgbtq-history; Karlyn Barker and Linda Wheeler, "Gay Activists Arrested at High Court," *Washington Post*, October 14, 1987, https://www.washingtonpost.com/archive/politics/1987/10/14/gay-activists-arrested-at-high-court/ec188d09-6f3f-4cda-89f6-d9c643b63e93/.

25   **October 13, 1990** "First Pride in South Africa," Working Class History, last edited July 19, 2022, https://stories.workingclasshistory.com/article/8528/1st-pride-in-south-africa.

26   **October 14, 1979** "National March on Washington for Lesbian and Gay Rights Collection," ONE National Gay and Lesbian Archives, USC Libraries, University of Southern California, https://oac.cdlib.org/findaid/ark:/13030/c80k2cz7/; Alan Young, "National March! on Washington for Lesbian and Gay Rights," official souvenir program, October 14, 1979, https://www.cristanwilliams.com/wp-content/uploads/2012/12/MOWprogram-1979.pdf.

27   **October 14, 1977** Michael Annetta, "October 14 in LGBTQ History," Lavender Effect, October 14, 2013, https://thelavendereffect.org/2013/10/14/october-14-in-lgbtq-history; "Anita Bryant Pied," Working Class History, last edited July 19, 2022, https://stories.workingclasshistory.com/article/8624/anita-bryant-pied.

28   **October 15, 1926** "Michel Foucault," Stanford Encyclopedia of Philosophy, last revised August 5, 2022, https://plato.stanford.edu/entries/foucault; "Michel Foucault," Confinity, accessed March 19, 2025, https://www.confinity.com/legacies/michel-foucault.

29   **October 15, 1952** Michael Annetta, "October 15 in LGBTQ History," Lavender Effect, October 15, 2013, https://thelavendereffect.org/2013/10/15/october-15-in-lgbtq-history; "One, Inc," LGBTQIA+ Studies: A Resource Guide, Library of Congress, accessed January 6, 2024, https://guides.loc.gov/lgbtq-studies/before-stonewall/one.

30   **October 15, 1973** Michael Annetta, "October 15 in LGBTQ History," Lavender Effect, October 15, 2013, https://thelavendereffect.org/2013/10/15/october-15-in-lgbtq-history; "Our History and Timeline," National LGBTQ Task Force, accessed September 15, 2023, https://www.thetaskforce.org/about/history/.

31   **October 16, 1854** "Oscar Wilde Born," Working Class History, last edited July 19, 2022, https://stories.workingclasshistory.com/article/8827/oscar-wilde-born.

32   **October 17, 1981** "Dykes in the Streets," Queer Events, accessed December 5, 2023, https://www.queerevents.ca/queer-history/canadian-history-timeline.

33   **October 17, 1995** Michael Annetta, "October 17 in LGBTQ History," Lavender Effect, October 17, 2013, https://thelavendereffect.org/2013/10/17/october-17-in-lgbtq-history; International Gay and Lesbian Human Rights Commission, "The International Tribunal on Human Rights Violations Against Sexual Minorities," program, October 17, 1995, https://www.iglhrc.org/sites/default/files/188-1.pdf.

34   **October 18, 1887** Annelise Orleck, *Common Sense and a Little Fire: Women and Working-Class Politics in the United States, 1900–1965* (University of North Carolina Press, 2017).

35   **October 19, 1991** "Cracker Barrel Target of Protest," *Daily Press*, October 19, 1991, updated July 20, 2019, https://www.dailypress.com/1991/10/19/cracker-barrel-target-of-protest; Morna J. Gerrard, "Bias Is Bad for Business: Carl Owens, Gay Rights, and the Fight Against Cracker Barrel," Georgia State University Library blog, May 17, 2017, https://blog.library.gsu.edu/2017/05/17/bias-is-bad-for-business-carl-owens-gay-rights-and-the-fight-against-cracker-barrel-by-william-greer/.

36 **October 19, 1998** Tyler Austin, "Today in Gay History: Matthew Shepard Political Funeral March," *Out*, October 19, 2016, https://www.out.com/today-gay-history/2016/10/19/today-gay-history-mathew-sheppard-political-funeral-march.

37 **October 19, 2008** "Who Are We?," Russian LGBT Network, accessed October 10, 2023, https://lgbtnet.org/en/about/.

38 **October 20, 1873** Victoria A. Brownworth, "Frances Kellor: The Lesbian Behind the Multiculturalism," *LGBTQ Nation*, October 25, 2018, https://www.lgbtqnation.com/2018/10/frances-kellor-lesbian-behind-multiculturalism/.

39 **October 21, 1917** Dudley Clendinen, "William Dale Jennings, 82, Writer and Gay Rights Pioneer," *New York Times*, May 22, 2000, https://www.nytimes.com/2000/05/22/us/william-dale-jennings-82-writer-and-gay-rights-pioneer.html.

40 **October 22, 1977** "Montreal Raids," Queer Events, accessed December 5, 2023, https://www.queerevents.ca/queer-history/canadian-history-timeline.

41 **October 23, 1965** Michael Annetta, "October 23 in LGBTQ History," Lavender Effect, October 23, 2013, https://thelavendereffect.org/2013/10/23/october-23-in-lgbtq-history; "Public Protest," *25 Years of Political Influence: The Records of the Human Rights Campaign*, exhibition, Cornell University, accessed February 13, 2025, https://rmc.library.cornell.edu/HRC/exhibition/stage/stage_12.html.

42 **October 24, 1981** Michael Annetta, "October 24 in LGBTQ History," Lavender Effect, October 24, 2013, https://thelavendereffect.org/2013/10/24/october-24-in-lgbtq-history.

43 **October 25, 1929** Mary Reinholz, "David McReynolds, Pacifist and Socialist Leader, Is Dead at 88," *Villager*, August 23, 2018, archived at https://web.archive.org/web/20190530160102/https:/www.thevillager.com/2018/08/david-mcreynolds-pacifist-and-socialist-leader-is-dead-at-88/.

44 **October 25, 1940** Kelly Aliano, "Life Story: Miss Major Griffin-Gracy," Women & the American Story, March 13, 2024, https://wams.nyhistory.org/end-of-the-twentieth-century/the-information-age/miss-major-griffin-gracy/.

45 **October 26, 2022** Sharon Zhang, "For the First Time, LGBTQ Candidates Are on the Ballot in All 50 States," *Truthout*, October 26, 2022, https://truthout.org/articles/for-the-first-time-lgbtq-candidates-are-on-the-ballot-in-all-50-states; "Out on the Trail 2022 Report," LGBT+ Victory Fund, accessed February 13, 2025, https://victoryfund.org/out-on-the-trail-2022/.

46 **October 27, 1970** Michael Annetta, "October 27 in LGBTQ History," Lavender Effect, October 27, 2013, https://thelavendereffect.org/2013/10/27/october-27-in-lgbtq-history.

47 **October 27, 2016** Alleen Brown, Will Parrish, and Alice Speri, "The Battle of Treaty Camp: Law Enforcement Descended on Standing Rock a Year Ago and Changed the DAPL Fight Forever," *Intercept*, October 17, 2017, https://theintercept.com/2017/10/27/law-enforcement-descended-on-standing-rock-a-year-ago-and-changed-the-dapl-fight-forever; Zaria Howell, "Indigenous Women and LGBTQ+ People Led Dakota Access Pipeline Protests. Five Years Later, They Reflect on Standing Rock," *19th*, May 20, 2021, https://19thnews.org/2021/05/Indigenous-women-and-lgbtq-people-led-dakota-access-pipeline-protests-five-years-later-they-reflect-on-standing-rock/.

48 **October 28, 2009** "Obama Signs Hate Crimes Bill into Law," *CNN*, October 28, 2009, archived at https://web.archive.org/web/20091031022948/https://www.cnn.com/2009/POLITICS/10/28/hate.crimes/.

49 **October 29, 2019** Steven Zhou, "Library Hosts Anti-Trans Rights 'Feminist,' Saying It Already Hosted Neo-Nazis, So Why Not," *VICE*, October 30, 2019, https://www.vice.com/en/article/59nakb/toronto-library-hosts-anti-trans-rights-feminist-meghan-murphy-saying-it-already-hosted-neo-nazis; "Protests Against Transphobia," Queer Events, accessed August 10, 2023, https://www.queerevents.ca/queer-histroy/notable-moment/2019-transphobia-library-protest.

50 **October 30, 1987** Michael Annetta, "October 30 in LGBTQ History," Lavender Effect, October 30, 2013, https://thelavendereffect.org/2013/10/30/october-30-in-lgbtq-history.

51 **October 31, 1940** Eric Marcus, host, *Making Gay History*, podcast, season 11, episode

1, "Craig Rodwell," November 3, 2022, https://makinggayhistory.com/podcast/craig-rodwell.

52   On Saturday, October 25, 1969, the *San Francisco Examiner* published journalist Robert Patterson's exposé on San Francisco's Folsom Street gay bars, clubs, and restaurants. Patterson called these queer spaces "deviate establishments" "that were "sad" and "dreary" sites for the "sick" ceremonies of "homosexuals," "transvestites," "drag queens," and "male prostitutes." Patterson also targeted San Francisco's transgender community, describing transgender women who frequented these bars "semi-males," "members of the pseudo-fair sex," "women who aren't exactly women," and "hybrid blossoms." See "The Dreary Revels of S.F. 'Gay' Clubs" at https://www.newspapers.com/article/the-san-francisco-examiner/155113954/.

53   **October 31, 1969** Marc Stein, "Guest Opinion: Recalling Purple Hands Protests of 1969," *Bay Area Reporter*, October 30, 2019, https://www.ebar.com/story.php?283715.

54   **October 31, 1969** "Queens Liberation Front," Working Class History, last edited November 29, 2023, https://stories.workingclasshistory.com/article/12668/queens-liberation-front.

55   **October 31, 1992** Meaghan, "Eating Fire: A Brief History of the Lesbian Avengers in NYC," *Off the Grid* (Village Preservation blog), November 12, 2014, https://www.villagepreservation.org/2014/11/12/eating-fire-a-brief-history-of-the-lesbian-avengers-in-nyc; "Fire-Eating Lesbians," *New York Times Magazine*, April 24, 1994, http://www.nytimes.com/1994/04/24/magazine/sunday-april-24-1994-fire-eating-lesbians.html.

November

1   **November 1970** "STAR House Founded," Working Class History, last edited July 19, 2022, https://stories.workingclasshistory.com/article/7652/star-house-founded.

2   **November 1, 1999** Peter Kurth, "'The Trouble with Normal' by Michael Warner," *Salon*, December 8, 1999, https://www.salon.com/1999/12/08/warner_7/.

3   **November 2, 1977** Michael K. Lavers, "Chile's First Openly Gay Elected Official Takes Office," *Washington Blade*, December 7, 2012, https://www.washingtonblade.com/2012/12/07/chiles-first-openly-gay-elected-official-takes-office/.

4   **November 2, 2012** Richard L. Rashke, *The Killing of Karen Silkwood: The Story Behind the Kerr-Mcgee Plutonium Case* (ILR Press, 2000).

5   **November 3, 1889** Lydia Zárate, "Amelio Robles, coronel transgénero de la Revolución mexicana," *Pikara Magazine*, September 13, 2016, https://www.pikaramagazine.com/2016/09/amelio-robles-coronel-transgenero-de-la-revolucion-mexicana/.

6   **November 4, 2008** Michael Annetta, "November 4 in LGBTQ History," Lavender Effect, November 4, 2013, https://thelavendereffect.org/2013/11/04/november-4-in-lgbtq-history-2.

7   **November 5, 1974** Michael Annetta, "November 5 in LGBTQ History," Lavender Effect, November 4, 2013, https://thelavendereffect.org/2013/11/05/november-5-in-lgbtq-history-2.

8   **November 6, 1903** "Hilde Radusch Born," Working Class History, last edited July 20, 2022, https://stories.workingclasshistory.com/article/10653/hilde-radusch-born.

9   **November 6, 2012** Chelsea Carter and Allison Brennan, "Maryland, Maine, Washington Approve Same-Sex Marriage; 2 States Legalize Pot," *CNN*, November 7, 2012, https://www.cnn.com/2012/11/01/politics/ballot-initiatives/index.html.

10   **November 7, 2017** Antonio Olivo, "Danica Roem of Virginia to Be First Openly Transgender Person Elected, Seated in a U.S. Statehouse," *Washington Post*, November 8, 2017, https://www.washingtonpost.com/local/virginia-politics/danica-roem-will-be-vas-first-openly-transgender-elected-official-after-unseating-conservative-robert-g-marshall-in-house-race/2017/11/07/d534bdde-c0af-11e7-959c-fe2b598d8c00_story.html.

11   **November 8, 1997** "ACT UP Accomplishments 1987–2012," ACT UP, accessed June 15, 2023, https://actupny.com/actions/.

12   **November 9, 1960** George Painter, "The History of Sodomy Laws in the United States:

Massachusetts," Sodomy Laws, accessed August 26, 2024, https://www.glapn.org/sodomylaws/sensibilities/massachusetts.htm#fn111.

13   **November 10, 1881** Jaime S.K. Starr, "The Jewish Transgender Couple Who Fell in Love and Escaped the Nazis," QueerAF, May 6, 2024, https://www.wearequeeraf.com/the-jewish-transgender-couple-who-fell-in-love-and-escaped-the-nazis; Kriti Mehrotra, "Charlotte Charlaque and Toni Ebel: What Happened to the Trans Women?," *Cinemaholic*, June 28, 2023, https://thecinemaholic.com/how-did-charlotte-charlaque-and-toni-ebel-die/.

14   **November 10, 1973** "Our History," Lambda Legal, accessed June 20, 2023, https://lambdalegal.org/history/.

15   **November 10, 1984** "LGBT+ Rights Protest in Rugby," Working Class History, last edited July 19, 2022, https://stories.workingclasshistory.com/article/8236/lgbt+-rights-protest-in-rugby.

16   **November 10, 2014** "The Hijra Pride," *Daily Star*, January 23, 2015, https://www.thedailystar.net/the-hijra-pride-61347.

17   **November 11, 1950** Joey Cain, curator, *Radically Gay: The Life of Harry Hay*, exhibition, San Francisco Public Library, accessed February 13, 2025, https://sfpl.org/locations/main-library/lgbtqia-center/radically-gay.

18   **November 12, 1963** "Stop the Church," ACT UP Oral History Project, accessed September 1, 2024, https://www.actuporalhistory.org/actions/stop-the-church.

19   **November 13, 1970** "First UK Gay Liberation Front Protest," Working Class History, last edited July 19, 2022, https://stories.workingclasshistory.com/article/8517/first-uk-gay-liberation-front-protest; Steven Feather, "A Brief History of the Gay Liberation Front, 1970–73," libcom, November 21, 2007, https://libcom.org/article/brief-history-gay-liberation-front-1970-73.

20   **November 13, 1970** Hugh Ryan, "The Incredible True Adventure of Five Gay Activists in Search of the Black Panther Party," *Harper's Bazaar*, June 8, 2021, https://www.harpersbazaar.com/culture/features/a36651331/the-incredible-true-adventure-of-five-gay-activists-and-the-black-panther-party/.

21   **November 14, 1969** Michael Annetta, "November 14 in LGBTQ History," Lavender Effect, November 14, 2013, https://thelavendereffect.org/2013/11/14/november-14-in-lgbtq-history-2.

22   **November 14, 1969** "Come Out!," website of John Lauritsen, accessed March 14, 2025, http://paganpressbooks.com/jpl/COMEOUT.HTM.

23   **November 14, 1985** "GLAAD History and Highlights," GLAAD, archived November 6, 2023, at https://web.archive.org/web/20231106085229/https://glaad.org/history/.

24   **November 14, 2012** Sue Englander, "Howard Wallace, 1936–2012," *Against the Current*, July–August 2013, https://againstthecurrent.org/atc165/p3942/.

25   **November 15, 1963** John D'Emilio, *Lost Prophet: The Life and Times of Bayard Rustin* (University of Chicago Press, 2004), 368–69.

26   **November 15, 1997** David W. Dunlap, "Jim Kepner, in 70's, Is Dead; Historian of Gay Rights Effort," *New York Times*, November 20, 1997, https://www.nytimes.com/1997/11/20/us/jim-kepner-in-70-s-is-dead-historian-of-gay-rights-effort.html.

27   **November 16, 1946** Tisa M. Anders, "Barbara Smith (1946–)," Black Past, June 25, 2012, https://www.blackpast.org/african-american-history/smith-barbara-1946/.

28   **November 17, 1962** James Baldwin, "Letter from a Region in My Mind," *New Yorker*, November 9, 1962, https://www.newyorker.com/magazine/1962/11/17/letter-from-a-region-in-my-mind; Pepper Stetler, "Picturing 'The Fire Next Time,'" *Ploughshares*, November 17, 2022, https://pshares.org/blog/picturing-the-fire-next-time/.

29   **November 18, 2001** "Community Rally Against Homophobia," Queer Events, accessed December 5, 2023, https://www.queerevents.ca/queer-history/canadian-history-timeline.

30   **November 19, 1980** Sam Moskowitz, "Remembering the Ramrod Massacre," *Off the*

Grid (Village Preservation blog), November 20, 2018, https://www.villagepreservation. org/2018/11/20/remembering-the-ramrod-massacre.

31 **November 20, 1910** Home page for the Pauli Murray Center for History and Social Justice, accessed February 13, 2025, https://www.paulimurraycenter. com; Naomi Simmons-Thorne, "Pauli Murray and the Pronominal Problem: A De-Essentalist Trans Historiography," *Activist History Review*, May 30, 2019, https:// activisthistory.com/2019/05/30/pauli-murray-and-the-pronominal-problem- a-de-essentialist-trans-historiography/.

32 **November 20, 1998** Michael Annetta, "November 20 in LGBTQ History," Lavender Effect, November 20, 2013, https://thelavendereffect.org/2013/11/20/ november-20-in-lgbtq-history.

33 **November 20, 1999** "The First Transgender Day of Remembrance Is Held," History. com, last updated November 19, 2024, https://www.history.com/this-day-in-history/ first-transgender-day-of-remembrance.

34 **November 20, 2019** Ajita Banerjie, "Why India's Transgender People Are Protesting a Bill That Claims to Protect Their Rights," *Scroll.in*, November 26, 2019, https://scroll. in/article/944882/why-indias-transgender-people-are-protesting-against-a-bill-that- claims-to-protect-their-rights.

35 **November 20, 2022** Imtiaz Ali, "Transgender Activists Demand Equal Rights, Protection in Pakistan's 'First' Trans Rights March in Karachi," *Dawn*, November 20, 2022, https://www.dawn.com/news/1722087/transgender-activists-demand-equal- rights-protection-in-pakistans-first-trans-rights-march-in-karachi; Sindh Moorat March (@MooratMarch), "For English Media/Audiences," X, November 16, 2022, https:// twitter.com/MooratMarch/status/1592795423789715456/photo/2.

36 **November 21, 2007** Todd Heywood, "Governor Prohibits Discrimination in State Employment on the Basis of Gender Identity and Expression," *Pride Source*, November 29, 2007, last updated September 12, 2023, https://pridesource.com/article/28233.

37 **November 22, 1958** Noreen Fagan, "Nate Phelps: Breaking the Mould," *Daily Xtra*, August 15, 2011, archived at https://web.archive.org/web/20140220201151/http:// dailyxtra.com/ottawa/news/nate-phelps-breaking-the-mould.

38 **November 21, 1870** Paul Avrich and Karen Avrich, *Sasha and Emma: The Anarchist Odyssey of Alexander Berkman and Emma Goldman* (Belknap Press, 2012).

39 **November 23, 1973** Michael Annetta, "November 23 in LGBTQ History," Lavender Effect, November 23, 2013, https://thelavendereffect.org/2013/11/23/november-23-in- lgbtq-history-2; John D'Emilio, *Sexual Politics, Sexual Communities* (University of Chicago Press, 1998).

40 **November 24, 1886** Mame Cotter, "Margaret C. Anderson, Founder of 'The Little Review,'" Literary Ladies Guide, March 22, 2021, https://www.literaryladiesguide.com/ other-rad-voices/margaret-c-anderson-founder-of-the-little-review/.

41 **November 24, 1967** "Biographical/Historical Information," home page of the Craig Rodwell Papers, Manuscripts and Archives Division, New York Public Library, accessed February 13, 2025, https://archives.nypl.org/mss/2606.

42 **November 25, 1950** "Aiyyana Maracle," University of Victoria Transgender Archives, accessed December 10, 2023, https://www.uvic.ca/transgenderarchives/collections/ maracle/index.php.

43 **November 26, 1957** "Nikoli, Tseko Simon (1957–1998)," glbtq: An Encyclopedia of Gay, Lesbian, Bisexual, Transgender, and Queer Culture, archived September 6, 2006, at https://web.archive.org/web/20060906001512/http://www.glbtq.com/social-sciences/ nkoli_ts.html.

44 **November 26, 2022** Alejandra Guzman, "Community Gathers to Remember Club Q Victims with Candlelight Vigil," *Fox 13* (Seattle), November 27, 2022, https://www.fox13seattle. com/news/community-gathers-to-remember-club-q-victims-with-candlelight-vigil.

45 **November 27, 1835** "Last UK Men Executed for Homosexuality," Working Class

History, last edited July 20, 2022, https://stories.workingclasshistory.com/article/9949/last-uk-men-executed-for-homosexuality.

46 **November 27, 2012** Amirah Sequeira, "AIDS Activists Expose Themselves and the Naked Truth About AIDS Budget Cuts," ACT UP, press release, accessed December 10, 2023, https://actupny.com/act-up-and-queerocracy-members-tell-naked-truth-to-speaker-boehner/.

47 **November 27, 2016** Charlotte England, "LGBT Protesters Take to Delhi Streets over Law Criminalising Homosexual Acts," *Independent*, November 27, 2016, https://www.independent.co.uk/news/world/asia/lgbt-protesters-delhi-anti-gay-sex-homosexual-acts-sodomy-law-377-pride-parade-a7442201.html.

48 **November 28, 1971** "1971," San Diego Pride, accessed February 13, 2025, https://sdpride.org/year1971.

49 **November 29, 2007** "Uruguay OKs Gay Unions in Latin American First," *Reuters*, December 18, 2007, https://www.reuters.com/article/world/uruguay-oks-gay-unions-in-latin-american-first-idUSN18540390/.

50 **November 30, 1999** Mac Lojowsky, "Comes a Time," WTO History Project, accessed June 5, 2023, https://depts.washington.edu/wtohist/testimonies/comesatime.htm.

December

1 **December 1, 1989** "Day Without Art," Visual AIDS, accessed November 10, 2023, https://visualaids.org/projects/day-without-art.

2 **December 1, 1998** Mattilda Bernstein Sycamore, *That's Revolting: Queer Strategies for Resisting Assimilation* (Soft Skull Press, 2008).

3 **December 1, 2017** S. Bear Bergman, "This Tiny LGBTQ Bookstore Is a Queer Haven in Small-Town Mississippi," *VICE*, August 16, 2021, https://www.vice.com/en/article/3aqyjn/tiny-lgbtq-bookstore-violet-valley-is-a-queer-haven-in-water-valley-mississippi; Jaime Harker, "A Message from Dr. Jaime Harker, Founder of Violet Valley Bookstore," accessed February 13, 2025, https://www.violetvalley.org/about.

4 **December 2, 1964** Michael Annetta, "December 2 in LGBTQ History," Lavender Effect, December 2, 2013, https://thelavendereffect.org/2013/12/02/december-2-in-lgbtq-history-2.

5 **December 3, 1946** Margalit Fox, "Allan Bérubé Is Dead at 61; Historian of Gays in Military," *New York Times*, December 16, 2007, https://www.nytimes.com/2007/12/16/nyregion/16berube.html.

6 **December 4, 1920** Elisa Rolle, "Queer Places: 33-23 171st St, Flushing, NY 11358, Stati Uniti," website of Elisa Rolle, accessed September 1, 2024, http://www.elisarolle.com/queerplaces/fghij/Jeanne%20Manford.html.

7 **December 5, 1642** "Legal Case: Elizabeth Johnson, Massachusetts Bay, December 5, 1642," from the collection "Colonial America: The Age of Sodomitical Sin, 1607–1783, by Jonathan Ned Katz," OutHistory, originally published 2012, accessed September 1, 2024, https://outhistory.org/exhibits/show/the-age-of-sodomitical-sin/1640s/legal-case-elizabeth-johnson-m.

8 **December 6, 2011** Neal Broverman, "World's First Full-Time Gay Male Leader: Belgium's Elio Di Rupo," *Advocate*, December 6, 2015, https://www.advocate.com/news/daily-news/2011/12/06/worlds-first-full-time-gay-male-leader-belgiums-elio-di-rupo.

9 **December 7, 1896** "Yoshiko Yuasa Born," Working Class History, last edited July 20, 2022, https://stories.workingclasshistory.com/article/10691/yoshiko-yuasa-born.

10 **December 7, 1984** "Leicester LGSM Fundraiser," Working Class History, last edited June 23, 2023, https://stories.workingclasshistory.com/article/11331/leicester-lgsm-fundraiser.

11 **December 8, 1986** "Little Sister's Bookstore Seizure," Queer Events, accessed December 5, 2023, https://www.queerevents.ca/queer-history/canadian-history-timeline.

12 **December 9, 1984** "Amelio Robles Ávila Dies," Working Class History, last edited July 20, 2019, https://stories.workingclasshistory.com/article/10887/amelio-robles-%C3%A1vila-dies.

13 **December 10, 1924** Michael Annetta, "December 10 in LGBTQ History," Lavender Effect,

December 10, 2013, https://thelavendereffect.org/2013/12/10/december-10-in-lgbtq-history-2; "Henry Gerber," Chicago Gay and Lesbian Hall of Fame, archived July 3, 2009, at https://web.archive.org/web/20090703190650/http://www.glhalloffame.org/index.pl?todo=view_item&item=18.

14   **December 10, 1984** Colin Clews, "1984. 'Pits and Perverts' Benefit Concert," Gay in the 80s: From Fighting for Our Rights to Fighting for Our Lives, May 27, 2013, https://www.gayinthe80s.com/2013/05/1984-pits-and-perverts-benefit-concert/.

15   **December 10, 1989** "Stop the Church," ACT UP Oral History Project, accessed January 5, 2024, https://actuporalhistory.org/actions/stop-the-church.

16   **December 11, 1948** Holland Cotter, "He Captured a Clandestine Gay Culture amid the Derelict Piers," *New York Times*, September 24, 2019, https://www.nytimes.com/2019/09/19/arts/design/alvin-baltrop-photographs.html.

17   **December 11, 1973** Dan Avery, "The Time Gay Activists Interrupted Walter Cronkite on the CBS Evening News," *Queerty*, June 5, 2012, https://www.queerty.com/the-time-gay-activists-interrupted-walter-cronkite-on-the-cbs-evening-news-20120605.

18   **December 11, 2023** Tim Pearce, "'Queers for Palestine' Protesters Shut Down Manhattan Bridge," *Daily Wire*, December 12, 2023, https://www.dailywire.com/news/queers-for-palestine-protesters-shut-down-manhattan-bridge.

19   **December 12, 1969** Michael Annetta, "December 12 in LGBTQ History," Lavender Effect, December 12, 2013, https://thelavendereffect.org/2013/12/12/december-12-in-lgbtq-history-2.

20   **December 13, 1922** "Founder," Imperial Council of San Francisco, accessed September 1, 2024, http://www.imperialcouncilsf.org/founder.html.

21   **December 14, 1974** "Remembering Michael Fesco," Saint Foundation, April 14, 2019, https://www.thesaintfoundation.org/community/2019/4/14/remembering-michael-fesco.

22   **December 15, 1961** Jack Halberstam, "Bio," website of Jack Halberstam, archived July 11, 2024, at https://web.archive.org/web/20240711203619/http://www.jackhalberstam.com/bio/.

23   **December 16, 1988** "Flashback: Disco Superstar Sylvester Died of Complications from AIDS (December 16, 1988)," *IN Magazine*, December 16, 2019, https://inmagazine.ca/2019/12/flashback-disco-superstar-sylvester-died-of-complications-from-aids-december-16-1988; Joshua Gamson, *The Fabulous Sylvester: The Legend, the Music, the Seventies in San Francisco* (Henry Holt, 2005).

24   **December 17, 1933** "USSR Re-Criminalised Homosexuality," Working Class History, last edited July 10, 2022, https://stories.workingclasshistory.com/article/8868/ussr-re-criminalised-homosexuality.

25   **December 17, 1970** Michael Annetta, "December 17 in LGBTQ History," Lavender Effect, December 17, 2013, https://thelavendereffect.org/2013/12/17/december-17-in-lgbtq-history-2.

26   **December 18, 1980** Michael Annetta, "December 18 in LGBTQ History," Lavender Effect, December 18, 2012, https://thelavendereffect.org/2012/12/18/december-18-in-lgbtq-history; George Painter, "The History of Sodomy Laws in the United States: New York," Sodomy Laws, accessed March 19, 2025, https://www.glapn.org/sodomylaws/sensibilities/new_york.htm.

27   **December 19, 1908** "Gisele Freund Born," Working Class History, last edited July 19, 2022, https://stories.workingclasshistory.com/article/9075/gisele-freund-born.

28   **December 20, 1957** Suyin Haynes, "You've Probably Heard of the Red Scare, but the Lesser-Known, Anti-Gay 'Lavender Scare' Is Rarely Taught in Schools," *Time*, December 22, 2020, https://time.com/5922679/lavender-scare-history.

29   **December 21, 1866** Michael Zimny, "The Winkte and the Hundred in Hand," South Dakota Public Broadcasting, June 6, 2016, https://www.sdpb.org/blogs/arts-and-culture/the-winkte-and-the-hundred-in-hand/.

30   **December 21, 1969** "Gay Activists Alliance Founded," Working Class History,

last edited July 19, 2022, https://stories.workingclasshistory.com/article/9364/gay-activists-alliance-founded.

31 **December 22, 1946** Kuwasi Balagoon, *Look for Me in the Whirlwind: From the Panther 21 to 21st-Century Revolutions* (PM Press, 2017); "Kuwasi Balagoon Born," Working Class History, last edited July 19, 2022, https://stories.workingclasshistory.com/article/9457/kuwasi-balagoon-born.

32 **December 23, 1954** "December," SF Gay History, accessed February 11, 2025, https://www.sfgayhistory.com/timeline/this-month/december.

33 **December 24, 1920** Rachel Tashjian, "A Brief History of Stormé DeLarverie, Stonewall's Suiting Icon," *GQ*, June 27, 2019, https://www.gq.com/story/storme-delarverie-suiting; William Yardley, "Storme DeLarverie, Early Leader in the Gay Rights Movement, Dies at 93," *New York Times*, May 29, 2014, https://www.nytimes.com/2014/05/30/nyregion/storme-delarverie-early-leader-in-the-gay-rights-movement-dies-at-93.html.

34 **December 25, 1908** Destiny Rogers, "1977: Quentin Crisp, Stately Homo of England," *QNews*, July 26, 2023, https://qnews.com.au/1977-quentin-crisp-stately-homo-of-england/.

35 **December 26, 1960** "Stuart Milk, Founder and President," Harvey Milk Foundation, accessed February 13, 2025, https://milkfoundation.org/about/advisory-board/stuart-milk.

36 **December 27, 1943** Julia Diana Roberton, "Martha Shelley—The Lesbian Who Proposed a Unified Front After Stonewall," *Velvet Chronicle*, August 31, 2020, https://thevelvetchronicle.com/martha-shelley-lesbian-who-proposed-unified-front-after-stonewall; Emily Kahn, "Lavender Menace Action at Second Congress to Unite Women," NYC LGBT Historic Sites Project, July 2020, https://www.nyclgbtsites.org/site/lavender-menace-action-at-second-congress-to-unite-women; "The Story of the Lavender Menace: The Protest for Lesbian Inclusion," Rainbow Stores, May 3, 2023, https://www.therainbowstores.com/blogs/blogs-guides/the-story-of-lavender-menace.

37 **December 28, 2009** Annie Kelly, "Gay Argentine Couple's Wedding Plans Divide an Entire Continent," *Guardian*, November 28, 2009, https://www.theguardian.com/world/2009/nov/29/latin-america-first-gay-wedding.

38 **December 29, 2018** Nick Duffy, "Transgender Pride March Takes Place in Pakistan," *Pink News*, December 31, 2018, https://www.thepinknews.com/2018/12/31/pakistan-transgender-pride/.

39 **December 30, 1977** Craig Jennex and Nisha Eswaran, *Out North: An Archive of Queer Activism and Kinship in Canada* (Figure 1 Publishing, 2020).

40 **December 31, 1918** "Marie Equi Guilty of Sedition," Working Class History, last edited July 20, 2022, https://stories.workingclasshistory.com/article/10360/marie-equi-guilty-of-sedition.

Index

"Passim" (literally "scattered") indicates intermittent discussion of a topic over a cluster of pages.

About the Contributors

Zane McNeill is the editor of *Y'all Means All: The Emerging Voices Queering Appalachia* (PM Press, 2022) and coeditor of *Deviant Hollers: Queering Appalachian Ecologies for a Sustainable Future* (University Press of Kentucky, 2024).

Riley Clare Valentine holds a PhD in political science from Louisiana State University. Their work focuses on care ethics critique of neoliberalism as well as analyses of political rhetoric.

Blu Buchanan is an assistant professor in the Department of Sociology and Anthropology at UNC Asheville. Their academic writing has appeared or is forthcoming in journals like *GLQ: The Journal of Gay and Lesbian Studies* and *PUBLIC: A Journal of Imagining America*, as well as edited volume chapters in *Black Feminist Sociology: Perspectives and Praxis* and *Unsafe Words: Queer Perspectives on Consent in the #MeToo Era*. They have also written extensively in the public sphere, particularly about movements to disarm campus police and confronting trans antagonism in the university.

Cindy Barukh Milstein, a diasporic queer Jewish anarchist, is the cocreator of *Paths Toward Utopia: Graphic Explorations of Everyday Anarchism*, the author of *Anarchism and Its Aspirations*, and the editor of anthologies such as *Constellations of Care: Anarcha-Feminism in Practice*, *Rebellious Mourning: The Collective Work of Grief*, *Deciding for Ourselves: The Promise of Direct Democracy*, and *There Is Nothing So Whole as a Broken Heart: Mending the World as Jewish Anarchists*.

Working Class History is an international collective of worker-activists who uncover our collective history of fighting for a better world and promote it to educate and inspire a new generation of activists.

ABOUT PM PRESS

PM Press is an independent, radical publisher of critically necessary books for our tumultuous times. Our aim is to deliver bold political ideas and vital stories to all walks of life and arm the dreamers to demand the impossible. Founded in 2007 by a small group of people with decades of publishing, media, and organizing experience, we have sold millions of copies of our books, most often one at a time, face to face. We're old enough to know what we're doing and young enough to know what's at stake. Join us to create a better world.

PM Press
PO Box 23912
Oakland, CA 94623
www.pmpress.org

PM Press in Europe
europe@pmpress.org
www.pmpress.org.uk

FRIENDS OF PM PRESS

These are indisputably momentous times—the financial system is melting down globally and the Empire is stumbling. Now more than ever there is a vital need for radical ideas.

In the many years since its founding—and on a mere shoestring—PM Press has risen to the formidable challenge of publishing and distributing knowledge and entertainment for the struggles ahead. With hundreds of releases to date, we have published an impressive and stimulating array of literature, art, music, politics, and culture. Using every available medium, we've succeeded in connecting those hungry for ideas and information to those putting them into practice.

Friends of PM allows you to directly help impact, amplify, and revitalize the discourse and actions of radical writers, filmmakers, and artists. It provides us with a stable foundation from which we can build upon our early successes and provides a much-needed subsidy for the materials that can't necessarily pay their own way. You can help make that happen—and receive every new title automatically delivered to your door once a month—by joining as a Friend of PM Press. And, we'll throw in a free T-shirt when you sign up.

Here are your options:

- **$30 a month** Get all books and pamphlets plus a 50% discount on all webstore purchases

- **$40 a month** Get all PM Press releases (including CDs and DVDs) plus a 50% discount on all webstore purchases

- **$100 a month** Superstar—Everything plus PM merchandise, free downloads, and a 50% discount on all webstore purchases

For those who can't afford $30 or more a month, we have **Sustainer Rates** at $15, $10, and $5. Sustainers get a free PM Press T-shirt and a 50% discount on all purchases from our website.

Your Visa or Mastercard will be billed once a month, until you tell us to stop. Or until our efforts succeed in bringing the revolution around. Or the financial meltdown of Capital makes plastic redundant. Whichever comes first.

About us

Working Class History is an international collective of worker-activists focused on the research and promotion of people's history through our podcasts, websites, books, and social media channels.

We want to uncover stories of our collective history of fighting for better world and tell them in a straightforward and engaging way to help educate and inspire new generations of activists.

Through our social media outlets with over two million followers, we reach an audience of over 20 million per month. So if you're on social media, you can connect with us in the following ways:

- Website: workingclasshistory.com

- Instagram: @workingclasshistory

- Facebook: facebook.com/workingclasshistory

- Twitter: @wrkclasshistory

- YouTube: youtube.com/workingclasshistory

- Mastodon: mastodon.social/@workingclasshistory

- Bluesky: @workingclasshistory.com

We receive no funding from any political party, academic institution, corporation or government. All of our work is funded entirely by our readers and listeners on patreon. So if you appreciate what we do, consider joining us, supporting our work and getting access exclusive content and benefits at patreon.com/workingclasshistory.

Y'all Means All: The Emerging Voices Queering Appalachia

Edited by Z. Zane McNeill

ISBN: 978-1-62963-914-7
$20.00   200 pages

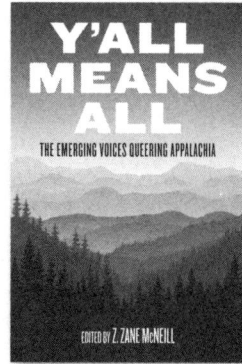

Y'all Means All is a celebration of the weird and wonderful aspects of a troubled region in all of their manifest glory! This collection is a thought-provoking hoot and a holler of "we're queer and we're here to stay, cause we're every bit a piece of the landscape as the rocks and the trees" echoing through the hills of Appalachia and into the boardrooms of every media outlet and opportunistic author seeking to define Appalachia from the outside for their own political agendas. Multidisciplinary and multi-genre, *Y'all* necessarily incorporates elements of critical theory, such as critical race theory and queer theory, while dealing with a multitude of methodologies, from quantitative analysis, to oral history and autoethnography.

This collection eschews the contemporary trend of "reactive" or "responsive" writing in the genre of Appalachian studies, and alternatively, provides examples of how modern Appalachians are defining themselves on their own terms. As such, it also serves as a toolkit for other Appalachian readers to follow suit, and similarly challenge the labels, stereotypes, and definitions often thrust upon them. While providing blunt commentary on the region's past and present, the book's soul is sustained by the resilience, ingenuity, and spirit exhibited by the authors, values which have historically characterized the Appalachian region and are continuing to define its culture to the present.

This book demonstrates above all else that Appalachia and its people are filled with a vitality and passion for their region which will slowly but surely effect long-lasting and positive changes in the region. If historically Appalachia has been treated as a "mirror" of the country, this book breaks that trend by allowing modern Appalachians to examine their own reflections and to share their insights in an honest, unfiltered manner with the world.

"These deeply personal and theoretically informed essays explore the fight for social justice and inclusivity in Appalachia through the intersections of environmental action, LGBTQA+ representational politics, anti-racism, and movements for disability justice. This Appalachia is inhabited by a queer temporality and geography, where gardening lore teaches us that seeds dance into plants in their own time, not according to a straight-edged neoliberal discipline."
—Rebecca Scott, author of *Removing Mountains: Extracting Nature and Identity in the Appalachian Coalfields*

Working Class History: Everyday Acts of Resistance & Rebellion

Edited by Working Class History with a Foreword by Noam Chomsky

ISBN: 978-1-62963-823-2 (paperback)
      978-1-62963-887-4 (hardcover)
$20.00/$59.95   352 pages

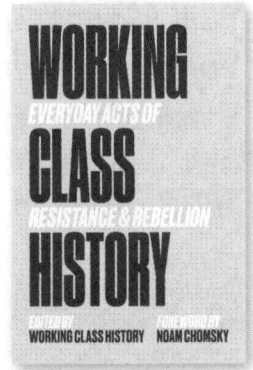

History is not made by kings, politicians, or a few rich individuals—it is made by all of us. From the temples of ancient Egypt to spacecraft orbiting Earth, workers and ordinary people everywhere have walked out, sat down, risen up, and fought back against exploitation, discrimination, colonization, and oppression.

Working Class History presents a distinct selection of people's history through hundreds of "on this day in history" anniversaries that are as diverse and international as the working class itself. Women, young people, people of color, workers, migrants, Indigenous people, LGBT+ people, disabled people, older people, the unemployed, home workers, and every other part of the working class have organized and taken action that has shaped our world, and improvements in living and working conditions have been won only by years of violent conflict and sacrifice. These everyday acts of resistance and rebellion highlight just some of those who have struggled for a better world and provide lessons and inspiration for those of us fighting in the present. Going day by day, this book paints a picture of how and why the world came to be as it is, how some have tried to change it, and the lengths to which the rich and powerful have gone to maintain and increase their wealth and influence.

This handbook of grassroots movements, curated by the popular Working Class History project, features many hidden histories and untold stories, reinforced with inspiring images, further reading, and a foreword from legendary author and dissident Noam Chomsky.

"*This ingenious archive of working class history, organized as an extended calendar, is filled with little and better known events. Reading through the text, the power, fury, and persistence of the working-class struggles shine. 'Working class' is broader than unions and job struggles, and rather includes all emancipatory acts of working-class people, be they Indigenous peoples fighting for land rights, African Americans massively protesting police killings, anticolonial liberation movements, women rising up angry, or mass mobilizations worldwide against imperialist wars. It is international in scope as is the working class. This is a book the reader will open every day to recall and be inspired by what occurred on that date. I love the book and will look forward to the daily readings.*"
—Roxanne Dunbar-Ortiz, author of *An Indigenous Peoples' History of the United States*